Children and the Capability Approach

Children and the Capability Approach

Edited by

Mario Biggeri
University of Florence, Italy

Jérôme Ballet
Université de Versailles Saint-Quentin-en-Yvelines, France

Flavio Comim
St Edmund's College, University of Cambridge, UK

First published 2011 by
PALGRAVE MACMILLAN

Palgrave Macmillan in the UK is an imprint of Macmillan Publishers Limited, registered in England, company number 785998, of Houndmills, Basingstoke, Hampshire RG21 6XS.

Palgrave Macmillan in the US is a division of St Martin's Press LLC, 175 Fifth Avenue, New York, NY 10010.

Palgrave Macmillan is the global academic imprint of the above companies and has companies and representatives throughout the world.

Palgrave® and Macmillan® are registered trademarks in the United States, the United Kingdom, Europe and other countries.

ISBN 978–0–230–28481–4

This book is printed on paper suitable for recycling and made from fully managed and sustained forest sources. Logging, pulping and manufacturing processes are expected to conform to the environmental regulations of the country of origin.

A catalogue record for this book is available from the British Library.

Library of Congress Cataloging-in-Publication Data
Children and the capability approach / edited by Mario Biggeri, Jérôme Ballet, Flavio Comim.
    p.   cm.
Includes index.
ISBN 978–0–230–28481–4 (hardback)
    1. Child development—Developing countries.   2. Child labor—Developing countries.   3. Poor children—Developing countries.
I. Biggeri, Mario.   II. Ballet, Jérôme.   III. Comim, Flavio.
HQ772.C46 2011
331.3′1091724—dc22   2011013737

10   9   8   7   6   5   4   3   2   1
20   19   18   17   16   15   14   13   12   11

Printed and bound in Great Britain by
CPI Antony Rowe, Chippenham and Eastbourne

Contents

Part III   Policy Implications

Part IV   Conclusions

List of Figures

List of Tables

Prologue

Kaushik Basu

Traditional welfare economics identifies a person's well-being with his/her command over goods and services. This naturally leads to a focus on the person's income, actual consumption and utility. An alternative and more pertinent route to describing well-being and human development is the "capabilities approach," developed by Amartya Sen (see, for instance, Sen, 1985), drawing on early works by John Stuart Mill, Adam Smith and even Aristotle. The capabilities approach tries to replace the traditional concern for commodities and utility with functionings and capability. The idea of capability is closely associated with freedom and the various opportunities that one has even if one does not actually exercise all those opportunities (see Basu and Lopez-Calva, 2010). The opportunities in this case refer to functionings, that is, what a person can be or do. It follows that a person's capability depends, in part, on factors external to the person, for instance, the income he/she has, the price of bicycles, the cost of healthcare, the opportunities that society he/she lives in provides him/her with, and so on. But it also depends on the person's own abilities, such as whether or not he/she has a handicap, the skills that he/she has, and so on.

Viewed in this manner the idea of capabilities is particularly relevant when evaluating the lives and well-being of children. What happens in childhood is intrinsically related to the capabilities with which an adult ends up. Adult skills and talents depend critically on childhood learning and experience. But even independently of these implications for later life, childhood and adolescence are periods deserving of agency and capability in their own right. But this idea, that children's capabilities are an important way of assessing their welfare and lifetime well-being, remains relatively unexplored in the literature. This book is one of the first comprehensive evaluations of this and, as such, a welcome addition to our shelves.

The opportunities for a child are determined by much more than objective indicators of physical well-being, school attendance and traditional suspects. Some years ago, I did a study using the results of tests done on slum children in Calcutta who went to a supplementary (that is, after-hours) secondary school called Anandan. The tests had been conducted by Anandan and I had access to the data. (The school as it happens is run by my sisters.) The data showed that, as a determinant of a child's cognitive and intellectual ability, a bigger influence than the child's household's income, wealth or even age was the status of the child at home. Did the child live with his or her parents? Did the parents talk to the child? These turned out to be more important determinants of a child's capacity and intellectual skill than the more regular variables like income and wealth.

Viewed in the capabilities framework, the problem of child labour also comes to acquire a new dimension. Being in the labour force not only robs a child of the joys of childhood and regular school education, it takes away the opportunity for the child to acquire the skills and mental and physical talents for future growth, the ability to do things and empowerment in general. Bringing capabilities into this picture thus creates an additional argument for placing restrictions on child labour.

Elsewhere (Basu and Van, 1998), the case was made not to give in to the instinctive urge that most of us have to demand a legal ban on child labour. This was based on the recognition that most parents in poor regions send their children to work only because of extreme poverty. They may be sufficiently poor that in the absence of child labour the household, including the child, would be driven to destitution and possibly starvation. We should of course work to banish such poverty but, if we do not do so, then simply banning child labour could hurt the very children we are trying to protect.

The argument here is that there could indeed be a case for legally banning child labour, but for that it would be necessary to ensure that certain preconditions were satisfied. For instance, child labour deserves to be banned where such a ban is likely to lead to a rise in adult wages sufficient to take the economy to a superior equilibrium where parents would, of their own accord, not wish to send their children to work. In such a situation, the parental contribution to child welfare would typically go beyond keeping the child out of the labour force to creating the environment that nurtured the child's capabilities. Such nurturing can happen consciously of course, but, as my slum study above demonstrates, it also happens as a consequence of other aspects of parental life. The analysis is also complicated by the fact that for parents inclined to impart good education and skills to their children, the decision is not just about whether to send the children to school or to work, but also about what kind of ethos to provide to the children at home.

These are complex matters that compel us to take nuanced positions on the subject of policy. I am glad that this book goes beyond traditional approaches to children's well-being and child labour by grappling with them through the capabilities approach. It is a rich book that draws on a broad range of disciplines, methodologies and perspectives and, crucially, includes the voices of children from several countries on many of the issues that matter to them. Consequently, the questions and conclusions emerging from this book are highly relevant for local, national and global policy debates. With what type of work (or other activities) and under what conditions can children develop valuable skills, attitudes and capabilities? How can we understand the relevance of the capability space and framework in assessing policies aimed at children's well being? Can we really think about the autonomy of adults without thinking about the autonomy of children? Should children be entitled to agency and participation? This book engages seriously and systematically with all these questions and is not just a thought-provoking read but, for those engaged in drafting legislation and crafting policy pertaining to children, an essential handbook.

References

Basu, K. and Lopez-Calva, L. F. (2010), "Functionings and Capabilities", in Kenneth Arrow, Amartya Sen and Kotaro Suzumura (eds), *Handbook of Social Choice and Welfare, Volume 2*, Elsevier, Amsterdam.

Basu, K. and Van, P. H. (1998), "The Economics of Child Labor," *American Economic Review*, 88(3): 412–427.

Sen, A. K. (1985), *Commodities and Capabilities*, North-Holland, Amsterdam.

Acknowledgements and Dedication

We would like to express our gratitude to Philippa Grand of Palgrave Macmillan and the anonymous referees for pushing us in this common effort.

During this period we have been privileged to receive comments and suggestions from a large number of people, all of which have been very useful to us. In particular, we would like to thank: Sabina Alkire, Paul Anand, Sabine Andresen, Bernhard Babic, Anou Bakhshi, Nicolò Bellanca, Simone Bertoli, Sara Bonfanti, Alejandra Boni Aristizabal, Giovanni Canitano, Giovanna Ceccatelli-Gurrieri, Fabio Cibecchini, Enrica Chiappero-Martinetti, Giovanni Andrea Cornia, David Crocker, MariaRosa Cutillo, Cristina Devecchi, Jean-Luc Dubois, Alex A. Frediani, Des Gasper, Andrea Ferrannini, John Hammock, Caroline Hart, Solava Ibrahim, Javier Iguiñiz, Filomena Maggino, Francesca Marchetta, Vincenzo Mauro, Fabio Cibecchini, Andrea Ferrannini, Martha Nussbaum, Hans Huwe Otto, Antonella Picchio, Mozaffar Qizilbash, Vittorio Rinaldi, Ingrid Robeyns, Fabio Sani, Marina Santi, Kailash Satyarthi, John Schischka, Nathalie Schoenberger, Amartya K. Sen, Lorella Terzi, Enrico Testi, Elaine Unterhalter, Polly Vizard, Franco Volpi, Melanie Walker, Holger Ziegler and Stefan Zublasing.

We are grateful to David A. Clark; we benefited substantially from his invaluable comments and suggestions on every chapter.

We wish to thank the Human Development and Capability Association (HDCA) and, in particular, its President, Professor Kaushik Basu, who kindly took part in one of our first meetings at the University of Florence, as well as the members of the Thematic Group on Children's Capabilities of the same association.

Last but not least, we would very much like to thank the children who participated competently and enthusiastically in much of the research reported in the book, and thus collaborated and contributed to it. To them and to our children (Andrea, Ambroise, Pietro Pio, Céleste and Marina) the book is dedicated.

Foreword

The capability approach – pioneered by Amartya Sen and with subsequent contributions by Martha Nussbaum and other scholars – has led to a large body of literature and a range of studies across many subjects – including development, social justice, welfare, poverty and social exclusion amongst other topics – as well as diverse disciplines. The approach puts the focus fairly and squarely on human beings – on what they can be and do in leading a valuable life. For many, however, like other approaches that focus attention on justice in terms of opportunity and freedom, application of the approach is usually focused on adults who are responsible for their actions and choices. But the reach of the capability approach extends beyond that. It has been applied in a variety of contexts covering our diverse humanity – including many disadvantaged and excluded groups – to whom it can give voice and power. Even more controversially, attempts have been made to apply it to non-human beings. An important set of contributions to this field has come from Mario Biggeri at the University of Florence, as well as his co-editors, Jérôme Ballet and Flavio Comim and their associates, including those in the vibrant and active Children's Thematic Group of the Human Development and Capability Association. This group has engaged in exciting, groundbreaking and pioneering work on children's capabilities and on empowering children by making their voices heard. The research strategy pursued by this group answers some doubts about some versions of the capability approach expressed by the very distinguished political philosopher, Susan Moller Okin in the context of gender. In the title of one of her last papers, in the context of recent work on poverty, well-being and gender, she asked: 'What counts? Who's heard?' The recent body of research on children's capabilities shows that the capability approach can listen creatively and carefully to those who are excluded or not usually heard. Early results from this emerging field of research have already shown how important it is – from both an epistemic and participatory perspective – to engage with and empower children. This book brings together a comprehensive body of work and includes contributions from several experts in this growing field. It makes an important contribution to this area of research, which should inform future work on human development, including work on policy where the voices of children are yet to make a significant impact.

Mozaffar Qizilbash
Professor of Politics, Economics and Philosophy
University of York
UK

Notes on Contributors

Tindara Addabbo is Associate Professor of Political Economics at the University of Modena and Reggio Emilia, Italy. Her main research areas are on the gender impact of public and social policies, measurement of well-being in the capability approach, employment and wage discrimination by gender, income distribution and quality of work. Amongst other essays she has published "Capability and functionings. A fuzzy way to measure interaction between father and child" (co-authors G. Facchinetti and G. Mastroleo) (in Saeed, K. Pejas, J. and Mosdorf, R. (eds) *Biometrics, Computer Security Systems and Artificial Intelligence Applications* (2007).

Rudolf Anich is Junior Researcher at the International Organization for Migration (IOM), Geneva. He graduated in Political Sciences at the University of Florence with a thesis on street children in Kampala. He obtained his MSc at Pavia University. During the research he acted as field coordinator.

Parul Bakhshi is a social psychologist with experience in the fields of education, gender and disability. She is currently an independent consultant and is working on assessments of inclusive education projects. She is also an honorary research fellow at the Leonard Cheshire Disability and Inclusive Development Centre, University College London. From 2004 to 2007, she was researcher and regional field manager for the National Disability Survey in Afghanistan research project, for which she designed the tools, carried out field work and contributed to extensive analysis on gender and vulnerability. Dr Bakhshi has also worked as a consultant on quality education for UNESCO and contributed to the writing of position papers to clarify definitions and improve efficiency and assessment of programmes. She is co-editor with Jean-Luc Dubois of a book on collective capabilities.

Jérôme Ballet is a researcher at the Institut de Recherche pour le Développement, France. He was previously Senior Lecturer in economics at University of Versailles. He is also member of the Fund for researches in ethics and economics (FREE) and editor of the review *Ethics and Economics* (http://ethique-economique.net). His main research fields are poverty and exclusion, ethics and economics. He has published in journals such as *Journal of Human Development, Ecological Economics, Journal of Economic Studies* and the *Journal of Environment and Development,* among others. He has been a consultant for UNDP and UNEP, and has done work for NGOs. He has coordinated a research project in Madagascar on household vulnerability.

Tridib Banerjee holds the James Irvine Chair in Urban and Regional Planning at the University of Southern California, USA. His research, teaching and writings focus on the design and planning of cities, and comparative urbanization. His publications include: *Beyond the Neighborhood Unit* (with William C. Baer, 1984); *City Sense and City Design: Writings and Projects of Kevin Lynch* (co-edited with Michael Southworth, 1990); *Urban Design Downtown: Poetics and Politics of Form* (with Anastasia Loukaitou-Sideris, 1998); and *Companion to Urban Design* (co-edited with Anastasia Loukaitou-Sideris, 2010).

Kaushik Basu is C. Marks Professor of International Studies and Professor of Economics and Director, Program on Comparative Economic Development at Cornell University, USA. Over the years he has held visiting positions at the Institute for Advanced Study (Princeton), CORE (Louvain-la-Neuve) and the London School of Economics (where he was Distinguished Visitor in 1993). He has been Visiting Professor at MIT, Harvard and Princeton, and Visiting Scientist at the Indian Statistical Institute. A Fellow of the Econometric Society and recipient of the Mahalanobis Memorial Medal, Basu has published scientific papers in development economics, game theory, industrial organization, political economy and the economics of child labour, and crafted the traveller's dilemma. In 1992 he founded the Centre for Development Economics (CDE) at the Delhi School of Economics, Delhi, and was the Centre's first Executive Director, until 1996. He is the editor of the *Oxford Companion to Economics in India* (2007). He is Editor of *Social Choice and Welfare*, Associate Editor of *Japanese Economic Review* and is on the Board of Editors of the *World Bank Economic Review*. In 2008, the Government of India awarded him the Padma Bhushan, one of the country's highest civil honors. He is President elect of the Human Development Capability Association.

Augendra Bhukuth is a researcher at Fonds pour la Recherche en Ethique et Economie, France. He works at the Centre de Recherche et d'Analyse de la Pauvreté au sein de la "National Empowerment Foundation" in the Republic of Mauritius.

Mario Biggeri is Associate Professor in Development Economics at the Department of Economics, University of Florence, Italy, and Director of the Master in Development Economics. His research interests include local development (clusters of small and medium enterprises and informal activities), child labour and capabilities, international cooperation, rural development, economies of transition, and Chinese and South Asian Development. He is the co-author of three books and co-editor of two. His papers have been published in several international journals. He worked for three years at UNICEF at the Innocenti Research Centre (IRC). He is a fellow of the

Human Development Capability Association (HDCA) and co-coordinator of the thematic group on "Children's capabilities".

Laura Camfield is Senior Researcher at Young Lives, a longitudinal study of childhood poverty, based at the Oxford Department of International Development, University of Oxford, UK. Laura has a PhD and MA in Anthropology from the University of London, and her research focuses on experiences of poverty, resilience and methodologies for exploring and measuring subjective well-being in developing countries. She was a research fellow with the Wellbeing in Developing Countries ESRC Research Group from 2002 to 2007 and coordinated its research in Thailand.

Flavio Comim is currently working for the United Nations Development Programme in Brazil coordinating its next National Human Development Report. He lectures in Human Development at the University of Cambridge and is a visiting fellow of St Edmund's College. He has published in journals such as *Review of Political Economy, History of Political Economy, Journal of Economic Methodology, Structural Change and Economic Dynamics* and *American Journal of Sociology*, among others. He has co-edited the books *The Capability Approach: Concepts, Measures and Applications* (2008) and *Capability and Happiness* (2008). He has been a Coordinating Leading Author of the Millennium Ecosystem Assessment and a Leading Author for the fourth Global Environment Outlook, produced by the United Nations Environment Programme.

Maria Laura Di Tommaso is Senior Lecturer in Economics at the University of Turin, Italy. Previous positions include College Lecturer in Economics at Robinson College, University of Cambridge and Research Associate in the Department of Applied Economics, University of Cambridge. Her interests are in the field of labour economics, micro-econometrics, the capability approach and feminist economics. Her work has appeared in the *Cambridge Journal of Economics, Economic Journal, Journal of Health Economics, European Journal of Political Economy, Journal of Population Economics, Applied Economics* and *Journal of Socio-economics, Labour*.

Marisa Horna received her degree in psychology from the Pontificia Universidad Católica del Perú. She obtained her Master in social policies focusing on children and adolescents at the Universidad Nacional Mayor de San Marcos, where she currently teaches. She specializes in vulnerable children (children in transitional status) and child worker issues. She is connected to IFEJANT. She is also the author of *Plan de Vida* [Project of Life] edited by Save the Children, dealing with social and self-agency.

Vittorio Iervese is Assistant Professor in the Sociology of Culture at the University of Modena and Reggio Emilia, Italy, and member of the Department of Languages and Cultures. He is founder of Cuscos – *Centro Universitario Servizi alla Cooperazione allo Sviluppo* [Cooperation for Development], of Cirsfia – *Centro Interuniversitario Ricerche sulla Famiglia, l'Infanzia e l'Adolescenza* [Family, Childhood and Youth] and member of the Board of *Forum: Qualitative Social Research*. His main areas of research and teaching are: social participation, the sociology of children, intercultural communication and conflict management. He participates in several international research projects on children's participation. He recently published with Claudio Baraldi (ed.) *Dialogue in Intercultural Communities* (2010) and "Mediating interactions among children in educational systems", in *Conflict Resolution Quarterly*.

Anne Kellock is a Senior Lecturer at Sheffield Hallam University, UK. She teaches on the Early Childhood Studies and Childhood Studies undergraduate degree programmes. She is a photographer and has a background in primary school teaching in England and New Zealand. She has been involved in visual research projects in the UK, New Zealand and Malaysia exploring the well-being of children through the use of photography and other participative techniques as part of her PhD and other funded projects. Her visual techniques have also been used with adults around problem-solving and well-being in the workplace.

Rebecca Lawthom is a Reader in Community Practice in the Department of Psychology at Manchester Metropolitan University, UK. She is a feminist and community psychologist and has published widely in areas such as life history methods, disability and psychology, community psychology and feminism. Recent works include *Researching Life Stories: Method, Theory and Analysis in a Biographical Age* (with Goodley, Clough and Moore, 2004), and an edited collection, *Disability and Psychology: Critical Introductions and Reflections* (with Goodley, 2006). A text in preparation is *Community Psychology: Critical Action and Social Change* (with Kagan, Burton, Siddiquee and Duckett).

Ferdinand Lewis is Lecturer at the College of Design, Construction, and Planning University of Florida, USA. He was Visiting Professor of Urban Planning at the School of Architecture and Planning, University of Buffalo, and was Adjunct Professor at the Roski School of Fine Arts, University of Southern California (Public Art Studies Program). He served on the Interdisciplinary Studies Faculty at the California Institute of the Arts for a decade. Dr. Lewis was also Lecturer at the University of Southern California Neighborhood Studies program, and at the USC School of Policy, Planning & Development.

Renato Libanora, is Lecturer in the Anthropology of Development at the University of Florence, Italy. His main themes of research are concerned with cultural, social and political changes in less advanced countries, with particular reference to conflict dynamics and peace-building processes, the informal economy and indigenous medicine, gender relationships and women's empowerment, protection of children, development and education. He has carried out field research and professional consultancies for the European Commission, Italian Ministry of Foreign Affairs, Save the Children and various other I/NGOS in Ghana, Uganda, Ethiopia, Malawi, Nepal, Sri Lanka and Liberia.

Stefano Mariani, economist and statistician, graduated at the University of Florence, Italy. Since 1995, he has worked at the Department of Statistics, University of Florence, as an expert in survey and questionnaire design, CATI interviews, database management and statistical elaborations.

Santosh Mehrotra, Director-General, Institute of Applied Manpower Research, Planning Commission, Government of India. He resigned from a senior staff position in UNDP to join the Planning Commission in September 2006. Head of Development Policy Division, Planning Commission until August 2009, and Head of the Rural Development Division, Planning Commission (2006–08); lead author of India's 11th Five Year Plan (2007–12). He also led the team that wrote India's Human Development Report 2011. He was Regional Economic Advisor for Poverty, Regional Centre for Asia, UNDP, Bangkok (2005–06), and chief economist, Human Development Report, UNDP, New York (2002–2005). He was Senior Economic Adviser, UNICEF New York (1991–1999) and then led UNICEF's research programme on developing countries at the Innocenti Research Centre, Florence (1999–2002).

After an MA in Economics (New School for Social Research, New York), and PhD at Cambridge University (1985), Santosh was Associate Professor of Economics, Jawaharlal Nehru University, Delhi (1988–1991). He has over 50 published papers in Indian and international journals, spanning his research interests: industry and trade issues, the informal sector, the impact of macro-economic policy on health and education, child well-being and poverty, and the economics of health and education. He currently holds the Parkin Visiting Professorship (2010–12) at the Centre for Development Studies, University of Bath, UK.

Katia Radja is a senior lecturer in Economics at the University of Versailles St Quentin-en-Yvelines and researcher at the Centre d'Etudes sur la Mondialisation, les Territoires et la Vulnérabilité (CEMOTEV) in France. She works mainly on family and gender issues, development and poverty, education and sustainable development issues.

Badreddine Serrokh holds a Masters in Management Engineering from the Solvay Business School (Université Libre de Bruxelles) in Belgium. He is a visiting research fellow at the Centre for European Research in Microfinance (Centre Emile Bernheim, Université Libre de Bruxelles). His research interest focuses on micro-finance, child labour, youth entrepreneurship and SME development. Professionally active in the field of international development and humanitarian aid, he has developed his field experience with various NGOs in countries within Africa, Asia and the Caribbean.

Yisak Tafere is a PhD candidate at the Norwegian Centre for Child Research, Norwegian University of Science and Technology, Trondheim, Norway. He has an MA in Social Anthropology and a BA in Philosophy from Addis Ababa University. He is the lead qualitative researcher for the project Young Lives in Ethiopia. His research has mainly focused on demobilization and reintegration of young soldiers, youth development, children and childhood poverty, intergenerational transfer of poverty and the socio-cultural construction of children's well-being.

Jean-Francois Trani is currently a senior research associate at the Leonard Cheshire Disability and Inclusive Development Centre, University College London, UK. In 2004, he initiated and defined the National Disability Survey in Afghanistan research project while he was technical advisor to the Minister of Martyrs and Disabled in Afghanistan. The objectives of the study were defined in view of the needs expressed by the various stakeholders and partners. Dr Trani also obtained direct support from the Ministry of Public Health (MoPH) and from the Central Statistic Office of Afghanistan to ensure national ownership of the survey. He introduced the use of the International Classification of Functioning, Disability and Health (ICF) defined by the World Health Organization (2001), and the capability approach elaborated by Amartya Sen and others to improve and standardize the measurement of disability in population-based surveys.

JungA Uhm received her PhD in planning from the University of Southern California in 2008. Her dissertation explored factors associated with children walking to school by examining transactions between children, parents and the environment. Her work in practice and research interest has focused on the planning and design of safe, healthy, and walkable environments. She currently works as a regional planner at the Southern California Association of Governments (SCAG), the largest metropolitan planning organization in the United States.

Part I

Introduction and Theoretical Perspectives on Children and the Capability Approach

1

Introduction – Theoretical Foundations and the Book's Roadmap

Flavio Comim, Jérôme Ballet, Mario Biggeri and Vittorio Iervese

Childhood and adolescence are periods in life that are distinct for a variety of reasons. It is during the early years of life that individuals experience the most important cognitive and emotional developments that subsequently shape their identity and world-views. The capabilities of children and adolescents are formed through social interaction and receptiveness within the household and broader environments, and constitute to a large extent the foundation of a human being's development. This means that understanding and assessing children's and adolescents' well-being cannot successfully be pursued by viewing them as miniature adults. Moreover, understanding adults' well-being might not be possible without reference to these early stages in life. As a result, what might appear to be a simple technical question – namely, what is the most appropriate way of assessing children's well-being? – may turn out to be a real challenge. To help address this challenge, this book develops the capability approach (CA) as a conceptual framework for understanding children's well-being.

There are several reasons why researchers and practitioners interested in the capability and human development approach should pay closer attention to children's issues. How can we think about human development without tackling child issues? A quick look at the Human Development Index reveals that two of its dimensions (namely, health and knowledge) are directly affected by what happens to children. Similarly, the realizations of several Millennium Development Goals relate specifically to children. Moreover "development" is a process that in many cases is especially relevant during childhood. What happens to children often leads to path dependency, and in some cases key capability failures may be irreversible in later life (e.g. stunting).

And yet, despite the efforts of some international agencies it seems that attention to children has not achieved the prominence it deserves. Even the most influential alternative development perspective of our generation – the

CA – has not yet adequately engaged with children's issues, although much has been written about education generally from this perspective (e.g. Walker and Unterhalter, 2007). This book aims also to bridge this gap by using the CA (as developed by Amartya Sen and Martha Nussbaum) to explore its significance and relevance for theory, policy and development practices regarding children.

Thinking about children's development is tantamount to thinking about poverty reduction. This is because:

- children are disproportionately represented among the poor in developed as well as developing countries;
- children often suffer irreversible forms of capability failure in terms of mental, physical, emotional and spiritual development;
- children are often misconceived as small-scale adults, which leads to the neglect of a wider range of development problems and challenges that depend on recognizing that young people have specific needs that evolve over their life cycle;
- children's low human development promotes inter-generational transfers of poverty; and
- children's well-being has a strong influence on many aspects of future development.

Like many other researchers, we think that the agenda of well-being assessment cannot be confined merely to the material aspects of life. Indeed, well-being in general has a multidimensional and immaterial character, and this is especially true in the case of children.

Within this context, the main objective of this book is to illustrate the case for putting children at the centre of the development studies agenda, seeing them as agents in the process of developing their capabilities and well-being. This involves engaging with a range of different fields including childhood studies, education, disability studies, urban planning, participatory methods and research and human rights. When children are acknowledged as subjects of respect and agency in society, a new vision of development can be achieved. Children also have an active role to play in promoting human development.

Although these reasons are more than enough to raise awareness among researchers, practitioners and policy makers, from a research perspective they are accompanied by two lines of academic enquiry that make the topic of children and capabilities a very important research issue.

The first explores the possible uses of the CA to investigate children's issues. Can the CA help us to think about the relevance of the particularities of being a child? Could synergies between the approach and children themselves result in new policies and strategies for improving the lives of millions of children in this world? It seems that there is room for further theorization of the CA by electing children as one of its objects of attention. In the same way, it appears that fresh light can be thrown on the promotion of public policies for children by using the approach. In this book, we hope to provide some idea of the potential contribution of the CA in various fields – from education, to disability studies, to urban planning via participation – since children as subjects with capabilities have a crucial role in society. Consequently, the CA, seen as a child-centred approach, offers important and constructive critiques of the dominant theories and often complements them in the analysis of children's issues and in establishing related policies.

The second line of enquiry is about how applying the CA to children can encourage a rethinking of the CA, challenging it far more intensely than we initially thought likely. Indeed, although the CA is a normative framework that can be used to evaluate children's issues, children's issues may also challenge the CA framework itself and force us to revise it. This means, for instance, ceasing to regard children as irrational or immature, and instead considering them to be active actors, agents and subjects of capabilities. Most importantly, having to investigate children's development forces us to take a more dynamic attitude to the CA.

Conceptualizing children as active agents and co-producers of their capabilities enables fresh insights into how capabilities can initially be built and subsequently assessed. One illustration might clarify this concept: when assessing the impact of educational systems on children using the CA, emphasis is given to outcomes; namely, whether children are able to read and write (understood as functionings). This might take us a long way from assessing the impact of these systems in terms of allocated resources to education or subjective perceptions. However, with a new conceptualization of children as individuals in the process of building their capabilities, a fresh perspective is brought into the analysis enabling us to consider the process aspects of human development. Instead of seeing children as irrational or immature, they can be considered as active actors and agents. Furthermore, the path of capabilities development followed by an individual combines elements of freedom with unfreedoms, due to path dependencies. A new horizon for the CA is therefore established when our main focus of analysis is children's capabilities.

Before entering into the book's contents we think that it is appropriate to introduce the concepts and theory related to the CA, as well as to reflect on how this framework may influence the dominant culture of childhood and vice versa.

1.1. The capability approach: a brief introduction

The CA, as developed by Amartya Sen (1985, 1999a, 2005) and Martha Nussbaum (2000) over the past two decades, has provided the intellectual foundation for a model of development that is both human and sustainable. It has focused on participation, human well-being and freedom as central features of development, combining ethics with economics.[1] This approach has been influenced and is influencing the cutting-edge thinking of development economists, sociologists, educationalists and anthropologists, among others, and has been used in many different fields and arenas of thought.

In general, the merits of the CA are more easily appreciated in theoretical rather than empirical terms. Its value for stimulating new ways of thinking about human development is undeniable, but its operationalization still represents a challenge in domains like health and education (see Comim, Qizilbash and Alkire, 2008) and in particular for assessing children's well-being. For example, concerning education Sen (1992, 1999a for instance) underlines the main role it plays in promoting capabilities. Nussbaum (1997, 2002, 2006) has more substantially developed this facet of the capabilities approach. Others researches have also reflected on these issues (for instance, Brighouse, 2000; Mehrotra and Biggeri, 2002; Saito, 2003; Swift, 2003; Unterhalter and Brighouse, 2003; Walker and Unterhalter, 2007). Nonetheless, the possibility of applying the CA to children has not yet been adequately explored.

Sen has written on a wide range of issues with reference to children and often takes children and young adults as a focal point.[2,3] However, there are few occasions where Sen has devoted full attention to children as the main object of analysis. Two of these occasions were in a speech at the Inter-American Development Bank and in an article for the *Indian Journal of Human Development*. In the first, Sen (1999b) discusses the relevance of investing in early childhood for social and economic development, and examines some childhood–adult connections from political, economic and social perspectives; while in the *Indian Journal of Human Development* article Sen (2007) concentrates on the relevance of child rights. Nussbaum, as discussed later, has often gone into issues regarding children as the subject of capabilities and agency, and the role of human obligations towards the most vulnerable (Nussbaum, 2000, 2006). Even before the creation of the Human Development and Capability Association (HDCA) in 2004, several theoretical and empirical papers have systematically explored this potentially rich field of research. Biggeri (2003) used the capability framework to rethink child labour definitions and issues, while Di Tommaso (2003) focused on the well-being of children in India using econometric analysis to measure capabilities. Schischka (2003) examined the impact of educational programmes for indigenous children in Samoa in the Pacific Ocean, while Comim (2009) has attempted to measure the expansion of children's capabilities.[4]

Sen and other *human development* scholars view development as the "expansion of capabilities" or "positive freedoms" (Sen, 1999a). Human beings are thus the ends of economic activity rather than merely means. When individuals are seen only as human capital they serve as means to achieve economic growth. However, when economic growth is seen as serving the interests of people, they become the ends of development. This is why "the capability approach proposes a change – a serious departure – from concentrating on the *means* of living to the *actual opportunities* of living in itself" (Sen, 2009: 17). Resources are indeed important for promoting the functionings and capabilities of children but only as instrumental means for human flourishing.

The essential idea of the CA is that social arrangements should aim to expand people's capabilities – their freedom to promote or achieve valuable beings and doings. Following Aristotle, the capabilities of a person have been associated with human flourishing, which suggests they can be realized in many different ways (Nussbaum, 2000). This image helps to capture the multidimensional nature of child development.[5]

Capability is defined as "the various combinations of functionings (beings and doings) that the person can achieve. Capability is, thus, a set of vectors of functionings, reflecting the person's freedom to lead one type of life or another... to choose from possible livings" (Sen, 1992: 40). Put differently, they are "the substantive freedoms he or she enjoys to lead the kind of life he or she has reason to value" (Sen, 1999a: 87).[6] *Functionings* are "the various things a person may value doing or being" (Sen, 1999a: 75). "The difference between a functioning and a capability is similar to the difference between an achievement and the freedom to achieve something, or between an outcome and an opportunity. All capabilities together correspond to the overall *freedom* to lead the life that a person has *reason to value*" (Robeyns, 2003: 63).

Therefore, the CA frames the range of experiences and life situations as "possible functionings". If a functioning is an achievement, whereas a capability is the ability to achieve, functionings are, in a sense, more directly related to living conditions, since they are different aspects of one's everyday life. Capabilities, in contrast, are notions of freedom, in the positive sense: what real opportunities you have regarding the life you may lead (Sen, 1987: 36); in this sense capabilities are both opportunities and capacities of individuals.[7,8]

The process aspect of freedom and empowerment are highly relevant. The concept of agency captures the ability to pursue goals that one values and has reason to value. We consider that the level of agency – as a measure of autonomous action and of empowerment in the context of choice – can vary according to age, especially for some capabilities (e.g. mobility).[9] As the CA is based on people's values (including children's), participation is one of the pillars of the approach.[10] It is important to note, however, that normally children are not consulted and in the meaning of an active actor in society given by the participation of adults. Children would probably define the meaning of being an active actor or citizen differently.[11]

The CA addresses human and social diversity positively. It allows for more flexibility and adaptation to different personal capacities (talent, skills and personal characteristics) and different cultural and societal contexts and thus "acknowledge[es] that different people, cultures and societies *may* have different values and aspirations" (Clark, 2006: 36). Other approaches often do not reflect the socio-economic realities of children's lives, their relationships with other group members in their communities (Feeny and Boyden, 2004: 18) or their values and priorities (Biggeri et al., 2006). In most social contexts "[t]he idea of them exercising rights autonomously is not only foreign but potentially undermining of family and community and even of child survival, since the child exists only as a part of a whole" (Feeny and Boyden, 2004: 18).[12]

Explicitly, what matters for children's well-being are their functionings and capabilities (Biggeri et al, 2006). Through the CA we are analysing what children are effectively able to do and to be, i.e. how well children are able to function with the goods and services at their disposal. Children may need different resources and policies to be able to enjoy the same basic capabilities and achieved functionings: a child, for instance, has very different nutritional requirements from an adult. As already mentioned, "the focus of the CA is not just on what a person actually ends up of doing, but also on what she is capable of doing, whether or not she chooses to make use of that opportunity" (Sen, 2009: 17).

In order to make this approach more dynamic, in Chapter 2 we present a new reading of capabilities looking at potential capabilities. This allows us to introduce the process of *evolving capabilities* incorporating the opportunity concept, the capacity concept and the agency concept that evolve over time. Although autonomy and agency are relevant in this process they do not mean independency and isolation, but interdependence and reciprocity, i.e. socialization.

Hence the development of each human being is the result of a complex interaction between genetic, household and environmental factors. The range of "possible functionings" for children, their "capability set", may thus be restricted due to their capacity, or be limited by their social and physical environment. Therefore, the ability to convert resources and commodities into capabilities and functionings depends on *conversion factors*. The conversion factors can be internal or societal/environmental. The "internal" conversion factors such as personal characteristics (e.g. physical conditions, sex, skills, talents, intelligence) allow individuals to convert resources and commodities (or their characteristics) into individual functionings. The conversion is also related to social factors (e.g. public policies, institutions, legal rules, traditions, social norms, discriminating practices, gender roles, societal hierarchies, power relations, public goods) and environmental factors (e.g. climate, geographical infrastructure). These factors can be related to the household's characteristics or to society. For instance, in the household, a mother's education typically enhances her children's opportunities for health and education. Indeed, the ability to convert resources and commodities into capabilities and functionings depends on individual and social conversion factors and typically, even more, on their parents' or caregivers' capabilities. Parents and women as mothers in particular are important in creating the household environment which allows children to flourish. The failure to create such a positive environment is often due not just to the parents' incapacity but to external circumstances which contribute to the perpetuation and upgrading of negative social capital, which often does not allow children to flourish or even survive.

In embracing this approach for children, we affirm that the child is a subject of agency and capabilities and that these need to be analysed through a distinctive "lens" (Biggeri et al., 2006). The main goal is to consider children as capable agents and to promote the active participation of children in society. But how is this approach related to the new sociology of childhood?

1.2. What do we talk about when we talk about childhood?

In recent times, thank to the resonance of historical studies such as that of Ariés (1960), it is widely accepted that childhood as a concept was first elaborated at the beginning of the modern age and then assumed different meanings and directions in the late modern age. According to this point of view, childhood is a historical construction that depends on the way children are treated in society. The theoretical and methodological question of the *history of childhood categories (ibid.)* had the praise of de-naturalizing childhood and bringing back the attention on children and their practices. Childhood thus can only be taken into account if it is considered contextualized in a specific culture and social structure.

Over the years there have been different descriptions that have modified the way of thinking of, and interacting with, childhood. Particular interests, traditions and ideologies can be found in each of these descriptions, which together provide different contemporary approaches to the study of the child. Considering the plurality of these approaches is a first step to reflecting on the question, what are we talking about when we speak of "childhood"?

A first distinction that can help us is the one that is classical in recent childhood sociology between "children's life" and "images of childhood" (James et al., 1998). If by "children's life" it is normally meant their social reality, their living and being active in a specific age and in a specific place, "images of childhood" by contrast is typically meant to convey the ideas and the representations that an age, social group or an individual has of children (which can have extremely important consequences for "real" children).

Everyone talks about children but finds themselves some distance from the reality they are talking about; in no way can they fully capture that reality. This hermeneutic circumstance, which is obvious, seems to be forgotten easily, in particular when it concerns children (Richter, 1987). We can thus try to distinguish between *children's culture* and *childhood's culture* (James et al., 1998), where the former represents the totality of the communications in which children are actively involved. Thus it is not a formalized and encoded culture, but a culture that affirms itself in the moment it expresses itself. Childhood's culture can be defined as all considerations, scientific or otherwise, that relate to children. It's the children that, with their considerations, give life to a children's culture; it's the adults that, with their conjectures, give birth to a childhood's culture (Iervese, 2006). The latter is different from the former by virtue of the presumption of representing more or less objectively children's reality.

Traditionally the dominant culture of childhood – especially in Western societies – gives particular relevance to two different approaches: (1) a *developmental* individualistic perspective, based on primary cognitive expectations concerning children's learning and (2) an *evolutionary* collectivist perspective based on primary relevance of attachment and affective dimension in children's socialization. Cognitive developmental individualism and affective evolutionary collectivism are mixed in a formula that explains children's social and personal lives: a child must be nurtured through an affective relationship and stimulated through a cognitive training; the mixture of these two social processes is considered successful for her or his socialization. The other side of this social representation is that an affective deprivation and a cognitive under-stimulation can be fatal for children's socialization, causing pain and deviance.

The dominant childhood's culture in recent years adopted a psycho-evolutionist paradigm that considered children as not yet complete (and to be completed) individuals, thus with a limited capacity for social action. Whether the child was considered as an object to be formed in view of a development, or as a source of instincts and internal drives, there was no consideration of its social participation and no idea that its meaning was historically and culturally build.

Classical sociology, both in the structural–functionalist version (represented by Talcott Parsons) and the symbolic interactionism account, focused itself on socialization processes that see the child as a naturalized object (a predefined structure subsequently determined in social interaction), instead of the main character of social processes (Parsons and Bales, 1955). In this approach we can see a connection between the sciences that deal with children and the general childhood's culture.

Following the theory of the social representation (Moscovici, 1984), the conception of childhood in the twentieth century can be interpreted according to the transformation of scientific theories (educational psychology of Freud and Piaget) in the dominating common sense in society. In particular, the naturalistic theory of psychometric development became the paradigm in the social treatment of children.

However, the mainstream culture of childhood has recently placed particular emphasis on children's self-realization (Prout, 2000) and on children's agency (James et al., 1998; Hallett and Prout, 2003). These new cultural presuppositions lead to the promotion of children's active participation, i.e. children's self-expression (Baraldi, 2008) and children's self-determination (Murray and Hallett, 2000). Promoting children's active participation means socializing children towards an "understanding of their own competencies" (Matthews, 2003: 274); that is, to a sense of responsibility and skills in planning, designing, monitoring and managing social contexts. This new narrative introduces a fundamental ambivalence in society: children are considered as either "being" or "becoming", either active or passive, either competent or non-competent. In interaction, the primacy of children's agency and self-realization is alternative to or mixed with the primacy of their instrumental usage to realize social aims (Prout, 2000).

Inside this cultural framework, promotion of children's social participation is very innovative. In fact, it is the third option with respect to the two sides of the traditional distinction between affective and cognitive dimensions. Above all, promotion of children's social participation avoids any reference to developmental and evolutionary perspectives, as it renounces to a temporal appreciation of childhood, which explains it in the light of either a common past (evolution) or an individual future (development), observing it in its actual existence, in its relationship with its social context. In this sense, this could be considered a genuine "capabilities perspective" (Sen, 1992). But what is the childhood's culture that can be evicted by the approach oriented by *capabilities*? What are the possible horizons?

In general, the distinction between childhood's culture and children's culture has become increasingly important from the moment in which the perspective that children are individuals who can reproduce both the adult culture and "incorporate" social norms, but also produce meanings and autonomous, unique and specific practices, has been developed. This perspective turns the idea of the incapability of children on its head: it is no longer claimed, for example, that the necessary condition to be admitted to participate is the demonstration of an adequate degree of development and of appraisal. It confirms instead the strict connection between participation, differentiated competencies and personal autonomy. Participation is the autonomy's expression and the individual expresses itself in autonomous ways by participating. Autonomy has sense only *in* social participation.

In this framework, the attention given to the control and valorization of the capabilities brings one, as far as children are concerned, to address not only the childhood's culture but in particular to make visible and active the children's culture by promoting their social participation.

Social participation may be observed as "visible action" in a public social space, produced in communication processes. Adapting a social system theory (Luhmann, 1984, 2002), communication can be defined as the coordination between action and understanding, creating information in a social dimension (Iervese and Rossi, 2009). Action is a component of communication, as it can exist only through understanding: one's action without others' understanding is deprived of social existence. Participation in communication may mean both understanding and action, but it is *visible* only as action. In fact, only action demonstrates participation, as understanding is not visible to others (understanding must be shown or demonstrated through action). Consequently, although individuals participate in communication by both acting and understanding, the idea of participation specifically implies that they are *active*.

Participation through action is common in communication processes. The term *social* participation, as it is generally used, implies something more than mere action: it implies that action is "public", that it is visible in the whole society (or community), as well as in particular interactive systems (like families or classes). In other words, "social" means (potentially) "visible for everybody", not only for a few "specialized" persons or roles (like parents, teachers, experts).

Social participation is a *visible action in public (societal) contexts*. For this reason, social participation is a clear manifestation of citizenship, intended as inclusion in a society, with full rights and opportunities.

Promotion is conceived as creation of environmental (social) conditions for an autonomous choice of participation. Promotion too is produced through communication. It is the creation of external (social) opportunities for a (social or individual) autonomous enhancement. The necessary conditions of promotion are (a) complete respect for autonomous choices and (b) renunciation of attempts to change choice perspectives from outside. Promotion of children's social participation is the creation of opportunities for children's active and visible action in society. Promotion tries to empower children's autonomous participation in social practices.

The study of children's capabilities cannot disregard the promotion of their active participation in the different social contexts. This for at least three reasons: (1) the competencies, resources and capabilities of a subject, in particular of children, are tied to the possibility of being acted, understood and being recognized as significant. In other terms, capabilities are strictly dependent on the forms (social and individual) and by the possibilities (environment) of *agency*; (2) the different forms of participation and the environmental conditions that enable its expression need to be valorized and sustained to enable them to reproduce over time: there are no "natural" *capabilities* (understood as opportunities) but only those socially built; and (3) different cultures and many social contexts that denote, and in which capabilities are built, can be considered only if they become visible along with the practices and the orientations that inspire them.

If these three points are not considered, there is the risk of tying the CA to a conventional and distant childhood's culture, incapable of taking into account cultural differences, different forms of expression and the social, political and environmental conditions that concern children. The attention given to a childhood's culture that takes seriously into account children's culture raises an important methodological problem, not only for those who do research, but also for those who conceive interventions and policies. Studying and working on childhood is neither easy nor trivial, as children do not have the opportunity to describe themselves on an equal footing with experts or have free spaces to describe themselves.

For this reason, those interested in children have to address the problem of which methods and techniques should be used to *give voice* to a childhood that is not able to speak for itself, by creating new instruments or trying to modify instruments already used in other scientific contexts. It follows that childhood researchers and policy makers should focus their attention on the ways children are involved and considered.

The central question, *what are we talking about when we are talking about childhood?* now becomes, *how do we talk about childhood and in which way do we relate ourselves to children?* This book attempts to address this question and provide insights into issues not usually considered by adults. Thus, from a capability perspective we need not only to ask whether children have the ability to be well educated, healthy, adequately housed and clothed and well integrated into the community, but also about the process of freedom itself.

1.3. The book's roadmap

We have seen that although some of the main problems addressed by human development policies are directly related to the promotion of children's capabilities, in the CA little attention is usually paid to the specific characteristics that result from being a child.[13] Therefore, if Sen's CA has attracted considerable attention, primarily in development and welfare economics, it remains under-theorized in relation to children as well as under-explored in terms of the practical applications and methodological developments that are vital for the approach. As a new approach for investigating child issues, there are inevitably several theoretical and empirical questions to consider before the CA can become operational. How can we understand the relevance of the capability space and framework in assessing policies aimed at children's well-being? Can the relevance of a capability change with the age of human beings? What is the role of agency associated with the age and maturity of the child? Can children define their capabilities? What are the relevance conversion factors? Is adaptation in terms of preferences or values explained by age? These and other questions are naturally tackled in different parts of this book.

Having said that, our collective efforts started in 2004 with the foundation of a thematic group to explore "Children's Capabilities" at a meeting held at the annual conference of the Human Development and Capability Association (HDCA).[14] It was a small but important occasion. New issues and challenges were identified and a sense of interdependence between different research agendas was created. The need for a book delving theoretically and practically into children's issues from a Capability Perspective was established.

The perspectives put forward here represent a serious interdisciplinary effort drawing on disciplines such as anthropology, economics, development economics, development studies, education, disability and gender studies, philosophy, sociology and urban planning.

The other 15 chapters included in this book explore children's issues from diverse theoretical, contextual and empirical perspectives, and look at children's functioning and capabilities related to issues and aspects of their lives such as child labour, education, participation, disabilities, poverty and freedom, situating them in daily life contexts, addressing the role of their environment, their relationships with peers, their role in society gender divide and measurement issues (among other things). The case studies reported represent international diversity, tackling issues in countries such as Afghanistan, Bangladesh, Ethiopia, India, Italy, Peru, Uganda and UK.

In this pioneering book we highlight the fact that the CA can provide significant theoretical underpinnings for the conceptualization and measurement of child well-being, human development and poverty, and for policy and practices regarding children in matters concerning them as both individuals and a group in society. It is important to note that the theoretical and practical marriage proposed by this book goes beyond the most obvious synergies. Rather, it claims that its policy implications can make a difference to the way that we think about human development and children's well-being. Thus, part of the book explores issues related to children's well-being and the other focuses on institutions for promoting children's well-being.

For simplicity the book is divided into four parts. The first part, which includes Chapters 1–3, builds on the theoretical foundations of the CA in relation to children's agency, well-being and well-becoming with reference to selecting domains for analysis. The second part of the book, which spans Chapters 4–10, is concerned with making the CA operational and consists of several case studies that develop methods and procedures for understanding children's agency, well-being and deprivation. Many of these chapters are concerned with measurement issues. The third part of the book, which incorporates Chapters 11–14, focuses on the policy implications of developing the CA for children and is supported by several novel case studies. The final part of the book summarizes the main conclusions.

In Chapter 2, the three editors present a general framework for understanding children's well-being based on the CA. Some of the main issues concerning children are raised, and a guide to interpreting the chapters of the book is provided. The aim of this chapter is to consider how the CA can fruitfully be used as a theoretical foundation for understanding children as subjects and agents of human development. This means considering children not simply as the recipients of positive freedoms, but as active social actors and agents within their communities with their own priorities, strategies, aspirations and potentials. In order to capture the development of children's capabilities, the concept of agency is examined and the concept evolving capabilities is introduced.

In Chapter 3, Mario Biggeri and Santosh Mehrotra define child poverty as the deprivation of basic capabilities and achieved functionings. If social or economic arrangements aim to promote capabilities, rather than income or resources, which capabilities should they promote? Indeed, the question of how to choose the most relevant domains (chosen for or by the children) is key to understanding child poverty, which is the authors' main argument. The authors explore briefly two procedures for selecting relevant dimensions, and use an open list of relevant capabilities to explore and compare the different methods used by the researchers; five methods that are generally used to choose and select domains are considered. The chapter is supplemented with two appendices: the first reviews the domains of child poverty and well-being based on various different approaches, while the second provides a concrete example of multidimensional child poverty. Making the CA operational, however, does not merely entail identifying and measuring "missing" dimensions of well-being. It involves a fundamental change in research design that begins with collecting information and continues with data elaboration methods (as described in Chapter 11).

In Chapter 4, Mario Biggeri and Renato Libanora propose tools and procedures for implementing the CA with respect to children's development. The first procedure considered addresses the problem of how to conceptualize and value children's capabilities, while the second is an evaluation tool. The tools and procedures proposed in this chapter follow on from the assumption that the selection of capabilities should be the outcome of a democratic process rooted in public scrutiny and open debate and, most importantly, that this is not exclusively the domain of adults but should be based on children's participation instead. An appendix describes the detailed questionnaire-based tools and methods used to aggregate ordinal and subjective data.

In Chapter 5, Rudolf Anich, Mario Biggeri, Renato Libanora and Stefano Mariani analyse capability deprivation amongst street children in Kampala, Uganda. The methodology augments the *ad hoc* survey presented in Chapter 4 with some qualitative participatory methods (photo essays, thematic drawings, life histories (peer interviews), mapping and focus group analyses). The data were collected from three groups of children: street children, ex-street children (i.e. "rehabilitated" children) living in institutions and a control group of children who had no "street experience". Policy implications are drawn from current policies and research findings.

In Chapter 6, Anne Kellock and Rebecca Lawthom invited children aged 8–10 to explore their own perspectives on emotional well-being using photography as a vehicle for expression (the children were attending British primary school classes). Photography was selected as a research tool as it is a rich visual medium for communicating ideas, and can be used to communicate thoughts and feelings creatively. Using the CA, they explore the things these children think they need to achieve functionings, whether commodities are important for this purpose and how their capabilities are applied in the process of assessment.

In Chapter 7, Marisa Horna Padrón and Jérôme Ballet explore child agency and identity formation. This chapter argues that children are endowed with a capacity for agency, including situations where they seemingly appear like mere victims, and examines the capacity for agency of children in a transitional situation on the streets of Peru. Their study has identified children and adolescents who perform various activities on the streets or in the midst of the traffic, and explores the impact of these on their capabilities.

In Chapter 8, Badreddine Serrokh investigates the still largely unexplored but prominent topic of micro-finance and street children. Could solutions be sought for the future of street children based on working arrangements? Serrokh analyses whether the provision of financial services is an appropriate tool for addressing their needs. Based on a participatory research in Bangladesh, the chapter highlights the necessity of a holistic programme in which financial services are provided along with vocational training and social services for street children. Moreover, he argues that savings and credit products need to be designed and delivered in a very specific manner in order to enhance the benefits for forgotten children.

In Chapter 9, Laura Camfield and Yisak Tafere analyse the differences between Ethiopian children in relation to their caregivers with regard to their understanding of what constitutes a good life, and what is needed to achieve it. They also consider whether the CA can bridge the gap between a shared local understanding of what constitutes a good life and universal prescriptions of international bodies, such as those of the United Nations Children's Fund (UNICEF), about what is "good for children". The authors use qualitative data from group interviews and activities with a subsample of children (between 11 and 13 years of age), caregivers and community informants participating in Young Lives, an innovative long-term international research project. The chapter concludes by contrasting discrepancies between the way children and adults understand what is "good for children", and exploring the extent to which they can be usefully understood within Nussbaum's meta-framework of central capabilities.

In Chapter 10, Tindara Addabbo and Maria Laura Di Tommaso look at the possibilities of using structural equation modelling to measure the capabilities of Italian children (6–13 years old) by matching two data sets (ISTAT and Bank of Italy). The chapter focuses particularly on capabilities in two areas – "Senses, Imagination and Thought" (such as their attitude towards education, attending art classes and other extra-curricular classes, such as computing and languages) and "Leisure and Play Activities" (such as how often children play in the playground, the games they play, their participation in sports classes). They use descriptive statistics, an ordered probit model and a structural equation model to investigate the relationships between these various indicators, the latent construct for capabilities and a set of covariates. In this way they undertake measurement using the CA.

In Chapter 11, Jean-Francois Trani, Parul Bakhshi and Mario Biggeri present an analytical and policy framework and policy implications based on the CA, which includes several concrete recommendations for research design and data collection and a case study regarding children with disabilities. In the first part of the chapter they review the main approaches to disability; in particular, they consider the individual model, the social model and the International Classification of Functioning, Disability and Health (ICF) framework through the lens of the CA before developing a framework as a guide for policy, data design and data collection. In order to understand the potential of the research framework, the authors report on an example based on data from an *ad hoc* survey carried out in Afghanistan by Handicap International. This survey is one of the first to attempt to apply the CA to disabled children.

In Chapter 12, Jérôme Ballet, Augendra Bhukuth and Katia Radja critically investigate the *education for all programme* focused on the situation of street children. Within this context, the CA can throw light on how to handle the access of street children to formal education. Any serious attempt to take the intrinsic value of education into account implies defining the quality of education in a way that is not restricted to its material and functional aspects. Quality too often remains centred on the positional and instrumental values of education. These findings have a number of policy implications, which are spelt out in turn.

In Chapter 13, Mario Biggeri, Augendra Bhukuth and Jérôme Ballet re-examine the definitions of child labour and child work through a critical use of the CA. The usual definitions are not usually centred on children, but tend to mimic adults' definitions, and downplay the gender issues. A new definition of children's activities based on the CA is proposed. This conceptual framework reveals shortcomings of the standard definitions and may reduce misconceived policy implications.

In Chapter 14, JungA Uhm, Ferdinand Lewis and Tridib Banerjee present a theoretical exploration of children's environmental capabilities by incorporating Kevin Lynch's ideas about the structure of a "good city" into the current discourse on Amartya Sen's Capability Theory. Using Lynch's performance dimensions as a normative framework, the chapter discusses how the design of the built environment could be better informed by current thinking on the CA, especially as it pertains to children and their development. The position adopted is likely to have a profound impact on the well-being of children and on childhood development. This chapter proposes that a capability-based evaluation of the built environment can offer policy makers, urban planners and designers a new conception of the "child-friendly environment", and a normative vision of how urban planning can impose, or remove, children's lack of freedom.

In Chapter 15, Flavio Comim elaborates on some of the core issues discussed in this book with special reference to emotions and parental caring during childhood. He also considers how key conclusions can be translated into practice.

The book concludes with Chapter 16, a brief set of final remarks identifying issues for future research and summarizes key policy lessons.

We hope that our readers will find this book illuminating and will subsequently build upon our attempt to develop the CA to explore children's issues, both conceptually and for policy purposes, by viewing children as real social actors endowed with the full range of human capabilities.

Notes

1. For a bibliography please see: http://www.capabilityapproach.com/index.php. See also Hawthorn (1987), Nussbaum and Sen (1993), Nussbaum and Glover (1995), Alkire (2002), Clark (2002, 2006), Saith (2007), Comim, Alkire and Qizilbash (2008), Deneulin (2009) and Chiappero-Martinetti (2009).
2. Sen regrets that India failed to reflect on the plight of the children while undertaking developmental activities: "The country has undoubtedly progressed in all spheres ... but the same has not been reflected in the welfare of children and their rights ... the schemes and programmes have more or less remained the same for the past one decade", he said delivering the keynote address in a seminar on child rights (New Delhi, 19 December 2006, PTI).
3. See also Sen (1998) on the role of infant mortality rates as an indicator of human development and of the success and failure of economic policies.
4. The first panel on children was held at the 2005 HDCA in Paris. The HDCA thematic group on "Children's Capabilities" was created at the same conference (see http://capabilityapproach.org).
5. Unfortunately, today – as at the time of Lycurgus in Sparta, Aristotle in Athens or at the time of Cicerone – we cannot say that the idea of "flourishing" is "deserved" for all children. This injustice is clearly visible in conflict areas, in extremely poor areas and often for children with disabilities.
6. HDCA_Briefing_Concepts.pdf at http://www.capabilityapproach.com/index.php. See also Comim et al. (2008).
7. This leads to the equal opportunity view (see Roemer, 1998) but from a multidimensional perspective. The freedom to be healthy, educated, well-nourished and integrated is intrinsically valuable regardless of whether the human being uses these capabilities as an instrument for other goals or not.
8. "There is no difference as far as the space is concerned between focusing on functionings or on capabilities. A functioning combination is a point in such a space, whereas capability is a set of such points" (Sen, 1992: 50).
9. "In this perspective, people are viewed to be active, creative, and able to act on behalf of their aspirations. Agency is related to other approaches that stress self-determination, authentic self-direction, autonomy and so on. The concern

for agency means that participation, public debate, democratic practice, and empowerment are to be fostered alongside well-being" HDCA_Briefing_Concepts.
10. "The single most important function of the capability approach is to make *explicit* some *implicit* assumptions in the Basic Needs Approach about the value of choice and participation (and the disvalue of coercion)" (Alkire 2002: 170).
11. For instance, in rural South Asia a child is part of a community if he/she contributes to the community with his/her time; but this does not allow him/her to become empowered or to participate in community decisions. Western societies recognize active citizens in the people that produce (in particular from the Industrial Revolution onward), but as children are not allowed to work they are not full citizens. This is clearly a contradiction. Furthermore, not being productive economically does not necessarily imply inactivity.
12. The reason Sen supports ethical individualism is that if the smallest fundamental unit of moral concern is any group – such as the family or the community – then analyses will overlook any existing or potential inequalities within these units (Deneulin, 2009). For instance, in some developing countries scrutinizing the well-being of individuals reveals the relative under-nutrition, or subordination, of female children.
13. A few exceptions can be found in the education field – see Walker and Unterhalter (2007) and Chapter 2 in this book.
14. Further information is available on the HDCA website, http://www.capability approach.com/

References

Alkire, S. (2002), *Valuing Freedoms. Sen's Capability Approach and Poverty Reduction*, OUP, New York.
Ariés, P. (1960), *L'enfant et la vie familiale sous l'ancien regime*, Libr. Plon, Paris.
Baraldi, C. (2008), "Promoting Self-expression in Classroom Interaction", *Childhood*, 15(2): 239–257.
Biggeri, M. (2003), "Children, Child Labour and the Human Capability Approach", paper presented at the 3rd HDCA Conference, 7–9 September 2003, Pavia University.
Biggeri, M., Libanora, R., Mariani, S. and Menchini, L. (2006), "Children Conceptualizing Their Capabilities: Results of the Survey During the First Children's World Congress on Child Labour", *Journal of Human Development*, 7(1): 59–83, March.
Brighouse, H. (2000), *School Choice and Social Justice*, OUP, Oxford.
Chiappero-Martinetti, E. (ed.) (2009), *Debating Global Society: Reach and Limits of the Capability Approach*, Fondazione Giangiacomo Feltrinelli, Milan.
Clark, D. A. (2002), *Visions of Development: A Study of Human Values*, Edward Elgar, Cheltenham.
Clark, D. A. (2006), "Capability Approach", in D. A. Clark (ed.), *The Elgar Companion to Development Studies*, Edward Elgar, Cheltenham, pp. 32–45.
Comim, F. (2009), "Assessing Children's Capabilities: Operationalizing Metrics for Evaluating Music Programs with Poor Children in Brazilian Primary Schools", in Reiko Gotoh and Paul Dumouchel (eds), *Against Injustice – The New Economics of Amartya Sen*, Cambridge University Press, Cambridge, pp. 252–274.
Comim, F., Qizilbash, M. and Alkire, S. (eds) (2008), *The Capability Approach: Concepts, Measures and Applications*, CUP, Cambridge.

Deneulin, S. (ed.) (2009), *An Introduction to the Human Development and Capability Approach: Freedom and Agency*, Earthscan, London.

Di Tommaso, M. L. (2003), "How to Measure Children's Well-being Using a Capability Approach? An Application to Indian Data through a Multiple Indicators Multiple Causes Model", paper presented at the 3rd HDCA Conference, 7–9 September 2003, Pavia University.

Feeny, T. and Boyden, J. (2004), "Acting in Adversity - Rethinking the Causes, Experiences and Effects of Child Poverty in Contemporary Literature", *Working paper series, WP 116*, QEH, Oxford.

Hallett, C. and Prout, A. (eds) (2003), *Hearing the Voices of Children: Social Policy for a New Century*, RoutledgeFarmer, London.

Hawthorn, G. (ed.) (1987), *The Standard of Living*, Cambridge University Press, Cambridge.

Iervese, V. (ed.) (2006), *La Gestione Dialogica del Conflitto. Analisi di una Sperimentazione con Bambini e Preadolescenti*, La Mandragora, Imola.

Iervese, V. and Rossi, E. (2009), "Conflict Mangament", in C. Baraldi (ed.), *Dialogue in intercultural communities*, John Benjamins, Amsterdam, pp. 29–74.

James, A., Jenks, A. and Prout, A. (1998), *Theorizing Childhood*, Polity Press, Cambridge.

Luhmann, N. (1984), *Soziale Systeme*, Suhrkamp, Frankfurt a.M.

Luhmann, N. (2002), *Das Erziehungssystem der Geselleschaft*, Suhrkamp, Frankfurt a.M.

Matthews, H. (2003), "Children and Regeneration: Setting and Agenda for Community Participation and Integration", *Children & Society*, 17: 264–276.

Mehrotra, S. and Biggeri, M. (2002), "The Subterranean Child Labour Force: Subcontracted Home Based Manufacturing in Asia" *Innocenti Working Paper no. 96*, UNICEF Innocenti Research Centre, Florence.

Moscovici, S. (1984), "The Phenomenon of Social Representations", in R.M. Farr and S. Moscovici (eds), *Social Representations*, CUP, Cambridge, pp. 3–70.

Murray, C. and Hallett, C. (eds) (2000), "Young People's Participation in Decisions Affecting Their Welfare", *Childhood*, 7(1): 11–25.

Nussbaum, M. (1997), *Cultivating Humanity. A Classical Defence of Reform in Liberal Education*, Harvard University Press, Cambridge, MA.

Nussbaum, M. (2000), *Women and Human Development: The Capabilities Approach*, Cambridge University Press, Cambridge.

Nussbaum, M. (2002), *Beyond the Social Contract: Towards Global Justice*, in "Tanner lectures on human values", Australian National University, Canberra, 12 and 13 November 2002.

Nussbaum, M. (2006), *Frontiers of Justice: Disability, Nationality, Species Membership*, Belknap Press of Harvard University Press, Cambridge, MA.

Nussbaum, M. C. and Sen, A. K. (eds) (1993), *The Quality of Life*, Clarendon Press, Oxford.

Nussbaum, M. C. and Glover, J. (eds) (1995), *Women, Culture and Development*, Clarendon Press, Oxford.

Parsons, T. and Bales, R. F. (1955), *Family, Socialization and Interaction Process*, The Free Press, New York.

Prout, A. (2000), "Children's Participation: Control and Self-realisation in British Late Modernity", *Children & Society*, 14: 304–315.

Richter, D. (1987), *Das Fremde Kind. Zur Entstehung der Kindheitsbilder des Buerglichen Zeitalters*, Fischer Vlg., Frankfurt a. M.

Robeyns, I. (2003), "Sen's Capability Approach and Gender Inequality: Selecting Relevant Capabilities", *Feminist Economics*, 9(2–3): 61–92.

Roemer, J. (1998), *Equality of Opportunities*, CUP, Cambridge.

Saith, R. (2007), "Capabilities: The Concept and Its Implementation", in F. Stewart, R. Saith and B. Harriss-White (eds), *Defining Poverty in Developing Countries*, Palgrave Macmillan, Basingstoke, pp. 55–74.

Saito, M. (2003), "Amartya Sen's Capability Approach to Education: A Critical Exploration", *Journal of Philosophy of Education*, 37(1): 17–33.

Schischka, J. (2003), "The Capabilities Approach as a Metric for Economic Development: An Application in Samoa", paper presented at the 3rd HDCA Conference, 7–9 September 2003, Pavia University.

Sen, A. K. (1985), *Commodities and Capabilities*, Elsevier Science Publishers, Oxford.

Sen, A. K. (1987), "The Standard of Living", in G. Hawthorn (ed.) *The Standard of Living*, Cambridge University Press, Cambridge.

Sen, A. K. (1992), *Inequality Re-examined*, OUP, Oxford.

Sen, A. K. (1998), "Mortality as an Indicator of Economic Success and Failure", *Economic Journal*, Royal Economic Society, 108(446): 1–25, January.

Sen, A. K. (1999a), *Development as Freedom*, OUP, Oxford.

Sen, A. K. (1999b), "Investing in Early Childhood: Its Role in Development", *Conference on Breaking the Poverty Cycle. Investing in Early Childhood*, Inter-American Development Bank, Washington, DC.

Sen A. K. (2005), Human Rights and Capabilities, *Journal of Human Development*, 6(2): 151–166.

Sen, A. K. (2007), "Children and Human Rights", *Indian Journal of Human Development*, 2(1).

Sen, A. K. (2009), "Capability: Reach and Limits", in E. Chiappero-Martinetti (ed.), *Debating Global Society: Reach and Limits of the Capability Approach*, Fondazione Giacomo Feltrinelli, Milan, pp. 15–28.

Swift, A. (2003), *How Not to Be a Hypocrite: School Choice for the Morally Perplexed*, Routledge, London.

Unterhalter, E. and Brighouse, H. (2003), "Distribution of What? How Will We Know if We have Achieved Education for All by 2015? Paper presented at the 3rd HDCA Conference, September, Pavia University.

Walker, M. and Unterhalter, E. (eds) (2007), *Amartya Sen's Capability Approach and Social Justice in Education*, Palgrave Macmillan, New York.

2
Children's Agency and the Capability Approach: A Conceptual Framework

Jérôme Ballet, Mario Biggeri and Flavio Comim

2.1. Introduction

The aim of this chapter is to explore the possibilities for fruitfully using the capability approach (CA) as a theoretical foundation for understanding children as subjects of human development. This means considering children not simply as recipients of freedoms, but as active social actors and agents in their communities with their own priorities, strategies and aspirations. By doing so, we hope to contribute to the current theoretical debate on the assessment of children's well-being with a simple and useful framework. Our overarching goal is to improve policies towards children's well-being.

Seeing children as subjects of capabilities means that we can consider them endowed with agency and autonomy, able to express their points of view, values and priorities. Therefore, the capabilities, choices and conditions experienced during childhood and adolescence crucially affect children's capabilities as adults. As stated by Sen (1999b: 4) the "... capabilities that adults enjoy are deeply conditional on their experience as children". Furthermore, deprivation of basic capabilities during childhood not only reduces the well-being of those suffering from them, but may have larger societal implications (Klasen, 2001). However, children are much more than future adults as they are already social actors before they become adults: more attention should be dedicated to the understanding of children's well-being for children themselves, rather than projecting them to future outcomes.

Nonetheless, according to Sen (2007), insofar as the process or *agency* aspect of freedom demands that a person should be making his or her own choice, that aspect of freedom is not particularly relevant to the human rights of children, except in some rather minimal ways (such as a child's freedom – and perhaps right – to get attention when it decides to scream the house down).[1] But the opportunity aspect of freedom is immensely important for children. What opportunities children have today and will have tomorrow, in line with what they can be reasonably expected to want, are a matter of public policy and social programmes, involving a great number of agencies. But, if the CA is based on people's values (including children's), participation should be one of the pillars of the approach.

We think that when using the distinction between the process and opportunity aspects of freedom, Sen is aware of the difficulty facing the CA with respect to children's participation. Children's participation supposes a minimal autonomy, a minimal capacity of self-determination. Therefore, integrating children's participation is a major stake. Also, Article 5 of the Convention on the Rights of the Child states that direction and guidance from parents or others with responsibility for the child must take account of the capacities of the child to exercise rights on his or her own behalf. This is quite in line with the CA and the capability concepts, which, in a certain sense, incorporate the opportunity concept, the capacity concept and the agency concept that evolve during time. The dynamic process of the three components of capabilities can be captured by the notion of *evolving capabilities* – which we present in Section 2.5 (Figure 2.1). In the case of children, from a practical perspective, this idea is quite close to the concept of *evolving capacities* presented by Lansdown (2005). More precisely "the concept of evolving capacities is central to the balance embodied in the Convention between recognising children as active agents in their own lives, entitled to be listened to, respected and granted increasing autonomy in the exercise of rights, while also being entitled to protection in accordance with their relative immaturity and youth" (Lansdown, 2005: 3). The child's capabilities are always present although their level may vary according to the age and maturity of the child.[2] Indeed, as Rogoff has suggested, "Instead of viewing children as separate entities that become capable of social involvement, we may consider children as being inherently engaged in the social world even from before birth, advancing throughout development in their skill in independently carrying out and organizing activities of their culture" (Rogoff, 1990: 22).

In this chapter, we concentrate on the methodological questions that emerge when one tries to apply the CA to children. In particular, we tackle the following questions: Does the CA readily apply to children's issues, or does it need to change? What kind of changes, if any, do children's issues imply for the CA? Does the CA complement other approaches? Does it promote children's rights?

The chapter is then structured as follows. In the second section, we investigate the self-determination hypothesis used by the CA, which also applies to liberal theories of justice. Of course the question of self-determination must be softened for children, but not abandoned. However, as the issue of choices is central in the CA, it naturally opens up the question of its applicability to children. In the third section, we recognize children as actors and we draw lessons for the CA. In the fourth section, we explore its relevance

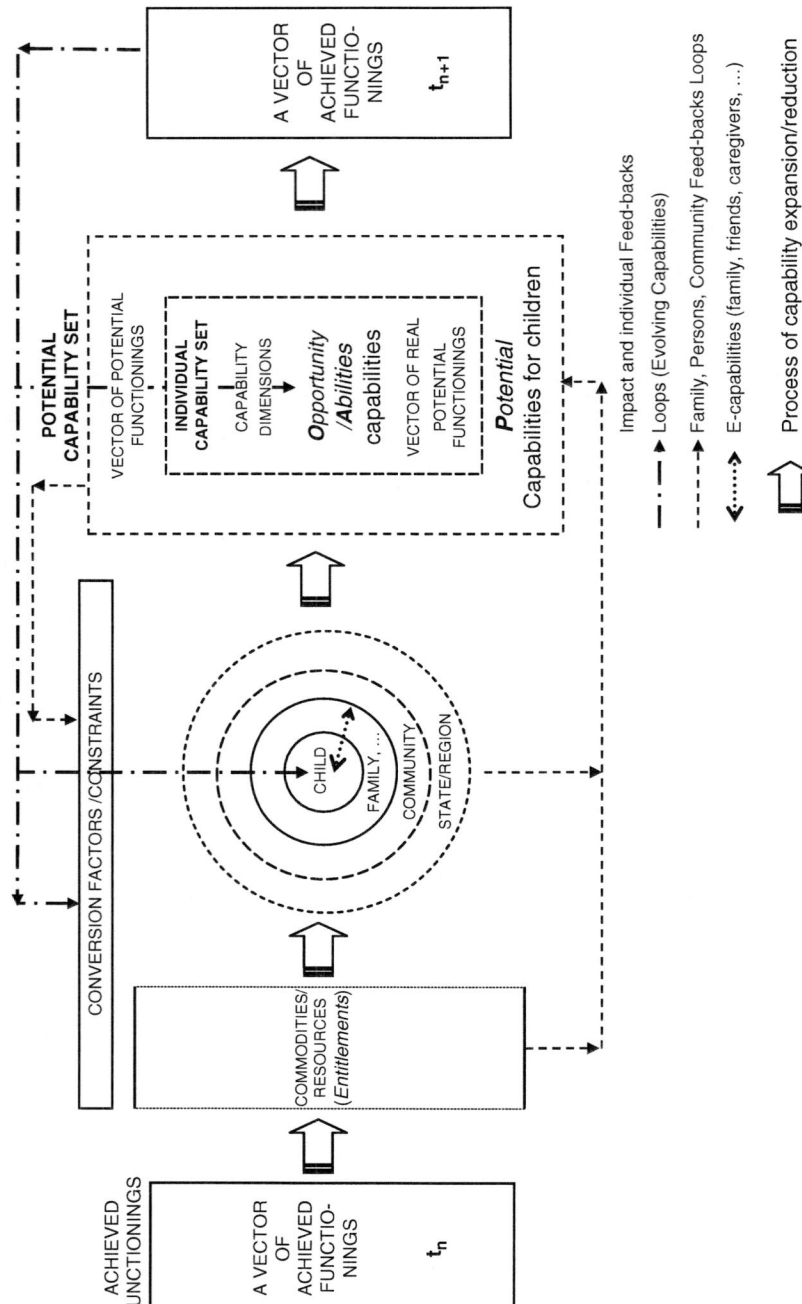

Figure 2.1 Capability Approach framework and evolving capabilities
Source: Our elaborations on Biggeri et al. 2009 and Trani et al. (chapter 11)

for addressing issues that are specific to children. In section five we underline the most challenging issues relating to the use of the CA for children, i.e. autonomy, agency and empowerment in a dynamic context. In the sixth section, we focus mainly on policy implications and how the CA can complement the human rights approach. The final section summarizes and concludes.

2.2. The question of self-determination and evolving capabilities

Applying the CA to assessing children's well-being is particularly delicate because one of the main features of the approach, namely its emphasis on agency and autonomy, is not self-evident. In fact, the CA obviously implies the individual's capacity for self-determination,[3] which may not apply to children. As Kymlicka (1992) observes, liberal theories of justice all agree on the principle of self-determination. They rely on the idea that the best way to promote individuals' interests is to let them choose the lifestyle that they wish to have. And if there is no agreement on the rights or resources required to pursue a conception of good, at least there will be general agreement about the principle of self-determination insofar as its negation would amount to treating individuals as unequal. Sen's CA encompasses this idea, especially when it makes a distinction between well-being freedom and agency freedom, the latter implying the person's capacity to exercise their own free will (Sen, 1987, 1992). After all, opening up the maximum number of choices for individuals is equivalent to supposing that they, alone, can judge what is good for themselves. What would be the use of freedom of choice if individuals were not in a position to benefit from it?

Should we consider that all individuals are entitled to this freedom of choice, including children? Saito (2003) quibbles about the possibility of applying the CA to children insofar as they are not mature enough to take decisions for themselves.[4] Typically liberal theories exclude children from their conceptual framework, as well as the mentally ill and temporarily disabled who, unlike other people, are the subjects of paternalistic benevolence. This exclusion rests on the inability of the individuals concerned to make choices for themselves, and thus implies their lack of cognitive capacity to decide on what is good for themselves.[5] Nussbaum (2006) argues that many of these liberal theories see social contracts as an agreement between equals and, whenever this rule is violated, equilibrium is restored by the exclusion of vulnerable groups.

Applying the CA to children therefore entails taking a stand with regard to their capacity for self-determination. We may certainly consider that freedom of choice does not apply due to children's lack of cognitive capacity to decide for themselves, but then the CA is reduced to a set of specific measures that provide children with opportunities without allowing any meaningful form of choice. Four different viewpoints can be identified – some of which are more problematic than others.

According to the first, the question of the children's mental attitudes is not central to their well-being although their functionings are. In that sense, self-determination is not a real problem since it is enough to consider what children actually achieve. This first point of view is nevertheless fairly reductionist, since the CA is reduced to investigating bare achievements.

According to the second point of view, the question of self-determination should not be addressed over the whole life cycle (but rather at an immature point in the life cycle), so that what actually needs to be taken into account is the autonomy adults acquire during childhood. Saito (2003: 26) interprets the CA along these lines. She argues that "when dealing with children, it is the freedom they will have in the future rather than the present that should be considered. Therefore, as long as we consider a person's capabilities in terms of their life-span, the CA seems to be applicable to children." This second point of view goes beyond the first by providing a guideline favourable to the development of the individual's autonomy in adulthood. Nevertheless, like the first, this second point of view does not seem sufficient to answer seriously the question of the place of autonomy as far as children are concerned.

The third point of view takes this kind of reasoning further. Note that this point of view is fully compatible with the other two, but it is more demanding. It, indeed, encompasses the two others whereas, conversely, it is quite possible to subscribe to one and/or both the first two points of view without subscribing to the third. It sets out to acknowledge a minimal self-determination principle for children. As a matter of fact, the exclusion of children from the principle of self-determination is fundamentally based on a view of individuals as having the moral capacity to determine their conception of good. Rawls (1980) expresses this point of view when he asserts that

> as free individuals, the citizens mutually recognise each other as being endowed with the moral capacity to have a conception of good. This means that they do not perceive themselves as being inevitably linked to the specific conception of good and its objectives which they espouse at some or other moment of their life. On the contrary, as citizens, they are regarded as being generally capable of revising and changing their conception on reasonable and rational grounds. The citizens can thus distance themselves from the different conceptions of good and endeavour to examine and evaluate their various ultimate objectives. (*ibid.*: 40).

This passage underlines two key aspects of liberal theories. On the one hand, the individual is rational and reasonable; on the other, these faculties enable him/her to reappraise their judgement. So, the exclusion of children, as well as of persons with mental disability, implies that they are neither rational nor reasonable, and are therefore not in a position to revise their judgement. In other words, the problem is not about making a bad choice but being in a position to revise this choice. After all, we are all confronted with bad choices, but the capacity to evaluate and revise choices is essential even more so when these affect our life and our conception of good. Nussbaum (2000: 78) expresses the same opinion when she asserts that the human capability of practical reason consists of "being able to form a conception of the good and to engage in critical reflection about the planning of one's life". The distinction between capacity to make choices and capacity to evaluate and revise choices is of some importance. The problem is not so much that children are unable to make choices, but that they might be unable to evaluate and revise the choices they make, i.e. act as capable agent. In many cases, however, this distinction is not taken seriously. Children have traditionally been regarded as totally vulnerable and dependent on their parents. Such a view is based on a sentimentalist and maternalistic cult (Boulding, 1979). For this reason, they are considered incapable of making choices, and paternalism implies that choices are made by parents. This reasoning firstly does not correspond to the situation of a great number of children in the world, since children are often able to evaluate and revise key aspects of their lives. Children start to learn to be independent from their parents from an early age.[6] Secondly, if the problem is not so much one of choice as one of choice evaluation and possible revision, then it is necessary to provide children with a choice space, instead of making choices for them, in such a manner that rational and reasonable decision making is favoured. The question is not to defend a strong self-determination principle for children but to acknowledge a weak self-determination principle. On the one hand, a strong self-determination principle would imply that the individual is the best judge of what is good for his- or herself insofar as he/she, more than anyone else, is in a position to evaluate and revise his/her judgement. On the other hand, a weak self-determination principle implies only that the individual is in a position to make choices but that the framework within which they make these choices must be defined so that their capacity for evaluation may develop and that certain, particularly harmful, choices may thus be eliminated. A weak self-determination is fully compatible with the notion of evolving capabilities previously mentioned.

In the fourth point of view, which gives more value to the previous three, we propose to assess children's evolving capabilities from their own point of view. The opportunity to exercise self-determination and autonomy evolves continuously over the life cycle. Children, according to their age and maturity, have a lot of scope to exercise their agency and self-determination (as we see in the next section). Therefore this area is different for adults and more interesting, as we said, and it is different for children according to their age and their maturity. Indeed, what the capability perspective does in well-being analysis is to enhance the understanding of the nature and causes of deprivation by shifting primary attention away from means to ends that people (children) have reason to pursue, and, correspondingly, to the freedoms to be able to satisfy these ends (Sen, 1993, 1999a). This means that different children may need different policies to be able to enjoy the same basic capabilities and actual functionings. For instance, the capacity to demand specific objects, toys, food or to move around the house may appear trivial from an adult's perspective, but may constitute big decisions and progress in the eyes of the child. For example, if a child of 6 embarks on a new adventure, to go on his or her own on a single journey, he or she might feel a big emotion, a mix of autonomy and agency that could be comparable to the first time for an adult flying in an aeroplane. The means to fulfil the story are different but the ends are the same. This means that different levels of well-being, agency and autonomy may be perceived by the same individuals at different points in their life cycle.

The question now is: Can individuals learn to be autonomous if they are not given any autonomy space? Or in other words, can we really think about the autonomy of adults without thinking about the autonomy of children?

2.3. Recognizing children as active agents

The view of children as social actors is now established in the literature (see Chapter 1, Section 1.2). This is based on evidence that contextualizes children as active rather than passive, and participants playing an active role in the lives of their families, communities and societies (see, for instance, Ballet et al., 2004; Feeny and Boyden, 2004). We recognize the exercise of agency by children in accordance with several empirical studies. For instance, Mayall (2000) shows that nine-year-old children in London are able to take charge of books, clothing and equipment for school, negotiate social relationships, organize homework and even offer support to their mothers in the aftermath of divorce, etc. Alderson (2001) points out that very young children exercise agency and exert power and persuasion over adults to get what they want. Punch (2001) also argues that children negotiate and renegotiate boundaries imposed by adults. Several of the chapters in this book emphasize children's agency (see especially, Chapters 5–8).

It is important to recall that the idea that children actively participate in their transition is not new. Within the psychological field, for instance, the Piagetian constructivist paradigm has taken for granted that children interact with the environment around them and develop through a process of equilibration (Piaget, 1978).[7] Also, some studies of social development have pointed to children's roles as social actors, meaning makers and participants in reciprocal exchanges (see, for instance, Schaffer, 1996 and Chapter 1, Section 1.2).

Sociological theories have contributed to this debate in two broad ways: on the one hand, they have shown how social structure is able to shape individual life; on the other hand, through the micro-analysis of the social process, they have highlighted the fact that each person participates in the creation of social life.[8]

Considering the relation between agency and theories of socialization, we can observe that the former represents an innovative element, letting us interpret socialization as a process taking place thanks to children's participation. If children are autonomously able to construct meanings drawing on the social processes they come into contact with, they are able to self-socialize (Luhmann, 1990).

Moreover, over the last 20 years, the importance of children's self-fulfilment has come to be accepted: institutions have started to acknowledge that children are endowed with agency and recognize the relevance of children's participation.[9] As Baraldi (2008: 37) argues, however, it's very difficult to reach the highest steps of the ladder (i.e. full participation), especially at an institutional level. In spite of the rhetoric and even when participation is encouraged, "a paradigm of socialization which emphasizes children's development towards a future of mature human being" (Kjørholt, 2002: 70) still dominates.[10]

2.4. Children as active actors but . . .

As with adults, the child's ability to convert resources or commodities into capabilities and functionings depends on *conversion factors*. Conversion factors can be internal and societal/environmental. As mentioned in Chapter 1, the "internal" conversion factors, such as personal characteristics (e.g. age, physical conditions, sex, skills, talents, intelligence) convert resources (or commodities) into individual functionings. In the case of children, age becomes a highly relevant factor in shaping their capabilities, especially as age is combined with a range of formal and informal social norms in different cultures and societies. The conversion is also related to *societal and environmental conversion* factors, that is social characteristics (e.g. public policies, institutions, legal rules, traditions, social norms, discriminating practices, gender roles, societal hierarchies, power relations, public goods) and/or environmental characteristics (e.g. natural environment, public infrastructure, climate).[11] The non-internal factors can be related to the household's characteristics or to society. For instance, at the household level, when a mother has a higher level of education, a child's opportunities in terms of health and education increase. Indeed, as pointed out by Sen, there are several freedoms that depend on the assistance and actions of others as well as the nature of social arrangements (Sen, 2007). Clearly, when we consider children – and, even more so in the case of infants or children with disabilities, caregivers' assistance becomes fundamental (see also Biggeri et al., 2011).

For these reasons we argue that children may have qualitatively different capabilities from adults and that they can attach different degrees of
relevance to the same capability. In other words, over a lifetime the relevance of capabilities changes for the individual (Comim, 2004; Biggeri et al.,
2006)[12] and, therefore, a child cannot be seen as a small-scale model of
an adult (White, 2002). Following Biggeri (2004) and Biggeri et al. (2006),
we emphasize five theoretical and practical considerations for evolving
capabilities.

First, the possibility of converting capabilities into functionings typically
depends on the decisions of parents, guardians and teachers, which implies
that the child's conversion factors are subject to additional constraints as
well as resources. Actually, even if we acknowledge that the child is not a
passive actor, his/her choice often represents a compromise (children and
parents often have different views and priorities, see in particular Chapter 9).
On the one hand, parents need to respect children's desires and freedoms
but, on the other, they have to assist children to expand or acquire further
capabilities, even though this may need to be done against their will (Biggeri
et al., 2006). In the task of educating their children, therefore, parents and
tutors can be either *autonomy supportive* (e.g. giving an internal frame of
reference, providing a meaningful rationale, allowing choices, encouraging
self-perspective) or *controlling* (e.g. pressure to behave in specific ways) (Ryan
and Deci, 2000). These two aspects can be in conflict if the child is not a passive actor, especially as age increases. Although sometimes the constraints
can be perceived by the child as negative or unjust, they can also be enabling
and supportive of their development. Therefore, while on the one hand children desire to be more autonomous, on the other they require parental care
(see Chapter 15).

Taking into account evolving capabilities strives, not to control children,
but to provide boundaries to support them. In doing so, it recognizes that
such boundaries are not fixed and are typically renegotiated by children.
Brighouse (2000) thinks along these lines when he makes a distinction
between autonomy-facilitating education and autonomy-promoting education. Autonomy-facilitating education, contrary to autonomy-promoting
education, is not aimed at passing on instrumental knowledge with a view
to developing choice autonomy in adulthood (in terms of employment
choices, for example), but attempts to develop freedom of choice in the
sense of a capacity to evaluate and revise choices (the policy implications
of this approach are discussed in Chapter 12).

The second point concerns the fact that the child's capabilities are partially affected by their capability set and achieved functionings as well as
the *entitlements* of their parents or caregivers to goods and services, which
results in a cumulative path-dependent process that can involve different
generations of human beings. For instance, there is often a link between
maternal health and nutrition and the birthweight and health of the child,

or between the mother's education and the child's education. Alternatively children may become subject to bonded labour because of their parents' actions, decisions or debts. More generally, the education of parents may affect a child's occupation.

If children's capabilities are affected by the inter-generational transfer of capabilities and the functionings and entitlements of their parents as an outcome of a cumulative path-dependent process, it follows that their capabilities may fail to expand through no fault of their own. In the worst case scenario "with their parents unable to feed, clothe, educate or protect their health, their only inheritance is destitution and deprivation" (Feeny and Boyden, 2004: 5). Thus, a poor household in a society characterized by an unequal distribution of resources (assets and income) may become trapped at a low level of human development and may require children, for instance, to work for generation after generation (Mehrotra and Biggeri, 2007: 21–26). There are no positive synergies – to affect their capabilities, functionings and their conversion factors – to break the cycle. Indeed the child repeats the experience of their parents, which is passed on from generation to generation. This reflects the absence of available choices for the child and mirrors Sen's notion of "development as freedom" (Sen, 1999a). In other words the child becomes a victim of inter-generational transfers of poverty, caught in a vicious circle, which is difficult for the household to overcome by themselves (Mehrotra and Biggeri, 2002).

The third possibility is common to all ages, but especially relevant for children, due to their high learning capacity and nutritional needs. It is connected, as already mentioned, to the interconnections between different functionings and capabilities and the synergies and outcomes of different instrumental capabilities, which is typically a positive sum. This is especially true at a young age, as rapid cognitive development can be facilitated or reduced by the presence or absence of instrumental capabilities such as being able to be adequately educated. This suggests that the absence of a key functioning or capability may constrain other capabilities and the capacity to evolve new capabilities.

For example, a child who is deprived of a capability such as being physically healthy (and related functionings) experiences the reduction of other potential capabilities, such as being able to have fun with friends or be adequately educated because he/she is unable to attend school. The functionings and capabilities are also constrained by conversion factors (child characteristics, e.g. personal impairment). The interactions and synergies through the conversion factors shape capability sets and thus the well-being of a child. In this sense, the CA helps us to identify the social constraints that influence and restrict well-being. Social norms or traditions expand or reduce the capability of individuals. For instance, in order to expand a female child's capabilities, set practices of empowerment in society and the improvement of specific social institutions could be required

(Mehrotra, 2002). This implies that, if there are constraints for capability as freedom to achieve something, a policy maker has to consider other functionings and the conversion factors connected. The synergies among functionings have important policy implications often undervalued by policy makers. In particular, there are two major types of synergies (at the micro level for the individual person and within the household, and at the meso and macro levels) among basic social services (BSS) and between BSS and income (Mehrotra and Biggeri, 2002, 2007; Mehrotra and Delamonica, 2007).

The fourth possibility concerns the life cycle and the importance of age in defining the relevance of a capability at a particular stage in life. This implies that a child could be the subject of different capabilities compared with adults and that the degree of relevance of these capabilities can vary according to age. Childhood foundations are complex and composed of different sensitive periods. Thus, studying the relation between age and capabilities could help us to discover impediments to a "decent life", so affecting the optimum timing of anti-poverty interventions (see for examples, Yaqub, 2002). The CA becomes a tool from a normative point of view by explaining the weaknesses or the constraints (including conversion factors) in the formation of a person's capabilities at the individual level as well as within a social group (see, for instance, Chapters 5 and 7).

An explorative study by Biggeri et al. (2006) based on a focus group discussion (FGD) explored some of these issues with reference to children's capabilities. The FGD was structured into two parts closely related to one another. The first part focused on age, capabilities and the degree of autonomy of choice; and the second part on definitions of child activities according to their impact on the child's well-being (for further details, see Chapter 13).[13] The process was conceived as follows: first, the children agreed on the age and capability categories. Secondly, they discussed the relevance of each capability according to their age grouping, and then according to their perceived degree of autonomy of choice. By doing so, they reached a common view and attributed a final assessment of the capability and related autonomy.

Although the results of the FGD have to be treated with caution, some general observations can be made (see Biggeri et al., 2006). The first is that the dimensions conceptualized by children during the survey constitute aspects of well-being that are usually neglected (see Chapter 3). The second is that the level of relevance of particular capabilities can vary according to age, while for the third the same is observed for the issue of related autonomy. Indeed, there is a strong age dynamic in child well-being and agency and autonomy have to be taken into account, and these vary according to the type of dimensions. The results indicate that each capability on the list is relevant for all children but, in many cases, the level of relevance varies according to age. In particular, the relevance of some capabilities (such as time autonomy and mobility) increases with age, while the relevance of others may decline with age (e.g. leisure activities). Furthermore, in contrast to capabilities, autonomy of choice increases as age rises and, as expected, the younger the age group, the less freedom of choice the child has. As we argued before, the lower degree of autonomy in their choices does not mean that younger children have no self-determination and agency. Children express their quest for autonomy and agency in different ways according to their age and maturity.

The fifth issue concerns the role of children in the construction of future internal and societal/environmental conversion factors as children, as future adults, parents and caregivers. Children, from this point of view, can be considered as a vehicle of positive change in building new social capital and contributing to the shape of future conversion factors and institutions. From this point of view, children as social actors are key resources for a better future.[14] Capabilities are evolving characteristics of human beings. Conversion factors can be either static or dynamic. The individual can change his/her internal conversion factors (change in the scale of value or in the perception of importance of opportunities, change in capacities) and, through participation and action in the social community, can modify social and environmental conversion factors thus influencing the well-being of other children (for instance, participating in defining services – see Chapter 6; for policies regarding child labour, see Chapter 13; or through urban planning, see Chapter 14). Therefore, the child can be at the centre of an intergenerational transfer of capabilities and, at the same time, as a future parent, a vehicle of change by shaping social institutions.

2.5. Revisiting the capability approach

It is worth considering not what can be learned about children using the CA, but what insights can be derived for the CA through the study of children. This is not a trivial issue. The CA has been viewed in the context of fully rational human beings with potential to be part of a social contract. Recently, Nussbaum (2006) has extended the approach to incorporate issues of disability and nature. It is relevant to see children in the same light, but thinking about children's capabilities adds several layers of complication, as we have seen.

To start with, children are not a unified category. A one-year-old child has limited capability shaped by neurological constraints, in contrast to, for example, an 11-year-old child, who has developed many capacities to understand the world. However, an 18-year-old teenager is much better prepared than both to relate with the world in several dimensions. And yet, all of them should be treated differently from adults who are better able to cope with many more aspects of individual and social life. So, the first layer of complication is that capabilities should be seen not within a static (as they usually are) but in a dynamic framework. In fact, strictly speaking, capabilities define merely an informational space, not a particular set of functionings. This means that as a framework, the CA only emphasizes the type of information required to produce a more complete view of peoples' well-being (although we know that references to well-being, from this perspective, also include agency).

When thinking about children, we should not be talking about static capabilities, but dynamic capabilities captured by the notion of evolving capabilities. This is a natural extension of the approach, given that the notion of capabilities refers to "potentials" (as functionings refer to "actualizations" of these potentials). But what are dynamic capabilities? Simply put, they are capabilities that change, that have a beginning, a flourishing and a transformation into something else, qualitatively different (Comim, 2004). For instance, a person's ability to communicate depends on several stages of cognitive and emotional development; and it is always inter-subjective. Seeing an elderly person speaking the language of teenagers is very unusual, because communication follows patterns that are appropriate, among other things, to age.

The Figure 2.1 illustrates the dynamic nature of the concept of capabilities. Following Biggeri et al. (2009) and Comim (2004), the CA can be seen more dynamically (see also Chapter 11) than usually presented in the literature (see, for instance, Sen, 1999a). The child is conceived at the centre of the development process (as in new social theory and in ecological theory, see, for instance, Bronfenbrenner, 1995, 1998) interacting and using entitlements available by their families, schools, communities and regional entities, such as the government. The process of capability expansion or of evolving capabilities starts from an initial set of achieved functionings of the child at time t_n. The process of resource conversion is very much affected by how different institutions, norms and cultures constrain or empower them, shaping the formation of a new set of functionings and capabilities that are inter-temporally distinct. The child's capability set (opportunity freedom, i.e. the vector of potential valuable and achievable functionings) is thus given by the resources/constraints, by his or her limited opportunities and by his or her own abilities. From the multidimensional capability set the choice will determine the vector of new achieved functionings at time t_{n+1}. The dynamic process is going to be influenced by feedback loops if seen as taking place in sequential periods of time.

It is important to call attention to the fact that the development of young children is crucially dependent on the attitudes of caregivers, family members and teachers. The emotional and cognitive development of children goes through different stages in which their decision making and agency is shaped by their life experiences and mimicking behaviour.

The dynamic of the CA is expressed by the feedback loops at the individual or child level. The achieved functionings of the child shape the future capability set of the child as well as the behavioural attitude of the child. The feedback loops are related to the family and community, which also influence the potential capabilities as well as resources and constraints that face the child and his or her behavioural attitudes. Given the new potential capabilities open to the child, the process of capability reduction and expansion continues (see Chapter 11 for a fuller discussion of collective action and policy implications).

For instance, it might be assumed that the plight of the female child in rural India is due to poor functioning in some dimensions. These low achievements could be constrained by lack of resources, large family size and restrictive social norm in the area. The potential capability set of the male children in the area is larger (there is a school for male children) than what seems available to poor female children. Lack of choice amongst female children may also be constrained by decisions taken by relatives on their behalf. A poor education is also likely to constrain autonomy, including social skills, technical abilities and power within certain personal relations at time t_{n+1}.

This will lead to a negative feedback loop for society and the relative services available in the area, which in turn will affect the capabilities of all female children as there will be little demand for formal female education. Lack of demand for female schooling may leave more progressive parents with relatively few choices.

As mentioned before, "[w]hile exercising your own choices may be important enough for some types of freedoms, there are a great many other freedoms that depend on the assistance and actions of others and the nature of social arrangements" (Sen, 2007: 9). During early childhood children's capability sets are shaped by conversion factors and perhaps even more by the capabilities of their parents and carers.[15] When the child is in his/her early childhood, the "external capabilities"[16] (i.e. given by informal human relationships, Foster and Handy, 2008) may play a central role and can be fundamental and instrumental in satisfying the basic capabilities of the child (see Biggeri and Bellanca, 2010). In this context it is relevant to reintroduce the concept of team agency. In some circumstances agency is expressed by a team or group composed of two or more individuals, as in the case of a mother and baby (see Biggeri et al., 2011).

In the context of children's capabilities, there is also an important challenge to the CA regarding the importance of autonomy *vis-à-vis* other important values. When children are very young their functionings are important, but their capabilities, understood here as their freedom to decide the best course of action to follow, are normally limited. In fact, small children test their limits all the time, and full decision making and freedom can only spoil them. This means that as much as we consider autonomy to be central within this approach, there is a case for at least inter-temporally limiting autonomy for "sustainability reasons". Thus, parents don't leave children with the decision to go to school but impose it as a *fait accompli*, with the understanding that the children who attend school today will be freer agents tomorrow. Could this challenge be extended to other issues addressed by the CA in which there is an important inter-temporal dimension related to capabilities? Might autonomy be one of these essential values?

Another layer of complication concerns the relationship between different agents. When thinking about children's well-being it is natural to wonder about the role of their parents or those responsible for them (see Chapter 15). This demands an understanding of how different capabilities are interconnected. In general, the CA follows a solipsistic line in constitutive terms, allowing social factors only an instrumental role. This has been widely discussed in the literature (see Sen, 1999a). As noted, children's capabilities depend to a large extent on their parents' and caretakers' capabilities, and the state's capability and so on. A challenge for the CA remains: How can we overcome its individualistic approach when thinking about children? Can we say, for example, that parent's capabilities are only instrumentally important for children?

Within this context it is important to understand how children form their normative ideas about what is good and bad or right and wrong. It seems reasonable to acknowledge that children are significantly influenced by their families, their schools and the messages that they hear in the media. The processes of value transposition from parents to children are mostly based on the normative judgements that children can absorb by seeing their parents act in their everyday life. The apparent gaps between what parents say and what they do are immediately shaped into a finer understanding of what values count in life. There are various bases on which children's choices and normative assessments can occur, but the least understood seems to be the one that traces them back to their family environments (see Chapter 15). The disengagement of parents can have long-term effects on children's emotional and cognitive development. The same could be said about the way that schools in recent times have become much more focused on the promotion of technical knowledge at the expense of social skills (see Chapters 6, 7 and 12). Are schools really providing children with the necessary skills to live in this world? Children's internalization of values is a complex process, but it is essential for recognizing them as autonomous beings. It is clear in this line of thought, however, that children's agency and autonomy should not mean independency or isolation, but interdependence and reciprocity.

Finally, it is worth mentioning that the agenda of human development is to a large extent dependent on the agenda of respecting children's basic capabilities: in its simplest form, the human development index (HDI) focuses on issues of education and life expectancy, both affected by what happens to children, especially in developing countries. If capabilities represent a multidimensional space or vectors of functionings, it seems reasonable to consider that our overall capability depends on our particular portfolio of positive freedoms (see, for instance, Chapter 3 on multidimensional child deprivation or Chapter 10 regarding measurement issues). How can these portfolios be developed over time? How can prioritizing children in thinking about human development shape the way we think about social policies? There is so much that we owe to children and their future, but there is a lot that we can learn from them as well.

2.6. Policy implications

Policies for promoting children's well-being are at the core of development plans and strategies. Monitoring based on the HDI is to a large extent influenced by it. Similarly, a large part of the Millennium Development Goals refers to the well-being of children. Many United Nations (UN) agencies specialize in the promotion of children's well-being. And yet, much remains to be done by recognizing, as already argued, that children should not be treated paternalistically as small-scale adults in the formulation of social policies.

It is important to recognize that children are endowed with different degrees of autonomy and that this core fact should be respected in formulating policies that are targeted at them as full citizens. In particular, these policies should encourage their proactive behaviour in decision-making processes. Indeed, fostering their participation is a key part in the process of evolving capabilities in order to take into account their priorities, values and aspirations. Furthermore, by doing so, an important essence of their development, namely, their agency, is being promoted with future positive consequences.

The implications for thinking about education can be dramatic. For instance, according to the CA, education should not be reduced to learning mathematics or developing literature skills (see Unterhalter and Brighouse, 2003; Walker and Unterhalter, 2007) but should tackle learning life skills and teach children to be more autonomous, cooperative and to interact with others instead (see also Chapter 10). Therefore, the main goal for any educational system should not be reduced to the mechanical transmission of instrumental skills (as important as they might be), but should promote learning environments where children can learn to flourish as human beings, dream and have aspirations in addition to learning how to read, write and count.

It follows that it is important to balance the expansion of intrinsic and instrumental capabilities. Both are relevant but often, as in the case presented in Chapter 8 on micro-finance for street children or in the case of child labour in Chapter 13, short-term *versus* long-term objectives can come into conflict, generating trade-offs. Should policy makers promote intrinsic and immediate capabilities or instrumental capabilities? There is no obvious answer and, in many cases, the response is driven by the necessity to overcome the deprivation of some capabilities (e.g. nutrition, and security) at the expense of other long-term goals. Again, the capacity to balance and complement short- and long-term perspectives is crucial.

2.6.1. The capability approach and children's rights

The Convention on the Rights of the Child (CRC) (1989), as a special case of the Human Rights Based Approach, constitutes the main reference for international organizations like UNESCO and UNICEF. While its relevance in terms of advocacy and awareness should be fully acknowledged (Sen, 2004, 2005, 2007), it is useful to recognize the limitations of the Human Rights Based Approach as a comprehensive tool for understanding children's issues and for policy proposals.

As a matter of fact, although some articles (such as Article 12) are broadly in line with the human rights approach to liberty[17] and relate well to new sociological approaches (see Chapter 1, Section 1.2) and the CA, most of the articles see children as passive actors following a paternalistic approach typical of the classic human rights approach.

Furthermore, invoking human rights (seen as the articulation of a commitment in social ethics) "tends to come mostly from those who are more concerned with changing the world than with interpreting it, to use a distinction made famous by that remarkable theorist-turned-political leader, Karl Marx" (Sen, 2007: 7). In other words, one of the concerns in using human rights discourse is that it runs the risk of bordering on advocacy at the expense of analysis (Mehrotra, 2002). In particular, the international rights legislation often does not reflect the socio-economic realities of children's lives, their relationships with other group members in their communities[18] (Feeny and Boyden, 2004: 18) and also their values and priorities. The use of the CA allows us to see children as diverse human beings experiencing a diversity of childhoods across different contexts and expressing different values in which they define their different ways as autonomous agents. Human rights continue to remain nominally, and therefore the guarantee of people's rights fails to get translated into real opportunities. For instance, the right to education will continue to remain a nominal right if all citizens in a country do not have the material means or the external opportunities to access educational systems (Alexander, 2004). With the CA in evaluating how well a society and individuals in that society are doing, we take into account both fulfilment of rights as well as other non-right considerations that together form social goals (*ibid.*). Furthermore, as already pointed out, the CA helps in understanding the interrelation among capabilities, between capability and functionings, and among functionings (and thus among rights). For instance, it is clear that the capability to be educated is linked to the capability to be well nourished, as school performance depends on the fact that children are sufficiently nourished.

Sen (2007) argues that the field of human rights has much to offer in exploring the role of freedoms in shaping one's well-being. Indeed, various forms of freedoms, such as freedom from hunger, from escapable morbidity or from premature mortality, can consolidate obligations that society has towards children. Sen (1995, 2004, 2005) also emphasizes that the CA can help to promote human rights. However, even if basic capabilities and basic rights are interchangeable, the CA still provides a more comprehensive framework for analysing and interpreting child development and well-being, as it allows us to explore the consequences of promoting rights.

Nussbaum (2006: 284) argues that "The capabilities approach is closely allied to the human rights approach" and that despite their differences, the capabilities approach is in fact "a species of the human rights approach". In fact, she emphasizes that the advantages of the capabilities approach, as she would call it, are more on the use of a particular language that lends precision and supplementation to the language of rights. But it is also true that many basic capabilities, as they appear in Nussbaum's list, overlap with core human rights, such as those concerning political liberties and free choice of occupation (among others). In the end, both perspectives refer to basic standards of humanity that should be fulfilled in the process of development.[19,20]

The CA can extend the human rights agenda towards notions of secure rights. It addresses positively the fact of human and social diversity. It allows for more flexibility and adaptation to different personal capacities (talent, skills and personal characteristics) and different cultural and societal contexts. Furthermore, the frequent use of the language of rights of all human beings, which can be seen in many practical arguments and pronouncements, has not been adequately matched by critical scrutiny of the basis and congruity of the underlying concepts (Sen, 2007: 2), that is, in the case of children, their participation. Indeed, if in principle Article 12 of CRC, and more recently other UN documents, indicate children as subjects of rights and participants in actions affecting them (Biggeri, 2004), in practice, no child has participated in drafting the Convention (Lewis, 1998; Feeny and Boyden, 2004) and, more generally, the rights were prepared during international conventions in a top-down fashion (Lewis, 1998), without roots at local level. Baraldi (2008) underlines that amongst over 40 articles only one concerns participation, while all the others are about the control of children (see also Chapter 3, Sections 3.2 and 3.3).

It follows that in the case of children, on the one hand human rights can be used as the main argument for defending a list of relevant capabilities for children (as in Chapter 3, Section 3.2) and on the other the CA can become a framework for normative evaluation and policy implementation. Therefore, it seems that the libertarian-inspired human rights approach and the CA can dialogue and complement each other quite well, with the first calling attention to the deprivations whereas the second can concentrate on their causes and assessment. Together, they can produce a cogent set of policy prescriptions.

2.7. Conclusions

The CA *per se* is a powerful framework for understanding children's well-being in terms of capabilities since we are forced to think about the complexities that characterize their lives.

Furthermore, the framework developed in this chapter and the concept of evolving capabilities constitute an important challenge to existing versions of the CA.

Childhood is a stage in life in which unique structures and capabilities matter and can evolve in different ways. It is not simply the fact that some capabilities can be more relevant than others as individuals get older. It is much more about understanding how children can be seen as autonomous beings, searching for agency, as adults do.

This means that children's well-being, following the CA, should be seen from a time-dynamic point of view. Normative assessment can also be seen as part of life cycles, following different timings in which policy interventions have a temporal dimension. Whenever children can participate as part of a solution for their problems, their capacity for agency is promoted.

This involves rethinking developmental complexities and tools for democracy in order to ensure inclusive citizenships (see also concluding chapter). If we seriously consider children's participation in decision-making processes regarding their well-being, then participation must take different forms according to their age. This means that we must be concerned with the formation of children's capacity for critical thinking and capability to aspire and must develop participatory methods that are suitable for different ages. As White (2002: 1101) argues, "there is no problem with the idea that (outsider) adults should be able to determine the best interest of (insider) children. In practice, however, there are often difficulties in the assumptions of superior understanding on the part of self-styled benefactors."

Notes

1. Even if this is the case, Sen argues that agency does not necessarily imply "control", as other people often operate the levers that expand choices (Sen, 1992, Chapter 3).
2. Age at last birthday is the parameter that international instruments generally use to define a child: "A child means every human being below the age of 18 years unless under the law applicable to the child, majority is attained earlier" (art. 1 of the UN CRC, Detrick, 1999). It is quite relevant to recognize that this demarcation has no social meaning in many parts of the world (Feeny and Boyden, 2004: 3).

3. Note that the notion of autonomy used here is synonymous with that of self-determination. It does not relate, strictly speaking, to the more complex notion of autonomy developed in Immanuel Kant's works.

4. Examples to the contrary are many and varied. For instance, the "speaking-out" surveys conducted by UNICEF (and the congress organized at the UN) underline that children are aware of their rights. The first Children World Congress on Child Labour organized by the Global March Against Child Labour (May 2004) emphasizes that children are the subject of capabilities (Biggeri et al., 2006), and most studies of the Bernard van Leer Foundation show children as social actor and agency since early childhood.

5. There is an obvious connection here between liberal theories and rationality. In fact, liberal theories are based on the assumption that the agents are rational. If, indeed, the individuals were not sufficiently rational to choose for themselves, it would then become legitimate for someone else to chooses for them (Sullivan, 1982; Jaggar, 1983; Unger, 1984).

6. "There is no lower age limit imposed on the exercise of the right to participate. It extends therefore to any child who has a view on a matter of concern to them" (Lansdown, 2001: 2). Indeed, there are many issues that very small children are capable of understanding and to which they can contribute thoughtful opinions (*ibid.*).

7. Erikson (1985) and Piaget (1978) emphasize the fact that child development is qualitatively different at different stages of childhood. At each stage, novel experiences challenge children to revise their ways of thinking in order to be able to explain new phenomena (Lippman et al., 2009).

8. As far as the first problem is concerned, notice that agency is perceived as a transition from nature to culture. However, it is accompanied by natural biological growth. According to Prout (2000) and other supporters of the theory of complexity, nature and culture represent elements that cannot be separated because they evolve together during children's growth. Baraldi (2008) argues that this fact results in the ambiguous character of agency meaning.

9. See Roger Hart's definition of participation (Hart, 1997) and O'Kane's analysis of the concept (O'Kane, 2003). Lansdown (2001) has argued that there are different levels of participation, according to which a child's capacity to influence events and his/her opportunities for personal development vary. She proposes a classification based on three stages, useful especially at an operational level: (1) consultative process; (2) participatory process; and (3) self-initiated process. Schier (2001) and Matthews (2003) have proposed two interesting scales in order to measure the promotion of participation in relation to child-adult.

10. According to the other point of view, a weak sense of agency can be considered as a primary phenomenon: it means that it's owned by children since their birth, when they show it through their smiles, gurgling, movements and looks, which express their expectations towards their interactions with adults (Baraldi, 2008). Assuming that even babies are endowed with at least weak agency implies that the relationship they create with adults, especially with the mother, has a reciprocal feature and adults' and children's action have to be coordinated (BvLF, 2004; Biggeri and Bellanca, 2010). Legerstee (2007) argues that the mechanism through which adults operationalize children's agency is the "emotional syntonization". Furthermore, children understand the people who look after them every day, think about what is going on around them and and enjoy new things and experiences (Makin and Whitehead, 2004).

11. Since the 1970s, Vygotsky has emphasized the role of social and cultural interactions in shaping children's cognition (e.g. Vygotsky, 1978).
12. On older people, see Lloyd-Sherlock (2002).
13. Eight children from South Asian countries (Nepal 3, Pakistan, 2, India 3) were invited to participate in the FGD. The group was composed of both males and females. All the children (one aged 13 years old, one 14, two 15 and four 16) were mature, and could understand each other and had sufficient English (five accompanying persons assisted in the FGD as well, to help in translation if needed, i.e. not as participants). All except one of the child delegates participating in the FGD were former child labourers who had new opportunities as a result of education and vocational training provided by rehabilitation centres or by the local civic organizations. Some of these children are still working to sustain their education fees. Clearly they did not need any introduction to the subject of child well-being and it is important to note that all of them were interviewed, both in their countries as well as during the three full days of the congress, where they had meetings on matters related to the issues of the FGD (see Biggeri et al., 2006).
14. According to children, leaders demonstrated lack of vision for children, and a disregard for the value of educating and protecting young people (UNICEF, Voice of Youth, 2003).
15. A good example is given by siblings; once the first child is literate, the second and third children learn to read, write and communicate relatively easily.
16. We may see external capabilities also as informal relationship capabilities given by affiliation and reciprocity. See also Mehrotra and Biggeri (2002).
17. According to this approach there is space for children to became active actors in the international and local contexts.
18. In most of social contexts "The idea of them exercising rights autonomously is not only foreign but potentially undermining of family and community and even of child survival, since the child exists only as a part of a whole" (Feeny and Boyden, 2004: 18).
19. An important dispute relates to the nature of the rights. Nussbaum claims (2006: 285) that the CA assumes entitlements that are considered "pre-political", and not simple products of laws and institutions. So, capabilities would be an essential feature of human species.
20. Following Dworkin's categorization the CA can be considered as a right-based approach. Dworkin (1977) proposes three categories of approaches for society evaluation: (1) a right-based approach considering that rights are the principle of justice; (2) a *conséquentialiste* approach considering only the consequences of policies and choices, even if some rights are violated; (3) and a duty-based approach, which starts from duties of individuals rather than rights.

References

Alderson, P. (2001), "Life and Death: Agency and Dependency in Young Children's Health Care", *New Zealand Children Issues*, 5(1): 23–27.

Alexander, J. M. (2004), "Capabilities, Human Rights and Moral Pluralism", *The International Journal of Human Rights*, 8(3): 451–469.

Ballet, J., Bhukuth, A. and Radja, K. (2004), "Capabilities, Affective Capital and Development Application to street child in Mauritania". Paper presented at the 4th HDCA Conference, 5–7 September 2004, Pavia.

Baraldi, C. (2008), *Bambini e Società*, Carocci, Rome.

Biggeri, M. (2004), "Capability Approach and Child Well-being", in *Studi e Discussioni*, 141, Dipartimento di Scienze Economiche, Università degli Studi di Firenze, Florence.

Biggeri, M. and Bellanca, N. (eds) (2010), "Dalla relazione di cura alla relazione di prossimità: L'approccio delle capability alle persone con disabilità", *Collana BiòTopi*, Liguori, Naples.

Biggeri, M., Bellanca, N. and Trani, J.-F. (eds) (2011), "From Cure to Care: Capability Approach to Rethink Policies on Persons with Disabilities", *ALTER European Journal of Research on Disability*, special issue.

Biggeri, M., Libanora, R., Mariani, S. and Menchini, L. (2006), "Children Conceptualizing Their Capabilities: Results of the Survey During the First Children's World Congress on Child Labour", *Journal of Human Development*, 7(1): 59–83.

Biggeri, M., Trani, J. F. and Bakhshi, P. (2009), "Le teorie della disabilità: una reinterpretazione attraverso l'approccio delle capability di Amartya Sen", *Studi e Discussioni* WP, DSE, Università di Firenze, Florence.

Boulding, E. (1979), *Children's Rights and the Wheel of Life*, Transaction Books, New Brunswick.

Brighouse, H. (2000), *School Choice and Social Justice*, OUP, Oxford.

Bronfenbrenner, U. (1995), *Developmental Ecology through Space and Time: A Future Perspective*, American Psychological Association, Washington, DC.

Bronfenbrenner, U. (1998), "The Ecology of Developmental Processes", in U. Bronfenbrenner, P. Morris, W. Damon and R. M. Lerner (eds), *Handbook of Child Psychology*, Wiley, Hoboken, NJ.

BvLF (2004), *Early Childhood Matters*, The Hague, The Netherlands: Bernard van Leer Foundation (review) 103, November.

Comim, F. (2004), "Time and Adaptation in the Capability Approach". Paper presented at the 4th HDCA Conference, 5–7 September 2004, Pavia.

Detrick, S. (1999), *A Commentary on the United Nations Convention on the Rights of the Child*, Martinus Nijhoff publishers, The Hague.

Dworkin, R. (1977), *Taking Rights Seriously*, Harvard University Press, Cambridge, MA.

Erikson, E. H. (1985), *Childhood and Society* (3rd edn), Norton, New York.

Feeny, T. and Boyden, J. (2004), "Acting in Adversity – Rethinking the Causes, Experiences and Effects of Child Poverty in Contemporary Literature", Working Paper Series, WP 116, QEH, Oxford.

Foster, J. E. and Handy, C. (2008), "External Capabilities", OPHI Working Paper Series.

Hart, R. (1997), *Children's Participation: The Theory and Practice of Involving Young Citizens in Community Development and Environmental Care*, UNICEF, New York.

Jaggar, A. (1983), *Feminist Political and Human Nature*, Totowa, NJ, Rowman & Allanheld.

Kjørholt, A. T. (2002), "Small is Powerful. Discourses on 'Children Participation' in Norway", *Childhood*, 11(1): 27–44.

Klasen, S. (2001), "Social Exclusion, Children and Education: Implications of a Rights-based Approach", *European Societies*, 3(4): 413–445.

Kymlicka, W. (1992), *Contemporary Political Philosophy: An Introduction*, OUP, Oxford.

Lansdown, G. (2001), "Promoting Children's Participation in Democratic Decision-Making" *Innocenti Insight*, UNICEF Innocenti Research Centre, Florence.

Lansdown, G. (2005), "The Evolving Capacities of the Child" *Innocenti Insight*, Save the Children-UNICEF, Florence.

Legerstee, M. (2007), *La Comprensione Sociale Precoce*, Raffaello Cortina, Milan (ed. or. 2005).

Lewis, N. (1998), "Human Rights, Law and Democracy in An Unfree World", in T. Evans (ed.), *Human Rights Fifty Years On: A Reappraisal*, Manchester University Press, Manchester, pp. 77–104.

Lippman, L. H., Moore, K. A. and McIntosh, H. (2009), *State of the Art of Positive Indicators of Social Well-being*, mimeo.

Lloyd-Sherlock, P. (2002), "Nussbaum, Capabilities and Older People", *Journal of International Development*, 14(8): 1163–1173.

Luhmann, N. (1990), *Sistemi Sociali*, Il Mulino, Bologna.

Makin, L. and Whitehead, M. (2004), *How to Develop Children's Early Literacy*, Paul Chapman, London.

Matthews, H. (2003), "Children and Regeneration: Setting and Agenda for Community Participation and Integration", *Children and Society*, 17: 264–276.

Mayall, B. (2000), "Intergenerational Relations and the Politics of Childhood". Paper presented at the Final Children 5–16, Conference, London, 20–21 October.

Mehrotra, S. (2002), "The Capabilities and Human Rights of Women: Towards an Alternative Framework for Development". Paper presented at the 2nd Conference HDCA, St. Edmunds, Cambridge.

Mehrotra, S. and Biggeri, M. (2002), "The Subterranean Child Labour Force: Subcontracted Home Based Manufacturing in Asia", Innocenti Working Paper no. 96, UNICEF Innocenti Research Centre, Florence.

Mehrotra, S. and Biggeri, M. (eds) (2007), *Asian Informal Workers: Global Risks Local Protection*, Routledge, New York.

Mehrotra, S. and Delamonica, E. (2007), *Eliminating Human Poverty: Macroeconomic and Social Policies for Equitable Growth*, Zed Books, London.

Nussbaum, M. (2000), *Women and Human Development: The Capabilities Approach*, Cambridge University Press, Cambridge.

Nussbaum, M. (2006) *Frontiers of Justice: Disability, Nationality, Species Membership*, Belknap Press of Harvard University Press, Cambridge, MA.

O'Kane, C. (2003), *Children and Young People as Citizens: Partners for Social Change*, Save the Children UK, South and East Asia Region.

Piaget, J. (1978), *The Equilibration of Cognitive Structures*, Blackwell, Oxford.

Prout, A. (2000), "Children's Participation: Control and Self-realization in British Late Modernity", *Children & Society*, 14: 304–315.

Punch, S. (2001), "Negotiating Autonomy: Childhoods in Rural Bolivia", in L. Alanen and B. Mayall (eds), *Conceptualising Child-Adult Relations*, Routledge-Falmer, London.

Rawls, J. (1980), "Kantian Constructivism in Moral Theory", *Journal of Philosophy*, 77(9): 515–572.

Rogoff, B. (1990), *Apprenticeship in Thinking: Cognitive Development in Social Context*, OUP, Oxford.

Ryan, R. M. and Deci, E. L. (2000), "Self-determination Theory and the Facilitation of Intrinsic Motivation, Social Development, and Well-being", *American Psychologist*, 55(1): 68–78.

Saito, M. (2003), "Amartya Sen's Capability Approach to Education: A Critical Exploration", *Journal of Philosophy of Education*, 37(1): 17–33.

Schaffer, H. R. (1996), *Social Development*, Blackwell, Oxford.

Schier, H. (2001), "Pathways to Participation: Openings, Opportunities and Obligations", *Children & Society*, 15: 107–117.

Sen, A. K. (1987), "The Standard of Living", in G. Hawthorn (ed.), *The Standard of Living*, Cambridge University Press, Cambridge.

Sen, A. K. (1992), *Inequality Reexamined*, OUP, Oxford.

Sen, A. K. (1993), "Capability and Well-being", in M. Nussbaum and A. K. Sen (eds), *The Quality of Life*, Clarendon Press, Oxford.

Sen, A. K. (1995), "Gender Inequality and Theories of Justice", in M. Nussbaum and J. Glover (eds), *Women, Culture and Development: A Study of Human Capabilities*, Clarendon Press, Oxford.

Sen, A. K. (1999a), *Development as Freedom*, OUP, Oxford.

Sen, A. K. (1999b), "Investing in Early Childhood: Its Role in Development", in *Conference on Breaking the Poverty Cycle. Investing in Early Childhood*, Inter-American Development Bank, Washington, DC.

Sen, A. K. (2000), "A Decade of Human Development", *Journal of Human Development*, 1(1).

Sen, A. K. (2004), "Elements of a Theory of Human Rights", *Philosophy and Public Affairs*, 32(4): 315–356.

Sen, A. K. (2005), "Human Rights and Capabilities", *Journal of Human Development*, 6(2): 151–66.

Sen, A. K. (2007), "Children and Human Rights", *Indian Journal of Human Development*, 2(1): 1–18.

Sullivan, W. (1982), *Reconstructing Public Philosophy*, University of California Press, Berkeley, CA.

Unger, R. (1984), *Knowledge and Politics*, Palgrave Macmillan, New York.

UNICEF (2003), *Voices of Youth*, The Bimonthly Newsletter, www.unicef.org/voy/.

Unterhalter, E. and Brighouse, H. (2003), "Distribution of What? How Will We Know If We Have Achieved Education for All by 2015?". Paper presented at the 3rd HDCA Conference, September, Pavia.

Vygotsky, L. S. (1978), *Mind in Society. The Development of Higher Psychological Processes*, Harvard University Press, Cambridge, MA.

Walker, M. and Unterhalther, E. (eds) (2007), *Amartya Sen's Capability Approach and Social Justice in Education*, Palgrave Macmillan, New York, Oxon.

White, S. C. (2002), "Being, Becoming and Relationship: Conceptual Challenges of a Child Rights Approach in Development", *Journal of International Development*, 14(8): 1095–1104.

Yaqub, S. (2002) "Poor Children Grow into Poor Adults: Harmful Mechanism or Over-Deterministic Theory?", *Journal of International Development*, 14(8): 1081–1093.

3
Child Poverty as Capability Deprivation: How to Choose Domains of Child Well-being and Poverty

Mario Biggeri and Santosh Mehrotra

3.1. Introduction

As mentioned at the beginning of the book, there are several reasons why child poverty[1] should be a much more important topic of development than it has been so far. At least five aspects are worth mentioning. First, children are disproportionately represented among the poor as they constitute a high share of the population in developing countries (from a third to a half), so reducing poverty necessarily means reducing child poverty. Second, child poverty, especially if persistent, often has irreversible effects for the current cohort of children, so there is a permanent pay-off from addressing them (in terms of mental, physical, emotional and spiritual development) (Mehrotra, 2006). Third, children are often hit hardest by poverty, household shocks and economic and social crises. Furthermore, reducing poverty for children by increasing their entitlements reduces future poverty, through an inter-generational transfer of poverty. Moreover, child poverty cannot be confined merely to the material aspects of children's lives (Biggeri et al., 2006). If poverty, in general, has a multidimensional character this is especially true for children, as the relevance of different domains changes according to age. For instance, to be able to move is arguably less relevant for an infant than for an eight-year-old child.

Although there are numerous approaches to conceptualizing, defining and measuring poverty (Roelen and Gassmann, 2008),[2] the five aspects identified above underline the need for children to be separated from their adult nexus, and treated on their own terms – only then can the true scale of their poverty be determined (Feeny and Boyden, 2003). Although identification and aggregation methods remain crucial for all approaches that aim to create a portrait of child poverty, "the vital issue with respect to these methods is how to capture children and child-specific issues by means of the poverty measure. The dependence of children on their direct environment for the provision of basic needs, the child-specific requirements in terms of basic needs and the need for specific information for the formulation of child-focused policies are important reasons that call for the development of child poverty approaches" (Roelen and Gassmann, 2008: 22).[3]

Furthermore, Feeny and Boyden (2003, 2004: 9) argue that the "tireless statistical obsession" prevents understanding childhood poverty as a process, and ignores how children perceive their situation and what their aspirations are for the future. It ignores the fact that they not only experience loss (of income, health or education) but also retain resourcefulness, courage and optimism (Feeny and Boyden, 2004; Mehrotra, 2006).

There has been an evolution in the approaches to child well-being and to conceptualizing, defining and measuring children's deprivations. The research trends show a shift from survival to well-being, from negative to positive, from traditional to new domains, all moving towards a composite index of child well-being (Ben-Arieh, 2008; see Appendix 3.1). For these reasons it is essential to expand the definition and analyses of child poverty beyond traditional conceptualizations. In this chapter, in line with previous ones, we define child poverty as the deprivation of basic capabilities and achieved functionings. According to Sen, "What the capability perspective does in poverty analysis is to enhance the understanding of the nature and causes of poverty and deprivation by shifting primary attention away from means to ends that people have reason to pursue, and, correspondingly, to the freedoms to be able to satisfy these ends" (Sen, 1999: 90).

The capability approach (CA) to poverty and human development considers income as a relevant means but, at the same time, it underlines the inadequacy of income as a proxy for the freedom of children. First, this is because in the capability perspective "low personal income is only one of the factors that influence the deprivation of basic capabilities" (Sen, 1998: 2). Moreover, children's access or "entitlement" to household income and resources is extremely marginal. Similarly, measures of income per household do not consider intra-household allocation and thus discriminate, for instance, against child health and nutrition.[4] In other words, the household head is not always benevolent.

The CA allows the measurement of well-being at the individual level and can therefore reveal intra-household and gender inequalities in well-being across different domains (Klasen, 2007). Moreover, in general, a resource-based approach presents other problems; for example, a child with disabilities may not be able to do many things that an able-bodied child can do with the same commodities. This means that different children may need different policies in order to enjoy the same basic capabilities and achieve the same functionings, many of which are instrumental to evolving capabilities.

Unquestionably, in the trade-off between simple but practical measurement *versus* complex but more informative evaluations, the CA embraces the latter (see Appendix 3.1). This raises the question of how to identify relevant functionings and capabilities. It follows that if identifying the poor is prior to aggregation, choosing relevant dimensions or domains[5] must be prior to identifying the deprived. Indeed, insofar as poverty researchers choose domains, they typically fail to make explicit their reason for choosing them (Alkire, 2008). Domains are particularly relevant in the CA since they are characterized by "multiple realisability" (Nussbaum, 2000) in the potential capability set of the child.

In considering the capabilities approach as a normative framework for analysing children's well-being and poverty, there are several questions that arise in selecting domains: what are these basic capabilities? How do we identify them? How can we define them in order to identify the poor children? Do these depend on how a society prioritizes different capabilities? How do we aggregate them?

In particular, the question of how to choose the relevant domains is the key to understanding child poverty and is the subject of this chapter. The main idea is to understand child poverty through the CA, that is, to create the space for children to conceptualize their well-being and prioritize different domains. If these actions are difficult or even impossible to imagine for very young children, as their agency and autonomy increases – according to the age and maturity of the child – child participation becomes more feasible but central to the analysis of their well-being (see Chapter 2). This is clearly in contrast to orthodox poverty analysis where children are seen only as passive actors dependent on others (Ben-Arieh, 2005). Of course, as mentioned in previous chapters, there are many freedoms that depend on the assistance and actions of others and the nature of social arrangements (Sen, 2007: 9). This is why basic capabilities (and fundamental human rights) cannot be ignored (especially for young children). Indeed, the material basis of well-being is also relevant to child poverty.

The chapter is structured as follows. In the second section we explore briefly two procedures for selecting relevant domains in the CA. An open-ended list of relevant capabilities is then used to explore and compare different practices among researchers. In the third section we present five methods generally used to choose and select domains. We consider their practical relevance for children, and examine the main strengths and weaknesses of each method and, where possible, compare the domains selected according to the different techniques. The last section reports the main conclusions and research implications. To illustrate, the sample of multidimensional poverty measurement amongst children in Afghanistan using the CA is reported in Appendix 3.1.

3.2. Selecting relevant capabilities for children

If we consider the capabilities approach as a normative framework for analysing children's well-being and child poverty, as we have done elsewhere (Biggeri, 2004; Biggeri et al., 2006), the procedures for selecting a list of relevant capabilities are central (Nussbaum, 2000, 2003; Robeyns, 2003b).

Nussbaum has developed her list of central capabilities as part of "political liberalism" that is supposed to have involved "years of cross cultural discussions" (Nussbaum, 2000, 2003).[6] Nussbaum's list is broadly universal and is intended to reflect common human values and experiences. She also has stressed that her list could be made more specific by local people, and some notable attempts have been made to identify capabilities in particular contexts (e.g. Clark, 2002, 2003; Ibrahim, 2009).[7,8] However, as Amartya Sen emphasizes, the problem does not lie with listing important capabilities themselves, but with endorsing a predetermined or fixed list of capabilities (Sen, 2005). Indeed, according to Sen, the selection of capabilities should be the product of a democratic process that includes public scrutiny and debate (Sen, 2004a, 2004b).[9] In Chapter 4 this account of deliberative democracy is discussed further and reconciled with Sen's (2006; 2009) idea of justice. Sen also argues that capability domains can be selected according to two criteria (Sen, 2004b). The first asks whether they are of special importance, i.e. if they should be regarded as basic capabilities. The second asks whether they influence society directly or indirectly. These criteria open up new spaces for investigating neglected domains for children.

At the end of the day, however, even if the analysis of well-being and/or poverty in the CA has the virtue of enriching the informational base for social assessments, this still requires techniques for identifying, prioritizing, measuring and comparing diverse capabilities in different situations (Alkire, 2008).[10]

In order to give researchers and practitioners a full overview of the operationalization of the CA, we present two complementary procedures that have emerged in the literature. The first procedure, suggested by Ingrid Robeyns, helps researchers to identify relevant capabilities in a general or more definite context of analysis (Robeyns, 2003a). The second, developed by the HDCA's Thematic Group on Children's Capabilities at Florence University (Italy) is helpful for those researchers and practitioners who work in the more definite context of analysis – as a social group, a local context or project action – to conceptualize capabilities at the local level, to form a consensus and to prioritize the different domains.

3.2.1. A procedure for the initial selection of capabilities

The procedure suggested by Robeyns (2003a, 2003b) helps researchers to think about and identify domains and capabilities both theoretically and pragmatically. It is based on four criteria (Robeyns, 2006: 356):

(1) *Explicit formulation*: Lists should be explicit and should be discussed and defended.
(2) *Methodological justification*: the method used to select the domains should be clarified, scrutinized and defended, while open to critique and modification.
(3) *Different level of generalities*: A two-stage "ideal–feasible" process holds that the list should be compiled at two levels; the first involves the selection of ideal domains, while the second aims to narrow down and modify the list in the light of what is practically feasible. This distinction is useful as practical feasibility can change in each reality.
(4) *Exhaustion and non-reduction*: the capabilities on the list should include all elements that are important. No dimensions or domains that are important should be left out.

These criteria are a sort of "check and balance" that help address the fact that every policy maker and researcher is situated in a personal context and therefore needs to take special care to avoid biases that are introduced by their (personal and disciplinary) background (Robeyns, 2006: 356).

In our original studies we applied this method as a first step for preparing an initial (open-ended) list of relevant domains for children (see Biggeri, 2004). Here we briefly report the result that will be drawn upon later. Indeed, in Section 3.3, we use this initial list to substantiate the five different methods to select relevant domains and to compare different list outcomes.

A group of experts on children's issues with different backgrounds and expertise[11] were involved in the initial two phases of the exercise. In the first stage, we selected relevant capabilities for evaluating child well-being and suggested a non-definitive and open-ended list. Then, in the second stage, we provided the reasons for our choices and related them to previous work on capabilities (namely, Nussbaum, 2000, 2003; Robeyns, 2003a)[12] and on literature on children's issues. The latter involved reflecting on the work of United Nations Children's Fund (UNICEF), United Nations Educational, Scientific and Cultural Organization (UNESCO), International Labour Organization (ILO) and the United Nations (UN). The third step involved choosing an appropriate level of abstraction. In our case, we have tried to capture the specific capabilities that are relevant for children and their broader social groups.

The fourth involves applying the rule of exhaustion and non-reduction. In other words, the selected capabilities should include all relevant domains for analysing child poverty, and none of these domains should be reducible to other items included on the list.

Table 3.1 Preliminary list of capabilities relevant for children (domains/dimensions)

1. *Life and physical health*: being able to be born, be physically healthy and enjoy a life of normal length
2. *Love and care*: Being able to love and being loved by those who care and being able to be protected*
3. *Mental well-being*: being able to be mentally healthy
4. *Bodily integrity and safety*: being able to be protected from violence of any sort
5. *Social relations*: being able to be part of social networks and to give and receive social support*
6. *Participation*: to participate in and have a fair share of influence and being able to receive objective information*
7. *Education*: being able to be educated
8. *Freedom from economic and non-economic exploitation*: being able to be protected from economic and non-economic exploitation*
9. *Shelter and environment*: being able to be sheltered and to live in a healthy, safe and pleasant environment
10. *Leisure activities*: being able to engage in leisure activities
11. *Respect*: being able to be respected and treated with dignity
12. *Religion and identity*: being able to choose to live or not according to a religion and identity*
13. *Time-autonomy*: being able to exercise autonomy in allocating one's time*
14. *Mobility*: being able to move*

Note: * in accordance with the age and maturity of the child.
Source: Our elaboration on Biggeri (2004).

Our proposed list of capabilities for children is presented in Table 3.1. Although similar to Robeyns's list (see footnote 12), our list contains some differences relevant for the analysis of children's well-being. Our results also confirm the difficulty of defining a universal list of capabilities for children using a procedure elaborated for other groups and purposes – namely gender inequalities amongst adults.

If the focus is on a specific domain (e.g. love and care), it may be possible to extend the analysis by exploring sub-domains (e.g. love and care of parents, siblings and other relatives or support from teachers, neighbours, friends or peers).

The main limitation of this procedure is that public scrutiny of the key stakeholders (in this case, children) is not taken into consideration. Nonetheless, this problem can be attenuated by employing the second procedure, which can complement this one (see Section 3.2.2).

It is also noticeable that some capabilities in contrast to others can be more "relevant" as age increases (this is intuitive and emerged from a focus group discussion with children; see Biggeri et al., 2006; see also Chapter 2, Section 2.4). Indeed, the presence of the asterisk in Table 3.1 implies that intuitively, and on the base of research experience, the relevance of the capability and agency may vary "in accordance with the age and maturity of the child" (whether the child is in her/his early childhood (from 0 to 5 years old), mid-childhood (6–10), early adolescence (11–14) or later adolescence (15–17)). For instance, it is possible that different ages may value in different ways each of the above-mentioned capabilities, although the process aspect of freedom tends to suggest that the full list of capabilities may be enjoyed only by the older category of children and from adulthood generally.

As mentioned Table 3.1 is intended as a preliminary, flexible and open-ended list of capabilities that is relevant for research, and can be used in conjunction with the capability framework to analyse child well-being.

3.2.2. A procedure to conceptualize capabilities and to prioritize domains

The second procedure has been developed by the HDCA's Thematic Group on Children's Capabilities at Florence University. Before we consider this procedure two other methodological points are worth emphasizing: (1) a good knowledge of the problems and the context of analysis is necessary; this can be achieved through both a literature review and participatory methods; and (2) the formulation of an initial open-ended list for children according to Robeyns' procedural criteria should incorporate focus group discussions with the primary stakeholders.

The aforementioned procedure is based on four principles which shape the core process of thinking, reflecting and participating, and aim to support stakeholders in their attempt to identify the central domains of their well-being. This process transforms into an instrument of public reasoning and allows for a first ranking of domains for practical uses.

> The core of the process is based on a progressive focalization of the child from his/her general opinions on values and well-being, shifting to his/her personal experience (internal focalization) regarding specific domains, capabilities and actual functionings. The child then moves towards a more general understanding of the dimensions of well-being within the community or group of children. This transforms the individual opinions into potential shared ideas. Finally, the child identifies a subset of capabilities that are considered to be of the highest relevance for children in their community. (See Biggeri and Libanora, Chapter 4, this book.)

Following Biggeri and Libabora (*ibid.*) the four steps employed are thus:

(1) Let the children conceptualize the capabilities dimensions without any interference.
(2) Focus on the personal achieved functionings for each dimension of well-being.

(3) Focus on community capabilities to define the relevance of each dimension.
(4) Let the children prioritize the different dimensions chosen.

The procedure has usually been delivered through a questionnaire. Although a questionnaire, for its internal coherence, could normally be too rigid to enhance and register processed knowledge, the focalization procedure proposed leads the subject to move through different levels of cognitive analysis until s/he reaches a final synthesis in the last stage.[13] Libanora and Biggeri developed the procedure through more participatory methods in the form of a game ("expedition game", Libanora and Biggeri, 2009, unpublished). Different rules, for example, in terms of the share of "consensus", can be used to validate the identification and the relevance of each domain for the children. For an example of the domains from our list, see Section 3.3.3 below and Chapter 5. The procedure is discussed at greater length in Chapter 4.

3.3. How to choose domains of child well-being?

In more general terms, Sabina Alkire (2008) has proposed a comprehensive review of studies to select relevant domains/dimension. She identifies five different methods or modes:

(1) existing data or convention;
(2) list based on consensus (public "consensus)";
(3) participatory processes (ongoing);
(4) assumptions, i.e. when the researcher has a clear view regarding the relevant domains drawn from a theory or from their own informed experience; and
(5) "expert analyses" of empirical data on values and preferences.

Furthermore, she argues that "there is no straightforward way for choosing how to choose domains of human well-being. What is very clear, immediately, is that these processes overlap and are often used in tandem" (Alkire, 2008, Section 6.6). Different methods can thus be combined (see, for instance, Vizard and Burchardt (2007), who combine legal and participatory approaches for the UK equality review).

Generally the selection of method(s) depends on the research objectives, operational processes (e.g. purposes of the analysis, short-term *versus* long-term policies, comparability *versus* local context, project *versus* programme) and practical constraints such as time, money, feasibility and capacity.

Although there is no straightforward way of deciding how to choose domains of human well-being, some selection methods are more promising than others for particular purposes. Different methods can be combined in order to overcome some of their limitations or to verify the validity of the results (i.e. triangulation).

3.3.1. Existing data or conventions

This selection method is mainly based on the use of existing data or convention. Usually the domains are chosen by researchers according to pre-designed questions – although in practice the domains are often chosen according to data availability (especially for developing countries). Indeed, the main concern of the researcher is often data availability, which has the effect of excluding important domains of child well-being or paying little attention to what these proxies/variables actually represent in terms of (human) values. This can bias the results of the research as well as the policy implications in many circumstances. For example, even conventional variables such as enrolment rates or years of education at school (used in empirical research to represent the education domain) exclude *a priori* informal education and fail to pay attention to the ways children are treated in schools, which may be the major factor affecting children's education and well-being.

The availability of good-quality data is an essential precondition for measuring child well-being through the CA and for analysing child poverty and social development. The CA needs a plural informational base. Relevant information has been collected by the Italian Statistical Institute (ISTAT) (see Addabbo Di Tommaso, Chapter 10) and through German, Swiss Swedish and UK panel surveys. Important progress has also been made in terms of developing techniques for measuring human well-being through the CA (Chiappero Martinetti, 2000; Robeyns, 2006; Brighouse and Robeyns, 2010; Chiappero and Roche (2009) consider measurement issues relating to empirical analysis).[14]

Almost all the empirical applications are restricted to the measurement of achieved functionings, although Chapter 10 is a rare exception.[15]

Applying the CA, however, does not just involve adding neglected domains to the analysis. It also demands a change in the research design starting from spans data collection, method of data elaboration, etc., as discussed in Chapter 11. This is also one of the reasons why *ad hoc* surveys that use the capabilities framework are important for obtaining the information and data required for analysis and offer the hope of influencing "official" surveys, censuses and policy planning.

At the aggregate level, especially for international comparison, an important source and base for the analysis of children's well-being and poverty is the statistical section of UNICEF's *State of the World Children* (published annually) and other reports of UN agencies such as UNDP, UNESCO and the World Bank. Most of these aggregate data come from household surveys undertaken by international agencies or national statistical offices (UNICEF, 2004).

The Multiple Indicator Cluster Survey (MICS)[16] is a tool developed by UNICEF for monitoring progress in the achievement of World Summit for Children (WSC) goals, and to monitor progress in relation to Millennium Development Goals (MDGs) that covers several domains.

Together with MICS, the World Bank's multi-purpose household surveys (Living Standards Measurement Study, LSMS/ Integrated Survey series and the Priority Survey series), ILO Statistical Information and Monitoring Programme on Child Labour surveys (SIMPOC), National Child Labour Survey (NCLS) and Demographic and Health Surveys (DHS) are important instruments for generating information on child well-being and poverty in developing countries. However, one has to allow for the fact that they differ in terms of scope and information/variables provided.[17]

Below we try to verify whether the data provided by the aforementioned surveys can capture the domains of child well-being, i.e. capabilities or better achieved functionings' sets, identified in Table 3.1.

Table 3.2 summarizes the results of our assessment by survey. The first column presents our preliminary list of children's capabilities, while the following columns assess the availability of relevant data (indicators or proxies) for gauging children's achieved functionings.

Most of the surveys contain some relevant information for measuring achieved functionings, but none of them capture the full complexity of child well-being across all relevant domains exemplified by our list. As we can see from Table 3.2, MICS2 collects useful information about life and physical health, body integrity and safety, and education that can be translated into indicators or proxies of achieved functionings. It also contains quite important information on freedom from economic and non-economic exploitation, shelter and environment, but only indirectly captures information on love and care, social relations, leisure activities and time autonomy. Moreover, it fails to address participation, respect, religious identity or mobility. The more comprehensive MICS3 questionnaire includes more detailed information. However it still does not contain information on participation, respect, religious identity and mobility.

Data sets from the other surveys, based on comprehensive interviews with a stratified sample of households, provide relevant information on children's achieved functionings.

The analysis of household survey questionnaires suggests that the informational base on children is well developed, although the available domains are limited due to data availability. Several domains need to be added to existing questionnaires. Even if we consider all the surveys mentioned above, some domains, such as social relations, participation, respect, identity, mental well-being and mobility, are under-represented or not covered at all, as we have shown.

For some domains, opinion polls are an alternative and interesting source of data. For instance, it is worth mentioning UNICEF's "speaking-out"

Table 3.2 Availability of information/data (for indicators or proxies) about children's achieved functionings by type of household survey

Achieved functionings of relevant children's capabilities domains	MICS2 (UNICEF)	MICS3 (UNICEF)	LSMS (WB)	NCLS (ILO)	DHS	"Speaking-out" service (UNICEF)	NDSA[a]
Life and physical health	••	••	•	•	••	–	••
Love and care	•*	•	•*	•*	•*	••	••
Mental well-being	–	•	–	–	–	••	••
Bodily integrity and safety	••	••	•	••	••	•	••
Social relations	•*	•*	–	–	–	••	•
Participation	–	–	–	–	–	••	•
Education	••	••	•	••	•	••	••
Freedom from economic and non-economic exploitation	•	••	•	••	•	–	•
Shelter and environment	•	•	•	•	•	•	••
Leisure activities	•*	•*	•*	•*	–	••	•*
Respect	–	–	•*	•*	•*	–	••
Religion and identity	*•	•*	•*	•*	–	–	•*
Time-autonomy	•*	–	–	–	–	–	••
Mobility	–	–	–	–	–	–	••

Note: •• reliable information[18]; • some information; * indirect information, e.g. information on the parents' religion and identity; – no information.
[a] National Disability Survey in Afghanistan.
Source: adapted from Biggeri (2004).

surveys, which ask some useful questions on domains overlooked by the surveys (see the penultimate column of Table 3.2).

One novel approach that goes some way to bridging the gap between theory and practice in the measurement of children's capabilities is the National Disability Survey in Afghanistan (NDSA), which is assessed in the final column of Table 3.1 and considered in Appendix 3.1 below (see also Bakhshi et al., 2006 and Chapter 11 in this book).

For a comprehensive application of the CA as a normative framework, additional information is required. First of all, data on means, such as household income, assets, education and health conditions are needed. In addition, information on each member of the household (especially the mother), on social services and on infrastructures should complement current data, as well as information on the institutional framework that may constrain the capability set of individuals, since they represent important "internal" and social/environmental conversion factors (see Chapter 1). Among the surveys considered, the LSMS seem to report most of the information on the means to achieve well-being (see Biggeri, 2004, Table 2.11).

However, the main limitation of this selection method is that researchers tend to use data without posing any question on the missing domains and even on the domains chosen. Indeed, "a weakness of this selection method is that it does not raise value issues. Thus it should be used only in conjunction with another method, unless the exercise is a technical test and will not provide the basis for practical recommendations" (Alkire, 2008). In Chapter 11 a concrete proposal for combining this approach with another principle is advanced (see, in particular, Chapter 11, Section 11.3 and Table 11.4).

Even if something is not measurable or does not appear in a data set (as is often the case with non-material well-being domains), it does not mean that these aspects are irrelevant. Unfortunately, most quantitative studies on children ignore this research issue and prescribe their policy implications only on the basis of available data, which are often incomplete and biased.

3.3.2. Lists based on consensus

This method involves identifying and using a set of domains previously established and have received widespread consensus.

Almost all the analyses of child issues refer to the UN Convention on the Rights of the Child (CRC) (1989).[19] For legitimacy purposes, it is important to remember that the CRC is, at present, ratified by 191 states. Domains of children's well-being are also captured by the Millennium Development Goals. Children explicitly figure in the first six goals, which relate to three separate domains: freedom from poverty/hunger, access to education and freedom from specific illness. Two goals are directly linked to children: achieving universal primary education (goal 2) and reducing child mortality (goal 4).

Other well-established goals are embodied in ILO conventions on the Minimum Age (ILO, n°. 138, 1973) and the Worst Forms of Child Labour (ILO, n°. 182, 1999) regarding freedom from economic and non economic exploitation.

There have been several attempts to structure/classify the articles of the CRC according to relevant domains (to our knowledge, not yet in the capabilities informational space).[20] This has been done, for instance, by UNICEF both theoretically and empirically as reported in Table 3.3 (UNICEF, 2004; see Santos Pais, 1999, for a similar list).

As with the previous selection method, an attempt is made to verify whether the articles of the CRC can adequately capture the well-being domains of children using the procedural criteria adopted earlier. The results,

Table 3.3   Terms of childhood considering children's rights

According to the Convention on the Rights of the Child, every child has the right to:	Articles*
Non-discrimination	2, 30
Action taken in their best interests	3, 18
Survival and development	6
Identity	7, 8
Family relations and parental guidance	5, 7, 8, 9, 10, 18, 21, 25
Protection from illicit transfer and illegal adoption	11, 21
Freedom of expression, thought, conscience and religion	12, 13, 14
Freedom of association and peaceful assembly	15
State protection of privacy, home, family and correspondence	16
Access to appropriate information	17
Protection from abuse and neglect	19
Special protection and assistance if deprives of the family environment	20, 22
Protection from armed conflict	22, 38–39
Special care if disabled	23
Health and access to health-care services	24
Benefit from social security	26
A decent standard of living	27
Education	28–29
Rest and leisure, play and recreation, culture and the arts	31
Protection from child labour, trafficking, sexual and other forms of exploitation, and drug abuse	32–36, 39
Protection from torture and deprivation of liberty	37–39
Dignity and worth, even if the child has infringed the law	40

* Articles refer to articles 1–40 of the Convention of the Rights of the Child. Those cited refer explicitly to children's rights of the obligations of States parties to children.
Source: Unicef (2004).

Table 3.4 CRC articles *versus* capabilities domains[21]

Children's capabilities domains	CRC articles	
	Direct	Indirect
Life and physical health	6, 23, 24, 25, 27, 29	(17), (19), (33), (37), (39)
Love and care	7, 9, 18, 20, 21, 26, 27	(3), (10), (22)
Mental well-being	23, 25, 27, 29, 37	(17), (19), (33), (39)
Bodily integrity and safety	19, 25, 26, 37	(23), (24), (39)
Social relations	15, 27, 29	(12)
Participation	12, 13, 15, 17, 23, 29	(40)
Education	13, 24, 28	(32)
Freedom from economic and non-economic exploitation	19, 32, 34, 36	(33), (35)
Shelter and environment	24(c), 27(3), 29(c)	
Leisure activities	31	(40)
Respect	16, 19, 23, 30, 39(2)	(2)
Religion and identity	8, 14, 29, 30, 31	(2), (7), (37)
Time-autonomy		(31), (37)
Mobility		(31), (37)

Source: for column 1, see Table 3.1

reported in Table 3.4, are extremely interesting and challenging as they show how it is both possible and fruitful to complement the CA and the Human Rights Based Approach (HRBA).[22]

In fact, the consensus-based lists have almost always been agreed upon by adults, without consulting children. More often than not, children did not take part in identifying criteria for assessing their own well-being. The CRC lists were prepared during international conventions, in a top-down fashion (Lewis, 1998), and lacked roots at the local level. Indeed, "there was no social movement preceding the granting of rights, indeed there was no participation by children at all in the formulation of the CRC" (Lewis, 1998).

Furthermore, these lists are sometimes disputed at the local level or rejected by the communities they are intended to serve. It follows that a consensus reached in this way may hide surrounding conflicts, may be inflexible to local circumstances and may not adequately involve key stakeholders and people. "It may also lead to the inaccurate conceptualisation of impoverishment where there actually is none, simply because the international rights legislation does not reflect the socio-economic realities of children's lives" (Feeny and Boyden, 2004: 18).

Article 12 of the CRC (1989) is a milestone in the advocacy of children's participation, as it defends the rights of the child to freedom of association and to peaceful assembly. The article argues that "there is no lower age limit imposed on the exercise of the right to participate. It extends, therefore, to any child who has a view on a matter of concern to them" (Lansdown, 2001: 2). The progress made in the human rights field and the ratification of the above-mentioned conventions have contributed to a step forward in the advocacy for children's rights and in definitively setting universal goals for children's well-being. The human rights language reminds us that children have justified and urgent claims to certain types of treatment, wherever she or he may live. In particular, the CRC and the UN document, "A world fit for children" (UN, 2002), presents a new ethical attitude towards children in which children are no longer recipients of services or beneficiaries of protective measures, but subjects of rights and participants in actions affecting them (see Chapter 2, Section 2.6.1).

Therefore, the main limit of the CRC is that, though endorsing the child's right to express his or her opinion freely and to have that opinion taken into account in any matter affecting the child, children have not been stakeholders in the process of defining it: "no children whatsoever participated in the drafting of the Convention" (Feeny and Boyden, 2004: 18).

It has to be acknowledged that, in recent years, UNICEF have attempted to increase children's participation substantially (UNICEF, 2002).

3.3.3. Participatory processes

Participatory processes could be a relevant method of selecting domains in the case of children, since they may lead to true public scrutiny and debate, i.e. to more exercise of democracy for children.[23] The participatory process can be applied with success at the local level and for community projects with children using different methods. Children themselves should participate in decisions about what it means to be poor and the magnitude of poverty, avoiding externally imposed standards.[24]

Although the results are relevant especially in local contexts, it is worth mentioning that participatory processes can be subject to distortions such as adaptive preferences (how can we ensure children's values don't reflect their personal circumstances?), mental conditioning (how can we be sure that children's values aren't shaped by manipulation, e.g. advertising programmes that promote eating tasty but chemically processed food?) or power (the most confident child can impose her/his view of well-being on other children). They may be driven by children of the local elite or, in our case, by older or more active children. Furthermore, if trust is low, "values" discussions may be superficial and misleading. The risk can be to "localise" too much (Nussbaum, 2003, see, note 6). For instance, the list can become a danger for children too "adapted" to some circumstances (see, for instance, Ballet et al., 2004 and Chapters 5 and 7, this book).[25]

In order to overcome, or at least to reduce, these problems some recommendations, theoretical and practical, can be taken into account such as control group and external check lists containing basic capabilities, and eventually prepared with the help of privileged observers to reduce the adaptive preference problem.[26] It is also necessary to address practical matters such as the use of local language and good preparation of facilitators.

Attempts to foster the democratic and participatory process on a large scale are carried out by UNICEF and other UN agencies, and by some international non-governmental organizations (NGOs) (Lansdown, 2005). However, these projects are only in their incipient stages. While there are many sociological and anthropological studies that use participatory methods in order to identify important domains for children, to our knowledge few studies have been carried out actively involving the subjects of the research themselves, by asking them to identify and conceptualize their capabilities domains and to value them (see, for instance, Clark, 2002; Camfield, 2006; and Chapters 5, 6 and 11 in the book).

This aspect evokes the issue of agency of children (van den Berge, 2006; Boyden and Levison, 2000; White, 2002; see also Camfield, 2006 and Chapter 2, this book). We are aware that children are too often characterized by voicelessness and powerlessness and are vulnerable to claims being made for them, claims that they have comparatively little scope to influence or dispute. Furthermore, "there is a powerful body of evidence showing how prevailing attitudes towards children, based on the view that adults know best and will act in their best interest, have failed many children. Many of these failures resulted from the refusal to listen to the voices of children themselves" (Lansdown, 2001: 3).[27] In the case of children, well-being and poverty research should also foreground subjective meanings and experiences, and also provide the background for interpreting "best interests" (Camfield et al., 2009).

As emphasized in the previous chapter, agency is a primary phenomenon: it means that it's owned by children since their birth, when they show it through their smiles, gurgling, movements and looks, which express their expectations towards their interactions with adults (Rogoff, 1990; Baraldi, 2008). In relation to such a participatory process, there is evidence showing that there are many issues that even very small children are capable of understanding and to which they can contribute with thoughtful opinions (Lansdown, 2005).

The level of children's participation can vary from light interaction to deep participation using different participatory tools (Hart, 1992). The tools used can also vary according to the local circumstances, the age and maturity of the children. They can vary from unstructured and participatory questionnaires to deep interviews, photo essay, mapping, focus group discussions, drawings, etc. Children's participation in the initial process and interim monitoring would contribute to improve project implementation.

The procedure described in Section 3.2.2, and with details in Chapter 4, uses a "light" participatory tool producing interesting results. For instance,

Table 3.5   Children's selected domains (Nepal, 2008)

a) Life and physical health
b) Love and care
c) Mental well-being
d) Bodily integrity and safety
e) Social relations
f) Participation/information
g) Education
h) Freedom from economic and non-economic exploitation
i) Shelter and environment
j) Leisure activities
k) Respect
*l) Religion (spirituality)
m) Religion and identity (tradition, culture)
n) Personal autonomy
*o) Personal autonomy (as agency)
p) Mobility
*q) Understand/interpret
*r) Plan/imagine/think

Note: * new domains not included in Table 3.1.

in the fieldwork in Nepal (September 2008) the domains conceptualized were those reported in Table 3.5, of which numbers 12, 15, 17 and 18 are different from those in Table 3.1 (see Libanora and Biggeri, 2009, unpublished).

3.3.4. Assumptions

The choice of domains can be based on assumptions. When the researcher has a "clear" view on the relevant domains (drawn from a theory or from their own informed experience), she/he is also able to present them transparently. For instance, in making assumptions regarding what people should value based on researchers' views or drawing on social theory, religion and so on, it is deeply desirable that these assumptions should be communicated so that they become the subject of public scrutiny (Alkire, 2008).

In developed countries the main domains of child well-being usually considered are health and survival, material well-being, education and personal development and social inclusion (Micklewright and Stewart, 2000), while in developing countries experts usually concentrate on various aspects of deprivation (Mehrotra, 2006).

As we have said, researchers' assumptions often use different approaches. In the case of children, for instance, Di Tommaso (2006) bases her choice on Nussbaum's list of central capabilities, which is mainly based on her philosophical background (see previous notes). Another example is given by the *State of the World's Children 2005* report (see Gordon et al., 2003 and UNICEF, 2004) where four domains – life and health (nutrition, sanitation, water), information, education and shelter and environment (shelter and water access) – are chosen and justified by a mix of human rights and basic need approaches (seven indicators are used for measuring the achieved functionings, see the appendix at the end of this chapter).

The risk of this method, as underlined by Alkire (2008), is to select domains based on implicit or explicit assumptions about what people do value or should value. These are commonly the informed guess of the researcher or may be drawn from conventions, social or psychological theories, philosophy, religion and so on.

In other cases, assumptions may be inaccurate and even detrimental. Indeed, they may perpetuate inaccurate assumptions and inaccurate academic conventions or may be asserted ideologically rather than subjected to scrutiny and reasoned debate (Alkire, 2008). The use of other methods could be relevant to handling these problems.

3.3.5. Empirical evidence regarding people's values (or "expert analyses")

Other important ways of selecting domains include the use of empirical data on values or data on consumer preferences and behaviours, or studies whose values are most conducive to mental health or social benefit (Alkire, 2008). Some studies about children are already available.

One interesting source of information, as mentioned in Section 3.1, is UNICEF's "speaking-out" surveys, which have the virtue of asking some questions related to specific domains of child well-being (UNICEF, 2003). These surveys (based on opinion polls) collect other information on indicators or proxies of children's achieved functionings, which are not common for the other types of survey (see Table 3.2). In fact, these surveys/opinion polls have been designated by UNICEF with the purpose of capturing specific child rights and thus are meant to cover areas of such relevant domains as love and care, mental well-being, social relations, participation and respect.

The *World Values Survey* has also given rise to a significant empirical literature on cross-cultural values. This worldwide network of social scientists is studying changing values and their impact on social and political life.

Moreover, a number of psychologists articulate normative values that, they argue (usually, but not always, on the basis of empirical evidence), are required for healthy human flourishing. In the same area there are a few studies carried out by neuro-economists and experimental economists, but which are not always focused on children, although there are a few exceptions.[28]

3.4. Conclusions

Most traditional measures of child poverty "tell us very little concerning the lack of opportunity and choice that appears and impinge heavily upon poor families, and that greatly undermines their ability to protect their children from hazards or exploitation by others. The idea that parents may themselves be willing exploiters of their children (and their labour in particular) is also ignored. If anything, therefore, poverty lines serve further to obscure children's experience of poverty, and are invoked less to meet the needs of the poor but rather to satisfy the " 'static and standardised wants of professionals' " (Chambers, 1992: 81; Feeny and Boyden, 2004: 8). Applying the CA necessarily enlarges the informational requirements, as it involves a shift in focus from child poverty in terms of resources to child poverty as deprivation of basic capabilities and achieved functionings (i.e. opportunities).

Furthermore, selecting relevant domains is necessary before any research or analysis into child poverty and well-being can be conducted. The selection method for choosing domains depends crucially on the research objectives and operational processes, as well as on practical constraints such as time, money, feasibility and capacity.

In this chapter we have explored five methods for selecting domains of child well-being. In order to improve the results of the selection process these methods can be, and often are, combined by researchers. We have also considered two procedures used in the literature on the CA to improve the selection process in the initial stage, and for the conceptualization and formation of consensus. Above all, the choice of relevant capabilities must be subjected to public scrutiny and choice, which includes involving the central stakeholders, children.

To conclude, neglecting relevant domains in the analysis of child poverty and well-being may lead to biased results and policy implications. In other words, all research should explain the reasoning behind the choice of domains used in the analysis and why some domains are excluded, and how this exclusion may affect the results of the research. Furthermore, it is evident that poverty thresholds and other deprivation indicators must be meaningful for the country/area under analysis, since wrong analyses may lead to wrong policies.

3.5. Appendix 3.1. Approaches to child poverty and an example of using the CA[29]

According to the literature (see, for instance, Corak, 2006; Mehrotra, 2006; Redmond, 2008; Roelen and Gassmann, 2008), the main approaches to child poverty are the monetary approach, the basic needs approach, the child rights-based approach,[30] the social exclusion approach,[31] the sustainable livelihoods[32] approach and the CA.

Within a scale from unidimensional to multidimensional measures, as described in Figure A.3.1, three different types of measures can be identified: (1) child poverty count measures (white boxes), (2) child poverty index measures (light grey) (3) and holistic child poverty measures (dark grey).

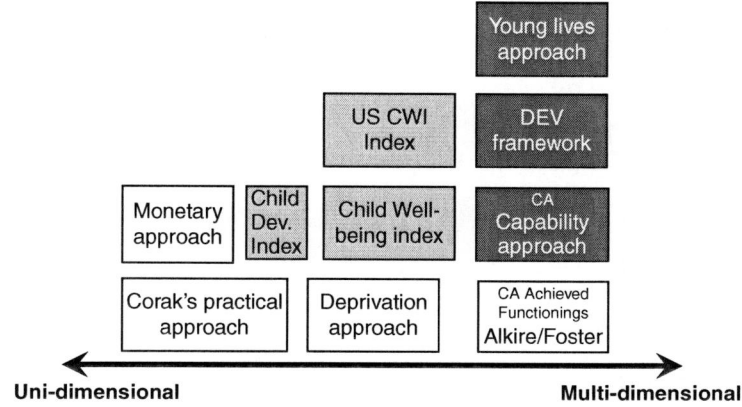

Figure A.3.1 From unidimensional to multidimensional child poverty measures
Source: Our elaborations on Roelen and Gassmann (2008: 21).

It is important to note that different domains are utilized by different child poverty approaches, as discussed by Biggeri et al. (2009) (see also, among others, Cummins et al., 2003; UNICEF, 2005; Bradshaw et al., 2006; Young Lives, 2006; UNICEF 2007; Save the Children UK, 2008; Barnes et al., 2009).

Biggeri et al. (2009) analysed child poverty in Afghanistan adopting the capability framework[33] and Alkire and Foster (2008) measure. Indeed, it is difficult to write about poverty in Afghanistan without considering children, who represent more than 60% of the population. The data utilized in this analysis are based on the National Disability Survey in Afghanistan (NDSA) carried out by Handicap International (Bakhshi et al., 2006). The NDSA was a one-off survey inspired by the CA and, thus, has investigated many domains of children's well-being typically overlooked in standard surveys.

In the analysis we apply the approach developed by Alkire and Foster (2008), which involves a poverty count measure based on a dual cut-off (for a brief introduction see Appendix 4.1). The term "dual" refers to the fact that it involves two different forms of cut-offs, one pertaining to single domains (so that many cut-offs must be selected) and the other relating to cross-cutting domains (where just one cut-off is required).

In Table A.3.1 we report the proportion of poverty for each of the ten domains.

The level of deprivation in some domains is particularly high. For instance, the lack of access to drinking water, shortage of assets, constraints to work or exclusion from school are very different domains of deprivation that, together, affect between 40% and 75% of all Afghan children.

Table A.3.1 Level of deprivation considering each dimension (5–14)

Dimension	Indicator	Cut-off	Dimensions from Table 3.1	Poverty (%) – single deprivation
1) Health	Access to good water	Well in residence/ compound/plot; covered well; open well and kariz; spring; river/stream; pond/lake; still water; rain water; tanker/ truck; other	1	65.1
2) Care	Who takes care of your child besides yourself?	lacks mother care	2	38.2
3) Family assets: material deprivation of the family	Does any member of your household own any of the following?	less than 6 assets	–	66.1
4) Food security: material deprivation of the children	How often does your household get enough to eat?	Often not enough food	1	34.7
5) Social inclusion	Based on 3 questions	Answer "yes" on at least one of the questions	4,5,6, 11	6.9
6) Education*	Has the person received some education?	Never attended school	7	34.7
7) Freedom from economic and non-economic exploitation and leisure activities	How many hours per day does your child spend on household tasks/ eldwork/work outside the house?	More than two hours of work	8,10	45.3
8) Shelter and environment	How many people per room are there in your household?	More than three people per room	9	27.5
9) Personal autonomy*	Based on 5 questions	Moderate difficulty	13	0.7
10) Mobility*	Based on 5 questions	Moderate difficulty	14	31.2

Source: Biggeri et al. (2009).
Note: values with the * are calculated without children aged 5–7.

Table A.3.2 Level and breadth of poverty for age 8–14

Cut-off (k)	Head count ratio H	$A=M_0/H$	M_0
1	0.987	0.366	0.362
2	0.935	0.381	0.356
3	0.759	0.423	0.321
4	0.493	0.489	0.241
5	0.264	0.567	0.150
6	0.133	0.634	0.084
7	0.036	0.725	0.026
8	0.009	0.804	0.007
9	0.000	0.900	0.000
10	0.000	N/A	0.000

Source: Biggeri et al. (2009).

In Table A.3.2 we report the values of the headcount (H) and of the adjusted headcount (M_0), which are based on the minimum number of domains (k) on which a child must be deprived to be considered poor.

The simple multidimensional headcount ratio is the proportion of children identified as poor (i.e. the number of poor children to the total number of children globally). As the number of domains (k) increases, the level of poverty diminishes.

The trend leads us to believe that with regard to one single domain of deprivation (i.e. the union approach), all Afghan children are poor. Even when we take into consideration two domains, the level of poverty is evident. If the poverty cut-off is four out of ten domains, 56% of the children are still poor.

In the third column, we report the adjusted headcount ratio M_0. The adjusted headcount ratio is the total number of deprivations experienced by all poor children divided by the maximum number of deprivations that could possibly be experienced by all individuals. In this way, M_0 summarizes information on both the incidence of poverty and the average extent of a multidimensional deprivation. In the fourth column the average depth of poverty among Afghan children is reported.

Notes

1. *The State of the World's Children 2005* (2004) proposes the following working definition: "Children living in poverty experience deprivation of the material, spiritual and emotional resources needed to survive, develop and thrive, leaving them unable to enjoy their rights, achieve their full potential or participate as full and equal members of society." This definition suggests that children experience deprivation with their hands, minds and hearts, and these aspects of their well-being are interrelated. For example, material poverty – in terms of starting the day without a nutritious meal or being forced to engage in hazardous labour – hinders cognitive capacity as well as physical growth. Living in an environment that provides little stimulation or emotional support to children, on the other

hand, can remove much of the positive effect of growing up in a materially rich household. By discriminating against their participation in society and inhibiting their potential, poverty not only causes child suffering – it also disempowers them (see Cornia et al., 1987).

2. Different approaches and methods to defining and measuring child poverty have different implications for policy and for targeting since they identify different children as being poor (White et al., 2009).

3. Camfield et al. (2009) outline some of the major debates regarding child poverty for three contrasting approaches to well-being: indicator-based, participatory and longitudinal research.

4. Child income poverty focuses on income through equivalence scale to take into account the household composition (Deaton and Paxson, 1997).

5. As in Alkire (2008), here "domain" and "dimension" are used interchangeably.

6. Nussbaum (2003: 41–42) presented the following list of central Human capabilities: (a) life; (b) body health; (c) body integrity; (d) sense, imagination and thought; (e) emotions; (f) practical reasons; (g) affiliation; (h) other species; (i) play; and (j) control over one's environment. For a critique, see Clark (2002, 2006) and Okin (2003), amongst others.

7. The question of whether there should be one universal list of domains, or whether multiple lists should be advanced from diverse human contexts, is a long-standing debate in the CA literature (Robeyns, 2003b; Alkire, 2005). This debate might be caricaturized as "having a [set?] list" *versus* "making lists for every occasion" (Alkire, 2008, Section 6.5). Here we argue that these two extremes can be reconciled.

8. As Alkire writes, "Nussbaum argues, as do others, that [the] specification of one 'list' of domains or central capabilities is necessary to make sure that the content of the CA carries critical force. If the approach is too open-ended then there is a real, practical possibility that the wrong freedoms will be prioritized and expanded." She writes, "[C]apabilities can help us to construct a normative conception of social justice, with critical potential for gender issues, only if we specify a definite set of capabilities as the most important ones to protect. Sen's 'perspective of freedom' is too vague. Some freedoms limit others; some freedoms are important, some trivial, some good, and some positively bad. Before the approach can offer a valuable normative gender perspective, we must make commitments about substance" (Nussbaum, 2003). See also Alkire (2008, Section 6.5).

9. To the best of our knowledge no lists of capabilities for children were reported in the literature before 2003. The first lists for children were advanced at the HDCA conference in Pavia by Biggeri (2003, 2004), Biggeri and associates (2006) and Di Tommaso (2006) (see also Saito, 2003). Maria Laura Di Tommaso (2006) adapts Nussbaum's list of central capabilities for children by choosing seven of her ten original capabilities (this route has been followed in Chapters 6, 8, 9, 10 and 14), while Biggeri et al. (2006) let children conceptualize the domains of their well-being (this list has been adopted in Chapters 3, 4, 5, 11 and 13). New entries can be found on the HDCA website. For further reading see Fattore et al. (2007).

10. Two other theoretical and practical exercises required for applying the CA are the "aggregation" (which can be interpersonal and/or intrapersonal) and the "formation of consensus" (Robeyns, 2006: 356–357).

11. These experts included development economists, anthropologists, sociologists, statisticians, demographers, psychologists, human rights defenders, UNICEF officers and experts, and NGOs practitioners (amongst others).

12. Nussbaum's list can be found in note 6. Robeyns (2003a) presents the following list for exploring gender inequalities amongst adults: (a) life and physical health; (b) mental well-being; (c) bodily integrity and safety; (d) social relations; (e) political empowerment; (f) education and knowledge; (g) domestic work and non-market care; (h) paid work and other projects; (i) shelter and environment; (j) mobility: being able to be mobile; (k) leisure activities; (l) time-autonomy; (m) Respect; and (n) religion (including the capability not to be religious).

13. Clark (2002, 2003) develops an approach based on a survey questionnaire that goes some way towards addressing these issues.

14. Anand (2008) and Volkert and Wüst (2009), using the GSEOP (German Socioeconomic Panel) data set for well-being analysis of very young children, looked at a range of different functionings and capabilities. An OECD programme led by Giovannini has been quite innovative in this direction. Details of other studies can be found on the HDCA website (www.capabilityapproach.org).

15. There are three main reasons (Robeyns, 2003b): (1) achieved functionings are (at least indirectly) observable, whereas the person's capability would also include all the opportunities including counterfactual options that were not chosen and are therefore unobservable; (2) whereas the achieved functionings are a vector of beings and doings, the capability set contains potential beings and doings, and it is not obvious how this set should be measured let alone be evaluated; and (3) the transition from achieved functionings to capabilities, the choice of which is a process in itself.

16. The MICS survey follows a stratified sample design building a national probabilistic sample, stratified by different geographic areas, departments and urban residences. The first round of MICS (MICS1) was conducted around 1995 in more than 60 countries. A second round of the survey (MICS2) was conducted in 1999–2001 to assess progress towards goals and objectives set for the year 2000 (around 65 surveys), and resulted in an increasing wealth of data to monitor the situation of children and women. The current round of MICS (MICS3) is focused on monitoring international commitments covering 101 indicators on several topics including nutrition, mortality and education, with data available by background characteristics (sex, ethnicity, household wealth, age, education, etc.) and disaggregated at the sub-national level (Cappa, 2007). MICS3 and MICS4 have been particularly designed for the monitoring of the MDGs and other international commitments on children rights. In particular, four of the indicators are specific MDG indicators designed to measure progress in specific millennium development targets: access to safe drinking water, access to improved sanitation, security of tenure and eviction and measles immunization.

17. It is possible to compare the data from different countries if the information is retrieved from same type of household surveys (e.g. LSMS). See, for instance, the website of the UCW Project, *Understanding Children's Work*.

18. "Good information" means that direct information is available on the domain. Some information means that there is indirect information on the domain that could be used in the analysis. Information on material poverty and values should be collected as well (see Chapter 11 and Biggeri et al., 2009).

19. Age at last birthday is the parameter that international instruments generally use to define a child: "A child means every human being below the age of 18 years unless under the law applicable to the child, majority is attained earlier" (art. 1 of the UN CRC).

20. "States Parties recognize the right of every child to a standard of living adequate for the child's mental, spiritual, moral and social development" (CRC, Article 27 (1).) (There is no definition of what an "adequate standard of living" is.) "The parent(s) or others responsible for the child have the primary responsibility to secure, within their abilities and financial capacities, the conditions of living necessary for the child's development" (CRC Article 27(2)). "States Parties, in accordance with national conditions and within their means, shall take the appropriate measures to assist parents and others responsible for the child to implement this right and shall in case of need provide material assistance and support programmes, particularly with regard to nutrition, clothing and housing" (CRC Article 27(3)).

21. We wish to thank Martha Santos Pais, David Parker and Leonardo Menchini (from UNICEF Innocent Research Centre) for their suggestions in May 2004. Apart from Article 27 (see previous note) the following rights are relevant: right to survival (Article 6); right to health care (Article 24); right to enjoyment of full and decent life for children with disabilities (Article 23); right to social security (Article 26); right to basic education (Article 28); right to protection from economic or sexual or other forms of exploitation (Articles 11, 32–35); and right to freedom of expression, thought, conscience, religion, association and information (Articles 12–17, 30).

22. On the one hand, human rights are not flexible enough to capture local contexts, while on the other they could offer a long-term perspective of specific rights and duties and an allocation of those duties. For a proposal on how to complement the two approaches see, for instance, Nussbaum (2003) and Sen (2004, 2005). Attempts to link the CA approach and the HRBA have been developed for adults by Nussbaum (1999), Alexander (2004) and Vizard and Burchardt (2007), amongst others (Tania Burchardt and Polly Vizard are developing one for children in the UK). For a tentative attempt to include participatory methods in the HRBA, see Jonsson (2003).

23. For instance, Clark (2002, 2003) uses a questionnaire method based on a survey in South Africa to understand perceptions of human well-being. See also Alkire (2002). Further studies are emerging, although to date unpublished; please see the HDCA website for the related thematic group.

24. Participatory approaches can also be used to define an appropriate minimum basket of commodities for the monetary approach; or a list of basic capabilities for the CA. Given the inequalities in voice and power that occur in participatory settings, extra safeguards should be introduced to ensure the integrity of the process.

25. On the adaptation problem, see Nussbaum (2000, Chapter 2), Teschl and Comim (2005), Qizilbash (2006) and Clark (2009, 2010).

26. Adaptation may not be a serious issue in many local contexts (see, for example, Agarwal, 2008; Clark, 2009).

27. Parents/tutors, for example, can be inspired by different motivations and they can be either autonomy supportive (for instance, giving an internal frame of reference, providing meaningful rationale, allowing choices, encouraging self-perspective) or just controlling (e.g. pressure to behave in specific ways) (see self-determination theory, e.g. Ryan and Deci, 2000).

28. Although the level of happiness can be a good indicator of people's well-being, it is not the same thing. Well-being is about capabilities and achievements. For

a review of theoretical and applied studies regarding lists of human values, see Alkire (2002, 2008, Tables 6.2–6.6) and Clark (2002, Chapter 3).

29. This appendix is written by Mario Biggeri, Jean-Francois Trani and Vincenzo Mauro and is largely based on Biggeri et al. (2009), which includes further discussion of these issues.

30. OHCHR developed a common set of rights that apply to most countries: being adequately nourished; being able to avoid preventable morbidity and premature mortality; being adequately sheltered; having basic education; being able to appear in public without shame; being able to earn a livelihood; and taking part in the life of a community. Implicit in the definition of poverty (based on the non-fulfilment of rights) is the assumption that governments have the legal responsibility to fulfil these rights, as the ultimate duty bearers (Minujin et al., 2006: 485). See also (Jonsson, 2003).

31. The concept of social exclusion describes the processes of marginalization and deprivation that can arise even in rich countries with comprehensive welfare provisions. It is a reminder of the multiple faces of deprivation. This approach focuses intrinsically on the processes and dynamics that allow deprivation to arise and persist, the structural characteristics of society and the situation of marginalized groups (Roelen and Gassmann, 2008).

32. This approach addresses issues of vulnerability, risk and insecurity. The means to combat these hardships are the assets that individuals, households and communities have. Assets, called "capital", include material and social resources of five types: physical, financial, human, social and natural (Moser and Norton, 2001).

33. See an interesting paper on Indian child labour and child deprivation by Jayaraj and Subramanian (2007).

References

Agarwal, B. (2008), "Engaging with Sen on Gender Relations: Cooperative Conflicts, False Perceptions and Relative Capabilities", in K. Basu and R. Kanbur (eds), *Arguments for A Better World: Essays in Honour of Amartya Sen*, Oxford University Press, Oxford, pp. 157–178.

Alexander, J. M. (2004), "Capabilities, Human Rights and Moral Pluralism", *The International Journal of Human Rights*, 8(3): 451–469.

Alkire, S. (2002), *Valuing Freedoms. Sen's Capability Approach and Poverty Reduction*, Oxford University Press, Oxford.

Alkire, S. (2005), "Why the Capability Approach", *Journal of Human Development*, 6(1): 115–133.

Alkire, S. (2008), "Choosing Domains: The Capability Approach and Multidimensional Poverty", in N. Kakwani and J. Silber (eds), *The Many Domains of Poverty*, Palgrave Macmillan, New York. MPRA Paper No. 8862, posted 26. May 2008. Online at http://mpra.ub.uni-muenchen.de/8862/

Alkire, S. and Foster, J. E. (2008), "Counting and Multidimensional Poverty Measurement", OPHI, Working Paper No. 7, Oxford Poverty and Human Development Initiative.

Anand, P. B. (2008), "Homo Faber: The Happiness and Capabilities of Very Young Children", Open University, Mimeo.

Bakhshi, P., Trani, J.-F. and Rolland, C. (2006), *Conducting Surveys on Disability a Comprehensive Toolkit*, Handicap-International, Lyon.

Ballet, J., Bhukuth, A. and Radja, K. (2004), "Capabilities, Affective Capital and Development Application to Street Child in Mauritania". Paper Presented at the 4th HDCA Conference, 5–7 September 2004, Pavia.

Baraldi, C. (2008), *Bambini e Società*, Carocci, Rome.

Barnes, H., Noble, M., Wright, G. and Dawes, A. (2009) "A Geographical Profile of Child Deprivation in South Africa". *Child Indicators Research*, doi:10.1007/s12187-008-9026-2.

Ben-Arieh, A. (2005), "Where Are the Children? Children's Role in Measuring and Monitoring Their Wellbeing", *Social Indicators Research*, 74: 573–596.

Ben-Arieh, A. (2008), "The Child Indicators Movement: Past, Present, and Future", *Child Indicators Research*, 1: 3–16.

Biggeri, M. (2003) "Children, Child Labour and the Human Capability Approach". Paper Presented at the 3rd HDCA Conference, 7–9 September 2003, Pavia.

Biggeri, M. (2004), "Capability Approach and Child Well-being", *Studi e Discussioni*, no. 141, Dipartimento di Scienze Economiche, Università degli Studi di Firenze, Florence.

Biggeri, M., Libanora, R., Mariani, S. and Menchini, L. (2006), "Children Conceptualizing Their Capabilities: Results of the Survey During the First Children's World Congress on Child Labour", *Journal of Human Development*, 7(1): 59–83.

Biggeri, M., Trani, J.-F. and Mauro, V. (2009), "The Multidimensionality of Child Poverty: An Empirical Investigation on Children of Afghanistan", Working Paper, OPHI, Oxford.

Boyden, J. and Levison, D. (2000), "Children as Economic and Social Actors in the Development Process", Working Paper 2000, No. 1, Expert Group on Development Issues, Ministry for Foreign Affairs, Stockholm.

Bradshaw, J., et al. (2006), "An Index of Child Well-being in the European Union", *Social Indicators Research*, 80(1): 133–177.

Brighouse, H. and Robeyns, I. (eds) (2010), *Measuring Justice: Primary Goods and Capabilities*, Cambridge University Press, Cambridge.

Camfield, L. (2006), "Why and How of Understanding 'Subjective' Well-being: Exploratory Work by the WeD Group in Four Developing Countries", WeD Working Paper 26.

Camfield, L., Streuli, N. and Woodhead, M. (2009), "What's the Use of 'Well-Being' in Contexts of Child Poverty? Approaches to Research, Monitoring and Children's Participation", *International Journal of Children's Rights*, 17: 65–109.

Cappa, C. (2007), "Understanding Children Wellbeing. Framework for the Assessment of Children Capabilities via Household Surveys". Paper Presented at the International Workshop on Children's Capabilities, Florence, 18–19 April.

Chambers, R. (1992), "Poverty in India: Concepts, Research and Reality", in B. Harriss, S. Guhan, and R. H. Cassen (eds), *Poverty in India: Research and Policy*, Oxford University Press, Bombay, pp. 301–332.

Chiappero Martinetti, E. (2000), "A Multidimensional Assessment of Well-being Based on Sen's Functioning Approach", *Rivista Internazionale di Scienze Sociali*, 2000(2): 207–239.

Chiappero Martinetti, E. and Roche, J. M. (2009), "Operationalisation of the Capability Approach, from Theory to Practice: A Review of Techniques and Empirical Applications", in E. Chiappero-Martinetti (ed.), *Debating Global Society: Reach and Limits of the Capability Approach*, Fondazione Giacomo Feltrinelli, Milan, pp. 157–201.

Clark, D. A. (2002), *Visions of Development: A Study of Human Values*, Edward Elgar, Cheltenham.

Clark, D. A. (2003), "Concepts and Perceptions of Human Well-being: Some Evidence from South Africa", *Oxford Development Studies*, 31(2):173–196.

Clark, D. A. (2006), "Capability Approach", in D. A. Clark (ed.), *The Elgar Companion to Development Studies*, Edward Elgar, Cheltenham, pp. 32–45.

Clark, D. A. (2009), "Adaptation, Poverty and Well-Being: Some Issues and Observations with Special Reference to the Capability Approach and Development Studies", *Journal of Human Development and Capabilities*, 10(1): 21–42.

Clark, D. A. (2010), *Adaptation, Poverty and Development*, forthcoming book, typescript.

Corak, M. (2006), "Principles and Practicalities for Measuring Child Poverty", *International Social Security Review*, 29(2): 3–35.

Cornia, G. A., Jolly, R. and Stewart, F. (1987), *Adjustment with a Human Face*, Oxford University Press, Oxford.

Cummins, R. A., Eckersley, R., Pallant, J., Van Vugt, J. and Misajon, R. (2003), "Developing A National Index of Subjective Wellbeing: The Australian Unity Wellbeing Index", *Social Indicators Research*, 64: 159–190.

Deaton, A. and Paxson, C. H. (1997), "Poverty among Children and the Elderly in Developing Countries", Research Program in Development Studies Princeton University, mimeo.

Di Tommaso, M. (2006), "Measuring the Well Being of Children using a Capability Approach: An Application to Indian Data", Child Working Papers, ChilD n. 05/2006.

Fattore, T., Mason, J. and Watson, E. (2007), "Children's Conceptualisation(s) of Their Well-being", *Social Indicators Research*, 80(1): 5–29.

Feeny, T. and Boyden, J. (2003), *Children and Poverty: A Review of Contemporary Literature and Thought on Children and Poverty*, Christian Children's Fund, Richmond, Virginia.

Feeny, T. and Boyden, J. (2004), "Acting in Adversity – Rethinking the Causes, Experiences and Effects of Child Poverty in Contemporary Literature", Working Paper Series, WP 116, QEH, Oxford.

Gordon, D., Nandy, S., Pantazis, C., Pemberton, S. and Townsend, P. (2003), *Child Poverty in the Developing World*, UNICEF, New York.

Hart, A. R. (1992), *Children's Participation: From Tokenism to Citizenship*, UNICEF, International Child Development Center, Florence.

Ibrahim, S. (2009), "Self Help: A Catalyst for Human Agency and Collective Capabilities", in E. Chiappero-Martinetti (ed.), *Debating Global Society: Reach and Limits of the Capability Approach*, Fondazione Giacomo Feltrinelli, Milan, pp. 233–266.

Jayaraj, D. and Subramanian, S. (2007), "Out of School and (Probably) in Work", *Journal of South Asian Development*, 2(2): 177–226.

Jonsson, U. (2003), *Human Rights Approach to Development Programming*, UNICEF, Nairobi, Kenya.

Klasen, S. (2007), "Gender-related Indicators of Well-being", in M. McGillivray (ed.), *Human Well-Being: Concept and Measurement*, Palgrave Macmillan, London, pp. 167–192.

Lansdown, G. (2001), "Promoting Children's Participation in Democratic Decision-Making", *Innocenti Insight*, UNICEF Innocenti Research Centre, Florence.

Lansdown, G. (2005), "The Evolving Capacities of the Child", *Innocenti Insight*, UNICEF Innocenti Research Centre, Florence.

Libanora, R. and Biggeri, M. (2009), "Report: Women's and Children's Capabilities at WF Nepal", Katmandu, Nepal, 12–20 September 2008, May, mimeo.

Lewis, N. (1998), "Human rights, Law and Democracy in an Unfree World", in T. Evans (ed.), *Human Rights Fifty Years On: A Reappraisal*, Manchester University Press, Manchester, pp. 77–104.

Mehrotra, S. (2006), "Child Poverty", in David Alexander Clark (ed.), *The Elgar Companion to Development Studies*, Edward Elgar Publishing Limited, Cheltenham, pp. 54–60.

Micklewright, J. and Stewart, K. (2000), "Child Well-Being in the EU and Enlargement to the East", Innocenti Working Paper, Economic and Social Policy Series, No. 75, Florence: UNICEF Innocenti Research Centre.

Minujin, A., Delamonica, E. E., Davidziuk, A. and Gonzalez, E. D. (2006), "The Definition of Child Poverty: A Discussion of Concepts and Measurements", *Environment & Urbanization*, 18(2): 481–500.

Moser, C. and Norton, A. (2001), *To Claim Our Rights: Livelihoods Security, Human Rights and Sustainable Development*, ODI, London.

Nussbaum, M. (1999), "Capabilities, Human Rights, and Universal Declaration", in B. H. Weston and S. P. Marks (eds), *The Future of International Human Rights*, Transnational Publishers Inc., USA, Ardsley , pp. 25–64.

Nussbaum, M. (2000), *Women and Human Development: The Capabilities Approach*, Cambridge University Press, Cambridge.

Nussbaum, M. (2003), "Capabilities as Fundamental Entitlements: Sen and Social Justice", *Feminist Economics*, 9(2–3): 33–59.

Okin, S. M. (2003), "Poverty, Well-Being, and Gender: What Counts, Who's Heard?", *Philosophy and Public Affairs*, 31(3): 280–316.

Qizilbash, M. (2006), "Well-Being, Adaptation and Human Limitation", *Royal Institute of Philosophy Supplements*, 81: 83–110.

Redmond, G. (2008), "Children's Perspectives on Economic Adversity: A Review of the Literature", Innocenti Discussion Paper No. IDP 2008-01, Florence: UNICEF Innocenti Research Centre.

Robeyns, I. (2003a), "Sen's Capability Approach and Gender Inequality: Selecting Relevant Capabilities", *Feminist Economics*, 9(2–3): 61–92.

Robeyns, I. (2003b), *The Capability Approach: An Interdisciplinary Introduction*, University of Amsterdam, Amsterdam.

Robeyns, I. (2006), "The Capability Approach in Practice", *The Journal of Political Philosophy*, 14(3): 351–376.

Roelen, K. and Gassmann, F. (2008), "Measuring Child Poverty and Well-Being: A Literature Review", Working Paper MGSoG/2008/WP001, Maastricht Graduate School of Governance, Maastricht University, January.

Rogoff, B. (1990), *Apprenticeship in Thinking: Cognitive Development in Social Context*, OUP, Oxford.

Ryan, R. M. and Deci, E. L. (2000), "Self-determination Theory and the Facilitation of Intrinsic Motivation, Social Development, and Well-being", *American Psychologist*, 55(1): 68–78.

Saito, M. (2003), "Amartya Sen's Capability Approach to Education: A Critical Exploration", *Journal of Philosophy of Education*, 37(1): 17–33.

Santos Pais, M. (1999), "A Human Rights Conceptual Framework for UNICEF", *Innocenti Essays*, ICDC/UNICEF, Florence.

Save the Children (2008), *The Child Development Index: Holding Governments to Account for Children's Wellbeing*, Save the Children, London.

Sen A. K. (1998), "Mortality as an Indicator of Economic Success and Failure", *Economic Journal, Royal Economic Society*, 108(446): 1–25.

Sen, A. K. (1999), *Development as Freedom*, Oxford University Press, Oxford.

Sen, A. K. (2004a), "Capabilities, Lists, and Public Reason: Continuing the Conversation", *Feminist Economics*, 10: 77–80.

Sen, A. K. (2004b), "Elements of a Theory of Human Rights", *Philosophy and Public Affairs*, 32(4), October: 315–356.

Sen, A. K. (2005), "Human Rights and Capabilities", *Journal of Human Development*, 6(2): 151–166.

Sen, A. K. (2006), "What Do We Want from A Theory of Justice", *The Journal of Philosophy*, CIII(5): 215–238.

Sen, A. K. (2007), "Children and Human Rights", *Indian Journal of Human Development*, 2(1): 1–12.

Sen, A. K. (2009), *The Idea of Justice*, Harvard University Press, Cambridge.

Teschl, M. and Comim, F. (2005), "Adaptive Preferences and Capabilities: Some Preliminary Conceptual Explorations", *Review of Social Economy*, 63(2): 229–247.

UNICEF (2002), *State of the World Children 2003*, UNICEF, New York.

UNICEF (2003), *Speaking-out Surveys*, UNICEF, New York.

UNICEF (2004), *State of the World Children 2005, Childhood Under Threat*, UNICEF, New York.

UNICEF (2005), "Child Poverty in Rich Countries", *Innocenti Report Card No. 6*, UNICEF Innocenti Research Centre, Florence.

UNICEF (2007), "Child Poverty in Perspective: An Overview of Child Well-being in Rich Countries", *Innocenti Report Card No. 7*, UNICEF Innocenti Research Centre, Florence.

United Nations (2002), *A World Fit for Children*. A/S-27/19/Rev.1. 12 July 2002, UNICEF, http://www.unicef.org/specialsession/documentation/documents/A-S27-19-Rev1E-annex.pdf

van den Berge, M. P. (2006), "Working Children: Their Agency and Self-organization", *Éthique et Économique/Ethics and Economics*, 4(1): 1–20.

Vizard, P. and Burchardt, T. (2007), "Developing a Capability List: Final Recommendations of the Equalities Review Steering Group on Measurement", Centre for Analysis of Social Exclusion, mimeo.

Volkert, J. and Wüst, K.(2009), "Early Childhood, Agency, and Capability Deprivation: A Quantitative Analysis using German Socio-economic Panel Data". Paper Presented at HDCA Conference, Lima, Peru.

White, S. C. (2002), "Being, Becoming and Relationship: Conceptual Challenges of a Child Rights Approach in Development", *Journal of International Development*, 14(8): 1095–1104.

White, H., Leavy, J. and Masters, A. (2009), "Comparative Perspectives on Child Poverty: A Review of Poverty Measures", Working Paper, No. 1, Young Lives, Oxford.

Young Lives (2006), "An International Study of Childhood Poverty", www.younglives.org.uk

Part II

Understanding Children's Capabilities: Methods and Case Studies

4

From Valuing to Evaluating: Tools and Procedures to Operationalize the Capability Approach

Mario Biggeri and Renato Libanora
University of Florence

As we have seen in Chapter 1, the operationalization of the capability approach (CA) has not been an easy task. While the CA has been used as an alternative programming and evaluative framework for projects carried out by NGOs in developing countries (Alkire, 2002; Ferrero et al., 2006; Frediani, 2007, among others), there is still a relative lack of tools and procedures available (Robeyns, 2006). Indeed, the evaluation and analysis of children's well-being can enrich the informational base for multidimensional social assessments in the space of capabilities. Nevertheless, this requires techniques for identifying, prioritizing, measuring and comparing diverse capability sets in different situations (see also Alkire, 2008).

Before the CA can become operational, an attempt must be made to identify the relevant capabilities that contribute to children's well-being. This topic has been extensively discussed in the first part of this book. In general, the selecting of methods depends on research objectives and operational processes such as the purposes of the analysis, short-term *versus* long-term policies, comparability *versus* local context and project goals and objectives *vis-à-vis* operational and practical constraints. In this chapter we present two integrated procedures that can be implemented by researchers and practitioners to operationalize the CA. The first can be used to start the process of prioritizing different dimensions of well-being in the capability space of a particular group of children. The second procedure is an alternative programming and evaluative tool for development projects.[1]

The tools and procedures proposed in this chapter flow from the assumption that the selection of capabilities should be the outcome of a democratic process rooted in public scrutiny and open debate (Sen, 1999, 2004a, 2004b). Indeed, as Amartya Sen emphasizes, "The problem is not with listing important capabilities, but with insisting on one pre-determined canonical list of capabilities, chosen by theorists without any general social discussion or public reasoning. To have such a fixed list, emanating entirely from pure theory, is to deny the possibility of fruitful public participation on what should be included and why" (Sen, 2005: 158). Thus the participation of the stakeholders is essential to the process and implies the reflection of subjects about their own condition, opportunities and constraints in their cultural, social, economical and political environments. The theoretical and philosophical foundations of the procedures proposed are based on rather innovative concepts within the CA such as "community capabilities" (see also Chapter 11) and the "impartial spectator" re-proposed in Sen's article "What do we want from a theory of justice?" (Sen, 2006: 232–234).

In this chapter we explore how a traditional survey methodology, based on the use of a questionnaire, can become part of a more dynamic and participatory process of self-assessment. In particular, we will illustrate how, through a focalization process stimulated by questions, children can identify dimensions of well-being as well as demonstrate reasoning in public, even at an early age. In other words, as argued in Chapter 2, there are many issues that even very small children are capable of understanding and to which they can contribute by thoughtful opinions (Boyden and Levison, 2000; Lansdown, 2001, 2005; White, 2002; Biggeri and Bonfanti, 2009). Furthermore, "there is a powerful body of evidence showing how prevailing attitudes towards children, based on the view that adults both know best and will act in their best interest, have failed many children. Many of these failures resulted from the refusal to listen to the voices of children themselves" (Lansdown, 2001: 3).[2,3]

Here we focus mostly on methodological aspects, although we also refer to research carried out among street children in Kampala, which is presented in depth in Chapter 5 (see also Biggeri et al., 2006; Biggeri, 2007) in order to illustrate how it can be applied to capability sets. For young children, qualitative participatory methods can be used to gather similar information (see, for instance, Biggeri et al., 2008; Libanora and Biggeri, 2009).

The rest of the chapter is divided into four parts. In the next section the methodological background is outlined, in the following two sections alternative methodologies are presented and in the last section the main conclusions are reported. Appendices summarize the core of the questionnaire (Appendix 4.1) and describe methods to aggregate multidimensional ordinal information (Appendix 4.2).

4.1. Methodologies

Operationalization is defined as the sequence of activities transforming a theoretical framework into standardized procedures applicable in practice, by users and beneficiaries. According to the CA, the focus in project design and social evaluation (including impact assessment) should be on what children are able to do and to be; and on what they value and have reason to value (Sen, 1999). This involves "... removing obstacles in their lives so that they have more freedom to live the kind of life which, *upon reflection*, they find valuable" (Robeyns, 2005: 3, emphasis added). Thus the subjective, cognitive and reflective position of children needs to be understood in view of the actual constraints and opportunities of their domestic, cultural, social, economical and political environments. In the words of Sen, "The CA to a person's advantage is concerned with evaluating it in terms of his or her actual ability to achieve various valuable functionings as a part of living. The corresponding approach to social advantage – for aggregative appraisal as well as for the choice of institutions and policy – takes the set of individual capabilities as constituting an indispensable and central part of the *relevant informational base of such evaluation*" (Sen, 1993: 30, emphasis added).

Along with the theoretical stances of Amartya Sen, throughout the 1980s a renewed emphasis has been placed on the agency of the "beneficiaries" of the interventions carried out by international agencies and non-governmental organizations (NGOs). Since the seminal work of Robert Chambers (1983), the concept and practices of "participation" and "empowerment" have evolved from Rapid Rural Appraisal (RRA), through the Participatory Rapid Appraisal (PRA), to Participatory Learning and Actions (PLA).[4] The common goal of all participatory approaches is to provide real decision power to the poor on development projects. Although several critics have revealed some political and epistemological limits of the participatory methods and practices (Rahnema, 1992; Escobar, 1995; Olivier De Sardan, 1995; Mikkelsen, 2005; Nelson and Wright, 2005), the subjective foundations of "processual knowledge" have been reaffirmed and valorised (Mosse, 1998). Mayoux and Chambers (2005) show that participatory methods can generate accurate quantitative data as well as local priorities and experiences of deprivation. In development terms, this means that the analytical space of projects needs to be scrutinized both for its capacity to provide subjective perceptions on changes and for the constructive role of the beneficiaries in enlarging their capabilities. The two faces of the well-being dimensional changes – one more objectively grounded (e.g. the availability of the school) and the other more subjectively performed (the perception of the enlargement of his/her capability set due to learning processes) – cannot be divorced from the evaluation process (Oakley et al., 1998; Oakley, 2001; Earle, 2004). Another consequence of a participatory approach to social and economic changes is that the development project or process is at least as important as the outcomes (Mosse, 1998). Therefore, the actual impact of any planned action should be measured in terms of how children's agency is enhanced and to what extent they are aware of it.

Thus agency and empowerment are the basis for the capability, participatory and Process Approaches (PA). They introduce new ways to combine quantitative and qualitative data, and subjective and objective perceptions. In their analysis of changes in development planning, Ferrero et al. (2006) also recognize the value of synergy between PLA and PA, the principles and the tools to operationalize the CA in the praxis of development.[5] Therefore, we argue that the adoption of methodological tools based on the principles of these different approaches is a relevant innovation in itself, useful for development scholars, practitioners and stakeholders. The methodology we have developed applies to a definite context of analysis such as development projects and wider programmes aimed at comprehensive human development.[6]

We are well aware that the quality of analytical and process knowledge of the CA, PLA and PA cannot be obtained by a single toolkit when looking at projects for children.[7] Therefore, researchers should always try to include other qualitative subjective data, obtained by collective assessments (role games, photo-mapping, focus groups) as well as quantitative data (household income, access to basic social services including objectively measurable variables).[8]

It has been argued that questionnaires can also be viewed as a "light" participatory tool (Hart, 1992). In light of our research experience we have prioritized the subjective evaluations made by the children we have interviewed, by using a "dynamic" questionnaire in order to cross-validate their evaluations with other relevant information. As a matter of fact, the procedures have been preceded or accompanied by a range of participatory tools (see also Lewis and Lindsay, 2000; Laws and Mann, 2004),[9] intended to allow children to participate and become active actors in the analysis.[10]

The operational procedure is based on four main stages, which constitute the core of the process of thinking, reflecting and participating in order to capture evolving capabilities from a multidimensional perspective. This should support stakeholders in their attempts to identify the most fundamental dimensions of their well-being (Clark, 2005). This process constitutes an instrument of public reasoning and allows for a first ranking of dimensions (prioritization) of well-being. The core of the process is based on a progressive focalization of the child from his/her general opinions on values and well-being, shifting to his/her personal experience (internal focalization) regarding specific domains, capabilities and actual functionings. The child then moves towards a more general understanding of the dimensions of well-being within the community or group of children. This transforms the individual opinions into potential shared ideas. Finally, the child identifies a subset of capabilities considered to be of the highest relevance for children in their community. These reflective procedures proposed are well matched with the procedural criteria of philosophical inquiry (Santi, 2009).[11]

Although a questionnaire is often considered an inadequate tool to register process knowledge and social relations dynamics, the focalization procedure we developed aims to reduce biases introduced by questionnaire-based research. We argue that using a questionnaire for participatory research can be effective. The questionnaire design and answering scheme can lead children through different steps of cognitive, subjective and collective analysis until they establish a synthesis at the last stage. Since the questionnaire is based on qualitative items, a central issue is the use of perception-based statistics as opposed to normatively derived objective measures. Such data raise difficulties to be overcome: for example, the child's choices may not reflect real desires, giving rise to the so-called "deformed desire" problem (Bertrand and Mullainathan, 2001).

This has been referred to as "valuation neglect" by Sen (1992) and "adaptive preference formation" by Elster (1982). These thinkers argue that both human perceptions and desires are influenced by personal, cultural and historical factors as well as by the current environment, personal expectations about the future and attitudes towards interaction in a given dialogical context (i.e. answering a questionnaire in a public space). Adaptation to one's own environment and personal circumstances can limit the capacity to reliably represent one's well-being and capabilities (e.g. Teschl and Comim, 2005).[12] On the other hand, adaptive preferences should not become an obsession since adaptation can have a positive influence on well-being and may generate resilience (Nussbaum, 2000; Clark, forthcoming). Indeed, there are many different types of adaptation and preference formation (Clark, forthcoming, especially Chapter 1), and the available evidence from social psychology and economics suggests that, in many cases, adaptation may not have serious consequences for value formation (Clark, 2009; Clark, forthcoming).

Therefore, the process we used to identify capabilities aims to address adaptation while exploring value judgements (Rawls, 1971).[13] This is achieved if the child manages partially to detach their preferences from his or her life experiences in order to become a "quasi-impartial spectator". It is worth noting that the "community capability set" might be neglected by (a large) part of the considered community (e.g. by children living in specific conditions such as slave children, or those subject to bonded labour in carpet weaving). Therefore, we need to refer to a control group in the analysis as "external impartial spectators" able to identify other – or to validate – potential functionings and opportunities (Sen, 2006, following Adam Smith in *The Theory of Moral Sentiments*, published in 1759). A control group can also help to address the possibility that a particular list may "localise" too much and reflect the muffled and distorted values of children who have adapted to straitened circumstances (Clark, 2009, note 13).[14]

Thus the capability set of the community is composed of individual, collective and social capabilities (Anand, 2007). This means that it is composed of all potentially valued functionings and opportunities that should be open to members of the community living in a given place and that are relevant for policy analysis (see Chapters 2 and 11). This comprehensive "community capability set" could be used as a reference for individuating the areas for practical uses. Nevertheless, we assume that these basic capabilities – and the corresponding human rights as entitlements – should always be included in this community capability set as they represent minimum requirements for well-being (Sen, 1999, 2005).[15]

Before describing the four steps of the first procedure in detail, a methodological issue needs to be raised. This is the need for accurate knowledge of the local context. To obtain this knowledge, one can proceed with a literature review, a collection of good practices, interviews with relevant stakeholders, role games, photo-mapping and visual cards. Games are particularly suitable for children in gathering situated information and to promote free expression and creativity.

4.2. Valuing capabilities and prioritizing dimensions

The following four steps are advocated (see also Biggeri et al., 2006):

(1) Let the children conceptualize the capabilities dimensions without any interference.
(2) Focus on the personal achieved functionings for each dimension of well-being.
(3) Focus on community capabilities to define the relevance of each dimension.
(4) Let the children prioritize the different dimensions chosen.

We generally shaped the process of thinking and reflecting in the form of a "dynamic" questionnaire, following a sort of step-by-step detaching/revealing process. The questionnaire's flexibility lies in the opportunity for the children to choose the relevant dimensions on which the questionnaire is built. The information is then aggregated to reflect the community's or sub-community's concerns (see also Appendix 4.2). As already mentioned, a control group is involved in the analysis as an important instrument for validation (particularly relevant as far as non-positive dimensions could be concerned) and for policy planning. The process is described in Figure 4.1, while the core section of the questionnaire is reported in Appendix 4.1 at the end of the chapter.

I) The first stage is characterized by the following question: "What are the most important opportunities a child[16] should have during his/her life?" The objective of this question is to identify which capabilities are relevant without limiting the possible answers with a predefined questionnaire. If the child mentions a capability that has not been identified earlier by the researcher, their answer is added to the list. If she/he mentions one that already is in the pre-codified list the answer is recorded only.[17] Therefore, the child participates directly in the elaboration of the questionnaire. This phase of the questionnaire allows the conceptualization and identification of the dimensions in the capability space.

II) At the second stage the child is asked about the actual functionings achieved, which involves drawing on personal experience. As shown in Figure 4.1, the child is then asked to evaluate each capability in turn. For example, in the case of health we asked: "Are you now enjoying good health (during your recent life)"? A Likert scale either from 1 (not at all) to 10 (fully) or based on pair items (e.g. 10, force choice method) is used to codify the answers (see Appendix 4.1).

III) At the third stage, the child is asked about the relevance of that specific capability/dimension for children in general (i.e. the broader community). This is because the individual capability set (the personal set of achievable functionings) may be of limited use for a child in need and because it could be influenced by adaptive preferences (see also Bertoli, 2006). Therefore we ask: "In your opinion how important/unimportant is being able to have good health for a child of your age (or your village, neighbourhood, school class)?" The aim of this question is to measure the relevance of each capability dimension for the whole group.

IV) At the last stage, the child is asked about other well-being dimensions she/he wishes to add. In order to obtain a partial ordering, we also ask the child about his/her preferences: "Among the aspects we discussed could you tell me which are the three most important opportunities a child should have during his/her life?" The aim is to identify the most relevant capabilities for the group. At the end of the questionnaire it is thus possible to draw a list of relevant capabilities defined by the children themselves, legitimated by the group (setting specific *a priori* vote rules), pointing out the level of achieved functionings (at both the individual and aggregated level, under some assumptions) and a first prioritization of the dimensions of well-being.[18]

A dimension in the capability space is validated if two conditions were satisfied: (1) at least one child identifies it spontaneously and (2) the majority of the children valued the dimension as either important or very important (specifically if three-quarters (75%) of the whole group identified the dimension as being important; note that simply a majority (>50%) could equally be used). This can be adjusted according to the goals of the research.[19] We report in Table 4.1 the results of all four stages of this procedure carried out during the First Children World Congress on Child Labour and Education, held in Italy by the Global March Against Child Labour (Florence, May 2004).[20]

As shown for stage IV in Table 4.1, the first five dimensions mentioned were "education", "love and care", "life and physical health", "freedom

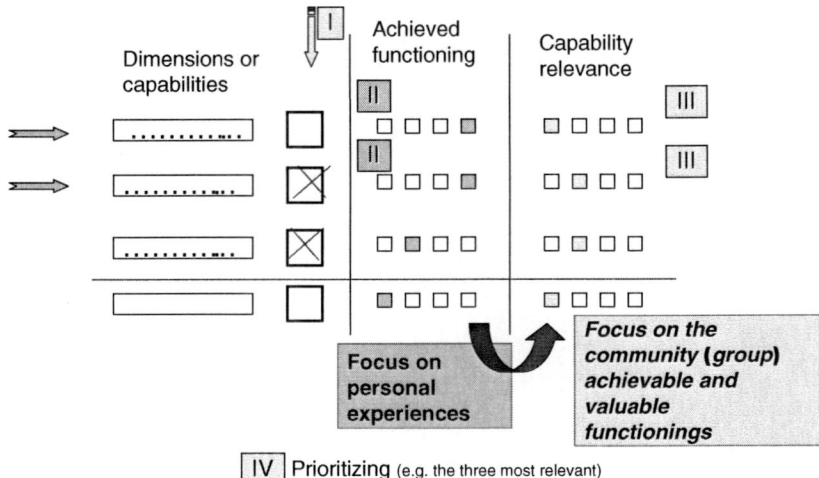

Figure 4.1   The four main passages (core section of the questionnaire)
Note: The children interviewed were not made aware of the "capability" concept, as care was taken to ensure that only general questions were asked during the course of the interview.[21]

from economic and non-economic exploitation" and "leisure activities", while other dimensions such as "mobility", "social relations" and "religion and identity" were almost neglected at the prioritizing phase, although the group considered them very important (see stage III). Through the process of focalization, the sample of children was able to give a clear indication of what they perceived as central capabilities for their development and well-being. For instance, "being loved and cared for" and "being able to play" were two of the most important dimensions for the children in our sample, which could be underestimated by many social scientists and policy makers. Moreover, the "education" and "life and physical health" dimensions that often constitute the focus of many development programmes have also been validated by children. These considerations are important as we can give different weight to different dimensions according to the priority given by the children interviewed.

Rethinking children's development and well-being through the CA opens new perspectives on children's studies. We might have difficulty interpreting some of our results (for instance, the low scoring of "shelter and environment"), but we nonetheless argue that a new debate on child participation concerning well-being and capabilities has been opened. In any case it is important to remember that this is a non-definitive list that needs to be integrated with other data sets comparing "objectively" some of the dimensions explored by the subjective perceptions of the children.[22]

Table 4.1 Results of the First Children World Congress on Child Labour and Education (as percentages)

Dimensions	Stage I	Stage II	Stage III		Stage IV
			Important	Very important	
1) Life and physical health	29.8	n.a.	21.2	76.0	34.6
2) Love and care	48.1	n.a.	13.5	83.7	51.9
3) Mental well-being	5.8	n.a.	14.4	82.7	9.6
4) Bodily integrity and safety	17.3	n.a.	20.2	73.1	5.8
5) Social relations	8.7	n.a.	51.0	41.3	3.8
6) Participation/ information	13.5	n.a.	16.3	81.7	18.3
7) Education	89.4	n.a.	5.8	92.3	73.1
8) Freedom from economic and non-economic exploitation	11.5	n.a.	11.5	87.5	25.0
9) Shelter and environment	13.5	n.a.	26.9	68.3	13.5
10) Leisure activities	34.6	n.a.	26.9	71.2	24.0
11) Respect	12.5	n.a.	15.4	79.8	11.5
12) Religion and identity	3.8	n.a.	49.0	32.7	2.9
13) Time-autonomy and undertake projects	11.5	n.a.	26.9	68.3	9.6
14) Mobility	3.8	n.a.	35.6	52.9	0.0

Note: n.a. not available.
Source: Biaaeri et al. (2006).

4.3. Evaluating a project

According to Sen (1992, 1999), policy and project actions intended to promote well-being should be evaluated in the space of capabilities rather than functionings. In other words, the evaluation should focus more on opportunities and agency than bare achievements. This means that a project is successful if it has expanded the capabilities of the beneficiaries in a holistic manner, beyond those domains targeted by the project. However, it is difficult to measure capability expansion or contraction in a wide informational space, and therefore the second evaluation procedure presented in this chapter assesses the impact of development projects on the capability space as it is perceived by the stakeholders (i.e. children and adolescents). This procedure consists of a sequence of questions articulated in four stages, in which a group of children is asked to evaluate their individual situation and those of the concerned group. The research measures the well-being impact of the development project. The main difference between this process and that described above is that here the evaluation of the project's impact occurs alongside the identification of well-being dimensions. The circularity of the previous analytical model (spontaneous identification, assessment of personal and collective values on the dimensions listed, and validation and prioritization) is now broken by shifting from the reflective experience of the children (as a social group) to a more practical field of activities and operators. In other words, we move from the theoretical value of a set of dimensions to the actual impact of an external intervention on the personal capability set of the children, as the children perceive it themselves.

Thus, the aim of the focalization procedure is not the validation of the initial list of dimensions by their spontaneous identification, or the selection made by the children along the process of responding to the questionnaire. It is rather the assessment of the priorities and modalities of intervention of an organization (for instance, an international agency or a local NGO) and its effective capacity in enlarging or reducing the space of capabilities of the targeted children.[23]

We still assume that the analytical base of the children's judgement is their holistic and subjective experience and reflection, which by all means are influenced by a variety of social, affiliation, affective and institutional contexts (i.e. conversion factors, see Chapter 1). In this case, however, we circumscribe their answers to a specific ground for enjoyment/limitation (functional evaluation) of some capabilities of the concerned children (as project's beneficiaries). Eventually this unfolding method allows us to ask the children to point out the first three dimensions of well-being for which the project should increase its efforts to expand their capabilities. As such, therefore, the procedural pattern is the following:

(1) The children identify the relevant capabilities without interference.
(2) For each dimension of well-being, they identify their actual level of functioning.
(3) They determine the impact of the project's activities on each dimension.
(4) They identify which capabilities the project should prioritize for intervention.

This procedure has some implications for the possibilities of establishing a direct analytical link between the subjective conditions of the subject who is initially judging his/her whole capability set and the impact of the project on his/her specific set of capabilities (as she/he perceives it). Let's clarify this point with an example from a project on health.

Following the identification of the most important dimensions of well-being, in the case of the health domain children were asked (step (2)): "Are you now enjoying good health (during your recent life)"? The answer is meant to identify the level of each child's functioning achievement in the health dimension. In step (3), children were asked to identify the project's impact on the health domain in terms of capability expansion or reduction. However, if the dimension is not clarified, there may be several conceptual difficulties or ambiguities in determining whether the child answering the question is considering:

(1) his/her clinical state of health (i.e. absence of diseases measurable by medical tools) or a balanced physiological development (measurable by scientific standards);
(2) the fact that she/he recently recovered from a serious illness and, although she/he could not be considered to be in "good health" clinically, she/he may feel that his/his health is good or very good in the "here and now"; or
(3) the possibility of having access to good doctors, drugs and hospitals in the event she/he suffers any disease or infirmity in the future.

In many cases a child is likely to combine all three considerations (physical condition, subjective perceptions of actual health and access to health services) when answering questions about his/her health. However, we can not exclude the possibility that some potential biases will interfere with reported health in the here and now.

Although the question is formulated and meant for the self-valuation of achieved functionings in the health domain, there will always be a degree of indeterminacy in assessing whether the respondent is consciously or unconsciously taking into account all three considerations that constitute the cognitive and experiential concept of "enjoying good health". We can refine the questions by asking for details on which basis the respondent is valuing his/her health (see below) or we can refer to some objective indicators of the subject's clinical history, although the latter will bring us away from the scope of our subject-focused methodological approach. Thus, the questionnaire yields the possibility of a holistic assessment in the capability space, but also focuses on specific dimensions. Indeed, each of the main dimensions should be further specified in two or more sub-dimensions. Therefore, if the researchers or stakeholders are interested in a specific dimension such as "love and care", it is possible to explore sub-dimensions by expanding the analysis using as many of those as needed: "love and care" by parents, siblings or other relatives, or by tutors, teachers, friends and so on (see, for instance, the questionnaire reported in Appendix 4.1 or Chapter 5, Table 5.2 for an example).[24]

Indeed, in step (3) we do not ask whether the project is performing well in a specific dimension, which is the traditional approach for evaluating development initiatives, but instead we ask them to evaluate the performance starting from a very *personal* point of view that has been elaborated above (step (2)): "Is the project affecting *your* possibility of enjoying good health? If yes, in which measure?" Thus the respondent will actually evaluate the relative performance of the project taking into account his/her personal achieved functioning in that dimension which, it should be recalled, represents the synthetic value of different ways to reflect upon it and the outcome of the interaction among personal attitudes, beliefs, family, local institutions and many other social actors such as teachers, friends, policemen, doctors, etc. Therefore, from the answers provided it is possible to evaluate the impact of the project in terms of expansion or contraction of his/her individual set of capabilities as she/he perceives it, rather than variation in the achieved functionings. A child who perceives a high degree of enjoyment of good health (8 on the numeric scale of achieved functionings) may negatively evaluate at the same time the impact of the project, i.e. in terms of capabilities reduction (say, 4 on the numeric scale). Alternatively the child may record a relatively high level of actual functioning and indicate that this is mainly due to the impact of the project, in which case the project will score highly too. The impact of the project is evaluated in terms of the expansion or contraction of capabilities in each dimension and in the whole set of capabilities listed in the questionnaire. We could also weight the dimensions according to their relevance, as identified by the children themselves in stage I. The aggregate results using a head count method can be, thus, represented as the share of children who attribute, for instance, a positive or very positive impact to the project in terms of capabilities expansion for each dimension identified in stage I (e.g. 70% of children perceived a positive or very positive expansion of capabilities) and for all the dimensions together. This helps us to capture more adequately the concept of evolving capabilities (see also Chapter 2).

Figure 4.2 shows the proportion of respondents who consider the impact of the project positive or very positive in terms of expansion of capabilities, which can be analysed for each dimension. For instance, the "side effect" of the educational activities of the project (which expanded for 80% of children) could be the reduction of mobility (almost 75% reported a reduction), while another indirect outcome is the enlargement of bodily integrity and safety.

In Appendix 4.2 we present possible methods for the aggregation of ordinal variables that are at the same time decomposable. Another possibility is to aggregate the results using an average. This is a controversial issue since the data are ordinal, although it is a commonly used method. For instance

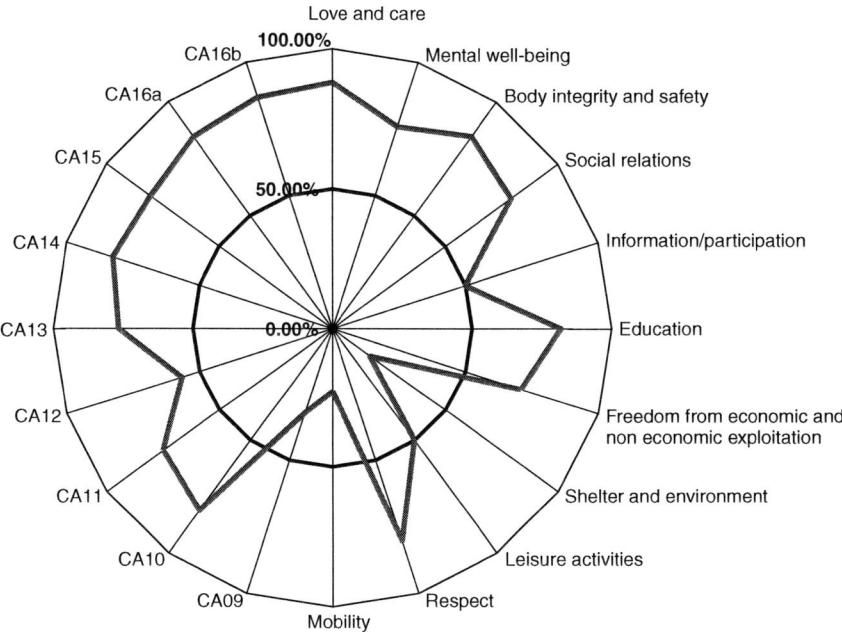

Figure 4.2 Proportion of children who consider the project results positive or very positive in terms of capability expansion (%)

in our example, according to the mean value the project has a positive impact. The overall impact can be calculated for subgroups, such as relatively deprived children (with lower achieved functionings) or by gender, to understand whether the project has been perceived by these specific subgroups as expanding their capabilities.

Figure 4.3 allows us to explore the results further. It shows the impact of a hypothetical project on two dimensions of well-being – education and respect. The vertical axis represents the expansion or contraction of capabilities, while the horizontal axis represents the children's achieved functionings. The two different intensities of grey of the bubbles represent the different dimensions (light for education and dark for respect). The bubbles are positioned on the base of a mean group score and the number/size of the group is given by the size of the group. Therefore, this figure shows that the project has a positive impact on children, considering that the larger bubbles are positioned in the expansion of capabilities quadrants. However, the largest bubbles are in the upper right quadrant, showing that the impact is more positive for less deprived children. In other words, the majority of those who were among the less deprived judged the impact of the project in a very positive manner for respect, while a minority felt a high negative

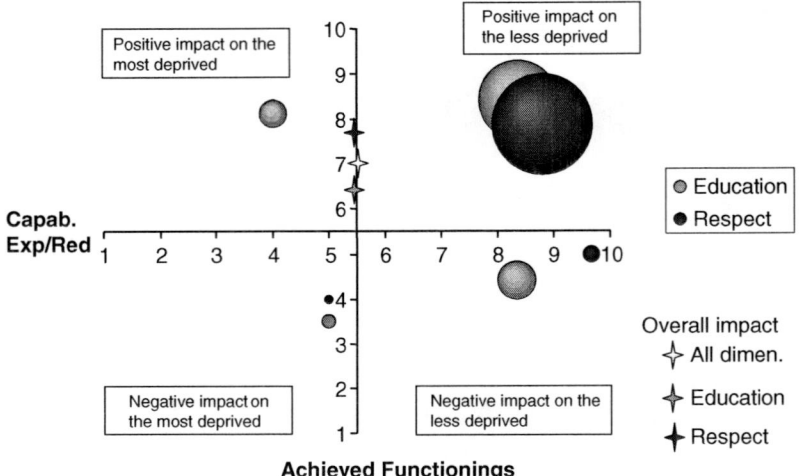

Figure 4.3   Project impact in terms of capabilities expansion/reduction according to the achieved functionings in two dimensions: education and respect (averages)

impact. There is also a very small percentage of respondents who perceived themselves as most deprived in the respect domains (dark grey bubbles), which has been affected negatively by the project (although in a moderate way). A similar story can be told for the education dimension (light grey bubbles), which also had a largely positive impact according to respondents (in particular the least deprived).

These results also imply that the project had a negative impact on the capabilities of a small minority of less deprived children. Although the distribution of the preferences according to the position of the children on the axis of the achieved functioning does not radically change the overall evaluation of the project, it introduces elements that contribute to a deeper understanding of the impact of such activities on individuals and small groups of targeted children.

Furthermore, the same figure represents the overall evaluation of the project in terms of capability expansion, as overall average values on the *y*-axis (white star, 7.1) and as average values for respect (dark grey star, 7.6) and education dimensions (light grey star, 6.4). In this respect, the project once again showed a positive impact in terms of capabilities expansion, especially for respect.

If we conceive the impact of the project in a holistic manner (as it should be using the CA), we may realize that the beneficiaries perceive the positive or negative (or neutral) impact of the project in various dimensions of life in which the project does not directly intervene.

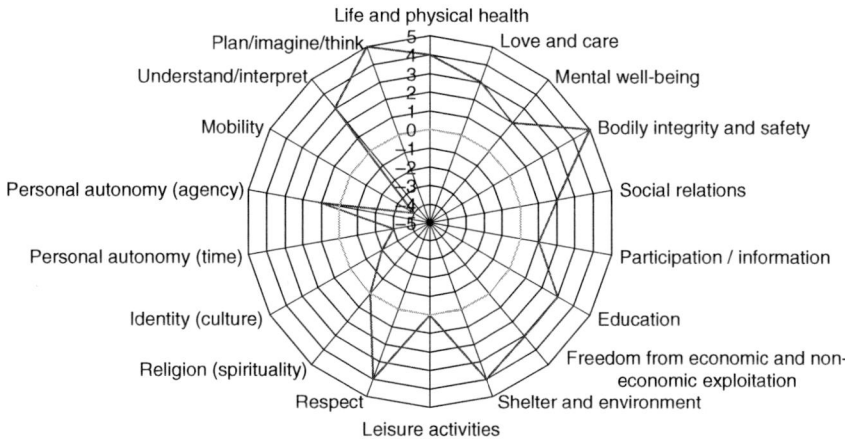

Figure 4.4   The project's impact on beneficiaries' capabilities (mean)

Figure 4.4 presents the data aggregated as a simple mean for each dimension using a transformed scale (spanning very positive (5) to positive impact (1), neutral (0), to negative (–1) and very negative impact (–5)).

4.4. Conclusions

The procedure presented in this chapter is a step forward in the enhancement of participatory methodologies in monitoring and evaluation exercises using the CA. However, there is always a certain degree of ambiguity in the answers provided by children (as with any other class of respondents), and thus a degree of caution in using the data and interpreting the diagrams presented above should be employed. We have repeatedly pointed out the need for control groups and for different participatory exercises and games in order to validate any data obtained with a questionnaire. The trade-off between detailed information and a holistic evaluation of the project should always look at the quality of information that the exercise is providing for the participants. This is a guiding principle of participatory exercises.

Children's legitimacy and ability in identifying their values or evaluating the impacts of the intervention (see also Van den Berge, 2006) constitutes a theoretical shift from the utilitarian framework and should lead to different subject-based welfare policies at the macro, meso and micro levels. As we noted, "choice, agency and empowerment", which often turn up as "buzzwords" of the aid industry, are concepts that scholars and professionals can still use if they are accurately scrutinized by the people (including children) affected by the planned interventions. Our methodological proposal goes in the direction of disclosing their meaning to the child beneficiaries of the initiatives, who are otherwise assumed to be lacking proper understanding of their conditions, opportunities, aspirations and means to realize them. Participatory processes and the CA can push forward the boundaries of social sciences and development organizations, showing the advantages of an involvement of economical and social actors, including those actors who are assumed to have fewer entitlements (Nussbaum, 2003) such as children, women, persons with disabilities, migrants, refugees and ethnic minorities.

In this regard simple graphics and accessible tables, like those shown above, are supportive devices for communicating the results to children. An additional effort should probably be made in this direction, exploring how questionnaire-based research should be effectively tuned to fully communicate the potentialities of this analytical tool; in this respect, the cognitive and cultural sensitivities of children of various ages who are living in different social and economical contexts and are experiencing adverse living conditions are key factors of analysis. According to our interpretation of the reflexive process enhanced by the dynamic questionnaire, the responding (while self-reflecting) child becomes aware of the many dimensions of evolving capabilities in which his/her life could be affected by the intervention. Evaluating each of them against his/her personal conditions and perceptions, the child gains the idea that the informational space of capabilities needs his/her active contribution. We have assumed that this active participation should be publicly and politically recognized as a relevant factor either in identifying the core capabilities that a determined group of children have reason to value, or in indicating the failure or the success of any intervention addressing their well-being.

Appendix 4.1. The questionnaire, core section on capabilities

CAPABILITIES SECTION

Q26 What are the most important opportunities a child should have during his/her life?

Note for the interviewer (Q26): do not read out; multiple answers; add capabilities not present in the list at the end

Note for the interviewer (Q27 and Q28): read out all the items one by one from the table below and for each of them ask the two questions Q27 and Q28

	Q26	Q27 Are you now … (during your recent life) The meaning is: how much have you been able to realize/achieve this functioning in your life, from 1 to 10? (where 1 = not at all and 10 = fully) (achievements) Fully not at all										Do not know	No answer	Q28 Is Project X affecting your possibility to (…)? Q29 if yes, in what measure? (where 1 = very negatively and 10 = very positively) (expansion or reduction of capabilities) Q28 Yes=1 No=0	Very Very Positively Negatively										Do not know	No answer	Q 30 In your opinion how important/unimportant is being able to (…) for a child of your age? (where 1 = unimportant and 10 = very important) (community capabilities) Very No or little important importance										Do not know	No answer
		10	9	8	7	6	5	4	3	2	1	88	99		10	9	8	7	6	5	4	3	2	1	88	99	10	9	8	7	6	5	4	3	2	1	88	99
1) Life and physical health Q26: mark if indicated Q27: enjoying good health [Q28 and Q30 enjoy good health …]	☐																																					
2a) Love and care loved and cared by your parents [be loved and cared …]	☐																																					
2b) Love and care loved and cared by your brothers																																						
2c) Love and care loved and cared by your tutors	☐																																					

	Q27 **Are you now…. (during your recent life)** The meaning is: how much have you been able to realize/achieve this functioning in your life, from 1 to 10? (where 1 = not at all and 10 = fully) **(achievements)**			Q28 **Is Project X affecting your possibility to (…)?** Q29 **If yes, in what measure?** (where 1 = very negatively and 10 = very positively) **(expansion or reduction of capabilities)**				Q 30 **In your opinion how important/unimportant is being able to (…)** for a child of your age? (where 1 = unimportant and 10 = very important) **(community capabilities)**		
	Q26 Fully not at all	Do not know	No answer	**Q28** Yes=1 No=0	Very Very Positively Negatively	Do not know	No answer	Very No or little important importance	Do not know	No answer
2d) Love and care **loved and cared by your friends**	☐									
3) Mental well-being **feeling happy**	☐									
4) Bodily integrity and safety **enjoying body integrity**	☐									
5) Social relations **participating in the activities of your family or neighbourhood**	☐									
6) Participation/ information **expressing your personal opinions and ideas and be listened to**	☐									
7) Education **attending school and non-formal courses**	☐									
8) Freedom from economic and non-economic exploitation **free from any form of exploitation**	☐									

9) Shelter and environment **living in a comfortable/safe home and clean environment**	□							
10) Leisure activities **having enough time to play**	□							
11) Respect **receiving respect and consideration from everybody**	□							
12) Religion (spirituality) **enjoining inner peace and spirituality**	□							
13) Religion and identity (tradition, culture) **attending religious celebrations and cultural festivals**	□							
14) Personal autonomy (time) **having enough time to do what you really like**	□							
15) Personal autonomy (agency) **having enough autonomy in decisions regarding you**	□							
16) Mobility **moving freely and visiting relatives or friends**	□							

	Q27 Are you now…. (during your recent life) The meaning is: how much have you been able to realize/achieve this functioning in your life, from 1 to 10? (where 1 = not at all and 10 = fully) (achievements)				Q28 Is Project X affecting your possibility to (…)? Q29 If yes, in what measure? (where 1 = very negatively and 10 = very positively) (expansion or reduction of capabilities)					Q 30 In your opinion how important/unimportant is being able to (…) for a child of your age? (where 1 = unimportant and 10 = very important) (community capabilities)		
Q26	Fully not at all		Do not know	No answer	Q28 Yes=1 No=0	Very Positively	Very Negatively	Do not know	No answer	Very No or little important importance	Do not know	No answer
17) understand/ interpret able to interpret (give meaning) the most important things that are happening to you and your life	☐											
18) Plan/imagine/think able to plan/imagine your life in the future	☐											
	☐											

Q31 Do you think we have forgotten any other important opportunity for a child?

Note for the interviewer: write down the new aspect; if it is not on the list or not mentioned in Q26 ask the questions Q27, Q 28, Q29 and Q30 again

Q32 Among the aspects we discussed, could you tell me which are the three most important opportunities a child should have during his/her life? *Note for the interviewer: record the capability or its number*	Q33 What is the most important thing the project could do to make life better for children in this area?
(a)	(a)
(b)	(b)
(c)	(c)

Appendix 4.2. Multidimensional impact measurement and analysis: aggregation methods[25]

In this appendix we present two aggregation methods considered in this chapter in greater detail. The methodologies were developed by Alkire and Foster (2008) and Mauro and Biggeri (2011, forthcoming), respectively.[26]

The Alkire and Foster method is also known as the "dual cut-off", where the term "dual" refers to the fact that it involves two different forms of cut-off, one pertaining to single dimensions (so that many cut-offs must be selected) and the other relating to cross-cutting dimensions (where just one cut-off is required; see Appendix 3.1 in Chapter 3).

The most important aspect of these methodologies is that they can be used with both cardinal and ordinal data.[27] Note that this is also the case for the procedures developed in this chapter. Indeed, in this procedure, the cut-offs for each dimension are given directly by the respondents. This reduces problems relating to the arbitrary determination of a single cut-off, but introduces potential bias by relying on subjective answers.

Hereafter, we report the values for the adjusted head count ratio (M_0) based on Alkire and Foster (2008). For comparing the analysis of capability expansion/reduction (M_v) see Mauro and Biggeri (2011, forthcoming).

Identification

Let Y be the $n \times k$ matrix containing the data (size of population n for k different variables), with generic entry y_{ij} representing the value of variable j observed for individual i. Let C be the $(k + 1)$ dimensional cut-off vector, where the first k elements correspond to the poverty thresholds that must be specified in order to identify a deprived individual with respect to the columns of matrix Y, and the last element of C, c_{k+1}, is an integer positive number representing the minimum number of dimensions on which a person must be deprived to be considered poor. A new matrix (G^0) is then defined as follows:

$$g_{ij}^0 = 1 \quad \text{if } y_{ij} < c_j$$

$$g_{ij}^0 = 0 \quad \text{otherwise}$$

The generic element (g_{ij}^0) represents an indicator for the deprivation status of individual i on dimension j.

Given the matrix G^0, it then becomes straightforward to identify a poor individual using the second form of cut-off across dimensions. Let

$$d_i = \sum_{j=1}^{k} g_{ij}^0$$

be the generic entry of vector D representing the number of dimension on which individual i is deprived. An individual is then identified as "poor" in achieved functionings if she/he is deprived in more than a certain number of dimensions.

Aggregation

Aggregation is an important issue in multidimensional analysis. A first, intuitive, measure can easily be derived from the number of poor people recognized in the dataset. Let Q be a n-dimensional vector with generic entry:

$$q_i = 1 \quad \text{if } d_i \geq c_{k+1}$$

$$q_i = 0 \quad \text{otherwise}$$

then, the quantity

$$H = \sum_{i=1}^{n} q_i / n$$

represents the proportion of poor people identified in the data. Although an easily understandable indicator, H does not satisfy an essential property, dimensional monotonicity: for a poor person i, H remains unchanged as d_i increases. To reflect this concern, a matrix G^{0*} is defined with generic entry

$$g_{ij}^{0*} = g_{ij}^{0} \quad \text{if } q_i = 1$$

$$g_{ij}^{0*} = 0 \quad \text{otherwise}$$

a new indicator, the (dimension) adjusted headcount ratio

$$M_0 = \sum_{i=1}^{n} \sum_{j=1}^{k} g_{ij}^{0*} / nk$$

is introduced. Note that $M_0 \in [0, 1]$ can be seen as the number of all the dimensions on which poor people are deprived, divided by its maximum possible value. This adjusted ratio satisfies the property of dimensional monotonicity mentioned above, as it increases according to any increase in the number of deprived dimension of a poor person. It is also poverty focused as it is invariant to changes in the value of d_i for a non-poor person (who remains non-poor). In other words, if a non-poor individual becomes more (or less) deprived on some dimension, but still remains identified as a non-poor, then the M_0 index does not change.

These methodologies allow us to preserve information at a single dimension level. From the perspective of the CA, a drawback of viewing multidimensional poverty through a unidimensional lens is the loss of information on dimension-specific deficits. Using an intermediate cut-off level for the number of deprivations that can assume values between the two extremes 1 and k is the natural generalization of the common identification methods as the union and the intersection approach, which can be seen as special cases where $C_{k+1} = 1$ and $C_{k+1} = k$.

Acknowledgements

The development of this procedure required a multidisciplinary team of experts. We would like to thank researchers at the University of Florence, including Nicolò Bellanca, Giovanni Canitano, Stefano Mariani, Leonardo Menchini, Simone Bertoli, Rudolf Anich, Sara Bonfanti, Enrico Testi and Stefan Zublasing, and the many students who participated in various sessions in Italy and elsewhere. We acknowledge the contribution of the HDCA thematic group on Children's capabilities. We also owe a debt of gratitude to Sabina Alkire, Jérôme Ballet, Parul Bakhshi, Enrica Chiappero Martinetti, Flavio Comim, David A. Clark, Washtina M. Haider, Santosh Mehrotra, Mozaffar Qizilbash, Ingrid Robeyns, Fabio Sani, Marina Santi, Diego Di Masi, Jean-Francois Trani, Alex Frediani, Franco Volpi and Melanie Walker for useful comments and suggestions. We are also grateful for the support of the Fondazione Culturale Responsabilità Etica of the Banca Popolare Etica (Italy). The usual disclaimers apply.

Notes

1. These tools have been applied in different contexts and with a different ranges of stakeholders.
2. Self-determination theory concerns the analysis of basic psychological needs for applying autonomy, competence and relatedness, and their relations with healthy development, motivation and health (Ryan and Deci, 2000). See also Chapter 2 in this book.
3. Agency is a primary phenomenon (Rogoff, 1990). It's owned by children since their birth, when they show it through their smiles, gurgling, movements and looks, which express their expectations towards their interactions with adults (Baraldi, 2008).
4. The core issue of the different approaches and toolsets, however, relies on the legitimacy and capacity of the (allegedly) poor and deprived villagers and squatters to overcome the iron bars of their cognitive, cultural, social and economical cages, and to provide new insights and awareness on their own constraints, opportunities and sustainable life's projects. The list of texts referring to participatory methods and analysis is impressive; however, for synthetic but comprehensive publications, see Chambers (1997), Kumar (2002), Mayoux and Chambers (2005) and Mikkelsen (2005).
5. Other researchers found that the use of participatory approaches increase the capabilities of the communities (Duraiappah et al., 2005).
6. Considering that children have less power than adults, maintaining a code of ethics during the research process is essential. The researcher is responsible for making sure that the research will not be harmful to the children and that participation in research is voluntary (ILO-UNICEF, 2000; Lewis and Lindsay, 2000; Lansdown, 2001; RWG-CL, 2003; Laws and Mann, 2004). The questionnaires, as well as the validity of a briefing manual, were tested in each survey. We then prepared a workshop of one or two days for training interviewers. The interviews were conducted directly with the children by interviewers; in most cases the help of interpreters was not needed.
7. See Bakhshi et al. (2006) for a comprehensive toolkit inspired by the CA for persons with disability.
8. Two other theoretical and practical steps required for applying the CA are the "aggregation" of data, (which can be interpersonal and/or intrapersonal), and the "formation of consensus" (Robeyns, 2006: 356–357). However the aggregation

problem has not yet been adequately addressed (Anand, 2007). On this see Appendix 4.2.

9. The first procedure has been systematically applied since 2004 by our research group at Florence University and a related HDCA thematic group on Children's Capabilities, while the second procedure has been tested from 2006 onwards. We applied this procedure in five research contexts: (1) in Italy – the first Children's World Congress on Child Labour (CWCCL) (Florence, May 2004); (2) in India – the Second CWCCL and Education (Delhi, September 2005), both organized by the Global March Against Child Labour (GMACL) and other grassroots associations (see Biggeri et al., 2006; Biggeri, 2007); (3) in Uganda, in research on Street Children (Kampala, March–April 2005, see also next chapter); (4) in India (Delhi, May–September 2008), evaluating the impact of Project Why on children with disabilities; and (5) in Nepal, evaluating the impact of Women Foundation on children and female victims of home violence (Kathmandu, September 2008).

10. See Hood (2005) and Fattore et al. (2007).

11. According to Marina Santi (2010), the procedural criteria of philosophical inquiry within the "Philosophy for Children" are the following: dialectical, dialogical, metacognitive, contextual, self-corrective, values oriented, judgement oriented, euristical, epistemical and generative/transformative (Santi, 2009). Some of these criteria can be found later in our procedure.

12. In order to overcome, or at least to reduce, the adaptive preference problem some theoretical and practical precautions can be taken, such as the establishment of a control group (i.e. children in the same geographical area but not involved in the project), external checklists and appropriate training of facilitators. In an explorative empirical investigation, we found that adaptation is reduced with the procedure developed by the group and that the level of adaptation varies among different dimensions. Clark (2002, 2003) also develops a questionnaire and survey methodology designed to address the adaptation problem while eliciting information about value judgements and identifying dimensions of poverty and well-being.

13. In other words it aims to drive the individual to the Freirian conscientization or "critical consciousness". People need to have access to knowledge to develop critical consciousness.

14. It is important to recognize that theoretical assumptions, as well, may not be accurate and even detrimental. As Sen writes, "a misconceived theory can kill" (1999: 209). Indeed, these may perpetuate inaccurate assumptions and inaccurate academic conventions or may be asserted ideologically rather than subjected to scrutiny and reasoned debate (Alkire, 2007).

15. Therefore, if pure theory cannot "freeze" a list of capabilities for all societies and for all time, irrespective of what the citizens (including children) come to understand and value (Alkire, 2008), this procedure would reduce the possible negative aspects of "making lists for every occasion".

16. Intended as a child in general, as part of a social group.

17. There is an initial open-ended list reflecting the research objectives, which should reveal fundamental dimensions in the capability space and may be used for codification at a later stage of the research. The process can be carried out through Robeyns' procedural criteria (2003a, 2003b), as mentioned in the previous chapter, or through focus group discussions with stakeholders, which are particularly effective for development projects. These further options whenever possible reinforce and consolidate the results of codification, increasing the capacity to clarify the contents of the different dimensions and pointing

out relevant sub-dimensions. In the case of difficulties in interpretation, the interviewer writes down the dimension at the end of the codified list.

18. Another way (very time consuming) could be to formulate a complete ordering.

19. We believe that our procedure goes further than that suggested by Sen (2005) for an open and public validation, as a necessary condition to confer legitimacy for the selection.

20. This research is based on interviews with 104 child delegates (see Biggeri et al., 2006).

21. The whole set of information collected in the survey is strictly confidential and is used for statistical purposes only. A brief manual covering the purpose of the research, ethical rules and how to conduct interviews and train interviewers was also prepared.

22. In this way some achieved functionings can be valued (measured, validated) against some specific proxies that translate them into "objective" numbers. Some well-being dimensions, usually the immaterial ones, are more difficult to measure objectively, and the proxies used in standard quantitative analysis can be misleading.

23. It could also be possible to formulate a questionnaire with two or more different situations to be assessed belonging, for example, to different cultural, social and political institutions. However we fear that the exercise of comparing different situations could divert the attention of children from their subjective conditions (in a holistic perspective) towards the interplay of two or more organizations.

24. Another example relating to child education is reported in the first column of Table 11.1 (Chapter 11). See also Young (2009: 290–295) on functional learning.

25. This appendix has been written by Mario Biggeri and Vincenzo Mauro (for further details, see Mauro and Biggeri (2011, forthcoming)).

26. For another interesting paper, see Chakravarty and D'Ambrosio (2006).

27. It is relevant to note that there are several problems related to data collection. The fundamental assumption is that every person interviewed interprets the question in the same way. For instance, the same question, if wrongly prepared, can be interpreted differently by different people. Furthermore, with subjective answers the ordinal scale can be misleading since one person/children may be very pessimistic and another very optimistic, i.e. the individuals adopt different scales. Questionnaire design can therefore be very relevant. For instance, in a current research in India we are using a common scale in order to have the same reference scale in a certain sense "anchoring" the ordinal scale. Furthermore we are using the vignette method to take into account to correct for individual-specific scale biases (Biggeri et al., 2010).

References

Alkire, S. (2002), *Valuing Freedoms. Sen's Capability Approach and Poverty Reduction*, OUP, Oxford.

Alkire, S. (2007), "Development: 'A Misconceived Theory Can Kill'", Oxford Poverty and Human Development Initiative, OPHI, Working Paper no. 11.

Alkire, S. (2008), "Choosing Dimensions: The Capability Approach and Multidimensional Poverty", in N. Kakwani and J. Silber (eds), *The Many Dimensions of Poverty*, Palgrave Macmillan, New York. MPRA Paper No. 8862, posted 26 May 2008 http://mpra.ub.uni-muenchen.de/8862/

Alkire, S. and Foster, J. E. (2008), "Counting and Multidimensional Poverty Measurement", Oxford Poverty and Human Development Initiative, OPHI, Working Paper No. 7.

Anand, P. B. (2007), "Capability, Sustainability, and Collective Action: An Examination of a River Water Dispute", *Journal of Human Development*, 8(1): 109–132.

Bakhshi, P., Trani, J.-F. and Rolland, C. (2006), *Conducting Surveys on Disability. A Comprehensive Toolkit*. Handicap-International, Lyon.

Baraldi, C. (2008), *Bambini e Società*, Carocci, Rome.

Bertoli, S. (2006), "The Circumstantial Contingency of Desires and Participatory Definitions of Well-being in the Capability Space", Working Paper 3/3, Dottorato in politica ed economia dei paesi in via di sviluppo, Università di Firenze, mimeo.

Bertrand, M. and Mullainathan, S. (2001), "Do People Mean What They Say? Implications for Subjective Survey Data National Bureau of Economic Research", Papers and Proceedings of the Hundred Thirteenth Annual Meeting of the American Economic Association, *The American Economic Review*, 91(2): 67–72.

Biggeri, M. (2007), "Children's Valued Capabilities", in Walker Melanie and Unterhalter Elaine (eds), *Amartya Sen's Capability Approach and Social Justice in Education*, Palgrave New York, Oxon, Chapter 10, pp. 197–214.

Biggeri, M. and Bonfanti, S. (2009), "The Capabilities Approach in Early Childhood: How Young Children Value Their Social Capabilities and Agency". Study paper for Bernard van Leer Foundation, The Hague, The Netherlands.

Biggeri, M., Bonfanti, S. and Conradie, I. (eds) (2008), "Children's Capabilities and Project Why, Reports on the results of the International Workshop on Children Capabilities and Participatory Methods, Human Development and Capability Association (HDCA)", September 4–9, New Delhi: 1–40.

Biggeri, M., Libanora, R., Mariani, S. and Menchini, L. (2006), "Children Conceptualizing Their Capabilities: Results of the Survey During the First Children's World Congress on Child Labour", *Journal of Human Development*, 7(1), March, 7(1): 59–83.

Boyden, J. and Levison, D. (2000), "Children as Economic and Social Actors in the Development Process", *Expert Group on Development Issues, Ministry for Foreign Affairs*, Working Paper No. 1, Stockholm.

Chakravarty, S. R. and D'Ambrosio, C. (2006), "The Measurement of Social Exclusion", *Review of Income and Wealth*, 52(3): 377–398.

Chambers, R. (1983), *Rural Development. Putting the Last First*, Longman, London.

Chambers, R. (1997), *Ideas for Development*, Earthscan, London.

Clark, D. A. (2005), "Sen's Capability Approach and the Many Spaces of Human Well-Being", *Journal of Development Studies*, 41(8): 1339–1368.

Clark, D. A. (2009), "Adaptation, Poverty and Well-Being: Some Issues and Observations with Special Reference to the Capability Approach and Development Studies", *Journal of Human Development and Capabilities*, 10(1): 21–42.

Clark, D. A. (2010), *Adaptation, Poverty and Development*, forthcoming book, typescript.

Duraiappah, A. K., Pumulo, R. and Parry, E-J. (2005), "Have Participatory Approaches Increased Capabilities?", International Institute for Sustainable Development (IISD).

Earle, L. (ed.) (2004), *Creativity and Constraints. Grassroots Monitoring and Evaluation and the International Aid Arena*, INTRAC Publications, Oxford.

Elster, J. (1982), "Sour Grapes: Utilitarianism and the Genesis of Wants", in A. Sen and B. Williams (eds), *Utilitarianism and Beyond*, Cambridge University Press, New York, pp. 219–238.

Escobar, A. (1995), *Encountering Development: The Making and Unmaking of the Third World*, Princeton University Press, New York.

Fattore, T., Mason, J. and Watson, E. (2007), "Children's Conceptualisation(s) of Their Well-being", *Social Indicators Research*, 80(1): 5–29.

Ferrero y de Loma-Osorio, G. and Zepeda, C. (2006), "Changing Approaches and Methods in Development Planning: Operationalizing the Capability Approach with Participatory and Learning Process Approaches". Paper presented at the Annual conference of the HDCA, Groningen.

Frediani, A. (2007), "Amartya Sen, the World Bank, and the Redress of Urban Poverty: A Brazilian Case Study", *Journal of Human Development*, 8(1): 133–152.

GMACL (2004), *Children's World Congress on Child Labour: Narrative Report*, Global March Against Child Labour, International Secretariat, Delhi, India.

Hood, S. (2005), "Reporting on Children's Well-being: The State of London's Children's Reports". Paper to Childhoods 2005 Conference, Oslo.

Hart, A. R. (1992), *Children's Participation: From Tokenism to Citizenship*, UNICEF, International Child Development Center, Florence.

ILO-UNICEF (2000), *Investigating Child Labour, Guidelines for Rapid Assessment*, A Field Manual, Simpoc, Geneva, mimeo.

Kumar, S. (2002), *Methods for Community Participation, A Complete Guide for Practitioners*, Vistaar Publications, New Delhi.

Lansdown, G. (2001), *Promoting Children's Participation in Democratic Decision-Making*, Innocenti Insight, UNICEF Innocenti Research Centre, Florence.

Lansdown, G. (2005), *The Evolving Capacities of the Child*, Innocenti Insight, UNICEF Innocenti Research Centre, Florence.

Laws, S. and Mann, G. (2004), *So You Want to Involve Children in Research?* Save the Children, London.

Lewis, A. and Lindsay, G. (eds) (2000), *Researching Children's Perspectives*, Open University Press, Buckingham.

Libanora, R. and Biggeri, M. (2009), "Report: Women's and Children's Capabilities at WF Nepal", Katmandu, Nepal, 12–20 September 2008, May, mimeo, unpublished.

Mayoux, L. and Chambers, R. (2005), "Reversing the Paradigm: Quantification, Participatory Methods and Pro-Poor Impact Assessment", *Journal of International Development*, II(17), March–April: 271–298.

Mauro, V. and Biggeri, M. (2011, forthcoming), Capabilities Expansion or Reduction? A Multidimensional Impact Measurement and analysis, mimeo.

Mikkelsen, B. (2005), *Methods for Development Work and Research. A New Guide for Practitioners*, Second Edition, Sage Publications, London.

Mosse, D. (1998), "Process-Oriented Approaches to Development Practice and Social Research", in D. Mosse, J. Farrington, and A. Rew (eds), *Development as Process. Concepts and Method for Working with Complexity*, ODI, Routledge, London.

Nelson, N. and Wright, S. (eds) (2005), *Power and Participatory Development: Theory and Practice*, ITG, London.

Nussbaum, M. (2000), *Women and Human Development: The Capabilities Approach*, Cambridge University Press, Cambridge.

Nussbaum, M. (2003), "Capabilities as Fundamental Entitlements: Sen and Social Justice", *Feminist Economics*, 9(2–3): 33–59.

Oakley, P. (2001) (ed.), *Evaluating Empowerment: Reviewing the Concept and Practice*, INTRAC Publications, Oxford.

Oakley, P., Pratt, B. and Clayton, A. (1998), *Outcomes and Impact: Evaluating Change in Social Development*, INTRAC Publications, Oxford.

Olivier de Sardan, J. P. (1995), *Anthropologie et Development. Essai en Socio-anthropologie de Changement Social*, Editions Khartala, Paris.

Rahnema, M. (1992), "Participation", in Sachs W. (ed.), *The Development Dictionary: A Guide to Knowledge as Power*, Zed Books, London.

Rawls, J. (1971), *A Theory of Justice*, Harvard University Press, Cambridge, MA.

Robeyns, I. (2003a), "Sen's Capability Approach and Gender Inequality: Selecting Relevant Capabilities", *Feminist Economics*, 9(2–3): 61–92.

Robeyns, I. (2003b), *The Capability Approach: An Interdisciplinary Introduction*, University of Amsterdam, Amsterdam.

Robeyns, I. (2005), "The Capability Approach: A Theoretical Survey", *Journal of Human Development*, 6(1): 93–114.

Robeyns, I. (2006), "The Capability Approach in Practice", *The Journal of Political Philosophy*, 14(3): 351–376.

Rogoff, B. (1990), *Apprenticeship in Thinking: Cognitive Development in Social Context*, OUP, Oxford.

RWG-CL (2003), *Handbook for Action-Oriented Research on the Worst Forms of Child Labour Including Trafficking in Children*, Regional Working Group on Child Labour, Bangkok.

Ryan, R. M. and Deci, E. L. (2000), "Self-determination Theory and the Facilitation of Intrinsic Motivation, Social Development, and Well-being", *American Psychologist*, 55(1): 68–78.

Santi, M. (2009), "Philosophers Goes to School. Some Constraints and Shared Eemarks", in E. Marsal, T. Dobashi and B. Weber (eds), *Children Philosophize Worldwide. Theoretical and Practical Concepts*, Peter Lang Verlag, Frankfurt, pp. 527–542.

Santi, M. (2010), "Inclusive Philosophy? Some Key-notes and an Educational Proposal to Promote Children Flourishing Life". Paper presented at the International Workshop on Children's Capabilities, September 2010, Amman, mimeo.

Sen, A. K. (1992), *Inequality Reexamined*, Clarendon Press, Oxford University Press, United States, New York.

Sen, A. K. (1993), "Capability and Well-being", in M. Nussbaum and A. Sen (eds), *The Quality of Life*, Clarendon Press, Oxford.

Sen, A. K. (1999), *Development as Freedom*, OUP, Oxford.

Sen, A. K. (2004a), "Capabilities, Lists, and Public Reason: Continuing the Conversation", *Feminist Economics*, 10: 77–80.

Sen, A. K. (2004b), "Elements of a Theory of Human Rights", *Philosophy and Public Affairs*, 32(4): 315–356.

Sen, A. K. (2005), "Human Rights and Capabilities", *Journal of Human Development*, 6(2): 151–166.

Sen, A. K. (2006), "What Do We Want from a Theory of Justice?" *The Journal of Philosophy*, CIII(5): 215–238.

Teschl, M. and Comim, F. (2005), "Adaptive Preferences and Capabilities: Some Preliminary Conceptual Explorations", *Review of Social Economy*, 63(2): 229–247.

Van den Berge, M. P. (2006), "Working Children: Their Agency and Self-organization", *Éthique et Economique/Ethics and Economics*, 4(1): 1–20.

White, S. C. (2002), "Being, Becoming and Relationship: Conceptual Challenges of a Child Rights Approach in Development", *Journal of International Development*, 14(8): 1095–1104.

Young, M. (2009), "Capability as an Approach to Evaluation of Learning Outcome from Local Perspectives", in E. Chiappero-Martinetti (ed.), *Debating Global Society: Reach and Limits of the Capability Approach*, Fondazione Giacomo Feltrinelli, Milan, pp. 267–299.

5
Street Children in Kampala and NGOs' Actions: Understanding Capabilities Deprivation and Expansion

Rudolf Anich, Mario Biggeri, Renato Libanora and Stefano Mariani

5.1. Introduction

This chapter, and the chapters that follow, present studies aiming to operationalize the capability approach (CA). In particular, in this chapter, in order to analyse the deprivation of capabilities of street children in Kampala, Uganda, and capabilities expansion (or reduction) of former street children participating in rehabilitation projects, the method of analysis developed in Chapter 4 (Section 4.2) is employed.

Street children[1] are amongst the most vulnerable population groups,[2] and are thus of increasing concern to international agencies and policy makers. Reports from major international agencies and non-governmental organizations (NGOs)[3] are exploring central issues regarding these children and document best practices. In Uganda, increasingly wide-ranging literature on child poverty has come forward, but little academic research on street children in Kampala[4] has been carried out, and none of these studies apply to CA. Indeed, at the time this research was designed, the only study that utilized the CA to focus on street children was that carried out by Ballet et al. (2004) in Mauritania, which suggested affective deprivation to be one of the principal causes of the phenomenon and one of the main poverty dimensions, with monetary poverty having an important but indirect role.

In the second section, we report the main characteristics of street children in Kampala and briefly review policy interventions enacted by government and local authorities, and actions by NGOs. In the third section, we present the research design and methodology used, i.e. the survey-based method (see Chapter 4, Section 4.2). In the fourth section, we present the main results, with a particular focus on the main dimensions of child well-being as identified by the street children of Kampala. We describe participatory methods that have been used to fully understand the level of deprivation of children's capabilities, and explore the space for policy intervention and the role of rehabilitation projects in expanding or reducing the capabilities of former street children (in terms of achieved functionings).

5.2. Street children and related policies in Kampala

5.2.1. Street children in Kampala

Although street children are considered a "new phenomenon", the "market boys", who have been found on the streets in Kampala since the early 1970s, were typically homeless children engaged in informal activities in order to survive (Farrant, 1970; Naliwaiko, 1990). Only later, during the 1980s, were they referred to as street children, following an increase in the number of homeless children in Kampala (Young, 2004). This upsurge in numbers was essentially a consequence of the liberation war against Idi Amin's dictatorship, which started in the late 1970s, and later the guerrilla movement led by Youweri Museveni against the second regime of Milton Obote, which brought a long period of political turmoil, internal insecurity and indiscriminate destruction of whole villages, schools and habitations. In addition, the famine among the Karamojong and the civil war among the Iteso increased the settlements in the slum areas around urban centres, where children were seen as a cheap labour force. The neglect and abandonment of children was further worsened by endemic HIV infection.[5]

The different categorization of vulnerable children (such as orphans, children at risk, child labourers) may help to identify "potential" street children and give some useful indication of reasons for moving to the street. Looking at the reasons behind children moving to the streets of Kampala, we see that although some children choose to live on the streets, the majority are forced to live there.

According to the literature and to our analysis, two groups of factors can be identified: push factors and pull factors. Push factors include civil war and conflicts with neighbouring states, as well as poverty and HIV, with its associated upsurge of disrupted or instable family structures. It is clear, as underlined by our study and confirmed by the literature, that violence often underlies the major push factors, which also include a lack of love and care by parents, domestic abuse and violence or the conflict in the region. For example, Young (2004) observes that almost 90% of the street children interviewed in her field study cited negative factors (mainly mistreatment by parents or guardians, parental death or poverty) as the main catalysts in their decision to move to the street. Others were driven by drought and famine in eastern Uganda, while some were fleeing from the LRA turmoil in northern Uganda or civil war in southern Sudan. Kasagga (1998) observes that the majority of street children in Kampala originated due to poverty and disrupted family structures; for locations such as Jinja, Mbale, Gulu, Arua and Cabale the phenomenon seems to be determined primarily by dislocations due to civil wars, while in border cities such as Malaba and Busia the high demand for cheap labour increases the number of children living on the street. Munene and Nambi (1993) discovered that the majority of wandering children in Kampala were as a result of broken families and massive poverty at home, combined with the political turmoil during the period from 1966 to 1985.

On the other hand, we find some pull factors, such as increasing urbanization, dominance of money and peer attraction. This latter refers to conditions, events or opportunities that influence and attract children to live on the streets, a kind of "culture of consumerism", as Lugalla and Mbwambo (2004) suggest. However, these aspects seem to be related to age, affecting mainly older children and youngsters.

However, it is relevant to emphasize that the different causes must not be considered singularly, but as a combination of social, economic, political, cultural, religious and biological reasons that influence and impinge on each other.

Once on the street, children as young as 5 surrender themselves to harsh living conditions. Life on the street subjects children to economic, commercial or sexual exploitation and other forms of hardships. Kasagga (1998) observes that 53% of the street children in Kampala live in Mengo-Kisenyi, which is a densely populated area characterized by an informal economy, which requires manual labour forces with little or no need of formal education. Main income-generating activities engaged in by street children include looking for scrap metal, collecting empty bottles or tins, cleaning cars or shoes, carrying heavy loads, selling plastic bags, working as housemaids, fetching water, transporting luggage, looking for customers for taxis and selling small items (Nassejje, 1992; Oloya, 1995; Anich, 2006). The proximity to the Owino Market represents another advantage, as it is the cheapest place to buy food. According to Mutongole (1996), many street children prefer to beg for money as it may represent an easier and safer method of earning money. For children who have just arrived on the streets and for those who have failed to find a job, begging or stealing remain the only alternatives for survival. Money is not necessarily spent on food, but also for other entertainment, such as watching films or drug abuse. Kasirye (1994) observes that many street children in Kampala smoke cannabis (*bhang*), chew coca leaves or sniff volatile substances, such as petrol (*bugoro*) or aircraft fuel (*mafuta*).

Several estimates[6] have been carried out to establish the number of street children in Uganda (GOU, 2003). In 2002, according to the Government of Uganda, the population of street children was estimated to be over 10,000; in 1999, Kampala "hosted" 2000 of these (National Council for Children, Uganda, 1999). In a follow-up study to the reports carried out by the NGO Friends of Children Association (FOCA), the number of street children in Kampala alone was estimated at 2500.

5.2.2. Policies implemented by government and local authorities

Until very recently, no specific government policies existed for street children,[7] only general policies and goals relating to the enhanced social development and living conditions of all vulnerable groups, including street children and youths.[8]

The Constitution of Uganda (1995)[9] provides a general framework that can serve as a basis for any practices and measures applied in addressing child poverty. However, as with many constitutional documents, this normative engagement lacks mechanisms for enforcing the associated rights.

Since 1990, the Ugandan Parliament has ratified the UN Convention on the Rights of the Child (CRC), which entered into force in September of that year. These and other commitments induced the Government to elaborate the *Children's Statute 1996*, which translates the rights declared in the UN CRC, as well as the African Charter on the Welfare and Rights of the Child, into a national legal tool.[10]

The main governmental actor was the Ministry of Gender, Labour and Social Development (MGLSD), whose leading role could particularly be seen in the implementation of the policies for Orphan and Vulnerable Children (OVC), structuring and staffing of the Department for Youth and Children Affairs and the National Council for Children (NCC) (MGLSD, 2003).

In 1993, the Government launched the *Uganda National Programme of Action for Children* (UNPAC), aimed primarily at improving health status and access to essential services such as education and sanitation, as well as the protection of child rights. The UNPAC is now part of Uganda's Comprehensive Development Framework, the *Poverty Eradication Strategy and Plan of Action* (PEAP) initiative. The PEAP started in 1997, in conjunction with an integrated monitoring system, and the second draft, which emerged in 2001, was accepted as Uganda's Poverty Reduction Strategy Paper (PRSP). As one of the main strategies of the PEAP is to increase the income of poor families, some suggestions for the revision procedure of the PEAP were prepared by the NGO Save the Children UK, which conducted a specific study on child poverty, partially concentrating on children's perceptions of poverty (Save the Children, 2002, 2003).

Similarly, the GOU instituted the *Poverty Action Fund* (PAF) in 1997, which is a fund intended to pool resources and channel them into poverty-reduction activities (Save the Children, 2002).

In 1997, *Universal Primary Education* (UPE) was introduced and the government committed to paying school fees for four children per family. In order to guarantee gender equality, the expenses of two boys and two girls per family would be covered. Nationwide enthusiasm was followed by a growing scepticism, as increased literacy was often obtained at the expense of school quality (Nuwe, 2001).

Another relevant initiative in relation to children's well-being is the *Probation and Social Welfare Office* (PSWO), which helps orphans and other children in difficult circumstances by referring or recommending them to one of the various NGOs offering assistance.

Recently, a programme entitled *Model for Orphan Resettlement and Education* (MORE) was developed effectively to educate and re-socialize children who have been living on the street (see Jacob et al., 2004).

Furthermore, it should be mentioned that the Uganda Country Programme of the World Food Programme (WFP) plays an important role in preventing children from migrating from rural areas to urban settlements, as well as in providing food assistance to orphans and street children in vocational training centres operated by other partners (MGLSD, 2003).

However, Government efforts remain mainly "theoretical" and juridical. The implementation level of the above-mentioned policies is still very poor, mainly due to the lack of resources. The capacity of the NCC to perform well has deteriorated, resulting in limited opportunities effectively to implement the UNPAC (MGLSD, 2004a). In addition, the lack of political will and poor coordination and collaboration between the various stakeholders working with children detract from the already limited resources available to support the increasing needs of children in Uganda.

5.2.3. Interventions of NGOs

Local and international NGOs have been concerned about the issue of street children in Kampala for a considerable period of time. Many of them have been dealing with the issue of child well-being, but few are dedicated specifically to the street children phenomenon. Though NGOs ideally work independently from the public sector, in order to avoid duplication and to facilitate good performance, it has been acknowledged that constructive and open communication and cooperation between the Government and NGOs, and amongst NGOs themselves, is essential. According to the second periodic CRC report of the Ugandan Government, around 70 NGOs are involved in addressing the problem of street children, primarily through the following activities:

I) *Resettlement* within their families and communities should be the ultimate objective, to be achieved in collaboration with the local Probation and Social Welfare Office. Thus, it is fundamental to maintain contact between a street child and his/her parents or other relatives. Street children, if it is feasible, should be reintegrated as quickly as possible, once parents or other relatives able to provide sufficient living conditions are identified. An orphan without any parent or relative needs some type of family structure (even one that does not involve actual blood relatives or home villagers) that could take care of him/her in substitution for his/her own family. As much as a child can receive love and care in a foster home, the family still remains the natural and best place for their balanced physical, emotional, social and cultural growth. Indeed, the *Children's Statute 1996* does not recommend institutionalization as an intervention approach. Alternative care options, such as children's homes, are considered for those children who cannot be reintegrated, but only as a last resort (MGLSD, 2004b). The latter is seen as a dangerous remedy, as by living with other children they may be exposed to violence or to deviant or socially irresponsible attitudes. Often, a child within an institution is not considered as a human being in need of particular care, but as merely one of many individuals hosted by the institution, and is thus often neglected. In addition, the continuous turnover of social workers employed in the centres makes it difficult for a child to create a bond with anyone, which often gives rise to frustration and isolation. Thus institutions should have a transitory role, where the child remains temporarily while the family or a substitute suitable is identified. In order to maintain their culture and language, the children hosted in an institution should be reintegrated into their communities, which have a responsibility to welcome them (Ministry of Relief and Social Rehabilitation, 1999). There are two types of resettlement: *urban* and *rural*. The latter refers to the previously described option, i.e. bringing a child back to his/her natural parents or other relatives within his/her home village. This approach is recommended for cases of young or "new" street children, where the conflict with their origins might be reconcilable. Urban resettlement, instead, concerns mainly children of a certain age (usually from 13 upwards) who are supported in renting a room (*mizigo*) in an area bordering Kampala.

II) *Counselling* aims at offering street children some alternatives to their daily living conditions. It represents an essential tool of mediation to sensitize children on specific issues such as hygiene, reproductive health education or even recreational activities of pedagogical value. The work is usually done by professional counsellors and social workers, while spiritual support is offered by religious figures or by the *baabas* (peers previously living on the street). *Peer counselling* has proved to be particularly suitable, due to the easy access of the *baabas* to their peers and their ability to act as a role model for those newly arrived on the streets, as well as for those who refuse to abandon the street lifestyle. The local church and missionaries provide important spiritual support to street children, teaching them moral values such as peace, solidarity and equality.

III) *Legal assistance* to those children involved in juridical questions, such as those with criminal charges or hereditary disputes, is particularly worthwhile, especially in the absence of their parents. To help children enjoy and defend their rights, so-called *"fit persons"* have been created. These figures are representatives of the community and are chosen by the local Community-Based Organizations (CBOs). In addition, they also help to resettle a child within his/her community. In the case of juveniles, it is noteworthy how *community service* appears to be a beneficial approach to restoring justice. A child accused of having committed a crime can, through this service, demonstrate his/her willingness to pay back the community for his/her misconduct. Simple apologies, financial reimbursement, different tasks such as digging, carrying rubbish or helping to cook, are all accepted. In this way, both the number of children entering the formal juridical system and the likelihood of recidivism diminish. In addition, community services serve to reduce prejudice and stereotypes regarding street children, but they also require accurate monitoring in order to avoid reprisals that may result in child exploitation.

IV) *Educational sponsorship* and *vocational training* are the main types of support offered by organizations. Children hosted in a centre for some time without being resettled into their community are usually sent to primary school, and sometimes sponsored also for secondary school and further studies. It seems that street children (especially those living on the streets for a long period of time) prefer vocational training and apprenticeships, due to the acquisition of practical, income-generating skills that can be utilized immediately and are in high demand in the informal sector. Boys are usually interested in carpentry or welding, while girls concentrate on tailoring and crafts. In this sense, vocational training increases the capacity of children to become independent and self-sufficient. Many also lack life skills, including personal and social competencies that allow an individual to be effective, active and constructive in society, e.g. by appropriately coping with emotions, stress and difficulties, and by engaging in communication and planning. The accrual of different working and life skills has a positive influence on self-esteem, active participation and behaviour change (MGLSD, 1999, 2000, 2002).

V) Some organizations have created *drop-in centres* in and around Kampala. Various activities take place in these centres, such as recreation, informal education, vocational training, health services, etc. On certain days, some centres distribute foodstuffs and offer clothes and free medical treatment. Similarly, some churches offer provisions, mainly on praying days. Sometimes, drop-in centres also offer temporary accommodation until a child can be reintegrated into his/her community. The various actors do not agree on the convenience of these drop-in centres. For many, this kind of aid implies an institutionalization of the phenomenon and is financially unsustainable. In particular, drop-in centres located in urban contexts are much discussed. On the one hand, they can be seen as providing support that enables children to survive on the street, creating an important meeting point for street children; on the other hand, they can be seen as actually sustaining a problematic issue. Many children turn from one organization to another, in an attempt to get as much as possible. Once a child receives sufficient aid to provide a living, he/she will rarely abandon the freedom that street life offers to return to the family situation from which he/she had previously fled. By providing particular goods and services to street children, drop-in centres can also inadvertently attract others. A number of organizations create their centres in a rural environment in order to reduce the influence of the street on those children rehabilitated in the centres.

In conclusion, it should be noted that not all street children look favourably on the assistance offered by NGOs. There is often a loss of trust and respect towards adults due to personal experience with their parents, step-parents or teachers, which may generate a negative attitude towards governmental agencies (including the Police, Local Defence Force and Kampala City Council) and charitable organizations. Persuading a child to act in their best interest might be a complicated task. Living on the street, the children learn to look after themselves and gaining their trust can take a long time. Nuwe (2001) observes that a significant number of street children feel exploited by certain aid organizations. According to them, some NGOs are more interested in getting financial resources from abroad than in the well-being of the children (Anich, 2006). Similarly, there is a growing conviction within civil society that the issue of street children persists in part due to the interest of some NGOs in keeping the phenomenon alive in order to receive additional funding. Some children place more trust in religious organizations, as they work on a voluntary basis and are not in need of project funding for their own survival. However, the religious organizations are often criticized for offering help and assistance directly on the street (as do some NGOs, as well). Their charitable and compassionate attitude might give additional incentive to children living in the rural neighbourhood of Kampala to migrate towards the town. Free services, such as medical treatment and material goods (e.g. clothes and foodstuffs), encourage a significant number of children to join the streets. Many of these opportunities are missing at home; in some cases, the parents themselves motivate the children to try their luck on the streets, or attempt to place a child with a NGO by introducing him/her as orphan. While in the short term this practice of compassion and charity might be necessary and useful in lessening the suffering of children living on the street, in the long term it contributes to the escalation of the phenomenon of street children in Kampala (Anich, 2006). Similarly, the MGLSD indicates that handouts or relief to children on the streets, such as money or food, should be avoided, unless linked to a rehabilitation plan, since unstructured handouts may have the adverse effect of attracting even more children to the streets. "Work with street children must be development-oriented, not relief-oriented" (MGLSD, 1999).

5.3. Research design and methodology

The research design and methodology was developed by a multidisciplinary team drawn from the HDCA Thematic Group on Children's Capabilities,[11] and the subsequent field research lasted six months, from January to

July 2005. The analysis of children's well-being from a CA perspective is multidimensional and holistic in nature, and thus requires different techniques for identifying, prioritizing, measuring and comparing diverse capabilities through children's active participation in the research.

By embracing Sen's (1999) CA as a normative framework, the system of values and the procedures of public scrutiny are applied, but a "control" is still necessary (as discussed in Chapter 4). Indeed, as Judith Ennew observes regretfully, "in Africa as elsewhere, the record is frequently flawed by researchers failing to use control groups, targeting only groups of children in the street as research subjects" (Ennew, 2003: 9). Accordingly, in order to safeguard the richness of the CA, while at the same time avoiding the misspecification of values and scrutiny, which are sometimes connected to adaptive preferences or resignation (Teschl and Comim, 2005), our study included a control group. Thus, three different groups of children were involved in the research:

I) *Children of the street*, or the so-called full-time street children. For these children, the street is their home and their only resource for survival.
II) *Rehabilitated street children*, who live in accommodation provided by NGOs or other associations for street children. These children have been rehabilitated in centres promoted by NGOs or similar institutions, where they receive accommodation, food, medical care and vocational training.
III) A *control group*: children of the same age and from the same geographical areas, who have never "experienced" life on the street.

By comparing these three groups, we are able to understand how children with different experiences and life conditions conceptualize and value relevant capabilities; and by investigating their actual functionings, spaces for policies and further evaluative exercises are revealed.

The sample design for each group/category of children was specifically elaborated. Given the lack of quantitative information available (insufficient for direct random sampling), we opted for a multistage sample design, taking into account the qualitative information available on street children and the institutions involved in their rehabilitation.[12] Thus, data collection was based on a two-stage sample design. The first stage involved the identification and selection of the areas where street children use to live.[13] An attempt was made to compile a list of all the NGOs and associations that rehabilitate street children in centres; however, it was not possible to assemble a complete, reliable and updated list of all these institutions, as some are very small or newly founded, while others have stopped operating or are not registered (Anich, 2006). Therefore, we decided to concentrate on institutions that had the following characteristics: (a) offer regular shelter; (b) provide education sponsorship and/or vocational training; and (c) have a good reputation and sufficient experience in the field. This resulted in a list of 12 NGOs (Anich, 2006).

The second stage of the sample design was based on a random selection.[14] The *size of the sample* was chosen *a priori* to comprise at least 50 children in each category/group, a sufficient number for acquisition of reliable data for statistical analysis.[15] The outcome of this sampling method is a good approximation of the respective statistical population present in Kampala during the research period. The interviews were conducted directly with the children, usually in their mother tongue.[16] As mentioned, the control group included local children who had never lived on the street. Five public schools were randomly selected, and within each school a random selection of children was made.

The survey-based method used in this study can be viewed as a "light" participatory process (according to the scale proposed by Kumar, 2002), and proved to be an efficient way to identify and select children's dimensions in the capability space. To our knowledge, at the time our research was conducted few participatory studies had been carried out that actively involved the subjects of the research in the identification and evaluation of their capabilities.[17]

This survey-based method uses a questionnaire[18] as a means of stimulating thought and participation. The child passes through a process of reflection, which helps them to focus upon, and detach themselves from, their past experiences. The procedure is discussed at length in Chapter 4 and is based on four steps that ask stakeholders to (1) conceptualize their capabilities; (2) report on their actual functioning achievements (across dimensions); (3) focus on social or group capabilities and move towards consensus on the relevance of these dimensions; and (4) start prioritizing the chosen dimensions.

The core section of the questionnaire on capabilities consists of four questions. The first stage was based on a fundamental open-ended question: "What are the most important opportunities a child should have during his/her life?" This question allows the researcher to identify which capabilities the child considers relevant without affecting the results. If the child mentioned a new capability (which was not included in the codified set) it was recorded at the bottom; if he/she mentioned one of those in the list, it was marked (in cases where interpretation was difficult, the interviewer added it as a "new" capability). In this way, each child could interact and participate directly in the formation of the questionnaire (Biggeri et al., 2006: 69–70). Since love and care were central in a previous study (Ballet et al., 2004), we decided to divide this dimension into sub-dimensions: "love and care" from parents, from brothers/sisters, from a tutor or guardian and from friends.

In order to record their individual level of achieved functioning in the second stage, we asked all children: "How much have you been able to achieve this ... in your life?" The child had to concentrate on his/her own experience and rate their achieved functioning as "not at all", "insufficient", "sufficient" or "fully".

In the third stage, our intention was to stimulate a process of reflection and abstraction in order to detach the child from his/her life experience as much as possible, i.e. to operate as a neutral spectator (Sen, 2006). Thus we asked the child the following question in relation to each capability: "In your opinion how important/unimportant is this opportunity for children during their life?" Each child had to choose whether, in his/her opinion, this opportunity/capability is unimportant, of little importance, important or very important for children in general (i.e. as a capability for a social group).[19] In the fourth stage, the final question aimed to identify the most relevant capabilities for a child.

We opted to validate a dimension as relevant in the capability space if two conditions were satisfied: (1) at least one child identifies it and (2) the majority of the children considered the dimension as either important or very important. This procedure is in accordance with Sen's idea (2004, 2005) of having open and public validation and scrutiny as a necessary condition to confer legitimacy on a selection.

The *ad hoc* survey was accompanied by four participatory research tools involving thematic drawings, mobility maps, photo-essays and life histories including peer interviews (Anich, 2006; Biggeri and Anich, 2009). These tools were experimental in nature and mainly used to improve our understanding of the socio-spatial life conditions of street children in Kampala. The results are reported here to complete the analyses and to validate the survey results.

5.4. Main findings

In this section, we report the core results derived from the questionnaire, i.e. the achieved functionings and the identified capabilities. Although resources or commodities are important for generating child functionings (as achievements) and capabilities (as freedom to achieve), they remain merely means for achieving valuable ends (Sen, 1999). The ability to convert resources and commodities into capabilities and actual functionings depends on *conversion factors*, which can be internal (personal), social and/or environmental (see Chapter 1). Policies at the individual, household and community levels must be oriented in this direction if we wish to expand the capabilities valued by street children (see, in particular, Chapters 2 and 11).

As already mentioned, the first stage of the questionnaire is concerned with the identification of relevant functionings and capabilities. All capabilities identified by at least one child are reported in Table 5.1. Around 20 children conceptualized four new categories of capabilities that were not directly codified prior to interviews and were therefore added at the end of

Table 5.1 Percentage of children identifying individual capabilities dimensions (survey 2005, Kampala, Uganda)

Capability	Total	Children of the street	Rehabilitated street children	Control Group
1) Life and physical health	82.9	83.0	87.3	78.0
2) Love and care	81.6	81.1	81.8	82.0
3) Mental well-being	18.4	30.2	14.5	10.0
4) Bodily integrity and safety	16.5	15.1	12.7	22.0
5) Social relations	22.8	26.4	14.5	28.0
6) Participation/information	13.3	15.1	10.9	14.0
7) Education	89.2	79.2	94.5	94.0
8) Freedom from economic and non-economic exploitation	16.5	20.8	10.9	18.0
9) Shelter and environment	31.6	34.0	30.9	30.0
10) Leisure activities	34.8	28.3	29.1	48.0
11) Respect	7.0	11.3	3.6	6.0
12) Religion and identity	10.8	3.8	5.5	24.0
13) Time autonomy and undertake projects	8.2	9.4	3.6	12.0
14) Mobility	10.1	11.3	10.9	8.0

Question: "What are the most important opportunities a child should have during his/her life?". Note for the interviewer: Do not read out; multiple answers allowed, add capabilities not present in the list of codified to the end.

the list. However, during the analysis of the questionnaires, the four categories were absorbed into the original codified list. For example, "national identity" as a new capability was later added under the "religion and cultural identity" category. All mentioned capabilities were legitimized by the fact that all were considered as important or very important by the majority of the children.

It is essential to highlight that some capabilities were more frequently mentioned than others, i.e. education, love and care, leisure activities, and life and physical health. The results show that all groups conceptualized the same categories of capabilities, suggesting that, in our sample, children's points of view across life experience and economic divides do not differ significantly. For instance, analysing the responses by the three categories/groups, we found that both the rehabilitated street children and the control group have very high shares for education, at 94.5% and 94%, respectively. Street children mentioned education slightly less, at 79%, although this capability was still ranked immediately after love and care, and life and physical health.

The second stage encouraged the children to concentrate on their own experiences (achieved functionings) for each dimension or capability identified (Table 5.2). The third stage investigated the relevance of each

Table 5.2 Percentage of functionings achieved by children (survey 2005, Kampala, Uganda)

Achieved functionings	Children of the street				Rehabilitated children				Control Group			
	Not at all	Insufficient	Sufficient	Fully	Not at all	Insufficient	Sufficient	Fully	Not at all	Insufficient	Sufficient	Fully
1) Life and physical health	35.3	31.4	23.5	9.8	3.9	9.8	29.4	56.9	0.0	16.1	14.3	69.6
2a) loved and cared by your parents	60.9	23.9	4.3	10.9	55.3	12.8	19.1	12.8	8.9	5.4	3.6	82.1
2b) loved and cared by your brothers	41.7	18.8	18.8	20.8	35.6	11.1	20.0	33.3	0.0	5.6	9.3	85.2
2c) loved and cared by your tutors	66.7	12.1	9.1	12.1	8.7	6.5	26.1	58.7	7.4	1.9	18.5	72.2
2d) loved and cared by your friends	2.0	22.4	40.8	34.7	0.0	7.8	41.2	51.0	1.8	5.4	26.8	66.1
3) Mental well-being	12.0	38.0	34.0	16.0	6.0	10.0	30.0	54.0	1.8	10.7	12.5	75.0
4) Bodily integrity and safety	16.0	42.0	32.0	10.0	5.9	5.9	33.3	54.9	7.1	14.3	17.9	60.7
5) Social relations	30.0	28.0	22.0	20.0	38.0	16.0	18.0	28.0	5.4	10.7	23.2	60.7

Table 5.2 (Continued)

Achieved functionings	Children of the street				Rehabilitated children				Control Group			
	Not at all	Insufficient	Sufficient	Fully	Not at all	Insufficient	Sufficient	Fully	Not at all	Insufficient	Sufficient	Fully
6) Participation/information	17.6	52.9	17.6	11.8	5.9	23.5	29.4	41.2	3.6	3.6	32.1	60.7
7) Education	74.0	12.0	6.0	8.0	24.0	8.0	8.0	60.0	7.1	5.4	1.8	85.7
8) Freedom from economic and non-economic exploitation	30.6	34.7	26.5	8.2	2.0	8.2	18.4	71.4	3.7	5.6	18.5	72.2
9) Shelter and environment	58.8	29.4	7.8	3.9	3.9	0.0	25.5	70.6	5.4	7.1	16.1	71.4
10) Leisure activities	12.0	14.0	24.0	50.0	2.0	11.8	17.6	68.6	5.4	16.1	16.1	62.5
11) Respect	25.5	45.1	25.5	3.9	6.0	2.0	48.0	44.0	5.4	23.2	44.6	26.8
12) Religion and identity	31.4	25.5	19.6	23.5	3.9	11.8	49.0	35.3	5.4	7.1	37.5	50.0
13) Time autonomy	5.9	9.8	21.6	62.7	2.0	23.5	23.5	51.0	8.9	41.1	12.5	37.5
14) Mobility	17.6	23.5	25.5	33.3	21.6	39.2	29.4	9.8	12.5	42.9	19.6	25.0

Question: "How much have you been able to realise/achieve this functioning in your life?" (achievement).

dimension/capability for children as a social group of human beings (Table 5.3). This sequence in the process of thinking should enable children to become partially detached from their life experience and scrutinize potentially valuable functionings, irrespective of whether they are achievable (the control group is necessary to gauge the extent and scope of any bias in the findings that might be related to adaptive preferences – see Section 4.2).

The interaction between these two stages can help in the design and programming and evaluation of programmes and projects intended to improve child well-being; if a capability dimension is highly valued but the level of functionings achieved is low, more efficient or additional policy interventions will be needed to fill the gap between what is valued and what is achieved. Similarly, it is also possible to investigate whether the rehabilitation programmes offered expanded or reduced the capabilities (i.e. opportunities) for the children. Although this exercise is not based on longitudinal data, it represents a useful cross-sectional evaluation exercise that provides two interesting results:

I) *All children seem to share the same values* (including street children, rehabilitated former street children and children in the control group). Each single capability identified in Table 5.1 was valued as important or very important by all the children interviewed (see Table 5.3).[20] It is relevant to note that at the end of the interview (when asked if there was any other opportunity not covered so far), 4 children out of 158 emphasized the capability of being economically independent, i.e. control over money and resources and the capability to work and be paid.

II) *The level of functionings achieved varies according to the child's life experience.* Street children exhibited low achievement levels, particularly in dimensions that clearly require policy intervention, such as life and physical health, love and care by parent and tutors, participation/information, education, freedom from economic and non-economic exploitation, shelter and environment, and respect. In particular, the love and care domain and sub-domains show very low emotional achievements (see Chapter 7 on agency and identity formation) or parental care (see Chapter 15 on the relevance of emotions) for street children. The improvement in some dimensions demonstrates the success of the work done by NGOs in supporting street children, such as in life and physical health, love and care by tutors, participation/information, education, freedom from economic and non-economic exploitation, shelter and environment, and respect. There are obviously certain spheres that are difficult for NGOs to reach, such as love and care by parents, although some progress in terms of reconciliation can be noted. The control group is in a different position, with significant achieved functionings, except in time autonomy and mobility, as school attendance and work at home do not leave much flexibility for other things. Indeed, street

Table 5.3 Relevance of capabilities for children, by percentage (survey 2005, Kampala, Uganda)

Capability	Children of the street				Rehabilitated children NGOs				Control Group			
	Unimportant	Little important	Important	Very important	Unimportant	Little important	Important	Very important	Unimportant	Little important	Important	Very important
1) Life and physical health	0.0	0.0	3.9	96.1	0.0	0.0	2.0	98.0	0.0	0.0	3.6	96.4
2a) loved and cared by your parents	0.0	0.0	2.0	98.0	0.0	0.0	3.9	96.1	0.0	0.0	0.0	100.0
2b) loved and cared by your brothers	0.0	2.0	2.0	96.0	0.0	0.0	3.9	96.1	0.0	0.0	10.7	89.3
2c) loved and cared by your tutors	0.0	2.2	0.0	97.8	0.0	0.0	3.9	96.1	0.0	0.0	5.4	94.6
2d) loved and cared by your friends	0.0	0.0	2.0	98.0	0.0	0.0	2.0	98.0	0.0	0.0	8.9	91.1
3) Mental well-being	0.0	0.0	2.0	98.0	0.0	0.0	2.0	98.0	0.0	1.8	7.1	91.1
4) Bodily integrity and safety	0.0	2.0	0.0	98.0	0.0	0.0	5.9	94.1	0.0	0.0	7.1	92.9
5) Social relations	0.0	0.0	15.7	84.3	2.0	0.0	12.0	86.0	0.0	0.0	12.5	87.5
6) Participation / information	0.0	0.0	2.0	98.0	0.0	0.0	2.0	98.0	0.0	0.0	5.4	94.6
7) Education	0.0	2.0	3.9	94.1	0.0	0.0	0.0	100.0	0.0	0.0	0.0	100.0
8) Freedom from econ and non-econ exploitation	0.0	0.0	10.2	89.8	0.0	0.0	2.0	98.0	0.0	0.0	3.7	96.3
9) Shelter and environment	0.0	0.0	2.0	98.0	0.0	0.0	0.0	100.0	0.0	0.0	0.0	100.0
10) Leisure activities	0.0	0.0	9.8	90.2	0.0	0.0	3.9	96.1	0.0	0.0	10.7	89.3
11) Respect	0.0	3.9	11.8	84.3	0.0	0.0	13.7	86.3	0.0	8.9	8.9	82.1
12) Religion and identity	2.0	5.9	5.9	86.3	0.0	0.0	9.8	90.2	0.0	3.6	1.8	94.6
13) Time autonomy	3.9	2.0	9.8	84.3	2.0	3.9	7.8	86.3	12.7	10.9	3.6	72.7
14) Mobility	0.0	5.9	7.8	86.3	2.0	7.8	7.8	82.4	8.9	10.7	10.7	69.6

Question: "In your opinion how important/unimportant is this opportunity for children during their life?".

children record very good achieved functionings in time autonomy (which includes the opportunity to undertake projects as a form of agency) and mobility. Many rehabilitated street children have much better achieved functionings in all dimensions except the latter two, since the children were obliged to start following different rules with the NGOs. Consequently, a kind of trade-off emerges: mobility and time autonomy may foster children's agency and are therefore relevant for their autonomy and empowerment, but they may also reduce the time devoted to instrumental capabilities (such as education and vocational training) and at the expense of shelter and security, which are relevant for present well-being and for the process of evolving capabilities. This can generate some trade-offs that need to be understood for short-term and long-term policies (see, for instance, the discussion in Chapter 11, Section 11.6, and Chapter 13).

The last interview question aims to select the most relevant capabilities. Without providing a complete ordering of all capabilities, we asked the children to select the three most relevant (Table 5.4). The results suggest that for street children the four most important were education (68.3%), love and care (51.7%), life and physical health (45.5%) and shelter and environment (37.2%), whereas for rehabilitated street children the most important were education (89.2%), life and physical health (60.8%), shelter and environment (53.2%) and love and care (34.2%). The control group mentioned education (84.2%), life and physical health (69.0%), love and care (57.5%) and shelter and environment (39.0%). All three groups agreed on the prominent importance of education, life and physical health, love and care, shelter and environment.[21]

Summarizing the results, we observed that children, independently from their life conditions and experiences, were able to conceptualize their capabilities and, in particular, that they valued them as important capabilities. Some of these dimensions were often ignored or not perceived as relevant in existing research, although they were seen as essential by children.

From a policy point of view, it is fundamental to recognize that street children exhibit low levels of functioning, which can be seen as capability deprivation, since they value those dimensions as important or very important. There are many dimensions in which the Government and NGOs can operate to reduce the level of deprivation and to improve the well-being of children, some of which children have mentioned in participatory research.

While NGOs were able to improve some dimensions of well-being for street children, there remains substantial scope for intervention by the Ugandan Government and public institutions, which constitute the missing actor in street children policy.

Table 5.4   Three most relevant capabilities for children, by percentage (survey 2005, Kampala, Uganda)

Capability	Children of the street	Rehabilitated street children	Control group
1) Life and physical health	45.5	60.8	69.9
2) Love and care	51.7	34.2	57.5
3) Mental well-being	8.3	0.0	4.1
4) Bodily integrity and safety	4.1	1.9	4.1
5) Social relations	4.1	0.0	0.0
6) Participation/information	12.4	9.5	2.1
7) Education	68.3	89.2	84.2
8) Freedom from economic and non-economic exploitation	10.3	0.0	2.1
9) Shelter and environment	37.2	53.2	39.0
10) Leisure activities	12.4	11.4	10.3
11) Respect	10.3	11.4	2.1
12) Religion and identity	8.3	11.4	4.1
13) Time autonomy and undertake projects	6.2	5.7	8.2
14) Mobility	12.4	7.6	6.2

Question: "Among the aspects we discussed could you tell me which are the three most important opportunities a child should have during his/her life?".

Free quality education and sanitation seems to be crucial and also instrumental for the evolving capabilities of the child. Shelter and a clean environment is another important issue, while love and care by tutors/guardians can partially or temporarily complement the lack of love and care by parents. Participation, respect and freedom from economic and non-economic exploitation are equally essential for a better future for street children.

The results obtained by the participatory research tools complement[22] the survey-based method (i.e. triangulation of data) and proved to be highly effective in enabling children to identify and express the relevant dimensions of their well-being, as well as in interpreting the outputs in terms of functionings and capabilities. For younger children, in particular, the participatory methods seemed to be the most appropriate means to access their point of view.

Love and care is considered by all children interviewed as one of the most relevant dimensions for their well-being (see Table 5.4). Indeed, the lack of love and care was identified by all four different participatory research tools as one of the main reasons for children to move to the streets. Low achieved functionings in terms of love and care are particularly evident in the maps drawn by street girls, but also within different life histories recorded by rehabilitated and current street children interviewing each other, as the following interview emphasizes.

A: [...] I come from Masaka.

Q: What made you to leave Masaka?

A: I just came with my mother.

Q: Your mother? Then where did she drop you?

A: We were staying together.

Q: So you were staying together! Then when you reached the town what did you do?

A: She got married to another man who later started mistreating me.

Q: Mistreating you?! Then you decided to go on the street?

A: No. He started mistreating me so badly by beating me whenever my mother was not available. So only after coming back I could tell her everything. This made her take me back to the village and my real fathers place, but again my stepmother started mistreating me in the same way (like the stepfather) and she even told to go back to my real mothers place and stay with her. So I went back to see my mother, but she was not there anymore. I had no one to stay with.

Q: *13 years old, and N., 15 years old, both street children, interviewing each other.*

In the drawings and photos, the lack of love and care is referred to indirectly. Apart from the drawings emphasizing the feeling of protection a church can provide, love and care seem to be absent for almost all the children involved in the research, apart from peer friendship. The data collected contain details on some situations characterized by the absence of love and care: in families with one or two step-parents (but sometimes also with natural parents), domestic violence is quite common, and community members, as well as public authorities (such as the Police or Local Defence Units), do not hesitate to behave in a rude fashion with children loitering around. This accentuates the importance of peer friendship but, at the same time, may show lack of parents' care. A sample of the data is reported in Tables 5.5 and 5.6.

In looking at shelter and the environment, through various participatory research tools we were able to elicit further knowledge on its importance and various shapes. Low achieved functionings can be seen as deprived capabilities once we consider the relevance the children gave to this dimension (see Tables 5.1, 5.3 and 5.4), thus underlining the central role that clean and safe accommodation plays for people living on the street, particularly children. Another example of deprivation of shelter and environment is captured by children looking for food.

Generally, each piece of data emphasizes deprivation (or temporary satisfaction) of more than one capability. Thus, they are particularly worthwhile, showing how different capabilities are interrelated in specific contexts (see, for example, the drawing in Figure 5.1 and photo in Figure 5.2, which help

Table 5.5 Participatory Rapid Assessment and the perception of capability deprivation: Thematic drawings

Thematic drawings	1) Life and physical health	2) Love and care	3) Mental well-being	4) Bodily integrity and safety	5) Social relations	6) Participation and information	7) Education
dkampi2a-drugs	X		x				
dkampi4-fetching							
dkampi5-drugs	x				X	x	
dkampi6				X			
dkaral	x			X			
dkara2				X			
dkara4a	x			X			
dkara5a	x			X			
dkara6a	x			X			
dkara7	X						
dkara8							
dkaydal-bad	x	x		X			
dkayda2-bad	x	x		X			
dkayda3-good	x						
dkayda4-bad			X				
dkayda5-good							
dkayda7a-bad	x	x		x			
dkayda7b-bad	X			x			
dkayda8-bad	x						
dkinl							
dkin3				X			
dkin4a+b							
dkin5a				X			
dkin5b-fetching	x						
dkin5c-box	x	x					
dkin6a-football							
dkin6b-mobility							
dkin7a-begging							
dkin8a-scrap							
duccl-activities	x						
ducc2a-scrap							
ducc2b-church		x			x		
ducc3-police	X			X			
ducc4-fightings				X	X		
ducc5-activities							
ducc6-police			x	x			

illustrate the relationship between shelter and environment, love and care, life and physical health and body integrity and security).

Sleeping on verandas, in empty boxes or near the dump depot, for example, can be extremely harmful to the health and safety of children. In such conditions, children have to struggle with cold and wet weather, and may be harassed or even beaten by community members or local authorities. They also risk imprisonment by police, sexual abuse or rape, and face illness and infections such as pneumonia. None of the data collected indicate sufficient adequate access to shelter or appropriate environmental conditions.

Thematic drawings	8) Freedom from economic and non-economic exploitation	9) Shelter and environment	10) Leisure activities	11) Respect	12) Religion and identity	13) Time autonomy	14) Mobility
dkampi2a-drugs							
dkampi4-fetching	X						
dkampi5-drugs							
dkampi6				x			
dkaral			x				x
dkara2					x		x
dkara4a				x			
dkara5a				X			
dkara6a							
dkara7	x						
dkara8			x	x		X	
dkaydal-bad	x	X		X			
dkayda2-bad	x	X		X			
dkayda3-good			X			x	x
dkayda4-bad		x					
dkayda5-good			X		x	x	x
dkayda7a-bad				x			
dkayda7b-bad		x					
dkayda8-bad		X					
dkinl	X						
dkin3	X	x					
dkin4a+b	X						
dkin5a		x					x
dkin5b-fetching	X						
dkin5c-box		X					
dkin6a-football			X			X	X
dkin6b-mobility							X
dkin7a-begging	x			X			
dkin8a-scrap	X						
duccl-activities	X	x		x			
ducc2a-scrap	X						
ducc2b-church		x			X		
ducc3-police							
ducc4-fightings							
ducc5-activities	x			x			x
ducc6-police				X			

Notes: X = strong impact x = impact. (a) Drawings selected from the total of 83 data pieces collected, the selection was made on the base of different aspects that the life on the street implies; (b) in bold the data piece shows in the paper; and (c) the shadows are used as follows: negative perception/capability deprivation █████ positive perception/achieved functioning.

Although mobility is not considered among the three most relevant capabilities (see Table 5.4), it was identified (explicitly as well as implicitly) by all of the participatory tools we utilized. In this case, we cannot speak of a capability deprivation (see also Table 5.2), as it is typically described as a benefit street life can give. In fact, low achievements in mobility were observed only when referring to the rules within a NGO and/or to family life before joining the streets. Freedom in terms of movement, as well as

Table 5.6 Participatory Rapid Assessment and the perception of capability deprivation: Mobility mapping, photo-essays and life histories

Tools	1) Life and physical health	2) Love and care	3) Mental well-being	4) Bodily integrity and safety	5) Social relations	6) Participation and information	7) Education
Mobility maps							
mkampi1	x						X
mkampi2					x		X
mkara1					x		
mkayda1		X			x	x	X
mkayda2		X		x			x
mkin1	X						
mkin2							
mkin3							
mucc2					x		
Photo essay							
frubbish	X	x					
frubbish2	X						
frubbish3	X						
fwater	X						
fwater2	X						
fbegging							
fdrugs	X		x				
fmarket	X						
f scrap							
fscrap2							
fscrap3							
fsleeping	x	x		X			
fstreetadults					x		
Life histories							
lh-friendship H		X	x	x	x	x	
lh- friendship S	X	x	X	X	x		
lh-drugs Kampi S	x	x	x	X	x	x	
lh-drugs Kampi K			X				
lh-money attraction H		X	X	x			
lh-money attraction S	x						
lh-money attraction N	x	x	x				
lh-scrap H		x	X				
lh-scrap S	x	x		x			X
lh-stealing S					x		
lh-stealing N							
lh-stepparents NGO H	x	X	X	X	x	x	
lh-stepparents NGO S	X	X	x	X	x	x	

time autonomy, offered by the streets, seems to represent a significant pull factor for children migrating to urban settings.

Observing the high number of different places frequented by street children every day (Figure 5.3), we can imagine how difficult it must be for a child rehabilitated at home or in a centre to follow strict rules regarding freedom of movement.

In summary, participatory research tools proved to be extremely useful for improving our understanding of children's capabilities and perspectives and for obtaining greater awareness of the different aspects of life that each

Tools	8) Freedom from economic and non-economic exploitation	9) Shelter and environment	10) Leisure activities	11) Respect	12) Religion and identity	13) Time autonomy	14) Mobility
Mobility maps							
mkampil					X	x	x
mkampi2			X		X	x	x
mkaral	x		X		X	x	x
mkaydal					X	x	x
mkayda2		X	x	X		x	x
mkinl	X		X		X	x	x
mkin2	X		X		X	x	x
mkin3						X	X
mucc2	x		X			x	x
Photo essay							
frubbish		x					
frubbish2		x					
frubbish3		x					
fwater		x					
fwater2		x					
fbegging		x					
fdrugs	X			x			
fmarket	x						
f scrap							
fscrap2	X	x					
fscrap3	X						
fsleeping	X						
fstreetadults		X					
Life histories							
lh-friendship H	x			X		X	
lh- friendship S	X	X		X			
lh-drugs Kampi S	x			X			
lh-drugs Kampi K				X		X	X
lh-money attraction H							
lh-money attraction S	X	X					
lh-money attraction N			X			X	X
lh-scrap H				x			
lh-scrap S	x			x			
lh-stealing S				X			
lh-stealing N						X	X
lh-stepparents NGO H				x			
lh-stepparents NGO S		X		X			

Notes: X = strong impact x = impact. (a) Mapping selected from the total of 20 data pieces collected, the selection was made to include the different group classification of children; (b) photos selected from the total of 105 data pieces collected, the selection was made on the base of different aspects that the life on the street implies; (c) life histories selected from the total of 27 data pieces collected, the selection was made on the base of different aspects that the life on the street implies; (d) the shadows are used as follows: ▬▬▬ negative perception/capability deprivation ▬▬▬ positive perception/achieved functioning.

capability dimension can represent (see Tables 5.5 and 5.6). By allowing children to take control of the research process without being influenced by the researcher's presence, it was possible to gather additional information that might otherwise be ignored.

Figure 5.1   Pavement drawing by K., a 12-year-old street child

Figure 5.2   Photo by S. (14) and L. (12), street children

The study also brings out some of the limitations of participatory research tools. However, these limitations can be regarded as a limit more of our research design than of the participatory approach itself, and can be overcome by fine-tuning these tools in the future.

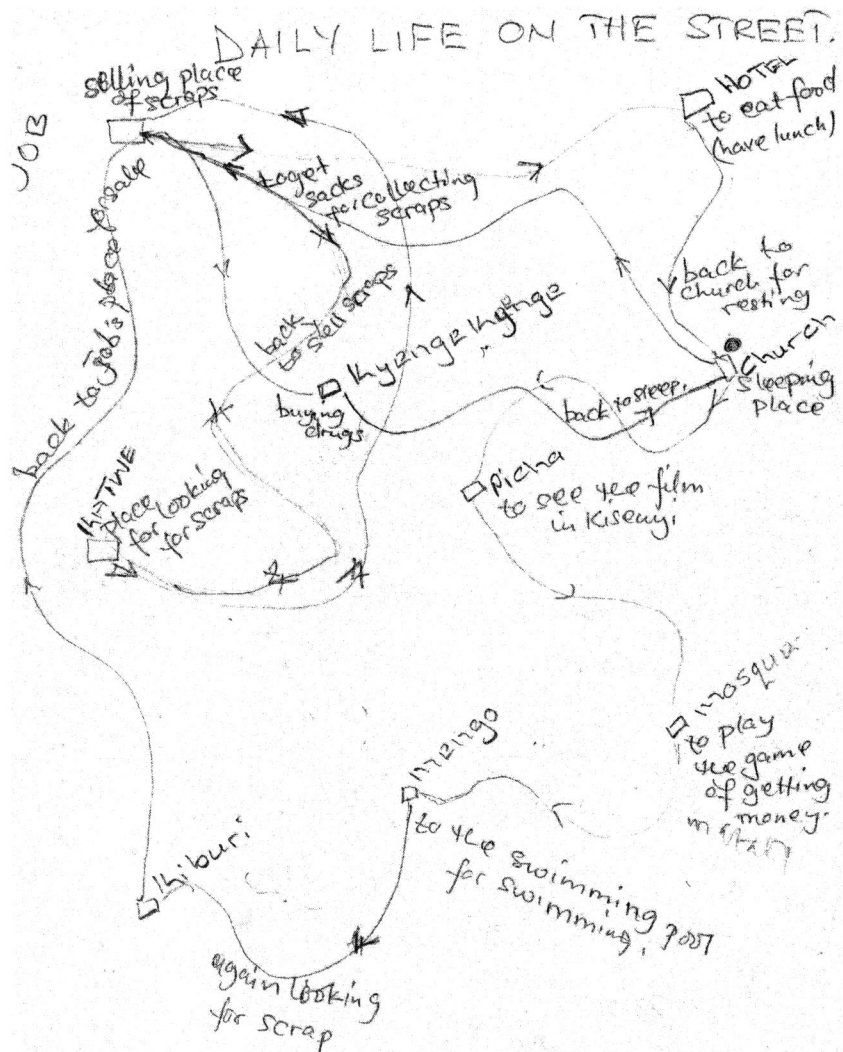

Figure 5.3 Mobility map elaborated by a group of rehabilitated street children, 10–15 years old

5.5. Conclusions

By stimulating the process of thinking and self-reflection, the adopted survey-based method helps children to conceptualize their capabilities and to choose relevant dimensions of their well-being. This methodology enriches the analysis by exploring more dimensions (i.e. the capability space), and unlocking a new complementary perspective. Indeed, the children participating in our research identified dimensions and issues (agency, autonomy, love and care) often not covered by other approaches, underlining the possible areas of interventions and trade-offs between daily/short-term policies and long-term policies.

Participatory research tools complement the survey-based method (i.e. triangulation of data) and proved to be highly effective in researching the socio-spatial conditions of street children in Kampala. They represent a useful methodology for increasing our knowledge of each capability, for validating our survey-based method and for furnishing valid material for further analysis and discussion. However, to become more effective, participatory research tools need to be further tailored to the framework of the CA.

Acknowledgements

The fieldwork was carried out by Mario Biggeri (research coordinator) and Rudolf Anich (field study coordinator); Renato Libanora and Mariani Stefano were involved in the research design and development of the methodology. The authors are extremely grateful to the children who participated in the research, and collaborated and contributed to the research project. The assistance of Lameck Muwanga, Semakula Musoke Henry, Opolot Roberts Imongot, Alutia Moses Zorran Brudd and the *baabas* in the field is also appreciated. We acknowledge the support of the University of Florence, the HDCA Thematic Group on Children's Capabilities, and the Fondazione Culturale Responsabilità Etica (the funds were donated by the family of Pia Paradossi, who was a much-loved member of Mani Tese Firenze).

Notes

1. Definitions of street children living in different contexts should take into consideration the perceptions of each single child on his/her living conditions (Wernham, 2001). Different authors (see, for instance, Aptekar, 1988; Lusk, 1992; Dallapè, 1996; Shanahan, 1998), used a general definition that utilizes various dimensions for categorization, such as time lived in the streets, absence of contact with a responsible adult, relation and involvement with own family, type of working engagement, number of deviant attitudes, etc. According to CIDA (2001), a more suitable term to use is "street-involved children", which "better" describes the large spectrum of relationships in which children engage the socio-economic, cultural and physical space of the street environment. For definitions of children "of" and "on" the street see the two chapters in this book by Ballet et al. and Serrokh.
2. See, for instance, MGLSD (1999); Wernham, (2001); UNICEF (2002); and UNESCO (2005).
3. Such as CIDA (2001); Save the Children (2002); UNICEF (2002).
4. For instance, Munene and Nambi (1993, 1996); FOCA (1999); Young and Barrett (2001a, 2001b); Jacob et al. (2004); Young (2004); Van Blerk (2005, 2006).

5. The prevalence of endemic HIV has resulted in a high number of orphans, estimated at around 116,000 children under the age of 15 years (UCOBAC, 1996).
6. Differences in numbers are related to diverging definitions (please see footnote 1) as well as to the difficulty in identifying street children.
7. A notable exception is "Practice Guidelines for Work with Street Children in Uganda", a small handbook prepared by the Department of Youth and Children Affairs, MGLSD (1999) to advise organizations working with street children in Uganda.
8. These policies further include the BECCAD (*Basic Education, Child Care, and Adolescent Development*), the PEARL (*Programme for Early Adolescent Reproductive Life*), YES (*Youth Entrepreneurship Support Programme*) and the PAP (*Poverty Alleviation Programme*), to mention a few (MGLSD, 1999).
9. Particularly relevant in relation to children's well-being are articles 14 (which includes access to education, health services, work, decent shelter, adequate clothing and food security) and 34 (which outlines a child's right to know and be cared for by his/her parents, right to basic education and protection from social or economic exploitation).
10. This statute is a vigorous juridical tool (complemented by the *Family and Children's Courts*), which helps to consolidate the legislation on children issues that was previously split into different acts. It primarily protects the fundamental rights of the children, but also identifies their duties towards society (Mbambu, 2000).
11. The research conducted was approved by the government body in charge of social research surveillance and followed standard ethical guidelines. The information collected in the survey is strictly confidential and is used for statistical purposes only and at aggregate level.
12. For this reason the best way to proceed is to ask expert "privileged observers" to identify those to be surveyed (Fabbris, 1990). The selection depends on experts correctly identifying those specific institutions required for the survey.
13. For details, please see Anich (2006); Biggeri and Anich (2009).
14. A small fraction of children of the street were selected through snowball sampling, since some children brought us the first friend they met after the interview.
15. We could not base the dimension of the sample on objective information; indeed, we had no *a priori* information reliable enough to use a confidence interval with an error margin.
16. Children of the street cannot be approached easily for interviews, and in particular for the application of participatory tools. Therefore, it was very important to find somebody who could bridge the gap between the research group and the street children. This person or persons would have to understand how street life works, know where children are staying and have gained the trust of the community. The *baabas* performed this role very well; they are former street children who have since matured and become fully reintegrated in society. These *baabas* have proved to be particularly responsible and are consequently employed by different NGOs in order to identify, sensitize and support current street children (Anich, 2006).
17. A notable exception is Clark (2002, 2003), who developed a questionnaire to explore perceptions of well-being (a good form of life) amongst the urban and rural poor in South Africa. See also Clark and Qizilbash (2008).
18. See Biggeri et al. (2006); Biggeri and Anich (2009); and Appendix 4.1. in Chapter 4.

19. The participant also has to value those dimensions identified by other children. Therefore, the resulting conceptualized capability set reflects the capabilities that all children value and have reason to value.
20. We expected this dimension to appear more frequently and, in particular, in the four stages of process. This issue also emerged during a focus group discussion in another research project, with children aged between 14 and 17 years of age (see Chapter 13, Section 13.3). The fact that it appears at the end indicates that, for a few children, it is probably a pragmatic response to their condition.
21. Very similar results were obtained by Biggeri et al. (2006) and Biggeri (2007). See also Chapter 4 (especially Section 4.2 and Table 4.1) in this book.
22. Indeed, they were not able to identify all the dimensions.

References

Anich, R. (2006), *Bambini di strada. Indagine sociologica di un recente fenomeno urbano attraverso le parole e le immagini dei bambini di Kampala*, Master Dissertation in Political Sciences, University of Florence.

Aptekar, L. (1988), *Street Children of Cali*, Duke University Press, Durham, NC.

Ballet, J., Bhukuth, A. and Radja, K. (2004), "Capabilities, Affective Capital and Development Application to Street Child in Mauritania". Paper presented at the 4th International Conference on the Capability Approach: Enhancing Human Security, 5–7 September 2004, Pavia.

Biggeri, M., Libanora, R., Mariani, S. and Menchini, L. (2006), "Children Conceptualizing Their Capabilities: Results of the Survey During the First Children's World Congress on Child Labour", *Journal of Human Development*, 7(1): 59–83.

Biggeri, M. (2007), "Children's Valued Capabilities", in Melanie Walker and Elaine Unterhalter (eds), *Amartya Sen's Capability Approach and Social Justice in Education*, Palgrave, New York, Oxon, Chapter 10, pp. 197–214.

Biggeri, M. and Anich, R. (2009), "The Deprivation of Street Children in Kampala: Can the Capability Approach and Participatory Methods Unlock a New Perspective in Research and Decision-Making?", *Mondes en Developpement*, 37(2): 73–93.

CIDA – Canadian International Development Agency (2001), *Action Plan on Child Protection: Promoting the Rights of the Children who Need Special Protection Measures*, The Canadian International Development Agency (CIDA), Quebec, Canada, Montreal.

Clark, D. A. (2002), *Visions of Development: A Study of Human Values*, Edward Elgar, Cheltenham.

Clark, D. A. (2003), "Concepts and Perceptions of Human Well-being: Some Evidence from South Africa", *Oxford Development Studies*, 31(2): 173–196.

Clark, D. A. and Qizilbash, M. (2008), "Core Poverty, Vagueness and Adaptation: A New Methodology and Some Results for South Africa", *Journal of Development Studies*, 44(4): 519–544.

Dallapè, F. (1996). Urban Children: A Challenge and an Opportunity, *Childhood*, 3(2): 283–294.

Ennew, J. (2003), "Difficult Circumstances: Some Reflections on Street Children in Africa", *Children, Youth and Environment*, 13(1).

Fabbris, L. (1990), "Problemi statistici nella utilizzazione di dati rilevati presso testimoni priviligiati", *Atti del Seminario di Studio Rilevazioni per Campione delle Opinioni degli Italiani*, Bressanone, 13 September: 89–115.

Farrant, M. (1970), "Market Boys of Kampala: A Survey", *East African Journal*, 7(10): 13–19.

FOCA (1999), *Baseline Survey on Fulltime Street Children in Kampala*, FOCA Friends of Children Association, Red Barnet, by El-Wambi, Muhumuza and Fehling, Kampala.

GOU (2003), CRC Second periodic report of State parties, August.

Jacob, J., Smith, T., Hite, S. and Yao Chen S. (2004), "Helping Uganda's Street Children", *Journal of Children and Poverty*, 10(1): 2–22.

Kasagga, V. S. (1998), *Socio-economic Factors Contribution to the Ever Increasing Number of Street Children within Kampala City. A Case Study of Mengo Kisenyi*, dissertation BA Degree in Social Work and Social Administration, Makerere University, Kampala.

Kasirye, R. (1994), *Paper on Drug Abuse*, Kampala.

Kumar, S. (2002), *Methods for Community Participation, A Complete Guide for Practitioners*, Vistaar Publications, New Delhi.

Lugalla, M. (2004), Street children and street life in urban Tanzania: the culture of surviving and its implications for children's health, in *International Journal of Urban and Regional Research* 23 (2), in Young Lorraine, journeys to the street: the complex migration geographies of Ugandan street children, in *Geoforum* 35.

Lusk, M. (1992), "Street Children of Rio De Janeiro", *International Social Work*, 35: 293–305.

Mbambu, D. (2000), *A Critical Analysis of the Legal and Institutional Framework for the Protection of Street Children in Uganda*, dissertation BA Degree in Law, Makerere University, Kampala.

MGLSD (1999), *Practice Guidelines for Work with Street Children in Uganda*, Street Children Desk, Department of Youth and Children Affairs (1999), Kampala.

MGLSD (2000), First periodic report on implementation of the CRC in Uganda.

MGLSD (2002), The National Action Plan on Youth, March.

MGLSD (2003), Mapping OVC Interventions in Uganda, October 2003.

MGLSD (2004a), National Strategic Programme Plan of Interventions for OVC 2005/6–2009/10, October, Draft.

MGLSD (2004b), Report on OVC. Rapid Assessment, Analysis and Action Planning Process (RAAAP), October.

Ministry of Relief and Social Rehabilitation (1999), *Child Care Open Learning Programme: Children with Special Needs*, GOU, Kampala.

Munene, J. C. and Nambi, J. (1993), *Operational Research on Street Children*, Department of Psychology, University of Makerere, Kampala.

Munene, J. C. and Nambi, J. (1996), "Understanding and Helping Street Children in Uganda", *Community Development Journal*, 31: 343–350.

Mutongole, C. (1996), *Survival Strategies of Street Children in Kampala City*, dissertation BA Degree in Social Work and Social Administration, Makerere University, Kampala.

Naliwaiko, A., (1990), "The Bag Boys: Nakasero Market Boys", occasional Paper Number 8, Makerere Institute of Social Research, Kampala.

Nassejje, S. (1992), *The Socio-economic Life of Street Children in Kampala*, dissertation BA Degree in Social Work and Social Administration, Makerere University, Kampala.

National Council for Children (1999), *Child Rights Monitoring Indicators*, MGLSD, Kampala.

Nuwe, A. D. (2001), *UPE and It's Impact on Kampala Street Children: A Critical Study*, dissertation BA Degree in Law, Makerere University, Kampala.

Oloya, J. (1995), *Feeding Practices of Kampala Street Children*, dissertation BA Degree in Social Work and Social Administration, Makerere University, Kampala.

Save the Children (2000), *Children and Participation: Research, Monitoring and Evaluation with Children and Young People*, Save the Children UK, London.

Save the Children (2002), *The Silent Majority: Child Poverty in Uganda*, Save the Children UK, London.

Save the Children (2003), *Suffering in Silence. The Plight of Kampala's Children*, Save the Children UK, Kampala.

Sen, A. K. (1999), *Development as Freedom*, OUP, Oxford.

Sen, A. K. (2004), "Capabilities, Lists, and Public Reason: Continuing the Conversation", *Feminist Economics*, 10(3): 77–80.

Sen, A. K. (2005), "Human Rights and Capabilities", *Journal of Human Development*, 6(2): 151–166.

Sen, A. K. (2006), "What Do We Want from a Theory of Justice", *The Journal of Philosophy*, CIII(5): 215–238.

Shanahan, P. (1998), "The Alternative Africa", *White Fathers-White Sisters*, 341: 4–15.

Teschl, M. and Comim, F. (2005), "Adaptive Preferences and Capabilities: Some Preliminary Conceptual Explorations", *Review of Social Economy*, 63(2): 229–247.

UCOBAC (1996), *The Vulnerable Child*, Kampala.

UNESCO (2005), *Children in Abject Poverty in Uganda. A Study of Criteria and Status of Those In and Out of School in Selected Districts in Uganda*, in collaboration with MPFED and MOES.

UNICEF (2002), *The State of the World's Children*, OUP, Oxford.

Van Blerk, L. (2005) "Negotiating Spatial Identities: Mobile Perspectives on Street Life in Uganda", *Children's Geographies*, 3(1): 5–21.

Van Blerk, L. (2006), "Diversity and Difference in the Everyday Lives of Ugandan Street Children", *Social Dynamics*, 32, 47–74.

Wernham, M. (2001), *An Outside Chance. Street Children and Juvenile Justice – An International Perspective*, Consortium for Street Children, London.

Young, L. (2004), "Journeys to the Street: The Complex Migration Geographies of Ugandan Street Children", *Geoforum*, 35(4): 471–488.

Young, L. and Barrett, H. (2001a), "Adapting Visual Methods: Action Research with Kampala Street Children", *Area* 33(2): 141–152.

Young, L. and Barrett, H. (2001b), "Issues of Access and Identity: Adapting Research Methods with Kampala Street Children", *Childhood: A Global Journal of Child Research*, 8(3): 383–395.

6

Sen's Capability Approach: Children and Well-being Explored through the Use of Photography

Anne Kellock and Rebecca Lawthom

6.1. Introduction

In this chapter we explore the utility of Sen's capability approach (CA) with primary school children. Capabilities are conceptualized in collaboration with children using a visual methodology. Photo-voice is a participative approach using photographs to elicit discussions around the photographic stimulus (Wang et al., 1998). Here, it is innovatively employed with children to engage with them and to capture alternative creative framings of well-being and capabilities. Sen's CA is utilized as an open framework (Robeyns, 2003) to visualize how children perceive their own capabilities and potential, both in terms of well-being and readiness to participate and learn in the school environment.[1] Indeed, Ballet, Biggeri and Comim (Chapter 2) discuss some of the complexities around children evolving capabilities. We argue that children's voice is important and is now recognized in policy contexts (e.g. UK Every Child Matters). Moreover, recent global work finds children's well-being low in Global North contexts (such as the UK).

Taking Sen's understanding, the human development of children can be seen as "an expansion of capabilities" or of "positive freedoms". Ballet, Biggeri and Comim develop a theory of children's capabilities in Chapter 2, Section 2.4. Of particular significance to this project is Biggeri's (2007) observation that, while capabilities can be converted into functionings, this process is dependent on the decisions made by parents, guardians and teachers. In educational settings, much of the process is adult controlled – in the present chapter, children are positioned as active agents in the photography and well-being project discussed. Within the school context, the balance of power needs consideration when discussing agency, capability and freedom (Agarwal, Humphries and Robeyns, 2003). Walker and Unterhalter (2007) argue that, within educational settings, we need to consider functionings (i.e. what is achieved) and not just capabilities. In this project, the process of involvement in photography allows a window on both functionings and capabilities. Other theorists (Nussbaum, 2000; Saito, 2003) have noted the centrality of schooling to the CA. Indeed, Terzi (2007) argues that the capability to be educated is inextricably linked to other capabilities as well as future ones.

Well-being is seen as multifaceted, including economic, demographic and environmental domains as well as educational opportunities, crime, health and happiness, etc. Well-being is also described as a phenomenon that is not only experienced by people, but also something that is created by people (Kagan and Kilroy, 2007). In this sense, we are investigating how children experience and create well-being and how their school environment plays a part in it.

We take well-being as an intricate experience that is to be understood in terms of context, as well as the many-sided definitions that are applicable. Robeyns (2003) explains Sen's argument that human diversity is also of central importance. Hypothetically, if all people were the same, the conceptualization of well-being would be the same as well. This is not the case as there are different conversion factors due to environmental or social issues, and thus capabilities and functions should be used in the evaluation of well-being. Within Sen's original formulation, the evaluation of individual well-being is non-utility based. Resources, whilst central, are only a means of enhancing well-being or advantage (Robeyns, 2003). Later work by Sen in Bruni et al. (2009) refers to the evidential role of subjective or utility information.

In terms of Sen's CA, well-being is viewed in terms of human capability reflecting the potential for well-being or well-being freedom in terms of achievable functionings (Sen, 1985; Robeyns, 2003; Clark, 2006).

Walker and Unterhalter (2007) use the scenario of 13-year-old girls who differ in capabilities with regard to mathematics. One girl has good teaching support but fails though lack of interest (preferring drama), while for another educational support is limited – her failure is due to restricted capabilities. However, in both instances, the girls' performance in mathematics is the same, although their capabilities are different.

Education is a fundamental part of children's lives, and the physical experience of being in school takes up a significant part of the time they have during childhood through to adolescence, and is therefore central to well-being (Sen, 1992). The application of Sen's approach with children (as agents) in a school setting sheds light on the complex relationship between utility and resources.

Walker (2005) describes the role that education plays as one that has the *potential* to expand abilities through opportunities. It is the way in which children use these opportunities that is of essence in the CA. In acting on opportunities and using the resources available, children may develop the competencies to achieve a fulfilling adult life. Yet, in contemplating the vast definitions available for well-being, fulfilment is only one part of that, as mentioned by Shah and Peck (2005) who indicate eudaimonic and hedonic well-being as two key types of well-being. Eudaimonic well-being incorporates personal development and fulfilment, whereas hedonic well-being addresses satisfaction and happiness.

In considering *capability inputs* (Robeyns, 2004), resources within education may be seen in simple terms as classrooms, books and computers and so on, yet these are not the key ingredients in being able to function. Resources are used by individuals in a journey towards their functions, and it is *how* resources are utilized Sen considers important (Walker, 2006).

Within the school environment, children are exposed to a range of play, learning and social situations that are aimed at their overall development (this is explained in Chapter 14 and can be extended to urban planning). Indeed, the role of education can be seen as intending to develop the abilities and expand the opportunities available to children, leading to the choices they make in life and adult life, based on their personal values and judgements (Walker, 2005; Clark, 2006).

As children are central to education and the "receivers" of all inputs within educational policies, it is important to gather child-centred perspectives of school experience. Aubrey and Dahl (2006) draw attention to the voice of children and the potential benefits of listening to children in the research context. They found in their study of children under the age of 11 years old that:

> ...children held clear, realiztic and indeed, sophisticated views about a number of aspects of their school environment, their teachers, their peers, their lessons and their behaviour, as well as the importance of their education. (*ibid.*: 34)

Aubrey and Dahl (2006) have utilized focus groups and some participatory methods to ascertain children's opinions – an effective approach that enables their voices to be heard. This focus on children as valid participants with voice is not recognized across disciplines and contexts. Underlining children's abilities in this area, Biggeri's (2007) work with children of different ages in different countries demonstrates that children can think and articulate their values and capabilities. Whilst this partly depends on life experience, all children who participated valued education as the most important capability (see Biggeri, 2007 and Chapter 5 in this book for further analysis with reference to different groups of children, including a control group). Similarly, this research project, through the use of photography, shows that children have rich opinions and draw on a range of experiences in the school setting. This creative and facilitative approach is pro-inclusive with children and increases the level of engagement and accessibility for all children (Wang et al., 1998).

In 2004 the UK Department for Education and Skills (DfES) issued a policy: Every Child Matters: Change for Children (DfES, 2004). The policy was
addressing children's well-being and was emphasizing the need for children's
voices to be heard. Indeed one of the precepts of the policy is the right to
participate. This step forward recognizes the important role that children
can play in building an understanding of what children want and need with
particular reference to the policy documents that are aimed at them. Utilizing children as participants in research (rather than subjects or objects of
research) allows richer understanding and relevance, rather like the voices
of other marginalized groups – women (Walker, 2006), subalterns (Spivak,
1988), the disabled (Ghai, 2003), the indigenous (Tuhiwai Smith, 1999) –
should not be dominated by homogenous white Global North perspectives.

One area where children's voices have been facilitated is through school
councils. School councils are set up in primary and secondary schools to give
children a say in matters that are important to them about the running of
their school (School Councils UK, 2008). Usually school leaders are elected to
be members of the council who voice the concerns of their classmates. Many
advantages are seen through school councils, including the development of
life skills and emotional literacy, improved relationships and more positive
behaviour.

It is recognized that pupils' voices within schools' councils can be tokenistic (Whitty and Wisby, 2007). Yet, there is a role for schools to provide a
more productive environment for their pupils' views to be voiced more seriously. Some of the key benefits outlined by Whitty and Wisby (2007) are that
of empowerment for pupils, improved educational achievement and health
and emotional well-being. However, this trend has been reliant upon verbal
communication rather than other modes of expression. The present study
proposes a rather different articulation of voice through the visual. As we
shall see, the main areas within the school setting for children to experience
well-being are feeling physically and emotionally safe in the school premises,
having positive and effective relationships with peers and (all members of)
staff, having confidence to take on a learning challenge and being able to
express their feelings about given situations. These fundamental aspects of
being at school may well facilitate the achievement of other functionings.

The four elements above are clearly important; however, the relationship
between these elements is poorly theorized. Whilst it is recognized that
some fundamental commodities such as basic needs are required, the wider
implications of opportunities are also investigated to comprehend children's
perceived notions of experiencing a full life (Streeten et al., 1981). There is
consideration into what the children use to achieve functioning, i.e. making
use of the commodities available and what those commodities might be. The
study also considers the aims and goals of children and looks into whether
they have the freedom to achieve these ends (Walker, 2005).

The ability to make rational choices is also considered. Sen (1992) discusses responsible choices, and the factors that can sway this may include social conditioning. For children, there exist a vast range of influences and at a young age, it is debated whether children are mature enough to make independent and responsible choices (Saito, 2003). The fact remains that children do make choices (which, from their perspective, they have reason to value) and are required to do so in their daily lives. These "choices" may seem small and tokenistic at times, but this small-scale reasoning affects their well-being (see Chapter 2, Section 2.2 and 2.3 in this book). Therefore, it seems necessary for schools and policy makers to make use of the views of children to ameliorate the learning environment to one that is "...*suitable for human flourishing...*" (Walker, 2005: 103).

With current UK government initiatives demanding the well-being of primary school children, the questions of *what is well-being?* and *from whose perspective?* naturally arise. This study seeks to question children and explore what they believe is important to achieve a productive and positive engagement within school. As there may be no definitive list of capabilities (as suggested by Sen), an open-ended version of the CA is utilized (Robeyns, 2003; Clark, 2006; Nussbaum, 2000; see also Chapter 3, Section 3.1).

6.2. The context of the study

In February 2007, the United Nations Children's Fund (UNICEF), a children's charity, published a report stating that the UK had the lowest levels of child well-being in the developed world (Boseley, 2007). This report assessed six areas of young people's lives, namely material well-being, health and safety, educational well-being, family and peer relationships, behaviour and risks and young people's own perceptions of well-being.

Readhead (2007) further explains that there is an *epidemic* of depression and self-harm for British teenagers that provoked new research into the pressures of modern living and school experience, including examination stress. Whilst such startling claims and statistics are of great concern, this research celebrates some of the more positive aspects of children's experiences and presents some useful policy implications.

The notion that British schoolchildren are not experiencing well-being or, indeed, *happiness* is not new. Seldon (2006) advocates a new method for teaching happiness within the Personal, Social and Health Education (PSHE) curriculum that has spread across the country. Seldon considers that children need to be able to know themselves, know their goals or aims in life and experience happiness. Such lessons involve emotional literacy and emotional intelligence, relationships and morals, with the intention of producing more balanced young people.

In policy terms, the Government Green paper "Every Child Matters", published in 2003, was quickly followed by the 2004 Children's Act, which in essence is legalization that underpins the *Every Child Matters* document. These policies were aimed at enhancing the well-being and life chances of all children and young people. Well-being is defined under five headings (Harris, 2006):

(1) Be healthy
(2) Be safe
(3) Enjoy and achieve
(4) Make a positive contribution
(5) Achieve economic well-being.

The policy framework implies that schools have a key role alongside partnerships within local communities (Harris, 2006). In this sense, the school environment is well positioned in coordinating partnerships, as well as in providing an arena for putting new legislation into practice.

Following considerable changes over generations within childhood experiences, Lewis (2006) argues that the classroom and playground are now the sole venues for learning. This stems from, for example, children no longer walking to school by themselves (as such naturalistic settings have been removed from the learning experiences of children due to parents' concerns for safety). Even taking the crucial importance of education in forming human capabilities into account (Sen, 1999), the education provided may have advantageous or disadvantageous effects that depend on its quality (Walker and Unterhalter, 2007.) In addition, despite these remarks learning does not occur solely within the school environment (Walker, 2006).

6.2.1. Overview of the English education system

To set this research in context, a brief overview of the state schooling system in England is considered. From the age of 3 to 5, children are at the Foundation Stage of education and learning is broken down into six key areas:

(1) personal, social and emotional;
(2) communication, language and literacy;
(3) mathematical development;
(4) knowledge and understanding of the world;
(5) physical development; and
(6) creative development.

Attendance at school commences with the first term after a child's fifth birthday. This means they will be at the Foundation Stage during their first year of school. As the children move from their first year (Reception) to year one, the

National Curriculum is introduced; learning is then divided into 12 separate subjects (3 core – English, maths and science – and 9 foundation subjects) through Key Stage One (up to 7 years old) and Key Stage Two (up to 11 years old) at the end of the primary school system.

It is in this setting, the primary school, where our research takes place. Whilst Sen (1992) views education as central to well-being, it must also be understood that schools are not the only place where education may take place.

Twelve children aged between eight and ten years participated in the qualitative research outlined below. In exploring children's perceptions of well-being, a range of activities have been employed to allow the children to explore ideas using conversation, drawing and photography. The activities will be described along with the findings.

6.3. Method

Photography was selected both as a rich visual media and for its potential. In brief, Berman (1993) argues that photography is accessible to a broader population than more traditional forms of media and has a universal attraction, as it plays a significant part in our daily lives. As such, it has a certain familiarity and is within the comfort zone of many as opposed to certain more traditional forms of art (Weiser, 2002).[2]

Photo-voice has become increasingly popular as a research tool over the last ten years. By using a simple technique of disposable cameras, participants can discuss their images and share their ideas collaboratively. Wang et al. (1998) recognized its many positive attributes, including its ability to build confidence and successfully communicate ideas visually. Photo-voice also holds great potential for those with learning difficulties or a lack of verbal fluency, leading to a sense of empowerment for those involved (Booth and Booth, 2003). Such skill development can also boost participant's – including children's – confidence in decision making (Walker, 2005).

In the case of this research, Polaroid cameras were used. During a pilot study children were found to appreciate the instant feedback from Polaroid cameras (as opposed to other forms of photography) and were able to use the images taken immediately in discussions and follow-up artwork. This low-tech approach was simple and effective, without any of the difficulties or complications that can occur using more advanced technology or waiting for film to be returned from processing. In another research project (Kellock et al., 2011), mobile phone camera technology was utilized with adults throughout the day to map well-being. Children in our study preferred the instant feedback provided by "old" technology.

The lead author is a trained primary school teacher with several years' teaching experience and a background in counselling psychology and training in visual arts and photography. In combining these skills and experiences, the research project has evolved. The research technique stemmed from previous research using photography as a problem-solving tool for adults as a visual methodology (Kellock and Lawthom, 2005).

During the research project in the primary schools, the children were exposed to a range of activities. For the most part, children worked in groups of three with the researcher within the school. Children were selected by the Head and teachers and identified as possibly benefiting from alternative forms of communication, as they were very quiet children who seldom participated in the classroom. The activities were aimed at assisting the children to communicate their ideas and thoughts, and took place regularly over a period of a few months. Some of these will now be explained.

The first activity is a tour of the school. During this time the children are responsible for a camera and they are asked to take photographs of significant or important parts of the school. This may take the form of anything they see as appropriate for them. These photographs are then arranged on a large piece of paper and annotated as to why the particular photograph was taken. For example, see Figure 6.1. The children took between eight and thirteen pictures each, as they wished.

Further activities included making vocabulary lists to describe different feelings; these were then acted out in freeze-frame photography. Short stories were also created on themes such as bullying or friendship, again using freeze-frame photography as a technique. The children created mind maps to show "OK" and "not OK" feelings in regard to specific situations within school, along with a design for the "perfect teacher".

An additional activity was the identity piece of art. The children collected visual images that they felt represented themselves and what was important to them and arranged them on a large piece of paper. These were done individually and it was up to the children how to execute this activity. The purpose of this was to see what the children believed reflected their identities or personalities and what was significant to them.

Alongside these activities and others, there was ample discussion and reflection on school life. This was done during activities and also in talking circles, passing around a toy to denote whose turn it was to speak.

6.4. Commodities highlighted by children and other resources used to achieve functioning

To consider how children conceptualize certain capabilities to examine how resources and opportunities function, we constructed a table (Table 6.1). This table also indicates when resources are not available or a bottleneck exists in working towards a function, and is illustrated with examples from the research project in the school. The capabilities in the table are also drawn from issues that the children brought up in relation to their own well-being.

Figure 6.1   *"This is where I read"* (free choice reading corner)

Table 6.1 is characterized by four capabilities, resulting from a thematic analysis of children's visual products and discussions about them. The capabilities advanced by the children are the abilities of being literate, being physically active, being a friend and of being creative. These capabilities are then examined in terms of their functions as being either achieved or not achieved, illustrated by children's examples. Opportunities are considered to be freedoms in the sense that they can aid functioning (Sen, 1999).

The barriers have been identified through discussions with the children. Whilst they have the freedom to experience, for example, being a friend, some of the time, there are occasions when this is not possible and this freedom is removed from their control. These remarks imply that the lack of

Table 6.1 Children's perspectives: Comparison of capabilities resulting in functioning or restricted functioning

	Capabilities			
	Being literate	Being physically active	Being a friend	Being creative
Opportunities (services and other resources)	Books, being taught to read, teaching time, reading time	Playground/area, PE equipment, friends, playtime	People, time with people, places to be with people	Creative materials, arts materials, people to share ideas with, time and space for development
Positive functions	Reading – for knowledge and fulfilment, fun, enjoyment, sense of achievement	Physical development, sporting skills, team skills, fun, health	Being a social being, interaction and communication skills, enjoyment, sharing, respect, making choices	Being a creative person, developing critical thinking, exploring self-creatively, self-esteem, enjoyment
Potential barriers	Reading level too hard, learning difficulties/disabilities, distractions in classroom, no reading time, no books, no desire to read, a shouting teacher	No playtime, no friends, no confidence to participate, no equipment, loss of playtime (punishment for misbehaviour), poor weather	No time to socialize, nowhere to go, not sufficient social skills, lack of self-confidence	No time for creativity or play, insufficient resources, lack of encouragement
Negative functions	Not being able to progress as a reader, not being fulfilled, not feeling good about self	Not being physically active/fit, not socializing with peers, not developing team skills, lack of self-esteem	Not having friends, not developing social skills, negative self-image	Being "squashed", not developing creatively, being bored

freedom to, for example, be literate, hinders children's learning and progress whilst, at the same time, causes a whole range of difficulties such as having a negative self-image. Therefore there is a structural, learning hindrance along with a psychological impact on the children.

The capabilities considered in Table 6.1 will be discussed in turn and illustrated with examples that the children have provided during the course of the research programme.

6.4.1. Being literate

The first area to be explored is that of "being literate". Being literate is a valuable capability and functioning that is affected by the capability set and achieved functionings of parents, teachers, etc. (Biggeri, 2007). The nature of resources and functions that are evident in the classrooms of English schools were investigated in this research programme. The first example here is illustrated by a child's photograph of the free choice reading area in the classroom. This image was taken by one of the children during the tour of the school and is, therefore, identified as an important place to the child; the annotation simply reads *"This is where I read"*. She enjoys reading and considers reading an important aspect of school life. Half of the children chose this area as one to take an image of, either in their own classroom or in the school library. The children said it was important to them to have quiet reading time, which is a pleasurable activity that they look forward to. The children also stated that they would appreciate more time doing this activity. The research questioned children's thoughts on what was important to them about their school experience, rather than eliciting preferences.

One of the positive aspects of this activity is that the children are able to develop their reading skills, a skill that will be depended upon through adult life. Furthermore, through selecting their own reading material, they are developing skills to make appropriate choices for their own satisfaction and possibly to challenge themselves.

Whilst, on the whole, the children enjoy this time and it is of educational benefit, there are some reasons why they can't do the activity more often. Within the table these are described under the heading "potential barriers", which includes lack of reading time due to issues of timetabling pressures. However, there are several other factors that make this time difficult for some of the children during follow-up discussions stimulated by the photographs.

The children had little patience for disruptive children who call out and are noisy, stating that, '... *they only do it for attention*', '... *they take up all the teacher's time*' and '... *are so noisy we can't concentrate*'. A further disruption to their quiet reading time was teachers shouting. This also upset the children as it is an unpleasant experience and puts them off doing their work or reading, even if the teacher wasn't aiming the shouting at them in particular.

In addition, some of the children disliked engaging in reading activities because it was described as being too hard. One of the older girls is achieving at an extremely high level in all subjects and is on the gifted and talented register, yet feels pressurized to work harder and finds it difficult to do her work in time. She explained that this pressure makes her angry. When asking what she feels like when she's completed the work, she doesn't feel a sense of accomplishment or a pride in the outcome, but a sense of relief that it's over and she can then do something else.

These blocks to children attempting to achieve their goal of quiet reading time are out of their control and have frustrating consequences. However, blocks do not occur continuously or all of the time. It is important to consider them and create potential ways of improving these experiences for the children.

6.4.2. Being physically active

Most of the children in the programme selected images of the playground, football area and netball posts as important places for them within the school grounds, as illustrated by the image below (Figure 6.2). The playground area is used during lunchtimes, playtimes and during physical education (PE) sessions. Lunchtime and playtime were identified by the children as important parts of the school day, when they are able to choose various play activities and decide how they spend their time independently. There are, of course, still rules to follow in the playground setting, yet from the children's point of view, there is pleasure in having this free time and freedom of choice.

The benefits of having time outside are clearly articulated by the children here, and discussed in the literature (Garrick, 2004). The children are able to practise a range of skills, such as physical development skills and socializing skills. It is a time when they have the opportunity to develop cooperative and sharing skills, friendship attributes and appreciate moral values. The freedom of choice during this time is, of course, interesting from the perspective of Sen's CA and is one of the few times during the school day that the children appear to experience this.

Yet, whilst this time is precious to the children there are circumstances when outdoor activities are not possible for several reasons. The UK weather certainly hinders outside playtime and PE at schools, and wet playtime (indoor playtime in the children's classrooms) is an experience not enjoyed by many. In Iceland and other Nordic countries there is more emphasis on the outdoor curriculum despite harsh weather. A further barrier to outside activity is on occasions where loss of playtime is allocated due to misbehaviour during class time. This is not a popular punishment with the children. And, again, there are also timetabling restraints in school that restrict time allocated to physical activities.

6.4.3. Being a friend

The notion of friendship or being a friend was described as a critical part of school life by most of the children involved in the study. Having time to

Figure 6.2 "*I took a picture of the football area because I like football*" (football play area)

be with friends and communicate with them is also crucial to social skills development. The next image (Figure 6.3) shows a place in the playground where one of the children likes to hang out with her friends during break times: "*This is where we go to talk in the playground*". This reflects two key sentiments that the child has selected, being with friends and having a space to talk with them. It seems apparent that despite a school being a large, shared space, the child has found a place in the playground to call her own along with her group of friends.

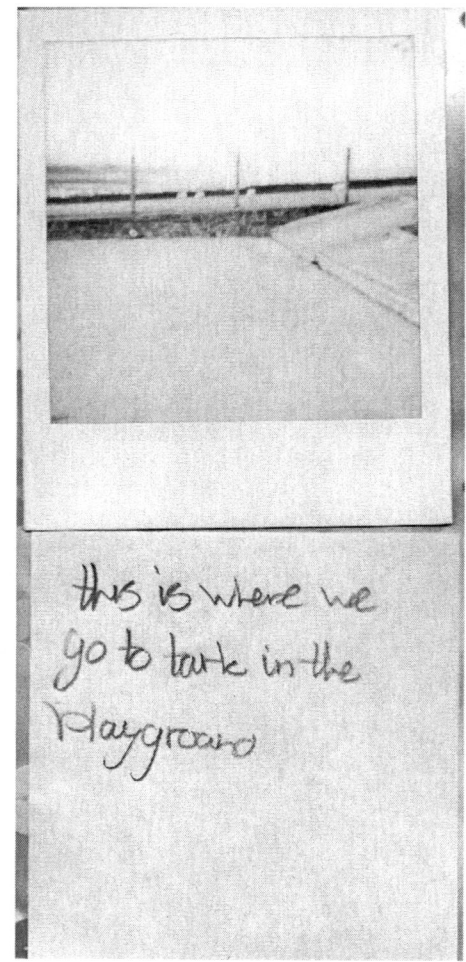

Figure 6.3   *"This is where we go to talk in the playground"* (quiet part of the playground)

Whilst time for friendship could be considered as something that could be experienced outside of school, it is an opportunity within school for such developments and social interaction to take place for many children. A lack of social skills may hinder this process for some, but it is an ideal location for skills to be practised. The explicit relationship between resources and capabilities is demonstrated here very clearly – photo-voice allows this kind of reflection to emerge.

Again, there is an element of choice here for the children concerning who they spend time with. During class time, children are often required to work in groups and rarely have the choice of who they work with. The opportunity of choosing who to spend time with is a rare occurrence. However, teachers may argue that allowing children to choose their partners for work-related tasks often results in limited output from the children. Below is a snippet of conversation taken from one of the sessions whilst the children made their charts to show different feelings at different times of the day:

Facilitator: *Are there any lessons where you pick who you work with?*
Child 1: *In art you get to ... er ... choose yer partner.*
Child 2: *Yeah in art..., but sometimes you don't get a partner if you're just sketching* [i.e. you are alone].

It seems that art is the only subject where children are allowed to make a choice concerning who they work with during class time. This also could be seen as a message to the children that art isn't a very important subject.

A place to be friends is important, and having sufficient time to spend with friends transpired to be of significance to the children involved in the study. The images shown in Figures 6.3–6.8 reflect some of the spaces that the children consider to be important to them.

6.4.4. Being creative

During the course of the research programme in school, almost all of the children expressed a desire to have more time to "play" and more creativity time. That is not to say that they would do less work, but that the work could involve more creative and practical elements.

In discussing subjects they particularly enjoyed participating in and talked about enthusiastically, activity seemed to be a key factor. Whether the subject was a core or foundation subject, the ability to do something within a lesson provided the children with much greater stimulation. For example, some children enjoyed taking part in practical experiments for science lessons, or being creative in art by painting or creating a piece of art. PE was also popular with most of the children.

Older children in the study reflected back on their time during Reception (first class) at school and recalled their enjoyment of the play activities provided. The home corner, sand and water trays were remembered fondly along with sadness that there was no longer any time in the school day to practise this kind of play.

Such play and creativity are imperative for developing broader skills, including sharing, communicating, exploring self in artistic activities, gross and fine motor skills and role play. Nussbaum (2000) notes that play is an essential capability that children need both to function and develop mature capabilities. However, the demands of the curriculum in the UK are such

Figure 6.4 *"I like it here because we get to use different instruments"* (musical instrument storage area in hall)

that there is little time to be given to this kind of development beyond the Foundation Stage. The imposition of a National Curriculum and testing has standardized learning, linking it to concrete outcomes, e.g. standard aptitude tests. This limits time available for creative play for primary school children, unlike younger children in the UK or those following approaches such as Montessori (Mooney, 2000) or Reggio Emilia (Brunton and Thornton, 2007)

Whilst children are demonstrating knowledge of their capabilities and, in some instances, their functioning, they do not necessarily experience the freedom to achieve or function as they desire. The research question here took place in school where preferences were less evident – we see children as competent agents who can express and reflect upon what they need for functioning (no child in this present study expressed a desire not to read or learn). Sen states that it is not what people have that is important, but what they do with their resources that is of essence (Robeyns, 2003;

Figure 6.5 *"I like this other bit of Class 1 because we got to play in the water"* (water play area in Reception)

Sharma, 2005). However, in certain circumstances, the freedoms to achieve and experience a fulfilling life are removed from children, by adults or the education system.

There is an interesting debate in the literature around the listing of essential capabilities (Nussbaum, 2000; Biggeri, 2007) or open-endedness around this. The findings above do not constitute an exhaustive list, nor are they meant to be. However, lists that do exist seem to share overlapping themes, for example knowledge and education, play, social relations and physical and mental health (Nussbaum, 2003; Robeyns, 2003; Biggeri, 2007).[3] These can be mapped onto our findings.

Figure 6.6   *"I love this area because it's brill!!!"* (the home corner in Reception)

6.5. Further findings

Amongst the issues already raised, there are other fundamental points children raised that connect with their well-being and are explored briefly below. These include the following, in order of significance:

- having support;
- having sufficient nourishment;
- having adequate resources;
- having their own space;
- having choice; and
- family and friends.

6.5.1. Having support

During discussions around well-being and what helps children be "OK" in the classroom, many of the children indicated that they required the support of an adult or, in some cases, their friends. This is not to say that the children are dependent workers or rely on help, but they needed to know that someone was there to support them in their work or with personal issues.

6.5.2. Having sufficient nourishment

Some of the children acknowledged that without sufficient food and water they would not be able to function adequately within school. One of the children said that she couldn't learn properly if she was hungry and needed her breakfast to help her wake up. However, some of the children said that *"other"* children would need nourishment to participate in school and didn't associate this with themselves.

6.5.3. Having adequate resources

When asked what they needed to participate successfully within school, the children immediately listed resources that they considered imperative to their learning, such as, a teacher, books, computer and pencils. They also acknowledged that if there were too many children in the class, this made it difficult for their teacher to talk to everyone and spend sufficient time with all of the children.

6.5.4. Having their own space

This links back to a previous image (Figure 6.3), in that the children have stated that they feel that having somewhere to call their own within the school was important to them. The image in Figure 6.7 below shows a picture called *"Me and my friends go under the coats"*. One of the children selected this as it is a part of the classroom where he plays with his friends and hides, in a den. While this activity is not really allowed, this is an important place for this child. Similarly, the image reproduced in Figure 6.8 shows a workspace of one of the children. The workspace is a given space from a teacher, yet there is a sense of ownership for the child (asserting the desire for comfort in one's own space, which may enable functionings).

6.5.5. Having choice

It is apparent from the selection of photographs taken by children, and through discussions with them, that having choice is important to them, although they have not verbalized this. There are several examples of activities that children consider important to them, and these all have an element of choice in them; they include playtime and reading time. Vaughan (2007) conceptualizes this as agency freedom – the ability to choose aspects valued by the individual (not necessarily by the school).

6.5.6. Family and friends

This last point has also been mentioned previously, in that friends have been identified as important to the children. However, when taking part in activities surrounding their identities, family became of central importance to most of the children. The family was recognized as a further source of support to some of the children, providing a sense of belonging and being with the family members.

It is noteworthy that the children participating were able to visualize and verbalize much richness – which seem linked to well-being (even if this is not a concept they would articulate).

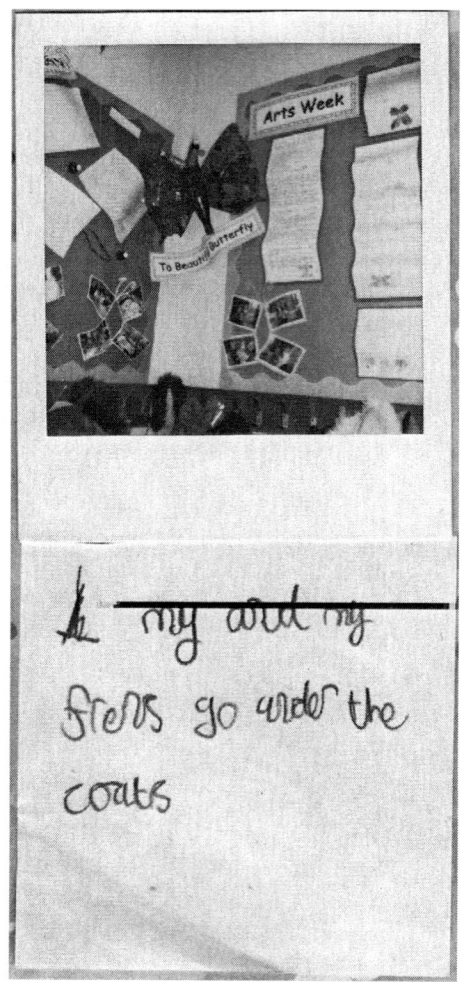

Figure 6.7   "Me and my friends go under the coats" (coat hooks in a classroom)

6.6. Conclusions

Whilst there is pressure on teachers and schools to get through an enormous curriculum at primary school, there seems to be a call from the children in the present study, saying that we need more time to play, more time to be with our peers and less testing. Children are being forced to grow up in primary schools very quickly and be independent workers, but it seems that some of them aren't ready for this. As stated previously, it is the older

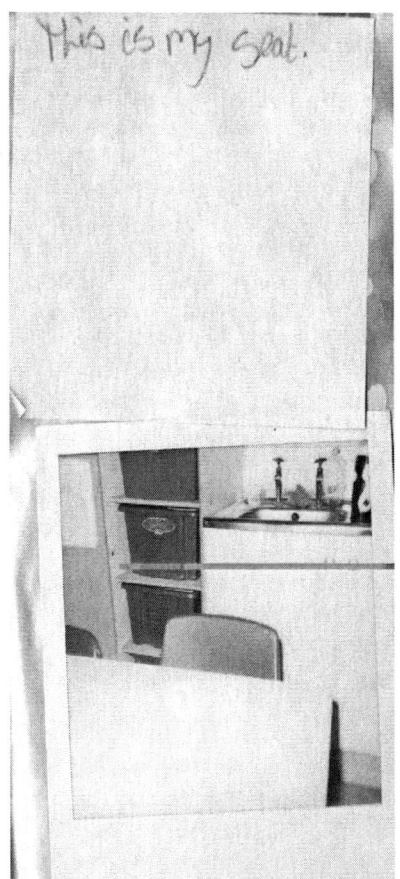

Figure 6.8 "*This is my seat*" (child's seat in a classroom)

children in particular that are asking for more time for the creative and physical activities.

The photo-voice technique has promoted dialogue between the children and the researcher that has brought about communication and understanding about well-being in the primary school from a child's perspective. The photographs enabled discussions to take place, and it was the children that took ownership of this process.

The children involved in this study articulated notions of well-being in terms of activities participated in, where this occurs and who it occurs with, along with an awareness of whether such activities are pleasurable, stimulating or meaningful. In addition, they recognize how well-being is influenced by issues outside of their control and they are able to express desires for improving given situations.

In addition to photographs and their narration verbally or with written annotation, the children created other pieces of art or visual text. This process also allowed time for contemplation and further deliberation of ideas or concepts. There appeared to be a double-barrelled outcome: the photography enabled discussions around well-being and the practical nature of taking part in the photography, moreover, these discussions gave a sense of well-being to the participants involved.

Schooling can be seen as a part of education and not wholly responsible for education; however, children are at school for a large part of their childhood and it is a critical time for their development as human beings. Sen (1999) has reinforced the importance of schooling to nurture future capabilities (see also Saito, 2003). We must consider carefully how education is delivered in the school setting and what is actually important (i.e. capabilities and functionings). Is it more important to acquire knowledge and skills in preparation for future careers, or to develop personal skills such as socializing, sharing and participating that will be of benefit to children as adults? A balance is required, of course, but if we are concerned with how people use the resources they have to function in everyday life, then perhaps there needs to be more focus in our schools towards developing creative and *person* skills.

The CA emphasizes the importance of capabilities and functionings. As Unterhalter and Walker (2007) note, this is not a homogenous notion of flourishing but a range of possibilities and choices. The present study indicates the competencies and recognition of lacking opportunities of young children (8–10). In this small-scale study they were able to articulate their concept of agency freedoms (Vaughan, 2007) and its impact on their well-being. This research reinforces the finding of previous chapters and demonstrates that children can, through appropriate methods, actively participate to conceptualize their valued capabilities and evaluate services, resources and barriers to their well-being on matters relating to school and their lives generally.

Notes

1. A PhD funded studentship was awarded to explore the role of visual methodology in exploring well-being in primary school settings. Participative techniques are being utilized in distinct contexts (UK and New Zealand) to afford greater understanding of pupil voice (Aubrey and Dahl, 2006).
2. Images portray a depth of information and allow participants to "speak" in ways perhaps not otherwise possible, delivering agency to those less often heard in the research setting, such as children (Bolton et al., 2001; Reavey and Johnson, 2008). Given the age group of participants in this study and the difficulty in articulating

feelings linguistically, a qualitative approach called photo-voice has been adopted to facilitate children's communication.
3. See also Alkire (2002), Clark (2002) and Saith (2007) for comparison of lists of capabilities, rights and needs.

References

Agarwal, B., Humphries, J. and Robeyns, I. (2003), "Exploring the Challenges of Amartya Sen's Work and Ideas: An Introduction", *Feminist Economics*, 9(2): 3–12.

Alkire, S. (2002), *Valuing Freedoms. Sen's Capability Approach and Poverty Reduction*, OUP, New York.

Aubrey, C. and Dahl, S. (2006), "Children's Voices: The Views of Vulnerable Children on Their Service Providers and the Relevance of Services They Receive", *British Journal of Social Work*, 26: 21–39.

Berman, L. (1993), *Beyond the Smile: The Therapeutic Use of the Photograph*, London: Routledge.

Biggeri, M. (2007), "Children's Valued Capabilities", in M. Walker and E. Unterhalter (eds), *Amartyr Sen's Capability Approach and Social Justice in Education*, New York: Palgrave Macmillan, pp. 192–214.

Bolton, A., Pole, C. and Mizen, P. (2001), "Picture This: Researching Child Workers", *Sociology*, 35: 501–518.

Booth, T. and Booth, W. (2003), "In the Frame: Photovoice and Mothers with Learning Difficulties", *Disability and Society*, 18(4): 431–442.

Boseley, S. (2007), "British Children: Poorer, at Greater Risk and More Insecure", www.society.guardian.co.uk, accessed 26 February 2007.

Bruni, L., Comim, F. and Pugno, M. (2009), *Capabilities and Happiness*, OUP, Oxford.

Brunton, P. and Thornton, L. (2007), *Bringing the Reggio Approach to Your Early Years Practice*, London: Routledge.

Clark, D.A. (2002), *Visions of Development: A Study of Human Values*, Edward Elgar, Cheltenham.

Clark, D.A. (2006), "Capability Approach", in D.A. Clarke (ed.), *The Elgar Companion to Development Studies*, Edward Elgar, Cheltenham, pp. 32–45.

Department for Education and Skills (DfES) (2004), *Every Child Matters: Change for Children* DfES/1081/2004, DfES Publications, Nottingham.

Garrick, R. (2004), *Playing Outdoors in the Early Years*, Continuum International Publishing Group Ltd, London.

Ghai, A. (2003), *(Dis) Embodied Form: Issues of Disabled Women*, Har Anand Publications Pvt Ltd, Delhi.

Harris, B. (2006), "Overview of Every Child Matters (2003) and the Children Act (2004)", *Pastoral Care*, June: 5–6.

Kagan, C. and Kilroy, A. (2007), "Psychology in the Community", in J. Haworth and G. Hart (eds), *Well-being: Individual, Community and Social Perspectives*, London, Palgrave Macmillan, pp. 93–109.

Kellock, A. and Lawthom, R. (2005), Photography and Problem-solving: A Participatory Approach, unpublished.

Kellock, A., Lawthom, R., Duggan, K., Mountian, I., Haworth, J.T., Kagan, C.M., Brown, D.P., Griffiths, J., Hawkins, J., Worley, C., Purcell, C., Siddiquee, A. et al. (2011) "Researching Real Life using Experience Sampling Method", in S. N. Hesser-Biber and P. Levy (eds), *The Handbook of Emergent Technologies in Social Research*, OUP, Oxford.

Lewis, J. (2006), "The School's Role in Encouraging Behaviour for Learning Outside the Classroom that Supports Learning within. A Response to the 'Every Child Matters' and Extended Schools Initiatives", *Support for Learning*, 21(4): 175–181.

Mooney, C.G. (2000), *Theories of Childhood: An Introduction to Dewey, Montessori, Erikson, Piaget and Vygotsky*, Redleaf Press, Minneapolis.

Nussbaum, M.C. (2000), *Women and Human Development: The Capabilities Approach*, CUP, Cambridge.

Nussbaum, M.C. (2003), "Capabilities as Fundamental Entitlements: Sen and Social Justice", *Feminist Economics*, 9(2–3): 33–59.

Readhead, P. (2007), "British Children Come Bottom of the EU Wellbeing League Table" www.esrc.ac.uk, accessed 26 February 2007.

Reavey, P. and Johnson, K. (2008), "Visual Approaches: Using and Interpreting Images", in C. Willig and W. Stainton-Rogers (eds), *The Sage Handbook of Qualitative Research in Pyschology*, Sage Publications Ltd, London, pp. 296–314.

Robeyns, I. (2003), "Sen's Capability Approach and Gender Inequality: Selecting Relevant Capabilities", *Feminist Economics*, 9(2): 62–91.

Robeyns, I. (2004), "Justice as fairness and the capability approach". Paper presented at the Fourth International Conference on the Capability Approach, University of Pavia, Italy, 5–7 September.

Saith, R. (2007), "Capabilities: The Concept and Its Implementation", in F. Stewart, R. Saith and B. Harriss-White (eds), *Defining Poverty in Developing Countries*, Palgrave Macmillan, Basingstoke, pp. 55–74.

Saito, M. (2003), "Amartya Sen's Capability Approach to Education: A Critical Exploration", *Journal of Philosophy of Education*, 37: 17–34.

School Councils UK (2008), "Benefits of School Councils", www.schoolcouncils.org, accessed 06 June 2008.

Seldon, A. (2006), "Lessons in Life: Why I'm Teaching Happiness", *Education and Health*, 24(2): 19–20.

Sen, A.K. (1985), "Well-being, Agency and Freedom", *The Journal of Philosophy*, LXXXII: 4: 179–221.

Sen, A.K. (1992), *Inequality Re-examined*, OUP, Oxford.

Sen, A.K. (1999), *Development as Freedom*, OUP, Oxford.

Shah, H. and Peck, J. (2005), *Well-being and the Environment: Achieving One Planet Living and Quality of Life*, New Economics Foundation, London.

Sharma, M. (2005), "Reifying Capability Theory in Disability and Rehabilitation Research", *Asia Pacific Disability Rehabilitation Journal*, 16(2): 125–135.

Spivak, G.C. (1988) "Can the Subaltern Speak?", in C. Nelson and L. Grossbery (eds), *Marxism and the Interpretation of Culture*, University of Illinois Press, Urbana, pp. 271–313.

Streeten, P.P, Burki, S.J., Haq, M.U., Hicks, N. and Stewart, F. (1981), *First Things First, Meeting Basic Human Needs in Developing Countries*, OUP, New York.

Terzi, L. (2007), "The Capability to Be Educated", in M. Walker and E. Unterhalter (eds), *Amartyr Sen's Capability Approach and Social Justice in Education*, Palgrave Macmillan, New York, pp. 25–44.

Tuhiwai Smith, L. (1999), *Decolonizing Methodologies: Research and Indigenous Peoples*, Zen Books Ltd, New York.

Unterhalter, E. and Walker, M. (2007), "Taking the Capability Approach Forward in Education", in M. Walker and E. Unterhalter (eds), *Amartyr Sen's Capability Approach and Social Justice in Education*, Palgrave Macmillan, New York, pp. 237–254.

Vaughan, R. (2007), "Measuring Capabilities: An Example from Girls' Schooling", in M. Walker and E. Unterhalter (eds), *Amartyr Sen's Capability Approach and Social Justice in Education*, Palgrave Macmillan, New York, pp. 109–130.

Walker, M. (2005), "Amartya Sen's Capability Approach and Education", *Educational Action Research*, 13(1): 103–110.

Walker, M. (2006), "Towards A Capability-based Theory of Social Justice for Education and Policy-making", *Journal of Education Policy*, 21(2): 163–185.

Walker, M. and Unterhalter, E. (2007), "The Capability Approach: Its Potential for Work in Education", in M. Walker and E. Unterhalter (eds), *Amartya Sen's Capability Approach and Social Justice in Education*, Palgrave Macmillan, New York, pp. 1–18.

Wang, C., Wu, K., Zhan, W. and Carovano, K. (1998), "Photovoice as a Participatory Health Promotion Strategy", *Health Promotion International*, 13(1): 75–86.

Weiser, J. (2002), "PhotoTherapy Techniques: Exploring the Secrets of Personal Snapshots and Family Albums", *Child and Family*, Spring/Summer, pp. 16–25.

Whitty, G. and Wisby, E. (2007), "Whose Voice? An Exploration of the Current Policy Interest in Pupil Involvement in School Decision-making", *International Studies in Sociology of Education*, 17(3): 303–319.

7
Child Agency and Identity: The Case of Peruvian Children in a Transitional Situation

Marisa Horna Padrón and Jérôme Ballet

Levison (2000: 125) asserts that *"Children are not considered to have human agency in that they are not viewed as contributing to the accomplishment of a purpose or results"*. She claims, however, that this point of view is erroneous and that children really are endowed with a capacity for agency, including in situations where they seemingly appear like mere victims (e.g. working children). Along these lines, this chapter examines the capacity for agency of children in a transitional situation on the streets of Peru. In particular, it explores one of the most relevant ingredients of the evolving capability concept outlined in Chapter 2 (Sections 2.2–2.5). In particular, it investigates the complexity of relationships between children and with adults that influences their agency and capacity for actions.

The field research identifies children and adolescents who perform various activities on the streets or in the midst of road traffic (e.g. playing, jigsawing, doing acrobatics, working, etc.). The concept of a *transitional situation* is used for children who may be considered to be simultaneously on the brink of ending up on the streets or remaining members of their families. The term *situation* emphasizes the fact that social and personal processes are dynamic insofar as critical processes involve risks, but also opportunities. The term *transitional* underlines the fluctuation of the children's experience, as well as the processes of change and emotional stresses in the development of affective bonds. The purpose here is to enhance the *transitional* aspect in which subjectivities are formed in the individual and social context of the persons considered in this study. In this sense, none of the children will be referred to according to their current situation (e.g. *street, abused, abandoned* or *displaced*, or any other term connoting victimization).

However, there is a strong tendency to regard children and adolescents as mere victims in a context where poverty affects them particularly. Sixty-six per cent of Peruvian children are poor, thirty per cent of them living in extreme poverty (UNICEF, 2006),[1] a situation some authors refer to as the *"poverty syndrome"* (e.g. Pimentel, 1996). A quarter of all under-five children suffer from chronic malnutrition. This figure is higher in Huancavelica (one of the poorest provinces), where one child out of two suffers from this condition. One child in four between the ages of 6 and 11 has to work, against one child in three between the ages of 12 and 17. The state does very little to make sure that Peruvian families have access to protein-, iron- and micronutrient-rich food generally (Barrón and Villar, 2007).

Even in such a seemingly terrible context, children prove to be in a position to develop strategies as agents and to shape their identity. Indeed, children and adolescents in a *transitional situation* use a wide range of capabilities, in spite of their material limitations. For example, social components include peers as well as close relations among children on the streets. Personal components of these resources are the body (visual discrimination combined with gross motor coordination) and cognitive skills (like coping and mathematical skills) fostered by the street situation.

Identity formation is a process springing from these capabilities, *affective* and *social bonds*.[2] Such a phenomenon involves more than socialization and mental health insofar as it entails the interplay among different functionings giving rise to other capabilities. The present study is based on the assumption that the childhood and youth cycles are important stages in which synergic processes are generated in terms of emotional development and identity structuring.

This chapter is organized as follows: Section 7.1 presents the theoretical background, relating child agency to identity; Section 7.2 describes the context and methodology of the study under consideration; Section 7.3 provides results and interpretation on child identity structuring; and finally, Section 7.4 puts forward remarks concerning emotional capabilities within the framework of identity development.

7.1. Theoretical framework: agency, capabilities and identity

Recognizing children as having the status of agents leads us to wonder about their capacities for action as agents. Giddens (1987: 3) views *agency* as *"the players' own capacity for action"*, i.e. the players' capacity to act and to project themselves into their action. Giddens' definition takes us back to Amartya Sen's positions on the *"real freedoms" of individuals"*. Sen thus makes a distinction between *well-being freedom* and *agency freedom* (Sen, 1999). The latter would permit the apprehension of individuals according to their aptitude for conceiving goals, commitments and/or values, i.e. their capacity to exercise their free will: "the ability of people to help themselves and also to influence the world" (Sen, 1999: 18). However, Sen mainly focuses on the general aims to which individuals lend importance or *"have reason to value"*. In doing so, he does not look much into the processes at play in the formation of such values and commitments, and so on what really is at the root of the person's capacity for action. This aspect of the approach proposed by Sen is particularly obvious as far as the question of identity is concerned. Identity is first and foremost a question of choice (Sen, 2004).

Of course, Sen acknowledges the role of constraints in the individual's choice capacity. "More generally, whether we are considering our identities as we ourselves see them, or as others see us, we chose within particular constrains. But it is not in the least a surprising fact – it is rather just the way choices are faced in any situation. Choices of all kinds are always made within particular constrains, and this is perhaps the most elementary aspect of any choice" (Sen, 2004: 15). On the other hand, Sen does recognize the importance of relations among individuals through identity. For instance, he asserts that "our focus on particular identities can enrich our bonds and make us do many things for each other and can help to take us beyond our self-centred lives" (Sen, 2006: 2). Relations are not perceived essentially as the foundations of identity though. Instead, they are regarded either as constraints in terms of identity choice or as life-enriching elements. Thus, even when he argues that the selected identity is not chosen on the basis of an "unencumbered" position, and that "choice does not require jumping out of nowhere into somewhere, but [it] can lead to a move from one place to another" (Sen, 2004: 18), Sen's view remains focused on a static perception of choice. This means that several identities may be chosen within a given context. Such an interpretation is closely akin to that of Markus and Nurius (1986), who consider that individuals are embedded in modern and open societies, having opportunity to choose one among a large set of identities, even though choice is not always easy and the loss of social markers may account for identity crises (Dubar, 2000).

Considering identity in a more dynamic perspective, we mean to highlight the role of biography (the past) and social context in the range of identity choices. It is not our intention to deny, though, that this variety of choice remains open-ended insofar as all individuals, including children, develop their own capacity for action with regard to their identity. The focal point we wish to underline is the fact that identity develops within the framework of both a multiple and restricted possibility trajectory. Put differently, if identity is a matter of choice, it never is a totally open choice. Furthermore, the individual's dependence upon the past is more or less strong according to the identity in which they have already cloaked themselves. This could explain the individual's broad adoption of a particular identity (Dubet, 2002). Following Sen, we shall first assume that identity is multiple and a subject of choice. We then propose a more dynamic view of identity, considering it through the idea of identity trajectory, which implies the notion of path dependency. This is related to the notion of evolving capabilities developed in Chapter 3.

In the first place, let us define an *identity choice space* as a set of feasible identities in a given social context. The definition of *identity choice space* may be interpreted in several ways. Firstly, the choice of an identity is associated with choice capacity through positive or negative emotional experiences (Ballet and Radja, 2005). Following Nussbaum (2000), we then consider that emotional capability plays a crucial role in terms of shaping identity and identity choice capacity. As Livet (2004: 52) notes: "The choice activity implies in itself a functioning scheme, which allows us to appreciate the feasible options offered, as well as their diversity."

Secondly, we do not deny that social context predetermines possible identities before the persons may be in a position to choose one among several identities. Individuals are embedded in a more or less strong social context where they are able to use strategies with a view to developing some particular identity rather than another. Here, the identity issue appears like a subtle game of identity development strategies allowing an individual to identify with a group while conforming to another. Identity thus refers to both strategies of conformity and distinction. This induces us to relate the issue of identity changes to the process of conformity and distinction across time. This dimension of identity takes us back to the notion of *"identity trajectory"* (Ballet and Radja, 2005).

The concept of *identity trajectory* refers to a transformation function of the identity space choice across time. As Livet (2004: 51) underlines: "The identity of an individual human being is not simply determined by what he is, but also by his capacity to transform himself." An identity trajectory is a transformation, or even sometimes a non-transformation, of identity across time. This idea is based on the assumption that identity is not unchanging. Of course, in some cases, the identity trajectory is limited or follows an invariant linear process, but this does not mean that it is unchanging.

A distinction can be established between two elements in the identity trajectory. Firstly, for an invariant given context, identity choices may change from one period to another. Secondly, a same identity choice is faced with changing contexts. The identity choice space over a given period of time is the combination of both elements. The identity trajectory then appears like a reflection of identity choices across time.

Following this pattern of identity choice capacity under path dependency constraint, we intend to examine, in the following sections, the identity construction of children in a transitional situation in Peru. We thus acknowledge that in situations that have contributed strongly to shaping their identity, these children remain in a position to develop their own identity strategy.

The streets become a pole of attraction as soon as they are free to be walked (see also Chapter 5 on pull and push factors). Children quickly learn to walk without getting lost, explore different places and realize how wide the opportunities are on the street. They learn from other children how to survive, how to make a day-to-day living and have a sense of freedom (by means of mobility) and choice (helping themselves to survive). They typically gain much experience, which empowers them to take care of themselves, learning how to survive until these experiences become part of their representations. This often contrasts sharply with what they left behind when they were sharing time with their families and at school.

7.2. Study context and methodology

7.2.1. The socio-cultural context

The fact that Peru is a multicultural, multi-ethnic and multilingual country makes the emergence of a unified national identity difficult and impedes the establishment of a National Project (Horna, 2005). Peru is a patriarchal, sexist and racist society, whose most excluded citizens have little political and economic power. This exclusion is socio-economic, cultural and political by nature, partly emanating from the government's colonial legacy (Quijano, 2005).

According to the latest UNICEF/INEI (2004) survey, 41% of people in Peru regard violence as an appropriate way to raise children. This adult perception, as Giddens (1999) points out, makes the household a most dangerous place for children. The child's primary socialization spaces – family, school and community – are in deep social crisis, which undermines social bonds between parents (or other adults) and children. Between 2500 and 3500 children and adolescents in Peru do not have a stable home. One of the main reasons why children run away from home is domestic violence (Jaramillo García, 2005): 41% of all parents punish their children through violence, thus repeating the way most of them (between 70% and 80%) were abused as children (Barrón and Villar, 2007).

Analysing the situation from a gender viewpoint reveals that the poorest girls and young women experience widespread discrimination. They are sexually abused (twice as much as boys), are malnourished and their work – which is typically domestic – is not valued. Two mothers out of six are teenagers. Adding this figure to the number of women who are heads of households (32%) brings to light the reproduction of "*female-based poverty families*" (Anderson, 2000) and the *vicious circle* of exclusion. Though adolescents are the subject of sex education programmes, the proportion of teenage mothers has nonetheless increased continually year after year (Horna, 2005).[3]

7.2.2. The methodological assumption

This study refers to new paradigms of knowledge that integrate the subjectivity and the rationality rooted in Aristotelian philosophy. As Albertina Mitjáns Martinez (from the University of Brasilia) underlines: "Capacities, reflections, values, aspirations, necessities, plans, projects, motivations, interests, self esteem, activities and intersubjective relations as many other psychological elements articulate themselves in configurations of strong emotional value, constituting the individual subjectivity" (*ibid.*, 2001: 241).

In a study on child labour and subjectivity, Mitjáns Martinez (2001) claims that these issues call for the definition and legitimization of several problems as research fields and part of theoretical debate. She further observes that the main tendency of scientific knowledge production is quantitative and descriptive. The fact that this tendency has, to a great extent, been prevalent in psychology explains why the socio-psychological research approach to working children favours the macro perspective. This makes it difficult to apprehend the concrete subject – child or youth – that is frequently described in a generic way which fails to bring out the complexity and diversity of the phenomenon.

In this perspective, Fernando González Rey (1999: 108) defines subject, subjectivity and intersubjectivity as "the organization of the sense and meaning that appear and organize in different forms and in different levels in the subject and it's personality, as in the different social spaces within he behaves". Subjectivity is a social construction and is a concept always related to society. It thus takes on a meaning and a sense, both in terms of individual and collective development, adding historical and biographical complexity to the concept of identity.

From this perspective, the identity of an agent is how freedom, choice and opportunities are constituted in his/her subjectivity, and also how the social context is constituted in meaningful organizers in the social space and in the personality. Socio-historical roots and our original culture's perspective add meaningful elements to the identity constitution.

The identity of an agent consists of two parts: the first relates to internal, nuclear, biographic, static representations (family and society adjudications), while the second relates to the intersubjective, narrative, dynamic part. This is the space where capabilities evolve from their static representation to the more dynamic, in which the agent stops being passive and becomes proactive regarding its own development (as discussed in Chapter 2, Sections 2.2–2.5). In this process, the identity trajectory changes from its passive, social external adjudicative form to one with more autonomy and internal references. This means a change in the self-definition, which is the basic element of an identity structure different from the former in which the basis was entirely or almost completely founded by family and social adjudications.

An objective derived from this study is to make visible the resources used by children and adolescents in a transitional situation in the subjective and intersubjective dimension space. These are the emotional capabilities used to explore and [inquire?] within their affective and social bonds in their social space. The ongoing integrative process allows them to articulate their opportunities, material resources, freedoms and choices. Through these, they are capable of responding to demands but, more importantly, are able to constitute their identity in a meaningful way.

From this point of view, the study under consideration here uses *intersubjective processes*. The resulting methodology is dynamic insofar as it clearly adjusts to the children's and adolescents' processes covered by the study.

7.2.3. Sample description and research procedure

This field research was conducted over several months among a sample of children.[4] This population is varied insofar as it encompasses children with different incomes, gender and ages. Here, our study focuses on boys aged between 8 and 17 years, with low-level income. The population considered in our research is representative of children and adolescents who perform activities on the streets of Lima, in the midst of the road traffic. Children are divided into two groups, the first consisting of children aged between 8 and 14 (n = 7) who stand on the corner of two main avenues (Javier Prado and Los Frutales); the second group consists of children aged between 15 and 17 (n = 7) who stand in a circular park opening out onto several streets that cross the main avenue, in a wealthy district of Lima. They come from the surrounding neighbourhoods of Ate-Vitarte and Manchay, where many immigrants from emergency zones settled in the 1980s and 1990s, in the aftermath of the surge of political violence. They divide themselves naturally among the spaces they use to perform their activities. Thus, while the former group of children stands on the corner of Javier Prado and Los Frutales main avenues, teenagers practise more complex performances in the above-mentioned circle park, within five minutes' walking distance.

In the first stage of the project, there were no specific unifying data about these groups: *children and youth in a transitional situation*. The figures with regard to working children and adolescents are not well defined, partly because the official definition of child labour is problematic (see Chapter 13). The children and adolescents considered here do not regard their activity as work, describing it rather as *performing art*.

In the second stage, we interacted directly with the target population,[5] which allowed us to discover more about the children's characteristics and perceptions in the midst of the road traffic. We then focused our attention on the children's relations with people around them, such as the store custodian or newspaper kiosk owner. The attitudes of car drivers and pedestrians are interpreted by children as a token of either approval or disapproval of their situation and behaviours.

The methods used consisted of interviews, focus groups and field observations. The general methodology involved active listening, respectful of the children's temporal and spatial understandings and preferences.

All of the participants (children or teenagers) use their own capacities within their own spaces to display their potentials. In doing so, they create synergy and strengthen other capacities. The first author of the chapter initially approached and observed the children and adolescents, reflecting on what she saw. She thus built up a space with a view to establishing an affective bond with them. However, she was always careful to let them take such an initiative.

The procedure was as follows. For almost 12 months, the first author of the chapter surveyed the children and adolescents on the street corners constituting their spaces/environments. At first (almost three months), she accompanied them and let them observe her in order to gain their confidence. At times, she brought some newspapers, puzzles and other graphic sources, which she let them use, if they asked. On occasions, when they wished to draw or to paint, she brought some fruit which she gave them at the end of the session. When asked, she let them know the reason for her presence. She briefly told them she was conducting a study about children and teenagers on the streets.

When the traffic lights turned green, the adolescents asked each car driver for money before letting them drive away; when the lights then turned red, they reverted to their routine activities in the midst of the road traffic. The author could talk to the children only once the vehicles were permitted to go off. At this stage, she offered to listen to them in exchange for some of their time, as they were performing their tricks on the streets. She was asked whether she was going to give them a tip, but she answered she could only listen to them.

She showed children and teenagers her voice recorder and camera. She said she needed such devices in order to record and remember what they told her. Her digital camera enabled her to take pictures that she immediately showed the children. Immediately, they asked her to take pictures of them, which she did; she was then in a position to take more photographs of the children in the act of performing their tricks. She always showed the children all of her pictures.

7.3. Results

The results of our research may be classified into four categories. The first category relates to the children's physical well-being conditions; the second is directly concerned with the physical and material aspects that permit the construction of the children's present identity; the third concerns the relations that impact on the children's identity in their current situation; and finally, the fourth category is connected with the way children perceive their destiny or aspirations giving rise to open possibilities of future identity trajectories.

Firstly, as regards material well-being, all children belong to families in extreme poverty. Most of them are children of single mothers or have step-fathers. All of them have been physically or psychologically abused by parents or teachers, although they deny parental ill-treatment. They think they must protect their parents from police persecution, which they themselves feel deeply when performing their activities on the streets. They say they use health services only for emergency purposes. They appeal to their neighbours or friends to get money for medicines.

Secondly, all of the children surveyed have gone through bad experiences that have marked their identity strongly (e.g. sexual abuse). Though these past events certainly have an influence on identity trajectories, they do not prevent children from developing their own identity, especially through their activity and group affiliation. In particular, children value numerous aspects of their activity on the streets, which gives them some sense of pride and self-esteem. Furthermore, most children enjoy their activity on the streets and in the road traffic. They like to meet peers, exercise abilities they do not usually have an opportunity to practise and feel free to purchase things that normally are unavailable to their families. Teenagers doing acrobatics claim they feel very good about their body. None of them think there is imminent danger in what they do, even though they sometimes fall while training or in front of cars. These adolescents have acquired some notion of care in terms of space orientation and nutrition, for example.

Thirdly, apart from their family and other children of the group, affective support is to be found in the neighbourhood, as well as in the close relations children establish with people around them, such as the store custodian or newspaper kiosk owner next to the street they use to perform their tricks. The children's activity also encompasses negative aspects. Thus, if their recognition by some people – and not only the tips they receive – encourages them to continue their practices, some other people reject them, especially when there is an intended police persecution against them. On the other hand, there also are people who adopt an overprotective attitude that is not favourable to the children's development. Instead of trying to integrate them and recognize their participation in public places, some authorities persecute, repress and victimize these children, which can lead to transgressions on both sides. Moreover, most children interact with peers – either at school or in the neighbourhood – who associate with gangs. Some of the children surveyed declare they are highly anxious about the closeness of gangs, especially because they regard them as a threat. However, certain children gradually come to feel the compulsion to associate with such gangs.

Fourthly, contrary to the commonly held representation of street children, all of them go regularly to school and are in touch with their family. They mostly trust their mothers, sisters and brothers-in-law, but also friends in their community. Besides, most of them assert they know very well what to do with the money they earn (e.g. helping their mothers, buying school supplies, trainers, clothes and other items). By way of illustration, a teenager revealed he intended to use the money he earned with a view to building a house, jointly with his other siblings. Children especially regard school supplies as important, believing these are essential to attending school. Nevertheless, most of the children surveyed would like to engage in another kind of activity insofar as they feel bad about police persecution and rejection by pedestrians.

All of these results bring to light identity trajectory dynamics. Children suffering from extreme material and affective deprivation do not have multiple alternatives to preserve or enhance their material situation. Street activities not only allow children to maintain partial schooling but also provide them with a means of identity construction. Thereby, children in a transitional situation do not regard themselves any more as mere victims of poverty and destitution. They develop a more positive view of themselves, valuing numerous aspects of their activity. Yet, such activity conceals strong identity tensions arising from the children's relations with other persons around them. On the one hand, the affective relations they have and gestures of approval they receive in their close street "entourage" help them to build a good image of themselves. On the other hand, the tokens of reprobation or disapproval with which they are frequently confronted give rise to more negative self-representations that tend to foster attraction for gangs. In a way, the bad image certain persons or authorities convey of them could drive these children to a mutual pattern of delinquency through association with gangs. Indeed, before accepting rejection submissively and lapsing into self-rejection, they prefer to reject those who reject them (Baumann, 2006). These negative aspects seem to prompt children to other aspirations though, as proved by the fact that they have not yet conformed to the image of delinquent projected onto them. The future identity of these children hinges on such tensions.

7.4. Concluding remarks

People in extreme poverty use different strategies that are rooted in their traditional networks. For example, the families of our sample population occasionally appeal to their neighbours in order to satisfy acute needs at a specific moment, or participate in soup kitchens when they lack food. The Spanish term *recurseo* refers to a strategy that consists in performing different kinds of activities so as to get small change or food. Children in a transitional situation are an illustration of the strategies the poor adopt with a view to changing their life.

As has been emphasized in our survey, a person's identity structuring is affected when parental support (parents, family, community) is lacking. In the case of the population considered here, the children's interaction with peers and other people important to them constitutes the bonds they may establish on the streets. In contrast, police persecution contributes to their marginalization, and so to their exclusion.

There are two ways children and adolescents take advantage of their activity on the streets. Firstly, the street enables them to enter a new space in their socialization process, a space they are generally denied. This space is an extension of the way their common sense has been formed. Children find in it what they do not have in their families and community. On the streets, they receive the care and stimulation they need to grow, a way of developing capabilities they do not find at school, where emphasis is always on linguistics and mathematics. Secondly, they develop capabilities where body, relaxation and tension prevail; not only motor abilities, but also body–mind functioning. The conversion of these physical abilities into mental processes shaping their identity benefits their development process and promotes integration of their mental structure. Furthermore, the social space that the street traffic opens up to children serves as a space of support – although improvised – for those who depend on momentary onlookers for their acrobatic performances.

In the research we examined the formation of agency and identity of children and youth. We found that the evolving capabilities of transitional children are strongly related to the capacity for action that is strongly connected to life experiences, to identity and to choice trajectories that are influenced by interactions with others.

The major subjective aspect is that these children are learning how to cope with their life situation in an active way. Integrating body–mind functioning entails acquiring the capacity to convert abilities from one dimension to another, which is important for identity structuring. In a society where children are treated roughly – both physically and affectively – it proves necessary to create mechanisms so as to reduce the negative effects of ill-treatment. It is essential as well to generate supportive spaces and to foster the children's identity development through new methods.[6]

This argues that it is necessary to develop school abilities together with *capabilities for self-worth life*. To this end, it is important to examine what conditions enable children and adolescents to develop their potential to the full. Optimal conditions for this do not exist at school. However, the educability of the human being opens up a horizon to *emotional capability development*. It is by accompanying and facilitating the identity structuring of children that their perception, feelings and actions will respond to reality, people around them and their environment within the framework of affective and social bonds.

In this sense, the *development of emotional capabilities* covers two dimensions: *conditions and spaces* where children and adolescents may develop their ability to acknowledge and voice their feelings, as well as to realize motivations and desires. As a research method, *autobiography*, is a way to acknowledge subjectivity. It allows the conscience to move around the pathless places in each child and adolescent. The second dimension is about *affective bonds* (close relations and social networks) that allow children to build up a collective project together, with a view to the desired changes in the social context.

In summary, this is about facilitating the process by which children and teenagers learn to express their emotions and opinions about the changes in their lives, aimed at improving their quality of life, promoting their education and health and working to better the conditions within their families and communities. A useful tool is facilitating and fostering participation and organization that promotes the collective and individual plans.

Regarding social policies, the fact that affective and social bonds networks constitute capabilities, and this has a strong impact on identity, leads to the conclusion that social policies may regulate integrally, not only the economic aspects, but take the advantage to create synergies among financial investment and the affective and social support system.

Notes

1. Transparencia, Idea, Ágora democrática y UNICEF. *La Niñez en las políticas de Educación, Situación y perspectivas*, p. 7.
2. According to his Bond Theory, Pichon-Rivière (1998) views the bond as a continuously moving and dynamic structure that comprises both the subject and object. Individuals are the result not of the action of instincts or internal objects, but of the interplay between the subject and external/internal objects – predominantly a dialectic interaction – expressed in certain behaviours.
3. Peru records the second highest maternal mortality rate in Latin America, as well as the highest percentage of adolescent mothers. Thirteen per cent of adolescents between the ages of 15 and 19 are mothers (Barrón and Villar, 2007). The most vulnerable and poorest teenagers and youths are adolescent mothers (UNFPA and MINSA, 2004). According to a radio broadcast from the Ministry of Education (22 April 2008), the second most common reason for school desertion is pregnancy. The most vulnerable and poorest teenagers and youths are adolescent mothers (UNFPA and MINSA, 2004).
4. Here we use the term "children" as defined in the Convention on the Rights of the Child. Childhood is the period between 0 and 18 years old, adolescents thus being included as well.
5. The study was conducted by the first author of the chapter.
6. The adolescents' break-dancing activity on the streets has become formalized through contracts with the municipality whereby they are given a space where they can teach their skills to younger children. In addition to physical skills, children are also taught to collaborate with others.

References

Anderson, J. (2000), *Trabajando por el Fortalecimiento de las Mujeres y la Igualidad de Genero*, UNIFEM, Lima.

Ballet, J. and Radja, K. (2005), "Emotional Capabilities as Identity Roots". Paper presented at the Workshop Identities and Capabilities, St Edmunds and Robinson College, University of Cambridge.

Barrón, J. and Villar, E. (eds) (2007), *Ausencias/Absences. Niños del Milenio*, Información para el Desarrollo, Lima, Peru.

Baumann, Z. (2006), *Wasted Lives*, Paidos, Buenos Aires.

Dubar, C. (2000), *La Crise des Identités. L'Interprétation d'une Mutation*, PUF, Paris.

Dubet François (2002), *Le Déclin des Institutions*, Seuil, Paris.

Giddens, A. (1999), *Un Mundo Desbocado. Los Efectos de la Globalizacion en Nuestras Vidas*, Runaway World, Edicions Taurus, Mexico.

Giddens, A. (1987), *Social Theory and Modern Sociology*, Stanford University Press, Stanford.

González Rey, F. (1999), *Comunicación, Personalidad y Desarrollo*, Editorial Pueblo y Cultura, Havana.

Horna Padron, M. (2005), *Plan de Vida. Un Programa de Vida para Proyectarse al Futuro* [Life Project Plan. A program to project yourself onto the future], Save The Children, Sweden, Lima.

Jaramillo, G. E. (2005), "Los maestros en la promoción y defensa de los derechos del niño", Instituto de Pedagogia Popular (IPP), Lima.

Levison, D. (2000), "Children as Economic Agents", *Feminist Economics*, 6(1): 125–134.

Livet, P. (2004), "La pluralité cohérente des notions d'identité personnelle", *Revue de Philosophie Economique*, 9: 29–57.

Markus, H. and Nurius, P. (1986), "Possible Selves", *American Psychologist*, 21(9): 954–969.

Mitjáns Martinez, A. (2001), "Trabajo Infantil y Subjetividad: una perspectiva necesaria", *Estudios de Psicología*, julio-diciembre, año/vol.6, número 002, Universidad Federal do Rio Grande do Norte, Natal, Brazil: 235–245. Red AL Y C. La Hemeroteca Científica en Línea en Ciencias Sociales. www.redalyc.com.

Nussbaum, M. C. (2000), *Women and Human Development. The Capabilities Approach*, Cambridge University Press, Cambridge.

Pichon Rivière, E. (1998), *Teoría del Vínculo* (Theory of the Bond), Ediciones Nueva Visión, Argentina.

Pimentel Sevilla, C. (ed.) (1996), *La Familia y sus Problemas en los Sectores Urbanos Pobres*, Centro Comunitario de Salud Mental, Lima.

Quijano, A. (2005), "Colonialidad del poder, eurocentrismo u América latina", in CLACSO (ed.), *La Colonialidad del Saber: Eurocentrismo y Ciencias Sociales. Perspectivas Latinoamericanas*, CLACSO, Buenos Aires.

Sen, A. K. (1999), "Investing in Early Childhood: Its Role in Development", Conference on Breaking the Poverty Cycle. Investing in Early Childhood, Interamerican Development Bank, Washington, DC.

Sen, A. K. (2004), "Social Identity", *Revue de Philosophie Economique*, 9: 7–27.

Sen, A. K. (2006), *Identity and Violence: The Illusion of Destinity*, W.W. Norton & Company, New York and London.

UNICEF/INEI (2004), *El Estado de la Niñez en el Peru*, UNICEF, Lima.

UNFPA and MINSA (2004), *Hacia el Cumplimiento de los Objetivos de Desarrollo del Milenio en el Peru*, ONU, Peru.

Transparencia, idea, Agora democrática y UNICEF (2006), *La Niñez en las Politicas de Educación, Situación y Perspectivas*, UNICEF, Lima.

8
Micro-finance, Street Children and the Capability Approach: Is Micro-finance an Appropriate Tool to Address the Street Children Issue?

Badreddine Serrokh

8.1. Introduction

The aim of this chapter is to use the capability approach (CA) to examine micro-finance as a tool to improve the well-being of street children in Bangladesh. In particular, it helps to throw light on a relatively new issue through fieldwork. Some of the policy implications of this chapter are discussed further in Part III of this book (especially Chapters 12 and 13).

Street children are usually perceived only as destitute, exploited and neglected beings. They are not considered as having human agency in the sense that they are not viewed as contributing to the accomplishment of a purpose or results (Levison, 2000: 125). This vision, taking its roots from the unthinking adoption of the "modern" Western conception of childhood, idealizes childhood as a privileged phase of life dedicated only to play and schooling, as a time in which children have the right to protection and education but not to autonomy or participation (Boyden et al., 1998). The archetypal child is therefore perceived as passive, dependent on his/her (nuclear) family for every need and without any meaningful responsibilities other than to develop into an adult (Moore, 2000). Because street children are not experiencing a proper (Western) childhood, they are pitied and viewed as powerless beings, rather than being considered as agents in their own right who are potentially capable, strong and resourceful people.

Although acknowledging how exposure to the multiple risks of street life enhances children's vulnerability, a recent movement of development psychologists has reacted to this pitying vision of street children by highlighting how they are active contributors to their development, attempting to make sense of their social world, being therefore not "*objects of concern*" but "*subjects with concern*" (Woodhead, 1999). They emphasize the importance of seeing children as subjects who "precisely because they are different from adults and have their own specific interests and needs, must be able to decide themselves about their affairs, and should be supported in this" (Liebel, 2004: 8; see also the other chapters in this book).

These considerations have policy implications. Whereas earlier interventions were aimed at rescuing the presumed destitute street child from the harmful life of the street through the provision of survival services, recent policies have been directed at changing the capabilities of those for whom street use is, to some degree, a positive aspect of their existence (Williams, 1993). Indeed, considering street children as agents themselves leads to focusing interventions on what matters to them and seeking solutions that are consistent with their livelihoods (Conticini, 2004; and Chapters 5 and 7 of this book).

This chapter investigates one type of intervention/instrument that enters into this new policy framework: micro-finance. Referring to the provision of small-scale financial services (primarily credit and savings) to poor and disadvantaged people (Robinson, 2001: 9), the micro-finance movement has witnessed a huge expansion worldwide. While considerable attention has been paid to adults, micro-finance recently enlarged its scope of interventions to children and youth on the basis that poor children need access to financial resources in order to build their capacity and increase their employability. In this context, street children have recently been provided with micro-finance and encouraged to undertake income-generating activities. Although this sort of programme may seem attractive, it raises a series of questions regarding its effectiveness in the long term and its impact on street children's well-being. Indeed, many argue that, even though we assume these children need financial services, providing these services may do more harm than good.

Tackling these questions requires a conceptual framework that can define and measure street children's well-being. In this chapter, as in the rest of the book, the CA developed by Amartya Sen is adopted. By emphasizing the importance of the expansion of human capabilities in the achievement of well-being, the CA stresses that the objective of any intervention should be to guarantee the freedom of a person "to lead the kind of life he or she has reason to value" (Sen, 1999: 87).

According to Sen, "Development consists of the removal of various types of unfreedoms that leave people with little choice and little opportunity of exercising their reasoned agency" (Sen, 1999: 12). Well-being is therefore not defined in utilitarian terms as wealth accumulation, but rather in terms of capability (freedom of choice) and agency (freedom of processes) expansion. However, as stated in Chapter 1, Sen's framework is usually applied to adults, not children. Therefore, the first challenge of this chapter is to discuss the dilemma that Sen's framework raises when applied to street children. Indeed, on the one hand, work appears to enhance the agency of street children, thanks to their ability to be agents of change for their own and families' well-being. On the other hand, this seems to conflict with freedom of choice, as street children appear to enter the labour market mainly because of structural constraints. Taking these points into consideration, we move on to develop an adapted CA framework that relies on street children's specific characteristics and seeks to expand their agency and capability within their constrained world.

After establishing this framework, we apply it to a sample of street children benefiting from a micro-finance programme in urban Bangladesh, with the objective of investigating its impact on their well-being. Thanks to a participatory methodology, we assess their level of demand for financial services and then examine the way street children use savings and credit, as well as the impact this has on their agency and capabilities. We find that street children do greatly need access to financial services, but that the use they make of them typically has a short-term impact on their well-being. Indeed, on the savings side, their ability to accumulate large sums of money in the long term appears depleted by the few profitable income-generating activities in which they are engaged. With regard to credit, many appear to invest in seasonal businesses, thus having a short-term impact. For those who did invest in long-term activities, problems linked to family intrusion or the profitability of the activity itself surfaced on several occasions.

The Bangladeshi organization studied in this chapter had the difficult task of engaging with these issues and realities; consequently, the programme faced some difficulties in its design. Leaving our field study, the last section analyses the conditions that need to be met by micro-finance programmes in order to generate a sustainable impact on street children's well-being. We propose a holistic micro-finance programme that accompanies financial services with vocational training and social services. We then conclude by presenting the main lessons learned through the analysis and provide some perspectives for the future.

8.2. The street children issue

Most people agree on the importance of the street children issue. However, what brings less agreement is to define with precision to what this notion refers. Indeed, because of the diversity of their backgrounds, street children are far from representing a homogeneous population. Hence, different definitions of the concept exist. One of the first definitions of "street children", which only came into general use after the United Nations' Year of the Child in 1979, can be traced back to Henry Mayhew's (1851) book, *London Labour and the London Poor* (see Scanlon et al., 1998). In the late 1980s, other definitions began to emerge, mainly in Latin America, where street children made a huge appearance in the public arena. Among these definitions, the most common one having gained credibility among practitioners and academics is the "ON/OF" terminology of UNICEF (1986). This binary terminology suggests dividing street children into two main categories: *"children of the streets"*, who live and work on the streets, 24/7; and *"children on the streets"*, who spend most of their daytime there, before returning to their families at night. The UNICEF typology is useful as long as its limitations are considered (O'Connor, 2003). Indeed, it still represents an umbrella term and the complexity of the phenomenon means that overlaps and grey areas exist (Hatloy and Huser, 2005),[1] leading local organizations to adapt the definition to their local context and some experts to define new categories, speaking for instance of 'children for the street' (Dunford, 1996). This difficulty in defining the concept of street children has a practical implication on the ability of governments and aid agencies to quantify their exact numbers and target policy interventions.

One common myth about street children is that they are 'orphans'. Surprisingly, studies estimate that 75% of street children around the world are "on" the streets (Shurink, 1993). Moreover, the majority of children "of" the streets still have their families but have run away from home, often in response to psychological, physical or sexual abuse (UNICEF, 2006: 41).

The literature examining the causes that drive children to the street stresses economic poverty as the main reason (Alexandrescu, 1996). However, evidence tends to show that non-economic factors, such as physical violence, play a crucial role (Conticini, 2004: 6–7; see also Chapters 5 and 7 of this book). Whereas the earlier assumptions identified two causes as mutually exclusive, poverty and family breakdown, the street children being either "throwaways" or "runaways", the new thinking about street children uses multifactor models (Foy, 2001). For instance, the model developed by Lucchini (1996) defines factors at the micro or individual level (such as desire for autonomy), the meso or family level (such as family violence) and the macro or country level (such as politics or the economy).

When on the streets, many children are found to be highly vulnerable to harassment, abuse and neglect. Involvements in criminal activities, violence from the police, drug addiction or sexual promiscuity are relatively prominent among them. Another significant source of vulnerability is the harassment faced by children in their work environment. Nevertheless, considering street children only through the looking glass of vulnerability might lead to a vision full of pity that neglects one of their most important shared characteristics: their capacities. Indeed, Blanc (1994: 340) argues that "to counter the negative perceptions of the street children, a new anthropological literature has emphasized the positive aspects of the street experience, and the new pride and confidence street work gives them". This view emerges from evidence which demonstrates that street children are active policy makers for themselves and that street life makes them develop resilience and adaptability, having therefore a high ability to thrive in difficult circumstances (Felsman, 1981). Moreover, many of them hold high moral principles and are found to have altruistic and caring behaviour (Ennew, 2000). In fact, supportive and cooperative peer relationships exist amongst them, generally as a replacement for natural family ties (Boyden, 1991; Lalor, 1999).

8.3. Street children, child work and the capability approach

Apart from being vulnerable and capable, street children share an additional characteristic: "working the streets to make a living" (Grundling and Grundling, 2005). As such, street children are considered as a direct subset of working children, being engaged in a wide range of economic activities that are situated mainly in the informal labour market.

Obviously, this characteristic widens the scope of debate on the issue of child work and calls for examination of the various opinions that surround this notion (see also Chapter 13). The current literature that looks into child work differentiates itself by its approach. Liebel (2004), referring to Myers (2001), highlights the existence of two perspectives. First, the *abolitionist perspective* advocates that children must never be allowed to engage in any form of economic activity and that childhood must be dedicated to school and play, with work consisting (only) of light chores in the home. It has been argued that this approach has done little to eradicate child poverty, which led to the emergence of a new movement of development psychologists (Moore, 2000). This movement attempts to show that abolitionism is based on the unthinking adoption of a Western conception of childhood, where the cultural aspect of child development is not taken into account. This gave rise to the appearance of the *"subject-oriented approach"*, which advocates the necessity of listening to children and allowing those who wish to work do so, unless the job is harmful. According to this view, decent work has a place in child development and can have positive effects, such as increasing their sense of responsibility and self-esteem. This replaces the narrow view of children's work as exploitation with a wider view that takes account of its multifactorial influences on children's growth and development (Boyden et al., 1998: 11). In such a context, it is possible that children seek and value work as a source of learning, social acceptance and self worth (*ibid.*). In the case of street children, Lucchini (1998) argues that these children are not content on the street if they are unable to pursue some concrete activity; that is, the child will feel ashamed of being on the street if he/she has nothing to do, and this inactivity causes boredom, the need for diversion and the feeling of being condemned.

These two approaches to child work have policy implications. An abolitionist perspective would support programmes that seek to rescue children from work, with the objective of integrating them in their presumed "natural" environment: school and family. In contrast, applying a subject-oriented approach would involve building upon the capacities of the street children with the objective of providing them with the opportunities and experiences enabling them to become economically productive and eventually self-supporting, to facilitate their survival in the world of work and independent living (Tolfree, 1998). This would therefore be a move "beyond conventions, towards empowerment" (Boyden et al., 1998: 87).

As we can easily see, the abolitionist and subject-oriented approaches, although different, have a common concern: the improvement of children's well-being. Still, the concept of well-being is very large and leaves a lot of scope for interpretation. A conceptual framework is therefore required to facilitate the conceptualization and measurement of well-being.

The CA proposed by Sen (1980, 1992, 1999) appears, in this respect, appealing (see Chapter 13 of this book). Developed as an alternative framework for analysing important concepts in development, such as standard of living, personal well-being and poverty, it criticizes traditional welfare economics that views well-being as either opulence or utility (Mitra, 2006). Following the CA (see Chapter 1), the objective of development should be to expand people's freedom, which Sen defines in two ways: the freedom related to *opportunities* that people face (capabilities or freedom of choice) and freedom related to *processes* that they control (their agency or freedom of processes). Capacities relate to being able to "do" or "be" things, thanks to their personal characteristics and social opportunities, whereas potentialities are the endowments in assets (i.e. capital equipment)[2] and in commodities (i.e. goods and services) that will be mobilized in order to achieve "functioning" and improve well-being. Capabilities are therefore people's real freedom to enjoy being and doing what they value and have reason to value (Sen, 1980, 1985, 1992). The second type of freedom that development should expand is process or agency freedom. This refers to the person's ability to act and bring about change and to pursue the goals that he/she values (Sen, 1999). It is the freedom to achieve whatever the person, as a responsible agent, decides he or she should achieve (Sen, 1985: 204) and is essential "in assessing what a person can do in line with his or her conception of the good" (Sen, 1985: 206). It recognizes people as responsible persons. As Sen highlights: "not only are we well or ill, but also we act or refuse to act, and can choose to act one way rather than another" (Sen, 1999: 190). In this perspective, he emphasizes that "people have to be seen...as being actively involved – given the opportunity – in shaping their own destiny, and not just as passive recipients of the fruits of cunning development programs" (Sen, 1999: 53).

Interestingly, if we apply this framework to the issue of working children, we could assert that the CA, in terms of process freedom, seems close to *the subject-oriented approach*. Indeed, as evidence tends to demonstrate that children choose to work in order to cope with the lack of family income, it could be asserted that children consider themselves as agents of change for addressing the poverty of their families. This agency, shaped by structural constraints, is said to have positive effects on children's well-being, but can be seen as a *second best solution* (Van Den Berge, 2006). Indeed, because children do not feel capable of changing the structural constraints that require them to work (e.g. lack of job opportunities for their parents), they look for solutions within their constrained environment, work being one of these. If we analyse the opportunity aspect of freedom (or *freedom of choice*), some problems appear. In fact, as work is mainly the result of the constraints they are facing, it can hardly be viewed as a choice they have made freely and appears, in this sense, in contradiction to the notion of *freedom of choice* (Ballet et al., 2006). Consequently, the CA would argue that, to address the issue of working children, policies should target these structural constraints (mainly through household income improvement). This would eradicate the need for children to work and enlarge the choices they have, permitting them to benefit from education instead of being active on the labour market.

This approach appears to be unsatisfactory when applied to the case of street children. Indeed, Ballet et al. (2006) raise two main problems. Firstly, it is difficult to accept the link between their parents' budget constraints and the consequences for their schooling. Indeed, violence imposed on children by their parents is one of the factors that force them onto the street (Conticini, 2004; Ballet et al., 2006). This makes it difficult to assume altruistic behaviour on the part of parents towards their children. Secondly, even though such an assumption may be correct in some cases, school is not always the best solution, as evidence tends to demonstrate that school violence is often at the heart of street children's predicaments (*ibid.*). Hence, acting on structural constraints appears ineffective for children already in street situations, but still essential in order to prevent street migration.

However, the CA could be of considerable value in the policy debates on street children if we reposition it within their constrained environment. Therefore, even though structural constraints exist, we need to go beyond these constraints and undertake a double analysis. Firstly, the capability aspect would require analysing, for the street children who have chosen to work in response to the constraints they are facing, how to expand their choices and opportunities within the labour market. Enhancing their opportunity freedom would therefore permit them to expand their universe of choice. Secondly, the agency aspect would call for developing policies that could enhance their ability to be agents of change for their own and their broader family and kin's poverty. On the other hand, we would need to assess the processes by which choices are made. Children must be able to make their choices independently and should be involved in such a process. Finally, if the choice is made to exercise an activity, the resulting gains should be enjoyed by the children.

Whereas the standard version of the CA provides few solutions to the policy debate on street children, as acting on the structural constraints through family income improvement would appear inefficient, the adapted CA framework we propose takes into consideration the constraints street children are facing and seeks, inside this universe, to improve street children's well-being through the expansion of their capabilities and agency. Some broader policy implications relating to education and children's activities are explored in Chapters 12 and 13).

8.4. Methodology

This chapter attempts to assess whether micro-finance is an appropriate tool for addressing the street children issue. Specifically, we seek to determine, firstly, the reasons underpinning the street children's need for financial services and, secondly, whether such a type of intervention has the ability to increase their well-being through the expansion of their agency and capability.

To do so, the chapter draws on field research undertaken between December 2005 and January 2006 (34 working days) in Dhaka, the capital city of Bangladesh, where an estimated 60% of the population lives below the poverty line,[3] with hundreds of thousands of street children being among them.[4] A total of 79 street children benefiting from the *Padakhep Mannabik Unnayan Kendra* (PMUK)[5] micro-finance programme were addressed by the study. The agency aspect of freedom had an impact on the methods used to collect data. As street children were considered as agents, they were urged to participate actively in the research thanks to the use of two specific child-friendly participatory research tools: participatory rapid appraisals (PRA)[6] and focus group discussions (FGD).

The sample structure comprised four categories of street children (following PMUK's classification), each category being divided, when possible, into three age groups (i.e. 8–12, 13–15 and 16–18) with an attempt made to achieve an equal distribution of girls and boys. An important point to highlight is that the objective was to capture the diversity of profiles existing in terms of demand and impact, not to undertake a complete impact assessment per category and age. Table 8.1 gives details of the sampling structure.

Furthermore, two PRA sessions gathered a total number of 38 participants, from all categories. An important constraint faced by the research relates to language, due to the dependence the researcher had on the Bengali translator's capacity to interpret. Some difficulties in retaining children who had to leave for work also arose.

The chapter presents the fieldwork results in two parts. The first part assesses the factors determining street children's demand for financial services, while the second discusses the impact of micro-finance on their agency and capability.

8.5. Results

8.5.1. Savings demand

Our data tend to demonstrate that street children are forward looking, and plan for their future financial needs with accuracy. Savings services were

Table 8.1 Sample structure

	Description	Definition	Number of FGD	Number of participants
Category 1	Working and living on the street day and night without their family	Their families are in the villages; left their families in Dhaka; or lost their families	5	37
Category 2	Working and living on the street day and night with their family	Children who are living with their families in a temporary house made of plastic or bamboo; they are found on the embankment of any metropolitan area of Bangladesh	2	11
Category 3	Working on the street during the day and returning to their family at night	Children who live in Dhaka with their uncles, aunts, grandmothers...	2	9
Category 4	Working and living on the street during the day and returning to their family at night	Children who live and work on the street during the daytime but return to their parents at night (settled generally in the slums of Dhaka)	3	22
TOTAL				79

viewed as an essential tool that enables them to meet these needs, which, following Rutherford (1999), are of three types: (1) *life cycle needs*, which refer to the predictable events that affect children, such as supporting their family or getting education; (2) *emergencies*, such as coping with the loss of a job; and (3) *opportunities*, like starting a business (see Table 8.2).

In deepening discussions, we found that the root of their demand for savings lies in street insecurity. Indeed, as their money is often stolen, they try to keep it safe by using three informal strategies.[7] Firstly, they use short-term devices, such as trousers or shoes, which are perceived as useful because these are quickly accessible, but inappropriate as money can easily be lost

Table 8.2   Factors determining demand for financial services

Savings demand	Credit demand
Street life insecurity, leading to the use of three informal strategies: (1) short-term devices; (2) informal financial intermediaries; (3) quick spending	Personal income-generating activities: (1) seasonal businesses; (2) long-term businesses
Future financial needs: (1) life cycle events; (2) emergencies; (3) opportunities	Families' income-generating activities

or stolen. The second strategy is informal financial intermediaries (such as mudbanks/piggy bank), but many street children face restrictions with regard to access, due to their perceived status as criminals in society. As such, we could assert that they do not have the social opportunity to access the services. Moreover, even when access is granted, it remains unsafe in their view, as many providers are said to disappear with the depositors' money or avoid giving returning money due to the absence of legal sanctions. For instance, street children expressed how police, along with the legal system, are often reluctant to protect their interests. As these two strategies provide them with little or no satisfaction, they use their last available tool: "quick spending". Al Amin, who is 13 years old, explains this behaviour in these terms: "If we don't have a place … to deposit our money, we know other street children will steal it from us. So, it's better to spend it quickly, before losing it."

In such a context, what may appear as money misuse from an external viewpoint is, in fact, a particular saving strategy resulting from the lack of access to safe places to store money. Consequently, street children enter a vicious circle. Because of their vulnerability, they are driven to spend their money quickly, preventing them from meeting their future financial needs and enhancing their vulnerability. In such a situation, the children, far from being the victim of robbery, may become the perpetrators. Stealing may therefore become a habit and, sooner or later, will negatively affect the child's well-being.

This vulnerability circle can be broken either by acting on the initial vulnerability factors, namely the insecurity of the street, or by setting up strategies enabling the street children to avoid misusing their money in the street environment. In this regard, micro-finance may help.

8.5.2. Credit demand

The mapping of street children's demand for credit, emerging from our participatory sessions, points to three main factors triggering demand, which can be subdivided. Firstly, street children desire access to credit in order to start their own income-generating activities. Here, the children's profiles were split between those who want to start seasonal businesses and those who wish to start a long-term business. Interestingly, the ones who stressed the desire for seasonal businesses had generally not yet completed the vocational training sessions provided by PMUK. However, when talking about their future, many of the same children expressed the desire to start a sustainable business after completing their training. The second factor driving demand emphasized the need to access capital in order for their parents to start or expand their businesses. This demand therefore correlates with the lack of credit available to their parents or with the better interest rate provided for the children's creditors. Finally, not all street children were expressing a need for credit; some still preferred to continue their formal education or start working as employees until they found the exact activity they wanted to do in the future.

Generally speaking, many children were expressing how access to credit was a way to expand their autonomy and free their lives from adults' choices, as it gave them hope and the capacity to build a better future. In order to assess these statements accurately, we discussed in a participatory session what they wanted to do in the future; two types of answer emerged. Some children wanted to become engineers, or doctors, or social workers, while others wanted to be business (wo)men and to become professionals in their actual or in an alternative type of activity. However, when delving more deeply into our discussions, we discovered that a large majority of children who highlighted the first type of answer distinguished between "*what they wanted to be*" and "*what they had to be*". An interesting point is that only a minority of children wanted to become an employee. Most preferred to start their own activities, voiced as a way of deliverance from the pressure of their employers.

A final element raised in the discussions is the limited access to credit gained before joining PMUK. Many street children did not have this opportunity before. Iglebaeck and Hassan (2005) confirm this finding and highlight, as is also the case for savings, that urban poor children have less access to credit facilities than their rural counterparts, but the little access they get is from people with whom they had working relationships. Moreover, the few who had this opportunity were obliged to pay an exorbitant interest rate.

8.5.3. Micro-finance, agency and capability

Capturing the impact of micro-finance on street children agency and capability requires, first, assessing the use they make of the financial services provided to them. The next step is to review these results in the light of the CA framework designed previously.

8.5.3.1. *Savings use*

The majority of street children save money in order to support their family, as testified by Bahrul, a 13-year-old boy (category 1) who left his village for Dhaka because he had to bear his siblings' educational costs (three brothers and one sister). Living first in his uncle's house in Dhaka, he was mistreated by his aunt and decided to flee and live on the street with other children. He then joined PMUK's programme and obtained a loan to start a cycle rickshaw service. He saves the profits until he has enough money to send to his family through a trustworthy person working as a bus driver.

This support is not unconditional though. In case of physical abuse, the child can refuse to support his family, as is the case of Aktar, a 16-year-old boy (category 3). Living in a village near Dhaka, he decided to flee from home with his two siblings after the death of his mother and the marriage of his father to a woman who constantly ill-treated them. Arriving on the streets of Dhaka, he went to live with his grandmother. Launching a business thanks to PMUK's loan, he uses his earnings to support his grandmother and siblings and, in parallel, saved money should an emergency arise. However, Aktar refuses to send money to his home village because of the presence of his stepmother.

Family support can be a real burden for some street children, especially the ones who live with their relatives, as shown by the case of Munna. Having left his parents in the village because of poverty, he is living with his uncle in Dhaka and works at a tea stall every day. This job provides him with 40–50 Tk (Bangladesh Taka) daily. From this amount, Munna has to meet several expenses: paying a monthly rent to his uncle (100 Tk a month), bearing daily family costs and supporting his parents in the village. For Munna, savings services were regarded as essential, otherwise "[his] *relatives will take all* [his] *money*".

Apart from these everyday expenditures, street children use their savings in order to cope with emergencies. As one child indicated during a PRA session: "*today we have a job, tomorrow we don't have it*". Indeed, crisis situations, such as income shocks following the loss of a job, are very common in their lives, and savings facilities were used in order to secure their livelihoods in unstable periods and to enable them to respond adequately to any crises that may occur in their lives. It is therefore an *ex ante* strategy to cope with shocks. For example, Kanchan (a 15-year-old boy, category 1) was working in a vegetable market until he lost his job. Then, the only means of survival available was the money he had saved. Without this, Kanchan would have surely been pushed to steal or to beg. Others, like Swapon (a 12-year-old boy, category 1), whose father died some years ago, left his mother because she ill-treated him. In order to survive, Swapon collects vegetables in a market and sells them. He buys at 8 TK a kilogramme and sells at 9 TK, this small profit enabling him to meet his present expenditures. But Swapon knows how uncertain his future is and therefore saves money. One day, Swapon had an accident in the street and had to undergo an urgent leg operation. He used 3000 TK from his savings account to pay the operation costs.

However, the notion of emergencies has a broader meaning for children who have closer relations with their families (mainly category 4). Examples abound, such as Shugon who withdrew some money from his savings account to pay for treatment for his sick mother, or Chahida for helping her parents when they faced financial problems with their business. Hence, the "emergencies" notion includes the family nexus, and not only the personal shocks street children may face.

Besides their life cycle and emergency needs, some street children use their savings in order to invest in income-generating activities. This appears to correlate with the compulsory savings strategy of PMUK, where street children are obliged to save a particular amount before benefiting from a credit.

8.5.3.2. Credit use

Three investment profiles emerged from the research. Some, like Sujon, a 13-year-old boy, receive small credit amounts and invest them in seasonal businesses. Driven to the street because of the abuses he faced from his father, he started to work in the vegetable and fish market as a "Minti" (i.e. carrier). Parallel to that, he received two small credits: (1) 30 TK to buy and sell chocolate in the street, generating a daily profit of 15 TK and (2) 70 K to buy and sell water during Ramadan,[8] with a total profit of 50 TK. As we can see, the main characteristics of these businesses are their short-term lifespan and the limited profit margin. This type of investment tends to be positively correlated to their degree of vulnerability: the more street children appear as vulnerable, the more they have a tendency to invest in seasonal businesses. From a sample of 19 street children living and working day and night without their family (category 1), we found the following figures in terms of credit investments: 37% in buying chocolate; 34% water; 18.5% vegetables, fish and fruit; and 10.5% cigarettes and cosmetics. The limited profits generated are then used to meet their personal and families' short-term expenditures.

Starting long-term businesses emerged as the second type of investment and mainly concerned those who had benefited from vocational training. As a matter of fact, the businesses launched were related to the training provided and credits were used, for instance, to purchase a sewing machine, buy electrical goods and create a tea stall. We remember the case of Aktar highlighted previously. Before starting his business, he was involved in hazardous jobs, until he benefited from a loan of 4000 TK (US$60) to open a tea stall. Generating good profits, it enables him to support his family financially. Aktar likes his work and now wants to expand his business.

Although success cases[9] can be encouraging, many street children face problems in their businesses. Chowdhurry, a 12-year-old boy, illustrates how family intrusion can be problematic. Receiving in January 2005 a credit of 2000 TK, he started his desired business: a vegetable shop. But as soon as his elder brother who was staying in the village heard about it, he came to Dhaka and took control of the shop. Chowdhurry was forced to leave his business and found a job he doesn't like in the cement factory, with the hope of re-opening a vegetable shop.

Other types of problems can arise, such as lack of profitability in investments. Raju, a 13-year-old boy who lives with his parents in Dhaka, loves mobile phones and quickly became an expert in repairs without any training. In 2005, he took a loan of 2000 TK (US$30) in order to buy repair materials and work with them in his cousin's mobile phone shop. This activity is very profitable to his cousin, but brings little income to Raju, as he is engaged as a "trainee". He therefore has to do extra work in order to reimburse his creditors.

For those with closer connections with their families (i.e. categories 2 and 4), their loans were invested in their families' non-seasonal businesses. The objective was to support their parents in starting or expanding their businesses, as is done by Chahida, a 17-year-old girl who is living with her parents in the slums of Dhaka. She received a credit of 2000 TK and gave it to her father, a physically disabled man, who started a potato chip business. She is helping him, besides working as a peer educator in PMUK. She likes her work, and wants to continue in this way.

However, this situation can raise problems, as in the case of Shumon who received a credit of 5000 TK and gave it to his father in order to start a grocery shop. He is working with his father, and the little money he receives as remuneration is used to reimburse the loan. Shumon does not like this situation and hopes to start his own grocery shop soon.

8.5.3.3. *Impact of micro-finance on children's agency and capability*

Analysing these findings in the light of the adapted CA framework provides some interesting observations (for a summary see Table 8.3).

Immediately, we note that street children are responsible agents who can undertake a careful assessment of the problems they are facing and seek solutions to them. Many fled from home because of physical abuse, hence knowing their rights and being able to take action to uphold them. However, we are not in a position to give a precise assessment of the increase or reduction in their well-being following their "migration".

Their initial agency is then enhanced thanks to the use they make of the financial services. Indeed, this access increases their ability to be agents of change for their own and their family's well-being. However, a concern can be raised over the lifespan of such impacts. With regard to savings, their ability to accumulate large lump sums of money over a long period of time, itself depending on the profits generated by their business activity, seems questionable. It is definitely problematic for those who are still involved in

Table 8.3 Summary of survey results

Financial services	Uses		Impact on well-being	
Savings	1.	Family support, if no physical abuse faced	1.	Gives them the ability to be agents of change for their own and family poverty
	2.	Meet personal emergencies emerging from the loss of a job or a sudden event occurring (accident)	2.	The ability to accumulate large lump sums of money is constrained by the limited profitability of their businesses
	3.	Meet family emergencies (mainly category 4)		
	4.	Future income-generating activities		
Credit	1.	Invest in personal businesses:	1.	Enhances their agency, but mainly in the short term
		1.1. seasonal businesses (mainly the most vulnerable street children)	2.	Some problems can arise: family intrusion, low profitability of the business
		1.2. long-term businesses		
	2.	Invest in family businesses (mainly categories 1 and 3).		

seasonal businesses. The same problem is witnessed for micro-credit, when street children invest in seasonal income-generating activities. It appears rather effective in the short term, but gives no real sustainable solution in the long term. Investing in their families' businesses seems to provide a better long-term solution, but freedom of choice is not really involved, as many of the street children in question (especially the older ones) want to start their own businesses. Finally, personal non-seasonal businesses would appear to be the most effective solution, but are questionable in terms of sustainability, as street children do not seem to keep their businesses viable in the long term.

Besides the ability to be agents of change, agency requires paying attention to the process by which choices are made in terms of access and use of financial services and gains. A programme that participates in the expansion of street children's agency should enable a high degree of participation and freedom in the way choices are made. Here, the problem of family intrusion that has been noted previously needs to be taken into consideration. Chowdhurry's case reveals how the financial gains of the business he launched thanks to credit were no longer controlled by himself, but by his elder brother. Interestingly, savings were expressed as a tool that enables them to protect their earnings from such intrusion, as in the case of children who save money in order to prevent their relatives taking all their money.

In addition to agency, the CA looks at street children's freedom to enjoy being and doing what they value and have reason to value, i.e. their capabilities. Micro-finance must therefore expand street children's choices and opportunities within the labour market. Our findings tend to demonstrate that micro-finance participates in such expansion, but mainly in the short term. Our analysis of demand factors emphasizes that street children who asked for credit generally desired to start their own long-term (non-seasonal) businesses, although their short-term goals were different – some desiring a credit for their families' businesses, others for survival. However, some success cases exist, where street children left a hazardous working activity for non-hazardous ones, with an increase in profitability and improved well-being.

Such considerations lead us to discuss this short-term *versus* long-term perspectives in terms of policy design and to analyse what micro-finance requires in order to facilitate an expansion of agency and capability in the long term.

8.6. Micro-finance, street children and the capability approach: short-term vs. long-term

8.6.1. Prevalence of micro-finance for street children

The beneficiaries of micro-finance interventions are mainly women. One of the reasons mentioned is related to the impact on children (Cheston and Kuhn, 2002). Children have, indeed, long been a priority of micro-finance interventions but, surprisingly, have not been directly targeted by such interventions (Foy, 2001). Indeed, thanks to its role of income generation and vulnerability reduction, micro-finance is said to be able to improve children's access to education, to enhance their nutritional and health status, reduce their need to work and even prevent them from having to turn to the streets to survive. This framework assumes that the impact of micro-finance will be beneficial only if the household (especially the mother) plays the role of interface. However, as pointed out by Nagarajan (2004: 2), "capital is assumed to flow from the family for adolescents (...) but family support is limited for orphaned and poor adolescents to access capital to start a business and to help accumulate assets".

Consequently, micro-finance interventions have recently broadened their scope to children and youth, as part of the new "Micro-finance for youth" framework being advocated by some youth-serving organizations (YSOs) and micro-finance institutions (MFIs).[10] Young people aged between 15 and 24 years number more than 1 billion worldwide, 85% being concentrated in developing countries where many are especially vulnerable to extreme poverty (ILO, 2006). According to ILO, youth unemployment accounts for approximately 41% of all 180 million unemployed persons globally.[11] As such, micro-finance is claimed to be a good solution for enhancing their employability. However, the prevalence of such micro-finance programmes remains quite low.

Regarding the specific case of street children/youth, the micro-finance programmes addressing them, although not numerous, have a global scope, being found in Asia, as well as in Africa and Latin America.[12] They are, for the most part, initiated by YSOs and built on the approach that perceives non-hazardous work as an essential vehicle of juvenile socialization, training and self-esteem, highlighting the necessity to listen to street children and consider them as capable human beings who know about their own affairs. This global scope extends our findings in terms of demand, since it appears that not only Bangladeshi street children express a need for financial services. Some may argue that such demand can be supply driven, in other words that the organizations create the demand by supplying their services, but this can hardly be defended as these organizations' philosophy is built on a subject-oriented approach.

YSOs indicate that micro-finance could be a valuable policy for addressing the street children issue. However, due to the particularity of the target population, they argue for the necessity of delivering micro-finance as part of a long-term development policy, where financial services are accompanied by additional services such as vocational training or social services.

8.6.2. Short-term *versus* long-term policies

Policies designed for intervening in the lives of street children depend largely on the way the beneficiaries are perceived. Indeed, due to the traditional approach that perceives street children as destitute, with no agency at all, policies in the past were mainly based on a short-term rescue strategy. As in the case of emergency programmes, the interventions were designed only for the provision of survival services such as food, shelter or health services. On the contrary, when street children are perceived as active policy makers for themselves and as agents with the right to express their preferences and choose between different options, interventions turn into a long-term approach aimed at "equipping street children with the skills and confidence required to reintegrate into society, fulfilling their human rights to self-realization and independence" (ADB, 2003: 6).

Micro-finance, as highlighted previously, needs to fall into this second category, especially for policy purposes. Indeed, delivering micro-finance as part of a short-term policy would mean, firstly, that the provision of savings and credit services to street children is just aimed at meeting their short-term financial needs. This means that the savings services would enable the child to store money for a short while in order to protect his/her money from theft. On the other hand, credit would represent a small loan assisting the child to start a seasonal business generating short-term profits. Secondly, this policy would considerably limit the positive impacts on street children, by focusing the few potential benefits on the short term and not proposing a sustainable solution to their predicament. Thirdly, this contradicts the capability framework that gives a central place to children's agency, as street children would still be perceived as destitute and not as agents who are forward looking.

The potential benefits of a long-term micro-finance programme for street children are multiple: helping the child build large lump sums of money; inculcating him/her with the habit of saving; increasing the child's agency thanks to the success of the business activity (self-esteem); and expanding his/her capability. This could create some negative effects, however, especially regarding credit. Firstly, if a street child fails in his/her business investment, he/she could decide to run away, hence losing the benefits of other services such as health or psychological counselling. Moreover, a failure could considerably deplete his/her self-esteem, hence negatively impacting his/her agency. Secondly, the street child could use the loan to buy drugs or weapons. Thirdly, if the child were in a position to join the formal education system, such services could limit his/her future freedom of choice. Finally, high indebtedness could also impact their well-being. In some cases the potential benefits may be outweighed by the costs.

Although these arguments are important to consider, we argue that a carefully designed micro-finance programme could avoid this damage to positive effects and that, alone, financial services are unable to create a long-term impact. Hence the importance of combining credit and savings services with additional services, especially training and life skills, which can be considerable in expanding street children's agency and capability in the long term.

8.6.3. Micro-finance and street children: designing a long-term intervention

8.6.3.1. Financial services

The core of a micro-finance programme lies in its financial services, generally comprising savings and credit. These products require a good design in order to create a positive effect on street children.

Firstly, a micro-savings scheme must help street children build financial capital and, in this way, expand their capabilities. For this, Rutherford (2002) emphasizes the importance for such a scheme to deliver reliable, convenient and flexible services. This means essentially to guarantee the security of the savings places, to deliver quick and accessible services and to allow voluntary deposits and withdrawals of any amount. Moreover, attention must be given to the provision of non-monetary returns in order to stimulate savings deposits, as well as accepting deposits of assets, such as working material for instance.

A micro-credit is characterized by a size, a term and an interest rate. The product needs to be characterized, firstly, by a small loan size, as this limits the risk of the child falling into high indebtedness as well as the risk of default for the provider. An amount between US$20 and US$100 seems appropriate. However, it must be adequately tailored to the needs of street children. Secondly, the term has to be flexible, allowing the child to extend initial deadlines if he or she is unable to meet initial repayments. Thirdly, the interest rate, called the "service charge" by a majority of street children programmes (both for economic and ethical reasons[13]), has to be low. The range of 5–15% seems to be the most commonly used among practitioners.

Then, a good targeting mechanism has to be implemented, by setting clear eligibility criteria, in order to create appropriate barriers of entry into the programme. This will avoid targeting street children who might not need credit or might not be able to make good use of the loan. This could be built on four criteria: (1) appropriate age; (2) membership time, in order to know the child before providing the financial services; (3) willingness, motivation and ability to start a business; and (4) feasibility of the business plan. Moreover, these criteria can include some collateral substitutes, such as compulsory savings (i.e. disbursing credit for those who have saved a minimum amount of money) or guarantors (such as a shopkeeper or another child).

Finally, an appropriate delivery mechanism will be essential. As such, three micro-finance mechanisms must be prioritized. Firstly, all YSOs highlight the importance of providing progressive lending, by starting small and expanding the loan size with the child's performance. The child's reliability will then be tested and this will increase his/her opportunity cost of non-repayment. Secondly, a frequent-repayment scheme (such as weekly) is a way for the institution to screen the child's ability and willingness to repay the loan. Last, but not least, one of the main characteristics of street children is their supportive and cooperative behaviour. Hence, some YSOs provide group lending, where the credit is disbursed to individual street children under the supervision of group members. The idea of peer support is to give the children the opportunity to share skills, opinions and ideas, supporting themselves and collaborating with one another to ensure the success of their respective businesses. This can enhance their self-esteem and self-confidence, as they feel they have a place and a role in society, and that their voice does count for something. However, some risks exist too, especially for the most vulnerable street children who maintain a hierarchy in their street relations. If micro-finance breaks this hierarchy, this can turn into non-supportive behaviour. This delivery process has thus to be carefully followed up.

Finally, involving guardians appears an essential element to the programme's success. It is important to guarantee that they approve of the child's participation in the programme, without interfering with his/her business, but supporting the child whenever he/she faces any problem. A monitoring system has to be initiated, though, in order to follow up family intrusion problems that may occur.

8.6.3.2. Holistic micro-finance programme

The minimalist micro-finance framework designed above needs to be completed by additional services in order to create a sustainable impact on street children's well-being. Indeed, even if motivated, willing and committed to starting a successful business, street children may lack the appropriate skills to do so. Vocational training, referring to an educational activity oriented to provide the necessary knowledge and skills for exerting a working activity (Casanova, 2003), appears to be an essential tool for achieving this objective. Following Kobayashi (2004), four types of vocational training need to be provided in two different phases. Firstly, the child should have the choice of following "production-oriented" training (such as mechanics or electronics) and/or "service-oriented training" (such as hotel management or restaurant servicing techniques). Once graduated from these training sessions, the child has two options: either work as an employee in a particular business or start his/her own business. In the second case, and only if the child satisfies the loan eligibility criteria raised previously, he/she will be provided with "entrepreneurship training" aimed at developing the personal, organizational and financial skills needed to start a business activity. This should include activities such as developing a business plan (one of our criteria in accessing credit), problem solving, stock control techniques and time management. Then, when the child starts a business, "management training" will seek to assist the child, after the launching of the business, in the challenges he/she may face in its management.

An essential notion that should frame this process is freedom of choice. Indeed, street children should be given the choice either to benefit or not benefit from these training sessions. Not all street children desire or need this support; some may still have the ability and willingness to join the formal education system, and this should be encouraged. Then, in the second phase, children should be able to choose the type of training they want. These two levels of freedom are essential and require the provider, firstly, to perceive children as responsible and capable beings and, secondly, to propose a large range of training sessions that build upon the existing skills of the child. Here there is a risk that such schemes may be subject to stereotyping, where girls are taught cooking and sewing and boys are trained in mechanics, which needs to be avoided (Ennew, 2000: 133). Moreover, not all children are potential entrepreneurs; some may only want or have the capacity to be employees. For the latter, savings services will help them to maximize returns from their jobs. Finally, Ballet et al. (2006) argue that the child's age must be as high as possible, as this process involves a defined trajectory for the child's future activity and in this way restricts their future freedom, mapping out their path.

After integrating these training components into our micro-finance framework, we need to turn to our third phase by incorporating the operational requirement of the programme: "social services" (see Figure 8.1). As outlined previously, even if street children have high capacities, they remain vulnerable, having basic and urgent needs to fulfil first. Although the fact of benefiting from financial services and vocational training can provide them with the ability to meet basic functionings (such as being well nourished or in good health) in the long term, some problems may still arise in the short term. Indeed, they need access to some immediate basic commodities, which generally comprise health, nutrition, education, psychological counselling and legal aid. These are provided in drop-in centres (DIC) (see Figure 8.1), where the child is also given shelter (day and/or night). However, in order to avoid problems of dependency, a good targeting strategy, with clear criteria for identification of the most vulnerable street children, has to be initiated. Furthermore, it is important gradually to downgrade the provision of social services as the child becomes more and more capable and autonomous.

When considering all these elements for the PMUK micro-finance programme, we notice shortcomings in the design of its financial services and some problems in the accompanying services. For instance, the majority of credits are not directly linked to vocational training and loan access criteria remain unclear, hence creating deficits in the targeting mechanism.

8.7. Conclusions

Recently, some government and youth organizations have coordinated their efforts in order to find effective and sustainable solutions for intervening in the lives of street children. By analysing the scope of micro-finance to address this issue, this chapter has attempted to bring new insights and enrich the range of solutions proposed.

The chapter argues that micro-finance has the ability to empower street children economically by providing them with tools that will enable them to take their own destiny in hand. Savings services can help them accumulate large lump sums of money for meeting their daily expenses, emergency and opportunity needs and, hence, to improve their future. Credit services, along with vocational training, can be highly valuable for enhancing the child's universe of choices and opportunities, protecting him/her from hazardous work and enlarging the child's future trajectory.

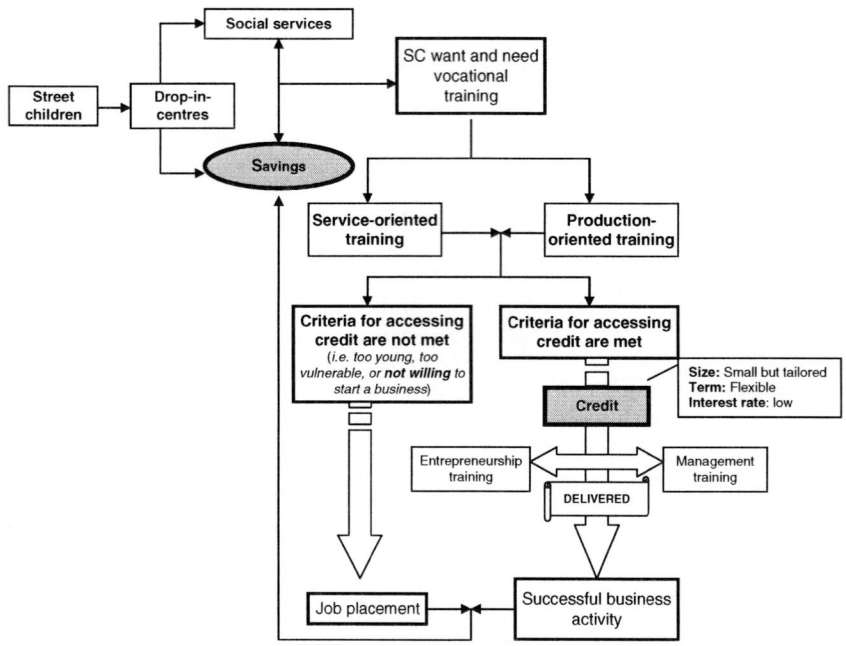

Figure 8.1   Micro-finance for street children framework

This can have considerable impact on children's agency too, as it can expand their ability to bring positive change to their livelihoods, hence expanding their self-esteem and self-confidence.

However, reaching such objectives requires a holistic intervention, combining carefully designed financial services with vocational training and social services. This can be very demanding on the management side, as the organization that chooses such an axis of intervention must have double expertise in the area of both "micro-finance" and "street children". This calls for thinking about effective partnerships between MFIs and YSOs. Moreover, this can be costly to administer and, thus, hardly financially sustainable. However, if well designed, it can minimize the level of subsidies needed and guarantee viability in the long term.

In addition to outlining such considerations, the chapter claims the importance of changing our conceptions about street children and child work in order to bring a new dynamic to intervention policies. Indeed, although working is not the result of a choice children would have made in an ideal living environment free of structural constraints, it still represents a choice made by many street children in order to improve their personal and family well-being within their constrained universe. We have explained how removing them from the labour market is not a sustainable solution in itself. Translating this into a policy perspective means that efforts should be concentrated on enhancing their capabilities in order to engage in decent work. It is important to point out that this issue is well captured in Part III of this book.

Micro-finance is not a panacea or miraculous solution to the issue. It remains an intervention tool that needs to go hand in hand with prevention mechanisms. It is therefore essential for governments and international organizations to raise concern about the predicament of street children and develop adequate prevention mechanisms. Finally, beyond the question of street children, this chapter aims to extend the scope of interventions, research and debate on micro-finance to other vulnerable groups of young people.

Acknowledgements

I would like to thank Daniel Traça, Jérôme Ballet, Mario Biggeri, Flavio Comim, Marc Labie, Christian Platteau and Angela Pollitzer for their comments on earlier versions. I am also grateful to Iqbal Ahmmed, PMUK staff and the street children who took part in our research in Bangladesh. I am responsible for all errors that remain.

Notes

1. For example, some "children of the streets" may have cut off all contact with their families, whereas others may still visit their families once in a while before returning to the street.
2. Capital equipment comprises several elements: financial, physical, human, social and cultural.
3. Centre for Urban Studies, quoted in Iglebaeck and Hassan (2005).
4. The Consortium for Street Children Worldwide estimated, in 2001, a total of 445,226 street children in Bangladesh, of which 75% are in Dhaka city and 53% are boys.
5. A Bangladeshi NGO, mainly specialized in the field of micro-finance.
6. A participatory tool that aims to identify the needs and perceptions of participants. It was used to analyse the street children's conceptions of money, savings and credit.
7. Before joining Padakhep and benefiting from access to savings services.
8. Ramadan is a Muslim celebration, lasting one month, where believers fast during the day and eat at sunset for spiritual reasons.
9. Other similar success cases appeared in the research. In order to limit the size of the chapter, we are not able to discuss them all.
10. By youth-serving organizations, we mean any organization serving at-risk youth and include child rights organizations. For MFI, we use the definition adopted by Rutherford (2002), who defines it as any NGO that provides financial services to low-income people, either as their exclusive business or as part of a wider programme of development.

11. By "unemployed", the ILO means any person without work who has made him/herself available for employment (ILO, 2006).
12. Examples include Street Kids International, the Children's Development Bank (Asia) and Pronats (Latin America).
13. It avoids becoming subject to formal regulation and the notion of "interest" implies profit, which is perceived as unethical in the context of working with children.

References

ADB (2003), *Working with Street Children: Exploring Ways for ADB Assistance*, Asian Development Bank, Manila, Philippines.

Alexandrescu, G. (1996), "Programme Note: Street Children in Bucharest", *Childhood, Global Journal of Child Research*, 3(2): 267–270.

Ballet, J., Bhukuth, A. and Radja, K. (2006), "Child labour, Human Rights and the Capability Approach". Paper presented at the HDCA Conference, Groningen.

Blanc, C.S. (1994), *Urban Children in Distress: Global Predicament and Innovative Strategies*, Gordon and Breach, Pennsylvania, PA.

Boyden, J. (1991), *Children of the Cities*, Zed Books Ltd., London.

Boyden, J., Ling, B. and Myers, W. (1998), *What Works For Working Children*, Sweden, Radda Barnen, Save the Children Fund Sweden.

Casanova, F. (2003), *Vocational Training and Labour Relations*, Cinterfor/ILO, Montevideo.

Cheston, S. and Kuhn, L. (2002), "Empowering Women through Micro-finance", in Sam Daley-Harris (ed.), *Pathways out of Poverty*, Kumarian Press, Bloomfield, Connecticut.

Conticini, A. (2004), *We Are the Kings. Managing, Protecting and Promoting Livelihoods on the Streets of Dhaka*, Institute for Development Policy and Management (IDPM), Manchester.

Dunford, M. (1996), *Tackling the Symptoms or the Causes? An Examination of Programmes by NGOs for Street Children in Nairobi*, Centre of African Studies, Edinburgh University.

Ennew, J. (2000), *Street and Working Children: A Guide to Planning*, 2nd edn, Save the Children Fund.

Felsman, J.K. (1981), "Street Urchins of Cali: On Risk, Resiliency and Adaptation in Childhood", Harvard University, MA: unpublished PhD thesis.

Foy, D. (2001), "Micro-finance and Street Children", unpublished master thesis, Institute of Development Studies, University of Sussex (UK).

Grundling, J. and Grundling, I. (2005), "The Concrete Particulars of the Everyday Realities of Street Children", *Human Relations*, 58: 173–190.

Hatloy, A. and Huser, A. (2005), "Report: Identification of Street Children, Characteristics of Street Children in Bamako and Accra", FAFO, Research Program on Trafficking and Child Labour.

Iglebaeck, M. and Hassan, E. (2005), "The Puzzle of Children and Their Money: Evidence from Bangladesh", final draft version, Plan International, Bangladesh.

ILO (2006), *The End of Child Labour: Within Reach*, ILO, Geneva, Switzerland.

Kobayashi, Y. (2004), *Economic Livelihoods for Street Children*, DAI Inc., Bethesda, MD.

Lalor, K. (1999), "Street Children: A Comparative Perspective", *Child Abuse and Neglect*, 23(8): 759–770.

Levison, D. (2000), "Children As Economic Agents", *Feminist Economics*, 6(1), 125–134.

Liebel, M. (2004), *A Will of Their Own: Cross-cultural Perspectives on Working Children*, Zed Books, London.

Lucchini, R. (1996), "Theory, Method and Triangulation in the Study of Street Children", *Childhood*, 3(2): 167–170.

Lucchini, R. (1998), "Sociologia de la supervivencia. El nino y la calle", Université de Fribourg, Suiza and Universidad Nacional Autonoma de Mexico, Mexico.

Marten P. Van Den Berge (2006), "Working Children: Their Agency and Self-organization", *Ethique et Economique*, 4(1), http://ethique-economique.net.

Mitra, S. (2006), "The Capability Approach and Disability", *Journal of Disability Policy Studies*, 16(4), 236–247.

Moore, K. (2000), "Supporting Children in Their Working Lives: Obstacles and Opportunities Within the International Policy Environment", *Journal of International Development*, 12: 531–548.

Myers (2001), "Valuing Diverse Approaches to Child Labour", in G.K. Lieten and B. White (eds), *Child Labour: Policy Options*, Aksant Publishers, Amsterdam.

Nagarajan, G. (2004), "Microbanking with Adolescent Youth", Asian Development Bank, newsletter of December 2004, accessible at adb.org/Documents/Periodicals/Micro-finance/finance-200454.pdf

O'Connor, S. (2003), "Hope and a Future: Empowering Street Children and Their Communities", Viva Network, accessible at http://www.viva.org/en/articles/haf.pdf

Robinson, M.S. (2001), *The Micro-finance Revolution: Sustainable Finance for the Poor; Lessons from Indonesia: The Emerging Industry*, The World Bank, Washington, DC.

Rutherford, S. (1999), *The Poor and Their Money: An Essay about Financial Services for Poor People*, The Department for International Development, New Delhi.

Rutherford, S. (2002), *Money Talks: Conversations with Poor Households in Bangladesh about Managing Money*, Institute for Development Policy and Management, University of Manchester.

Scanlon, T.J., Tomkins, A., Lynch, M.A., Scanlon, F. (1998), "Street Children in Latin America", *BMJ Journal*, 316: 1596-600.

Sen, A.K. (1980), "Equality of What?", in S. Memurrin (ed.), *The Tanner Lectures on Human Values*, University of Utah Press, Salt Lake City.

Sen, A.K. (1985), "Well-being, Agency and Freedom", *The Journal of Philosophy*, 82: 169–221.

Sen, A.K. (1992), *Inequality Re-examined*, OUP, Oxford.

Sen, A.K. (1999), *Development As Freedom*, Knopf Press, New York.

Shurink, W. (1993), *Street Children: Working Document*, Human Science Research Council, Pretoria, South Africa.

Tolfree, D. (1998), *Old Enough to Work, Old Enough to Have a Say: Different Approaches to Supporting Working Children*, Radda Barnen, SCF Sweden.

UNICEF (1986), *Children in Especially Difficult Circumstances: Exploitation of Working and Street Children*, United Nations Children Fund, New York.

UNICEF (2006), *The State of the World's Children 2006: Excluded and Invisible*, United Nations Children Fund, New York.

Williams, C. (1993). "Who Are 'Street Children'? A Hierarchy of Street Use and Appropriate Responses", *Child Abuse and Neglect*, 17: 831–841.

Woodhead, M. (1999), *Is There a Place for Work in Child Development?*, Save the Children Publication, Stockholm, Radda Barnen.

9
'Good for Children'? Local Understandings *versus* Universal Prescriptions: Evidence from Three Ethiopian Communities

Laura Camfield and Yisak Tafere

9.1. Background

Worldwide there have been many studies about understandings of well-being (reviewed in Alkire, 2002; Camfield, 2006), i.e. what constitutes and contributes to a life that people have reason to value in particular contexts.[1] As we have seen in Chapters 2 and 3 of this book, concepts and even domains of well-being may vary across different contexts or according to age, which implies that children's participation is central for understanding their capabilities. This chapter reports differences between Ethiopian children and their caregivers in expressed understandings of a good life and what is needed to achieve this. It also explores whether the capability approach can be used to bridge the gap between shared local understandings of a good life and the universal prescriptions of global bodies such as UNICEF on what is 'good for children'. The chapter uses quantitative and qualitative data from *Young Lives*, a longitudinal study of childhood poverty. These comprise group interviews and activities with a subsample of children (aged 11–13), caregivers and community informants from three urban and rural communities who explore what constitutes well-being or a good life for children in their community.[2] The qualitative data are supplemented by analyses of responses from children and their caregivers to questions on their values, aspirations and experiences of subjective well-being in the second round of the *Young Lives* survey.[3]

The chapter begins by reviewing literature on understandings of well-being in Ethiopia and describing the methods used to generate the data reported in Section 9.3. It then contrasts the diverse understandings of children and adults and explores the extent to which they can be usefully understood within Nussbaum's meta-framework of central human capabilities selected because of its claimed universality.

The CA pioneered by Sen and Nussbaum has influenced conceptualizations of well-being, although Sen refuses to ground and potentially limit the approach with a definitive list of basic capabilities and thresholds for their achievement in the manner of theories of human needs (see also Chapters 1 and 3). Sen argues persuasively that "pure theory cannot 'freeze' a list of capabilities for all societies for all time to come, irrespective of what the citizens come to understand and value", because "first, we use capabilities for different purposes, [...] second, social conditions and the priorities that they suggest may vary [...and] third, public discussion and reasoning can lead to a better understanding of the role, reach and the significance of particular capabilities" (2005: 158–160). As an extension of this approach, Nussbaum proposes a list of ten "Central Human Capabilities", such as affiliation and play, that "supply a moral and humanly rich set of goals for development, in place of 'the wealth and poverty of the economists', as Marx so nicely put it" (Nussbaum, 2003: 36). However, not only the achievability of Nussbaum's list, but also its cross-cultural validity and applicability to different groups (e.g. elderly people, children) has been questioned and requires further exploration with different groups in diverse settings[4] (Clark, 2002; Menon, 2002; Gough, 2004; Robeyns, 2005: 198–199). For example, Biggeri et al. (2006) have asked children to develop a corresponding list (see Chapters 3 and 5 of this volume), which comprises education, love and care, life and physical health, and leisure.

Biggeri et al.'s approach (see Chapters 4 and 5) illustrates the potential of participatory methods in mediating between the "thin" and "thick" approaches to the capabilities of Sen and Nussbaum, which Lavers describes as "combining the merits of a wide range of human capabilities and a broad vision of human flourishing, evident in Nussbaum's work, and the greater potential for underpinning international and inter-cultural consensus of Sen's" (2008: 132). The wide range of "goods" considered necessary for well-being in Ethiopia, according to data collected by the Economic and Social Research Council (ESRC) Well-being in Developing Countries Research Group (WeD) confirms Lavers' premise that "daily food is not the sole priority of the community members [...]. As such it is hard to justify any claims that asking people in Ethiopia what goals they have reason to value does not relate to the local reality as their sole focus is on day-to-day survival" (*ibid.*: 135). The group-based work with children and adults in Ethiopia reported in this chapter also challenges orthodox understandings of well-being, and one of the purposes of the chapter is to explore the extent to which a CA to well-being increases the power of existing methodologies.

Clearly understanding the "capability space" in different societies is important for understanding what people are then able to achieve, particularly in resource-constrained environments such as Ethiopia. The interpretation of the CA presented in Chapter 2 emphasizes children's role as "active social actors and agents in their communities with their priorities, strategies and aspirations". It acknowledges that adult capabilities are conditional on childhood experiences and that autonomy, for example, can be strengthened by participating in group activities involving reflection and debate. It also introduces dynamic or "evolving" capabilities that are at the heart of the balance in the United Nations Convention on the Rights of the Child (UNCRC) between children's agency and their entitlement to protection. The approach recognizes firstly that children's capabilities may differ from adults and that their relevance will vary across contexts and life stages: "capabilities define merely an informational space, not a particular set of functionings" (Chapter 2, this book). Secondly, different children may need different policies to enjoy the same basic capabilities and achieved functionings, depending on their own capacities and on social norms and arrangements – attaining freedoms is not just a matter of exercising individual choices.

Numerous empirical studies have applied the CA to select indicators to measure poverty and well-being (e.g. Chiappero-Martinetti, 1996, 2000; Anand et al., 2005; Clark and Qizilbash, 2008), some in relation to children (Di Tommaso, 2006; see also Chapters 3 and 10 in this book). Further work has also been done on operationalization by Alkire (2007a, 2007b) and Robeyns (2003). For example, Alkire highlights the value of "ongoing deliberative participatory processes" similar to those described in the methodology section in selecting dimensions for measurement, setting weights and thresholds and aggregating data (see Biggeri and Mehrotra, Chapter 3 in this book). In Ethiopia, adult understandings have typically been collected through Participatory Poverty Assessments (Rahmato and Kidanuo, 1999; Ellis and Woldehanna, 2005) and more recent work by WeD using structured questionnaires (Lavers, 2008) and measures (Woodcock, 2007). Although the findings of the studies show common elements – health, economic independence, behaving well, having religious faith and relationships in the family and community – they also demonstrate considerable diversity by location, gender, religion, socio-economic status and life stage. Far less work has been done with children in Ethiopia on their understandings of well-being, although two recent studies by Tekola et al. (2008) and Tafere (2007, unpublished) produced interesting insights. For example, Tafere's comparative analysis of two urban communities from *Young Lives* demonstrated the perceived importance of *social relationships, personal characteristics, engagement with environment* and *spirituality*, while Tekola's use of community maps with children in Addis Ababa generated interesting information about well-being and ill-being in relation to education. Tekola's findings support those of an earlier national study by UNICEF (Conticini et al., 2005; see also Chapter 5), which identified *education* as the main "dream" of children aged 5–17 because it was seen as "key to having a better life, getting out of poverty, 'becoming someone' and being able to help other vulnerable children" (*ibid.*: 11).

9.2. Methodology

This section describes the two main methods used to collect the data analysed in this chapter: quantitative child and household questionnaires and qualitative group activities and interviews.

9.2.1. Quantitative data

Young Lives administered questionnaires to children and their caregivers in 2002 and 2006. This chapter uses data from the 2006 survey (*n* = 979[5]), as this addresses aspirations and expectations directly and was collected one year before the qualitative research. The caregivers' questionnaire covers parental background, household composition and activities and, most importantly for this chapter, caregiver perceptions and attitudes. The child questionnaire focuses on children's activities, experiences and relationships; this chapter analyses data on children's feelings and attitudes, relationships with parents and perceptions of school and work.

9.2.2. Qualitative data

9.2.2.1. Sites

Five sites were selected to capture ethnically based regional difference and enable comparison between the capital and a smaller urban centre (see Camfield and Tafere, 2009 for a description of this process). These included two urban sites (Addis Ababa and a regional capital) and three rural, two of which were relatively remote. The data analysed in this chapter come from three sites:[6] *Akilit Tera* (urban, Addis Ababa region), *Leki* (near-rural, Oromia) and *Semhal* (remote-rural, Tigray).

I. *Akilit Tera* is a densely populated community in the national capital (14,066 inhabitants) that is ethnically and religiously diverse, albeit with a predominance of the *Amhara* ethnic group and Ethiopian Orthodox Christians. Indicators of absolute poverty were low and respondents reported good access to healthcare and education. They nonetheless perceived themselves as poor relative to others in the community, suggesting the presence of material inequality. *Akilit Tera* is located next to the city's fruit and vegetable market, which affects the inhabitants both positively and negatively: there are many economic opportunities for adults and children (e.g. street vending or renting buildings for storage), but the area is dirty due to rotting fruit and vegetables, young women reported harassment in public spaces and caregivers were concerned that their children were exposed to activities such as prostitution, gambling and the consumption of alcohol and drugs.
II. *Leki* is a comparatively small (2835) and ethnically homogenous community of predominately *Oromiffa*-speaking Orthodox Christians, with a few Muslim families. It has good natural resources (for example, irrigated

fields for vegetable growing, a lake for fishing) and a temperate climate, but is nonetheless materially poor and has poor access to healthcare and education. Girls in particular were employed growing onions and tomatoes, which were sold in *Akilit Tera* market.

III. *Semhal* is of similar size to *Leki* and is also ethnically homogenous, with exclusively *Tigrinya*-speaking Orthodox Christians. However, it is more remote as the nearest town is two to three hours' walk, and the road is usable only in the "dry season". Respondents were materially poor and had limited access to services and domestic utilities. Male educational participation was low, as boys were needed to herd cattle.

9.2.2.2. Sample

Equal numbers of boys and girls were sub-sampled in each site using additional criteria such as access to schooling, whether the household was female or male headed, and orphanhood. The sub-sampled children were compared with the young lives sample of older children in the five sites to see whether there were systematic differences that needed to be taken into account in analysis (see Camfield and Tafere, 2009). For example, sub-sampled children were slightly more likely to have engaged in paid work and reported a work-related injury in the previous four years. They were also more likely to consider their household poorer than others and less likely to aim for university.

9.2.2.3. Methods

The data analysed in Section 9.3 come from two sources: firstly, separate group interviews with caregivers and male and female community informants (for example, government employees, elders) on understandings of well-being and transitions, using focusing questions such as "How are children expected to spend their time?" or "Tell me some local sayings/proverbs that relate to children", etc. Secondly, a group activity called the Well-being Exercise conducted independently with five boys and five girls aged 11–13 at each site. The Well-being Exercise came from a toolkit of methods developed by the authors for application in diverse cultural contexts (Crivello et al., 2008). It explores what children consider a "good" or "bad" life for children of the same age and gender, living in their community and what they identify as sources of risk and protection. Children drew pictures individually of children experiencing good or bad lives, and explained their meaning to the group, often eliciting critical or challenging responses (for example, whether a 12-year-old child was too young to chew *chat* – a mild narcotic). This was followed by a collective discussion with children's suggestions written on a flip chart divided into columns for "good life" and "bad life", so that suggestions could be more easily turned into "indicators" that the participants ranked.

Individual children's ideas and rankings were recorded and followed up in individual interviews (not reported here).

Careful attention was paid to the composition of the research team and the nature and scheduling of activities, to enable respondents to feel more relaxed with the researchers. Informed consent was obtained at the start of the project; however, the team regularly checked participants' willingness and reminded them of their right to disengage whenever they wanted to, which was exercised on several occasions (Morrow, 2009).

9.3. Results

9.3.1. Quantitative

The analysis of the child and household questionnaires was carried out using the whole sample,[7] and further analyses were done for subgroups of gender,[8] location (rural *versus* urban) and perceived socio-economic status (grouped as poorer than other households in the community, average and richer than other households in the community). Most sections appeared in both the child and household questionnaires and the data could therefore be compared, for example, on the value of education; future aspirations relating to school and work; and two indicators of subjective well-being. We have also reported i) a section on perceptions of school from the child questionnaire, as education was a component of a good life for children in all sites, and ii) a section on important qualities for children, future expectations and the ages at which children are expected to make certain key transitions, from the household questionnaire, as these provide useful background. Most of the data were ordinal, so the significance of differences could not be tested with parametric stastistics. However, this was done for the subjective well-being indicators and the ages for key transitions using independent sample *t*-tests or ANOVA with a *post hoc* Scheffe test, as appropriate.

9.3.1.1. *Children's perceptions of schooling and work*

When children were asked what the best things about school were, the most common response was "learning useful skills" (34.1%, range 29.5%–36.6%), followed by "teachers are good" (20.8%, range 17.9%–24.1%). When asked about the worst things, the overwhelming response was "nothing" (27.7%, 20.6%–34.8%), and this response was particularly common among girls (34.8%), perhaps indicating their awareness of the gender disparities in access to education that exist at all levels.[9] The second most common response was "students fighting" (18.4%, 15.8%–22.4%). Conversely, in the group activities children, particularly girls, talked at length about shortcomings in the school infrastructure (for example, dirt, the absence of drinking water and toilets), and also about teacher absenteeism and violence. There are some interesting differences between groups; for example, "lack of toilets" is more of a concern for girls (7.4%) than boys (2.8%), which reflects fears about sexual violence in mixed or isolated toilets articulated by girls during the community mapping activity. "Lack of [drinking] water" is similarly a greater concern in rural (10.4%) than in urban areas (5.4%). This is partly because urban schools are in better repair, but also because in some rural areas children travel up to an hour and a half to attend school and so cannot return home if they need water or food during the day.

9.3.1.2. Adult perceptions of (a) important qualities for children to have; (b) future expectations; and (c) appropriate ages for key transitions

Respondents were asked to endorse three qualities from a potential 14 from the internationally validated "Value of Children" scale (Mayer et al., 2006) as the most important for children to have. All groups chose the same qualities with only minor variations in percentages, namely hard work (mean 24.4%), independence (mean 18.3%) and religious faith (mean 13.1%). Respondents across all groups also reported similar future expectations from their children, even where they had migrated for education, work or marriage. For example, while on average 82% of respondents expected their children to continue living close to them, over 95% expected some degree of financial, practical and emotional support, both for themselves and their other children, and 91% expected help with family work. Urban respondents were most likely to expect the child to continue living close by, rural least likely. This did not necessarily indicate an interruption of relationships, as rural respondents were more likely than urban to expect their children to care for their younger siblings, and for them when they became old. Perhaps unsurprisingly, respondents from poorer households were most likely to expect financial support from their children in the future, and this expectation is supported by similar assertions from children, particularly in relation to their mothers. There were also few significant differences in the ages at which children were expected to make key transitions or fulfil certain responsibilities (Table 9.1), even though these came out strongly in community focus groups (Tafere and Camfield, 2008) and girls were expected to marry and have children earlier than boys. Rural children were also expected to become financially independent and leave the household earlier than urban ones, which may reflect differences in their parents' educational aspirations, as discussed later in this section.

A more significant difference was that between the ages parents reported as appropriate for key transitions and the ages when these typically take place, according to the Ethiopian Demographic and Health Survey (DHS, 2005). For example, although the household questionnaire reported the expected marriage age for boys as 27.4 years, and for girls 25.6 years, according to DHS the median age at first marriage was far lower for both groups. There was also a large difference between the ages of men and women: the median

Table 9.1 Caregivers' preferences regarding the timing of key transitions

Caregiver	Urban	Rural	Poor	Average	Rich	Male	Female
Age [NAME] should earn money to support household	22.9[1] (4.24)	22.2 (4.65)	22.7 (4.22)	22.5 (4.68)	22.1 (4.40)	22.8 (5.04)	22.1 (3.87)
Age [NAME] should leave full-time education	21.1 (4.24)	20.8 (3.72)	20.8 (4.31)	20.9 (3.54)	21.3 (4.50)	21.2 (4.15)	20.7 (3.70)
Age [NAME] should be financially independent	23.9** (4.43)	23.0** (3.88)	23.3 (3.67)	23.3 (4.10)	23.3 (3.66)	23.3 (4.43)	23.4 (3.80)
Age [NAME] should leave household	24.9** (5.35)	23.7** (4.05)	24.2 (4.95)	24.2 (4.51)	24.2 (4.95)	24.5 (5.16)	23.9 (4.03)
Age [NAME] should get married	27.1* (6.30)	26.1* (4.95)	26.3 (6.27)	26.6 (5.26)	26.4 (5.16)	27.4** (5.93)	25.6** (4.93)
Age [NAME] should have a child	29.0 (6.63)	28.1 (5.36)	28.2 (6.87)	28.5 (5.65)	28.4 (5.00)	29.4** (6.46)	27.5** (5.09)

[1] Age in years (standard deviation). Significance level: $**p = <0.001$; $*p = <0.01$.
Source: Young Lives round 2 survey data.

age for women aged 20–24 was 18.1 years and for men aged 25–29 it was 24.2 years.[10] Similarly, the median age for women aged 25–29 to have their first child was 19.2 years, rather than the 29 years proposed by respondents in urban areas. Finally, although the expected age for leaving full-time education ranges between 20.7 and 21.3, in reality only 2.4% of men have post-secondary education and 1.4% of women. According to DHS, even in the highest wealth quintile the median years of schooling are only 4.2 for women and 6.7 for men.

9.3.1.3. Comparing responses to the same questions in the child and household questionnaires

Children and adults were presented with two hypothetical scenarios where a family in their community has a 12-year-old son or daughter who is attending school full-time: "The family badly needs to increase the household income, one option is to send the son/daughter to work but the son/daughter wants to stay in school. What should the family do?": 93.2% of children and 94.7% of adults felt the son should stay in school and 93.4% of children and 93.1% of adults felt the daughter should stay in school. There was little variation in responses in both surveys (range 91%–97% for both questions), although the adults were slightly more likely to favour the son, while the children had no clear preference.

Nearly all children (98.8%) described formal schooling as "essential" in their future life, and the range was again very small (98.1%–99.4%) (for similar results, see Chapter 5). This was mirrored by the scores of adult respondents who did not have formal schooling (mean 95%, range 94.1%–95.5%). Respondents who had received schooling were less certain of its value, for example, while 89% of urban respondents thought that schooling had been "essential" in their life, this view was shared by only 77.4% of rural respondents. Believing that schooling was essential was inversely correlated with socio-economic status: 88.8% of respondents from poor households expressed this, compared with only 79.7% from rich households. This may relate to either the quality of local schools or the types of skills they foster to support children's futures.

All these results suggest a normative consensus about the value of education, which is evident in survey responses to (educated) enumerators, but may not be reflected in practice. Nonetheless, there are variations in the level of education that children and their parents would like them to attain. For example, although overall 70.1% of children would like to complete university (73.9% for parents), the figure falls to 62.5% for children in rural areas (67.8% for parents), compared with 80.5% in urban (82.8% for parents). There is a similar difference in the aspirations of children from poorer households: 59.4% expect to go to university (68.5% of parents), compared with 75.6% of children from richer households (84% for parents). Although child and parent responses show similar patterns, in all cases parents are more ambitious than their children, and this is particularly evident in the responses of parents from poorer households.

There is little variation in what children think they will be doing aged 20, as the main choices are doctor (27.7%) or teacher (22.2%), with teacher, which requires slightly less education, being more popular for children in rural areas (31.7%) than urban (7.9%). Despite the assertions of older boys in individual semi-structured interviews, footballer (or "sportsman") averages only 1.3%. Doctor was also the most popular choice for caregivers (range 25.5%–30.3%), with the exception of respondents from urban or richer households who wanted their children to be university students (24%–29.2%).

The most striking differences between groups are in the variables that measure the extent to which people are experiencing a good life as they define it (Table 9.2), namely the respondent's perception of their current position on the "ladder of life" (an adaptation of Cantril's self-anchoring ladder [1965] where the top (9) represents the "best possible life" and the bottom (1) the worst), and where they think they will be in four years time. For children the mean scores for these variables are 4.26 (SD 1.87) and 6.12 (SD 1.97), and for adults 3.74 (SD 1.58) and 5.59 (SD 1.93). While adults score consistently lower than children, suggesting that they feel less positively about their current and future lives, perhaps more important to note is that both groups are currently well below the conventional scale midpoint of 6 (e.g. see WHO HSBC, 2001/2002). Children and adults who perceive their households as "average" or richer than others score progressively higher than those who see their households as poor, and the same pattern applies when households are grouped using expenditure quintiles. However, there were no significant differences between boys and girls, or the caregivers of boys and girls. Perhaps unexpectedly, the scores for rural children are significantly higher than for urban.

The main reasons given by children for moving up the ladder of life are "education" (19.7%) and "work harder" (21.8%), with some differences in priority between groups. For example, children in urban areas see education as more influential than those in rural areas: 25.2% *versus* 15.8%. "Work harder" was also the most important reason given by caregivers (mean 38%, range 34.8%–42.0%). Education was barely mentioned by caregivers than 1% of caregivers felt that being unable to improve their skills had moved them down the ladder. The belief that working hard will raise you up the ladder rises with wealth status (35.2% poor, 38.0% average, 42.0% rich), perhaps reflecting a realistic appraisal of the barriers to social mobility by poorer respondents. Respondents with sons or from rural areas are also more likely to believe working hard will help them move up the ladder (41.2% *versus* a mean of 38.0%). "Making less money" or having a "poor" or "irregular" job are the three main reasons given by children for moving down the

Table 9.2   Mean scores for current and future position on the "ladder of life"

	Urban	Rural	Poor	Average	Rich	Male	Female
Current position on ladder							
Children, mean (SD)	3.84**	4.55**	3.08**	4.40**	5.62**	4.23	4.29
	(1.70)	(1.92)	(1.67)	(1.58)	(1.88)	(1.91)	(1.83)
Adults, mean (SD)	3.35**	4.00**	2.89**	3.86**	4.68**	3.71	3.77
	(1.45)	(1.60)	(1.47)	(1.39)	(1.63)	(1.62)	(1.53)
Position in 4 years							
Children, mean (SD)	5.96	6.24	5.11**	6.25**	7.30**	6.01	6.24
	(1.91)	(2.01)	(1.91)	(1.85)	(1.66)	(1.93)	(2.01)
Adult, mean (SD)	5.21**	5.83**	4.70**	5.71**	6.47**	5.46	5.71
	(1.83)	(1.95)	(1.91)	(1.79)	(1.86)	(1.85)	(2.00)

Significance level: $**p = <0.001$; $*p = <0.01$.
Source: *Young Lives* round 2 survey data.

ladder in urban areas (total 51.3%, compared with 29.5% in rural areas), and poor harvest in rural areas (29.9% *versus* 1.4% in urban areas). Poor education (composite of "being poorly educated", "can't improve skills" and "have to leave education early") is also a more important reason for moving down the ladder in urban areas (21.7%) than rural (12.7%), although there are only minor differences by gender and socio-economic status. "Poor health status" is important for children from poor households (22.2%), reflecting the devastating impact of household illness on income and educational opportunities. Poor health status is also a concern for caregivers from poor households (19.1% gave it as a reason for moving down), although not having a good job was more important (21.9%).

9.3.2. Qualitative

9.3.2.1. Group activities with children

The analysis for this section used data from the Well-being Exercise, which was carried out separately with boys and girls in the three sites described earlier. It reports both the content of the discussions around good and bad lives or living well or badly, and the ranking of indicators that took place at the end of the activity. Due to the size of the sample, we have focused on differences between the responses of groups of girls and boys, and groups taking place in rural and urban areas.

9.3.2.2. Content

While the Well-being Exercise raised common themes, for example, education, these were specified differently in different sites and by different groups of respondents. In *Semhal* and *Leki*, the main concern was access to education, especially for girls (or boys with no younger siblings to herd cattle) and, to a lesser extent, educational materials. In *Akilit Tera*, however, the focus was on educational quality in many different dimensions (teaching, sanitation, class sizes, etc.) and there was a lively debate in the girls' group about the relative merits of private and state-funded schooling. For example, the private school has "adequate services like tap water and clean toilets and classrooms", and while the government school provides lessons in the evenings as well (enabling working children to attend), children are sent home during the frequent power cuts.

Children's behaviour was also a common theme (for example, being obedient, not fighting) and their comments were highly moral in tone. One example given was a vivid description of the destitute child who has a bad life because he "lives by wandering from house to house to steal" and after a period of imprisonment "[becomes] rich because of theft".[11] In the urban site comments related mainly to how the child's behaviour might affect their interactions with others. One boy described how if a boy fought with his parents he would not be supported in continuing his education, or even if he became sick: "His parents do not pay school fees for him because they don't like him; it is not because they don't have the money but because of lack of good family relations."[12] Relationships outside the family were also valued, and in *Akilit Tera* were considered important for social mobility. For example, many children emphasized the importance of having friends from school, rather than the local area: "His friends are from his surroundings and have bad behaviour. His friends are not clever so he is not clever too. [...] He and his friends are lazy in their education."[13]

Other common themes were work and its relation to all the other important domains of life, which included having a good appearance: "[having] no clothes means it becomes difficult to go out of home and you cannot go anywhere for work".[14] While all respondents were aware of status differentiations, children in *Akilit Tera* seemed to feel this more keenly and described experiences of inequality with great insight:

> [The well-being girl] has pen, exercise book, good living condition, uniform, can get adequate food, and can attend in private school. Her parents can afford the school fee and can fulfil what she wants to have. However, the ill being girl cannot get pen, pencil, bag, cloth and food. She is attending classes in government school. [...] A girl who is not doing well may join the private school but she cannot get what she needs like her well being friends since her family is poor economically but they can only afford her school fee. But the well-being girl can get what she wants to have [the same] as her friends.[15]

One of the most exciting dimensions of the exercise was the lively debate it generated, which can also be seen in the section below on the well-being ranking. This was particularly apparent in *Akilit Tera* where, although consensus was reached on the basic indicators (after two and a half hours of debate), there were still differences in the priority accorded to them. This is evident from the researchers' notes on the children's rankings of indicators of ill-being: "For Bekele losing parents is the first important indicator of ill-being, for Berhanu it is lack of proper follow up from family, for Beniam it is lack of proper education – a child who does not learn will finally be a thief, [...] for Tessema, all are equally important", etc.

9.3.2.3. Ranking

Once children had generated indicators of well-being or ill-being from the discussions described above, they were asked to rank these in order of importance. The ranking was recorded by the notetaker, who also noted any differences in opinion (for example, in *Akilit Tera* where respondents could agree on the five most important indicators, but not the order in which they should be placed). There are few differences between girls' and boys' indicators, although girls in *Semhal* mention having a separate kitchen, which would reduce eye irritation caused by cooking over wood in a poorly ventilated room. Although girls and boys in *Semhal* agree on the importance of good clothing, attending school and cleanliness as indicators of well-being and ill-being, there is a greater divergence in their views of a good life than in other communities. This suggests differentiated trajectories for girls and boys with associated differences in concerns; for example, girls mention getting sufficient food (e.g., not having to go to school without breakfast), being encouraged to study, having time to play and being asked their opinion and shown respect as signs of a good life, which may indicate that these things are absent. Boys are more concerned about good behaviour (for example, not stealing, fighting, being "foolish" or disobedient), health and having a loving and peaceful family.

In *Leki* education is only mentioned once as an indicator of well-being (by girls) and is ranked sixth (the most important indicator was food for girls and land for boys). In *Akilit Tera* both boys and girls rank education as the main indicator of well-being or ill-being. Girls also mention access to educational materials, and one girl ranked "having to attend a government school" as the second most important indicator of ill-being. Boys and girls mention being an orphan, which seems to be a particular concern of boys, and having sufficient food, and girls also mention shelter. As in *Angar*, boys mention not getting advice or "follow-up" from their families, which is implicitly linked to showing good or bad behaviour.

9.3.2.4. Group interviews with adults

The group interviews explored adult understandings of well-being and ill-being for boys and girls aged 5–6 and 11–13. Valued dimensions of well-being in all sites for children of any age and gender were (a) having material security, specifically being able to satisfy basic needs such as food and clothes; (b) experiencing good and harmonious family relationships, characterized by love, affection and care; and (c) receiving advice and moral guidance. Adults also mentioned having access to education and appropriate work that does not interfere with this; living in a good physical environment (i.e. clean with plentiful natural resources); and having personal character-istics such as confidence, sociability and cleanliness that enable children to relate well to others. Site-specific dimensions included the importance of pure water in the rural sites, and in *Akilit Tera* having educated parents who can advise and teach their children.

There were also some interesting gender differences in responses (Table 9.3); for example, male respondents in all sites mentioned play – having materials, spaces and time for recreation, which was not mentioned by women. Conversely, women highlighted the importance of having both

Table 9.3 Differences in understandings of well-being between male and female groups in different sites

	Akilit Tera – urban	Semhal – remote rural	Leki – near-rural
Men	Being calm and broad in their perspective Time to study and play	Plays well with others Good academic performance Plump and physically mature (girls), physically strong (boys) Boys should feel equal to peers, perhaps even start to feel "proud" and "look down on others" (enhanced confidence through starting to farm)	Local places and materials for recreation Having well-behaved friends and learning from them Early religious tuition and participation in church activities Becoming a good citizen Supervising girls to avoid early intimacy with boys and discouraging early marriage
Women	Not being an orphan Healthcare	Having both parents Girls should be able to Healthcare (a) keep clean during puberty and be prepared for menstruation; (b) marry and have children, even if this involves leaving school; (c) make choices in their lives and not be pressurized by parents	Having both parents Family wealth Healthcare

parents and access to healthcare while men mentioned health only in the sense of a resource to achieve goals (the difference between intrinsic and instrumental capabilities is discussed in Chapters 1 and 2).

Table 9.4   Differences in understanding of ill-being between male and female groups in different sites

	Akilit Tera – **urban**	**Semhal – remote rural**	**Leki – near-rural**
Men	No long-term support from government or community Resentment at not having what their friends have	No places for recreation No kindergarten (women also identify lack of care as problem) Preference for traditional medicine over modern (indicates poor parenting) Husbands waste family resources	No recreational spaces
Women	Parents separated or children orphaned by HIV/AIDS Poor sanitation, difficult for girls to keep clean Elderly household head Unemployed adults setting bad example in household No TV or money to watch TV Education – no time to study, going to government school rather than private, no extra tuition Limited access to healthcare, having to use traditional healers	No parents Effect on education of burdensome work within and outside household, e.g. young children herding instead of going to school, girls working too hard to study	Orphan or without a father Shyness, difficulty relating to others Effect of comparing self with rich children on subjective well-being

Common understandings of ill-being included (a) the absence of the dimensions of well-being listed above (e.g. basic needs such as food and parental care); (b) ill-health or disability incurring large medical expenses; and (c) feeling inferior to or resentful of others. Participants also mentioned inability to learn due to poor-quality tuition, lack of time, physical weakness through overwork or lack of food, etc; large, disharmonious families; and, related to this, poor parenting leading to mutual disrespect between parents and children and a lack of role models. These factors were seen as culminating in living and working on the street, leading to exposure to drugs, crime, violence, prostitution, etc.,[16] or risks of overwork, beating and sexual abuse at home. The differences between men and women (Table 9.4) were almost the same as those described for well-being, with the addition of concerns relating to education among women in two of the three sites.

9.4. Discussion

Trying to specify Nussbaum's list (first column in Table 9.5) using the data reported in Section 9.3 illustrates the historical and cultural specificity of capabilities such as "not having one's emotional development blighted by fear and anxiety" (Nussbaum, 2003: 41). It also shows the difficulty of relating concepts from "the realm of ideal theory" (Robeyns, 2005: 207) to real data. While the task might have been easier had we translated Nussbaum's list and asked people to indicate their level of importance, or discuss how they would be understood in their community, this might have compelled people to find something to say about aspects of life that were irrelevant or alien. It could also reduce the extent to which they felt able to talk about their own conception of a good life, something Clark (2002) addressed by combining open and closed-ended questions in his South African survey.

The data collection exercise described in Section 9.2 is not without flaws, as fundamental aspects of a good life such as being alive in the first place are so obvious that they do not need articulation. The same may be true of "being able to have attachments to things and people outside ourselves" (Nussbaum, 2003: 41), as the reverse is rarely an option in non-Western societies (Uyan-Semerci, 2007). Other areas that were barely mentioned included having control over one's environment and experiencing positive emotions. Both of these are central to a particular understanding of the individual as "a bounded, unique, more or less integrated motivational and cognitive universe [. . .] set contrastively against other such wholes and against its social and natural background" (Geertz, 1983: 59). This concept of the individual is clearly only "common sense" in the historical and social context in which Nussbaum was brought up. Christopher (1999) similarly criticizes the inclusion of emotions and environmental mastery in a supposedly universal measure of psychological well-being as "the assumption that the emotional state is important to, if not determinate of, well-being, ties in with an individualistic moral vision that sees happiness as the yardstick of the good life" (p. 143). It also supposes "a particular view of the world as [. . .] disenchanted, without deeper purpose or telos" (p. 147) and therefore able to be manipulated, controlled and mastered. An alternative view, expressed

Table 9.5 Specification of Nussbaum's list of central capabilities using data from children and adults in three Ethiopian communities

Nussbaum category	Children's specification	Adults' specification
Life	–	–
Bodily health	Good house (e.g. corrugated iron roof, separate kitchen), adequate food, personal hygiene, access to healthcare, physically strong and plump	Balanced diet, pure water, physical health – strong and plump, personal hygiene, clean house with sleeping area, sanitation, sufficient sleep, access to healthcare when sick
Bodily integrity	Not sexually harassed or assaulted (girls)	Not beaten or overworked, avoiding early marriage and being prepared for menstruation, family planning
Senses, imagination and thought	Access to good-quality education (e.g. in a private school in urban areas), educational materials, time to study	Access to good-quality education (e.g. extra tuition in urban areas), educational materials, time to study, religious tuition and opportunities for religious participation where available
Emotions	BARELY MENTIONED, except in relation to behaviour towards others	Having a peaceful mind, being broad and calm in their perspective, appearing/feeling equal with other children, feeling "proud" and "looking down on others" (boys, remote rural site)
Practical reason	Access to television and telephone to "educate and bring new ideas", respected and consulted by parents, encouraged in their education, good behaviour, personal characteristics such as curiosity, confidence and sociability	Encouraged to think freely, having educated parents who can "follow up" their children's study and give good advice, able to distinguish good from bad, being taught to live in a good way
Affiliation	Having parents, receiving love, advice and support from family, agrees with and helps parents – doesn't quarrel with them	Having parents, receiving care, guidance, support and protection from families, respecting parents and accepting advice, accepted, valued and respected by parents and the community, peaceful relationships in the family, having well-behaved friends and good relationships in the community, opportunities to marry early and have children (girls, remote rural site)

Other species	BARELY MENTIONED, except in relation to having a clean environment at home, school and in the community	BARELY MENTIONED, except in relation to having a good, clean environment with a pleasant climate and plentiful natural resources
Play	Having places to play outside the street, "going to entertaining places", time to play outside work, study and chores	Local places and materials for play, money for boys' recreation
Control over one's environment in a material and political sense	BARELY MENTIONED, except in the sense of freedom from harassment and assault	BARELY MENTIONED, except regarding having work appropriate to age and gender that can be combined with education and recreation

by many participants in this research, saw emotions as relevant only in so far as they supported or impeded relationships, and the environment as something over which people had relatively little control at any level, although it was always possible to control the way in which one responded to it.

While with a little creativity it was possible to fit almost all the aspects considered important into Nussbaum's list (Table 9.5), there were some areas discussed by respondents that either did not fit or could not be slotted in without obscuring their centrality in people's accounts. Examples of these are "appearance", e.g. having good, clean clothes and shoes and neat hair. This is valued as a concrete expression of family prosperity and care; for example, buying children new clothes at national holidays and dressing their hair with butter, or oil in *Akilit Tera*. "Material security" was important, but mainly because it enabled children to appear or feel equal to others, and parents to express their care by buying them "everything they needed", often through personal sacrifice (this relates to the arguments advanced in Chapters 2, Section 2.4 and 15).

Finally, having "personal characteristics" such as patience, confidence and sociability that enable children to relate well to others were valued, as was "good behaviour" or "liv[ing] in a good way", which was encouraged by parents, and in *Semhal* by religious teachers.

The results of trying to use Nussbaum's list in this way support the arguments of Robeyns (2003) and Alkire (2007a, 2007b) in favour of the "weak" critique of Sen.[17] Robeyns argues that Sen should not endorse one specific list of relevant capabilities, which might not be helpful in all situations (e.g. kitchen garden projects in Bolivia *and* health-related poverty assessments in

Niger, Alkire, 2007a). Instead, there should be "systematic methodological reasoning [...] on how such a selection could be done" (Robeyns, 2003: 191) and transparency about how consensus was reached. Similar reflections are made by Biggeri et al. in Chapters 3 and 4 of this book. This chapter advocates not a single, static list of capabilities, which in any case risks misinterpretation or cooption when it is specified in different contexts, but a "capabilities process". This should recognize the importance of "identifying and prioritising the freedoms people value" (Alkire, 2007a: 2) while retaining an awareness of questions such as "which judgements are informed, how to determine value, who determines value and how to resolve conflicting value claims" (*ibid.*). The process should also be sensitive to the material and political barriers to attaining valued capabilities, not only in a legislative sense (e.g. "having the right to seek employment on an equal basis with others", Nussbaum, 2003: 42), but also in relation to everyday power relationships in homes and communities that impact particularly strongly on children.

Notes

1. This is the definition of well-being used throughout the chapter, which maps more closely to the holistic understandings of respondents' than interpretations that limit it to welfare, wealth or standard of living. Please note that it is closer to Sen's definition of agency (standard of living, "sympathies" and "commitments") than well-being (Sen, 1987).
2. The qualitative research took place in 2007 and 2008 in five Ethiopian sites ($n = 250$) to capture ethnically based regional difference.
3. The household, child and community questionnaires were administered in 2002 and 2006 to 1000 children who were born in 1994–1995 across 20 sentinel sites in the five largest regions of Ethiopia (Amhara, SNNP, Tigray, Addis Ababa and Oromia).
4. In her defence, Nussbaum (2003) argues that the list is open-ended, intentionally abstract, primarily heuristic ("we need to have an account, for political purposes of what the central human capabilities are, even if we know that this account will always be contested and remade", p. 56), and does not license state intervention or suggest that people have to function in particularly ways, merely that they should be able to do so if they so wish (pp. 42–43).
5. The sample comprised 495 boys and 484 girls, 583 of whom came from rural areas and 396 from urban.
6. The original names of the communities have been replaced with pseudonyms.
7. $n = 979$ for the child questionnaire and $n = 980$ for the household. These analyses were repeated using just the qualitative sample ($n = 60$), but no significant differences were found.
8. In the case of the household questionnaire this was the gender of the child, not the respondent, which illustrates how expectations for children are shaped by the child's gender, but not how these are shaped by the identity and experiences of the respondent.

9. Figures from the Ethiopian Demographic and Health Survey (2000) report that 62.1% of girls who are old enough to have completed primary school have never been to school (EFA, 2007: 49), although this figure is declining.
10. 25–29 was the youngest age group recorded for men; the median age of first marriage for women aged 25–29 was even younger, at 16.6.
11. Afework, 12-year-old boy, *Semhal*.
12. Berhanu, 13-year-old boy, *Akilit Tera*.
13. Bekele, 13-year-old boy, *Akilit Tera*.
14. Well-being ranking by boys from *Leki*.
15. Abebe, 13-year-old girl, *Akilit Tera*.
16. The dangers of street life were mainly mentioned in *Akilit Tera*.
17. Nussbaum's approach is characterized by Robeyns as a response to the "strong" critique that "if Amartya Sen wants his version of the CA to have bite for addressing issues of social justice, he has to endorse one specific and well-defined list of capabilities" (Robeyns, 2005: 195).

References

Alkire, S. (2002), *Valuing Freedoms. Sen's Capability Approach and Poverty Reduction*, OUP, New York.

Alkire, S. (2007a), "Choosing Dimensions: The Capability Approach and Multidimensional Poverty", Chronic Poverty Research Centre Working Paper #88.

Alkire, S. (2007b), "Multidimensional Poverty: How to Choose Dimensions" in Maitreyee, *Maitreyee, the e-bulletin of the Human Development and Capability Association, no. 7*, February 2007: 2–4.

Anand, P., Hunter, G. and Smith, R. (2005), "Capabilities and Well-being: Evidence Based on the Sen-Nussbaum Approach to Welfare", *Social Indicators Research*, 79: 9–55.

Biggeri, M., Libanora, R., Mariani, S. and Menchini, L. (2006), "Children Conceptualising Their Capabilities: Results of a Survey Conducted during the First Children's World Congress on Child Labour", *Journal of Human Development*, 7(1): 59–83.

Camfield, L. (2006), "Why and How of Understanding 'Subjective' Well-being: Exploratory Work by the WeD Group in Four Developing Countries", WeD Working Paper 26.

Camfield, L. and Tafere, Y. (2009), 'No, Living Well Does Not Mean Being Rich': Diverse Understandings of Well-being among 11 to 13 Year Old Children in Three Ethiopian Communities, *Journal of Children and Poverty*, 15(2): 117–136.

Chiappero-Martinetti, E. (1996), "Standard of Living Evaluation Based on Sen's Approach: Some Methodological Questions", *Politeia*, 12: 43–44.

Chiappero-Martinetti, E. (2000), "A Multidimensional Assessment of Well-being Based on Sen's Functioning Approach", *Rivista Internazionale di Scienze Sociali*, 108(2): 207–239.

Christopher, J.C. (1999), "Situating Psychological Well-Being: Exploring the Cultural Roots of Its Theory and Research", *Journal of Counseling & Development*, 77(2): 141–152.

Clark D.A. (2002), *Visions of Development: A Study of Human Values*, Edward Elgar, Cheltenham.

Clark, D.A. and Qizilbash, M. (2008), "Core Poverty, Vagueness and Adaptation: A New Methodology and Some Results for South Africa", *Journal of Development Studies*, 44(4): 519–544.

Conticini, A., Kui, W.L. and Tsadik, W. (2005), *We Have a Dream: Children's Visions, Vulnerabilities and Rights in Ethiopia*, UNICEF, Addis Ababa.

Crivello, G., Camfield, L. and Woodhead, M. (2008), "How Can Children Tell Us About Their Well-being? Exploring the Potential of Participatory Approaches within the Young Lives Project", *Social Indicators Research*, 90(1): 51–72.

Di Tommaso, M.L. (2006). "Measuring the Well Being of Children Using a Capability Approach an Application to Indian Data", CHILD Working Papers wp05_06, CHILD – Centre for Household, Income, Labour and Demographic economics – ITALY.

Education for All (2007), *Education for All Global Monitoring Report*, Strong Foundations: Early Childhood Care and Education. UNESCO (http://unesdoc.unesco.org/images/0014/001477/147794E.pdf).

Ellis, F. and Woldehanna, T. (2005), *Ethiopia Participatory Poverty Assessment 2004–05*, Ministry of Finance and Economic Development (MoFED), Addis Ababa, October: 73 (also available at: http://siteresources.worldbank.org/INTETHIOPIA/Resources/ppa_ethiopia.pdf).

Geertz, C. (1983), *Local Knowledge*, Basic Books, New York.

Gough, I. (2004), "Human Well-being and Social Structures: Relating the Universal and the Local", *Global Social Policy*, 4(3): 289–311.

Lavers, T. (2008), "Asking People What They Want or Telling Them What They 'Need'? Contrasting A Theory of Human Need with Local Expressions of Goals", *Social Indicators Research*, 86(1): 129–147.

Mayer, B., Agache, A., Albert, I. and Trommsdorff, G. (2006), "Value of Children and Intergenerational Relations. Cross-cultural Equivalence of Instruments". Unpublished manuscript, University of Konstanz, Konstanz, Germany.

Menon, N. (2002), "Universalism without Foundations? Review of Nussbaum", *Economy and Society*, 31(1): 152–169.

Morrow, V. (2009), "The Ethics of Social Research with Children and Families in Young Lives: Practical Experiences", Working Paper 53, Oxford: Young Lives.

Nussbaum, M. (2003), "Capabilities as Fundamental Entitlements: Sen and Social Justice", *Feminist Economics*, 9(2/3): 33–59.

Rahmato, D. and Kidano, A. (1999), "Consultations with the Poor: A Study to Inform the World Development Report 2000/2001 on Poverty and Development", (National Report, Ethiopia), Addis Ababa.

Robeyns, I. (2003), "Sen's Capability Approach and Gender Inequality: Selecting Relevant Capabilities", *Feminist Economics*, 9(2–3): 61–92.

Robeyns, I. (2005), "Selecting Capabilities for Quality of Life Measurement", *Social Indicators Research*, 74(1): 191–215.

Sen, A. (1987), "The Standard of Living", in G. Hawthorn (ed.), *The Standard of Living*, CUP, Cambridge.

Sen, A. (2005), "Human Rights and Capabilities", *Journal of Human Development*, 6: 151–166.

Tafere, Y. (2007, December), "Children's Understanding of their Wellbeing: Evidence from Young Lives Qualitative Research in Two Urban Communities in Ethiopia". Paper presented at the 6th Conference of the Ethiopian Society of Sociologists, Social Workers and Anthropologists (ESSSWA), Addis Ababa.

Tafere, Y. and Camfield, L. (2008), "Community Understandings of Children's Transitions in Ethiopia: Possible Implications for Life Course Poverty", Young Lives Working Paper 41.

Tekola, B., Griffin, C. and Camfield, L. (2008). "Using Qualitative Methods with Poor Children in Urban Ethiopia: Opportunities & Challenges", *Social Indicators Research*, 90(1): 73–87.

Uyan-Semerci, P. (2007), "A Relational Account of Nussbaum's List of Capabilities", *Journal of Human Development*, 8(2), 203–221.

Woodcock, A. (2007). Validation of the WeDQoL-Goals-Ethiopia: Goal Necessity and Satisfaction Scales and Individualised Quality of Life Scores: Report to the WeD Team. Bath: Wellbeing in Developing Countries Research Group, University of Bath.

10
Children's Capabilities and Family Characteristics in Italy: Measuring Imagination and Play

Tindara Addabbo and Maria Laura Di Tommaso

10.1. Introducing children's capabilities

In the capability literature, there has been increasing concern about how to choose and define capabilities (Nussbaum, 1999; Robeyns, 2003) and specifically children's capabilities (Phipps, 2002; Saito, 2003; see also Chapters 3, 4 and 9, this book). Phipps (2002), for instance, compares the well-being of children in the USA, Canada and Norway by measuring ten specific functionings (low birth-weighting, asthma, accidents, activity limitation, trouble concentrating, disobedience at school, bullying, anxiety, lying, hyperactivity). She utilizes some descriptive statistics and shows that Norwegian children have better outcomes than US and Canadian children. The paper of Saito (2003) explores the possible relation between capabilities and education; she mentions Sen's interview on the application of the CA to children.

> If a child does not want to be inoculated, and you nevertheless think it is a good idea for him/her to be inoculated, then the argument may be connected with the freedom that this person will have in the future by having the measles shot now. The child when it grows up must have more freedom. So when you are considering a child, you have to consider not only the child's freedom now, but also the child's freedom in the future[1].

Nussbaum (2003) argues that the CA should endorse a theory of social justice where the subjects are not only "fully cooperating members of society over the course of a complete life".[2] This argument applies to children.

> So I believe that we need to delve deeper, redesigning the political conception of the person, bringing the rational and the animal into a more intimate relation with one another, and acknowledging that there are many types of dignity in the world, including the dignity of mentally

disabled children and adults, the dignity of the senile demented elderly, and the dignity of babies at the breast. ... We thus need to adopt a political conception of the person that is more Aristotelian than Kantian, one that sees the person from the start as both capable and needy – "in need of a rich plurality of life-activities" to use a Marx's phrase, whose availability will be the measure of well-being. (Nussbaum, 2003: 54)

Therefore, following Nussbaum, in order to conceptualize children capabilities, we consider children as subjects (see also Chapter 2, in this book).

This chapter explores the possibilities of using structural equation modelling to measure the capabilities of Italian children. We focus on two capabilities taken from Nussbaum's universal list (that also feature in the lists presented in Chapters 3 and 4) that are relevant for evaluating children's well-being in Italy:

(1) senses, imagination and thought (SIT); and
(2) leisure activities and play (LAP).

These capabilities were both chosen because they are relevant for children's development, they seem to be less developed in Italy compared with OECD countries (UNICEF, 2007) and they show high variance across Italian regions.

We use Nussbaum's definition for the capability of senses, imagination and thought (SIT) because it is very broad; it includes education but also other important elements for the development of children's minds. Nussbaum defines this capability as:

Being able to use the senses; being able to imagine, to think, and to reason – and to do these things in a "truly human" way, a way informed and cultivated by an adequate education, including, but by no means limited to, literacy and basic mathematical and scientific training; being able to use imagination and thought in connection with experiencing and producing expressive works and events of one's own choice (religious, literary, musical, etc); .... (Nussbaum, 1999: 41)

This is a basic capability for the development of children. The quality of education both in primary schools and kindergartens plays a crucial role in children's cognitive development (Clarke-Stewart and Allhusen, 2005). Attending a kindergarten has a positive effect on children's cognitive ability, and this effect is higher in poorer households (Waldfogel, 2002; Magnuson et al., 2004). Positive effects of pre-compulsory education on children's cognitive development have been found to be significant (although subject to diminishing returns) up to the age of 16 (Goodman and Sianesi, 2005).[3]

The other capability that we analyse in this chapter includes leisure activities and play (LAP). The role of this capability in defining children's well-being is essential. Nevertheless, these kinds of functionings are not easily observable. Psychologists stress that it is not only important to assess the quantity but also the quality of playing activities. This capability is strongly correlated to other children's capabilities like social interaction and education. Not playing alone requires interaction with other children, parents or with other individuals. This capability differs across regions which are characterized by different types of schools and leisure activities. One element to be considered is the reduction in time devoted to unstructured (not organized) leisure time.

In this chapter we try to measure the aforementioned capabilities utilizing Italian data on 6–13 year-old children. In Section 10.2, we analyse Italian child education and labour conditions. In Section 10.3, the relation between income and children's outcomes is explored. In Section 10.4, we outline the econometric model. We apply a Multiple Indicator Multiple Causes model (MIMIC), which is the simplest structural equation model. Structural equation models (SEMs) are particularly suitable for measuring capabilities, because they link latent unobservable variables to observed variables and to measurement errors. Capabilities are theoretical constructs that are intrinsically unobservable. MIMIC models allow the use of multiple indicators of the analysed capabilities and, at the same time, they allow us to analyse the effects of some covariates on children's capabilities. Section 10.5 explains the data set that is the result of matching two data sets: the 2000 Bank of Italy Survey on Income and Wealth and the 1998 Italian National Statistical Office (ISTAT) FSS (Famiglie, Soggetti Sociali e Condizione dell'Infanzia[4]). Finally, results are presented in Sections 10.6 and 10.7.

10.2. Italian child education and labour

According to a compounded index of some measures of school achievement at age 15, the percentage of 15–19-[5]year-old children in education and the percentage of 15–19-year-olds not in education, training or employment in Italy ranks that country 23rd out of 24 OECD countries (UNICEF, 2007). The other dimensions analysed by UNICEF (2007) concern material well-being (14th position), health and safety (5th), family and peer relationships (1st position), behaviour and risks (10th) and subjective well-being (10th). The UNICEF educational well-being index utilizes the PISA (Programme of International Student Assessment) 2000 survey. Italy (together with Spain, Portugal and Greece) is at the bottom of the list of OECD countries in terms of reading, mathematics and scientific literacy. The percentage of Italian 15–19-year-old children in education (another measure included in UNICEF educational index) is also very low (18th).

Dropout rates in primary school for the school year 2002–2003 were on average 0.08%, with little variation across areas; dropouts in secondary schools in the year 2002–2003 were more heterogeneous across regions: 0.10% in the North, 0.59% in the South and 0.55% in the islands. High school dropout rate in school year 2001–2002 comprised 3.77% in the islands, 2% in the South of Italy and around 1% in the Centre-North (Ciccotti et al., 2007).

Attending a kindergarten has a strong influence on future school performance. In Italy, kindergarten attendance increased from 5.8% in 1992 to 9.9% in 2005 (Ciccotti and Sabbadini, 2007). However, although increasing, the attendance rate of children younger than 3 is still far from the 33% target fixed by the European Union (Ciccotti et al., 2007). This figure shows a high variance across regions: 2% in Calabria (a southern region) and 24% in Emilia Romagna (a central region with a good regional social welfare system) (Ciccotti et al., 2007). These figures are correlated with a high variance of the availability of nursery schools across regions (Istituto degli Innocenti, 2002); the lowest figures are to be found in the South.

On the other hand, 104.4% of 3–5-year-old children attended kindergarten in the school year 2003–2004, with a low variance across regions[6] (Ciccotti et al., 2007). However, the number of those children who did not have school lunch at kindergarten was higher in the southern regions and in the islands (Ciccotti and Sabbadini, 2007: 15).

With regard to primary schools, we note that there is high variance across regions in the availability of "full-time" schools whose timetable includes afternoons (2% in Palermo and 90% in Milan) and tend to be more compatible with parents' work commitments, given the relatively low availability of part-time work in Italy in comparison with other countries.[7] Moreover, not all schools provide lunch: Ciccotti and Sabbadini (2007:16), using data from the ISTAT multipurpose survey for the year 2005, show that 75.8% in the North West have school lunch, 65.5% in the North East, 64.9% in the Centre, 25.5% in the South and 17.2% in the islands. These differences are mainly due to a lack of funding for schools in the South and to heterogeneous policies across regions.

An important issue in assessing the capability of leisure and play is to what extent the child is free from paid or unpaid work. There has been increased concern over the amount of work performed by Italian children. According to the ISTAT 2000 survey, 14.7% of young people from 15 to 18 years of age in Italy had work experience before they were 15 years old; that percentage is higher for males (18.8%) than for females (10.4%) and in the North East (20.1%) than in the Centre (9.9%), the South (14.7%) or the islands (13.2%). The higher the secondary school grade, the lower the percentage of those who had work experience before the age of 15 (Moretti, 2004).

10.3. Some evidence on the relation between income and children's outcomes

According to the literature, family income has a positive effect on children's cognitive and social development in many ways. Income determines investments in children's human capital (Blau, 1999; Taylor et al., 2004);

income is correlated with parental education and better neighbourhoods; and higher-income families have a lower probability of falling into economic hardship and experiencing its stressful consequences (Elder et al., 1985; Taylor et al., 2004).

Nevertheless, using sibling data from the Panel Study of Income Dynamics on 1364 households following children from birth until at least age 20, and using a fixed-effects estimator to control for omitted variables that might be correlated with family income and child outcomes, Levy and Duncan (2000) show that the effect of family income on children's completed years of schooling is very low; moreover, only family income at early childhood (0–4 years) positively and significantly affects children's schooling.

By using NLSY (National Longitudinal Survey of Youth) data (the matched mother–child sample), Blau (1999) finds that the impact of family income on 0–3-year-old children's motor and social outcomes, as well as cognitive and language outcomes for 3–7-year-old children, is higher for permanent rather than current income. In addition, the effect of income is non-linear (this is not consistent with the hypothesis that income effects are higher at lower income levels).

Taylor et al. (2004) focus on outcomes on 15–16-year-old children when, according to existing literature (Duncan and Brooks-Gunn, 1997), income effects should be larger. They use longitudinal data from the National Institute of Child Health and Human Development's (NICHD) *Study of Early Child Care* (SECC). They find that the income effect is similar to the effect of other variables that the literature finds related to children's outcomes (like maternal verbal intelligence), by using repeated measures of children's outcomes and assessing their relative weight at different points of income distribution. The inclusion of other control variables decreases the size of the income effect and, using random effects estimates, the size of income effect is smaller than by using Ordinary Least Squares estimates, and permanent income effects are higher than current income effects. Chevalier et al. (2005) use Labour Force Survey data and instrumental variables to estimate a significant effect of permanent income in reducing dropout rates at age 16. Policy implications call for alleviating financial constraints that prevent children in disadvantaged environments from improving their education (Plug and Vijverberg, 2003), and for the importance of investing in children from disadvantaged environments, especially in the early years (Heckman and Masterov, 2007).

10.4. MIMIC and evaluation of children's well-being

Any attempt to make the CA operational must address the measurement of the abstract unobservable multidimensional concept. One such attempt is the latent variable approach including principal components, factor analysis and SEMs.[8] MIMIC models are the simplest form of

SEM. The first two models provide estimates of the latent variables but are silent on the factors influencing these variables (capabilities in our context). MIMIC models represent another step in this direction as they include exogenous "causal" variables for the latent factors. More complex SEM models allow for feedback mechanisms where some of these causal factors not only influence human development but are also influenced by it. Previous chapters that utilize SEMs to estimate well-being within a capability framework include Kuklys (2005), Di Tommaso (2007) and Krishnakumar (2007). The seminal contribution of Kuklys (2005) contains the first theoretical model of capabilities applied to SEM. Krishnakumar and Ballon (2008) utilize SEM to estimate the capability of being educated and adequately sheltered using Bolivian data. Di Tommaso (2007) estimates the well-being of Indian children defined in terms of capabilities.

The principal advantage of this approach is that it does not rely on exact measurement of the capability. This is an advantage because capabilities are *per se* latent unobservable variables. They are a theoretical construct of which we can only observe some indicators. Each indicator represents a "noisy" signal of the capability.[9]

The MIMIC approach allows us to think of this model as comprising of two parts: two structural equations, one for the capability of Senses, Imagination and Thought (SIT) and one for the capability of Leisure Activities and Play (LAP) (which relates the two latent capability variables to the causes); and two measurement equations that allow each capability to be measured in terms of multiple indicators.

For each of the indicators chosen to represent a latent construct, a weight (a factor loading) will be estimated. This weight represents how much each specific functioning counts in explaining the latent variable (either SIT or LAP) relative to other functionings.

10.4.1. Model specification

In order to estimate the model outlined above we introduce some notation. The measurement part of the model is as follows:

$$Y^I = \Lambda^{Y^I} Y_1^* + \varepsilon_1 \qquad (1)$$

$$Y^{II} = \Lambda^{Y^{II}} Y_2^* + \varepsilon_2$$

where $Y^I = \left(Y_1^I, Y_2^I, Y_3^I, \ldots, Y_m^I\right)'$ is a vector with m elements representing an unobserved independent indicator of the SIT capability Y_1^*; and $Y^{II} = \left(Y_1^{II}, Y_2^{II}, Y_3^{II}, \ldots, Y_m^{II}\right)'$ is a vector with n elements representing an unobserved independent indicator of the LAP capability Y_2^*.

$\Lambda^{Y^I} = \left\{\Lambda_1^{Y^I}, \Lambda_2^{Y^I}, \Lambda_3^{Y^I}, \ldots, \Lambda_m^{Y^I}\right\}'$ denotes a $m \times 1$ parameter vector of factor loadings, with each element representing the expected change in the respective indicators following a one unit change in the latent variable Y_1^*.

$\Lambda^{Y''} = \{\Lambda_1^{Y''}, \Lambda_2^{Y''}, \Lambda_3^{Y''}, \ldots, \Lambda_m^{Y''}\}'$ denotes a $n \times 1$ parameter vector of factor loadings, with each element representing the expected change in the respective indicators following a one unit change in the latent variable Y_2^*.

ε_1 is a $m \times 1$ vector of measurement errors, with Θ_{ε_1} denoting the covariance matrix and ε_2 is a $n \times 1$ vector of measurement errors, with Θ_{ε_2} denoting the covariance matrix.

Moreover we let these two capabilities be correlated with correlation coefficient equal to $\rho_{\varepsilon_1\varepsilon_2}$. In addition, we outline the structural part of the model. We posit that the latent variables Y_1^* and Y_2^* are linearly determined by a common vector of observable exogenous variables $x = (x_1, x_2, \ldots, x_s)'$ and a stochastic error $\varsigma = (\varsigma_1, \varsigma_2) =$ giving,

$$Y_1^* = x'\gamma_1 + \varsigma_1 \qquad (2)$$
$$Y_2^* = x'\gamma_2 + \varsigma_2$$

where γ_1 and γ_2 are $s \times 1$ vector of parameters.

Examining equations (1) and (2) therefore, we may think of our model as consisting of two parts: the first part is the structural equation (Eq. 2) and the second part is the measurement equation (Eq. 1), which reflects the fact that the observed measurements are imperfect indicators. The structural equation specifies the casual relationship between the observed exogenous causes and the two capabilities. Combining (1) and (2), the reduced form representation is written as

$$Y^I = \pi_1 x' + v_1 \qquad (3)$$
$$Y^{II} = \pi_2 x' + v_2$$

where $\pi_1 = \Lambda^{Y'} \gamma_1'$ is the $m \times s$ reduced-form coefficient matrix for SIT; $\pi_2 = \Lambda^{Y''} \gamma_2'$ is the $n \times s$ reduced-form coefficient matrix for LAP; and $v_1 = \Lambda^{Y'} \varsigma_1 + \varepsilon_1$ and $v_2 = \Lambda^{Y''} \varsigma_2 + \varepsilon_2$ are the reduced-form disturbances.

The application of this model to our data set will allow us to estimate the parameter γ_1 and γ_2, the factor loadings (weights of each indicator in the respective latent variables), $\Lambda^{Y'}$, $\Lambda^{Y''}$, and the correlation coefficient, $\rho_{\varepsilon_1\varepsilon_2}$.

10.5. The data

The capabilities SIT and LAP cannot be measured directly, since primary data sources are not currently available; we are therefore forced to use secondary data sources. However, not all the relevant variables are available in one data set and therefore we have used two data sets[10]: the ISTAT multipurpose survey on family and children's conditions (FSS98) and the Bank of Italy Survey on Income and Wealth (FSS88) provide information on children's education, play and leisure activities, the socio-demographic structure of families and childcare provided by relatives and parents according to the type of activities in which the children are involved. However, FSS98 lacks information on family income and so we have recovered information on income by using propensity score matching techniques, matching ISTAT 1998 FSS (Famiglie, Soggetti Sociali e Condizione dell'Infanzia) with the Bank of Italy 2000 SHIW (Surveys on Household Income and Wealth). For this purpose we have used a micro-procedure inspired by propensity score matching (Addabbo et al., 2007; see also Rubin, 1977; Rosembaum and Rubin, 1983; Dehejia and Wahba, 1999).

The resulting data set (BFSS98 in the following discussion) contains information about 3–13 year-old children who live in families where both parents are present. The number of children is 2031, with roughly equal numbers of girls ($n = 1011$) and boys ($n = 1020$).

10.6. Measuring functionings of "senses, imagination and thought" and "leisure and play activities"

We restricted our sample to 6–13-year-old children because we are interested in children of school age. The resulting sample contains 1626 observations (of which 52% are from female participants).

BFSS98 provide information on children's attitude towards education. Table 10.1 shows higher values in terms of attitudes towards education for girls than boys with regard to effort and performance (measured in terms of results obtained).

Table 10.1   Attitudes towards education, by sex (percentages)

	Children 6–10		Children 11–13	
	Girls	Boys	Girls	Boys
Indolent, no effort	1.9	3.9	2.0	4.1
Only some topics he/she likes	7.8	11.1	10.8	9.4
Enough effort to attain pass mark	15.4	18.8	14.2	24.0
Good results but could do better	34.1	37.9	29.7	30.4
High level of effort and excellent results	40.9	28.3	43.3	32.1
Total	100	100	100	100
Observations (n)	434	503	301	280

Source: BFSS98 data (merging of two data sets, ISTAT Multipurpose Survey 1998 and Bank of Italy 2000 SHIW). The variable "attitude towards education" is the reply to the following question: "What is your child's attitude towards education?"

In Table 10.2, we control for a set of family, environmental and individual variables by estimating ordered probit models: the dependent variable is ordered in terms of the attitude towards education, from being indolent and showing no effort to showing excellent results and a high input of effort. The only statistically significant (at the 5% level) estimates for 6–10 year-old children are the dummy variable for being a boy (negative effect), the number of siblings (negative), homework with the mother (positive), having a

Table 10.2   Ordered probit estimates on attitudes towards education

	Age 6–10	Age 11–13
Boy	−0.345** (−3.27)	−0.237 (−1.77)
Centre-North	0.166 (0.74)	−0.259 (−0.78)
Number of brothers or sisters (child included)	−0.199* (−2.16)	−0.186 (−1.54)
Absent from school for more than 59 days	−0.269 (−0.70)	−0.400 (−1.66)
Weekly hours of school	0.018 (1.71)	−0.008 (−0.60)
Private school	0.353 (1.65)	0.857** (3.67)
Experimental class	0.123 (0.70)	−0.029 (−0.16)
Homework with father	−0.082 (−0.63)	0.368 (1.93)
Homework with mother	0.254* (2.30)	−0.007 (−0.05)
Homework with brothers/sisters	0.182 (1.05)	−0.143 (−0.60)
Homework alone	0.199 (1.89)	0.363* (2.40)
Father "white collar"	−0.118 (−0.71)	0.329 (1.57)
Father manager	0.319 (1.39)	0.283 (1.25)
Father self-employed	−0.202 (−1.27)	0.139 (0.71)
Mother "white collar"	0.087 (0.48)	−0.313 (−1.37)
Mother manager	−0.526 (−1.85)	−0.712* (−2.13)
Mother self-employed	0.210 (1.04)	−0.182 (−0.56)
Father unemployed	0.088 (0.23)	−0.015 (−0.03)
Mother unemployed	0.630 (1.58)	0.016 (0.04)
Mother housewife	0.147 (0.71)	−0.110 (−0.38)
Father graduate	0.019 (0.10)	−0.194 (−0.78)
Father high school	0.124 (0.95)	−0.179 (−0.95)
Mother graduate	0.488* (2.21)	0.352 (1.18)
Mother high school	0.039 (0.29)	0.096 (0.46)
Log equivalent household income	0.049 (1.02)	−0.085 (−0.87)
Father weekly paid hours of work	0.005 (1.30)	−0.001 (−0.18)
Mother weekly paid hours of work	0.018** (2.99)	0.003 (0.36)
Mother weekly unpaid hours of work	0.037* (2.02)	0.004 (0.13)
Incidence of kindergarten in region	0.080 (0.53)	0.259 (1.11)
High interaction between parents	0.391 (1.70)	−0.194 (−0.56)
Observations (*n*)	940	566

Robust z statistics in parentheses; * significant at 5%; ** significant at 1%.
Source: BFSS98 data (merging of two data sets, ISTAT Multipurpose Survey 1998 and Bank of Italy 2000 SHIW).

Table 10.3 Paid activity attendance (%) by child's sex, age and area

Area	Children aged 6–10		Children aged 11–13	
	Girls	Boys	Girls	Boys
North West	57	39	48	53
North East	64	44	55	45
Centre	45	48	59	39
South	20	34	25	30
Islands	25	17	20	29
Total	42	37	41	39
Observations (*n*)	481	534	310	301

Source: BFSS98 data (merging of two data sets, ISTAT Multipurpose Survey 1998 and Bank of Italy 2000 SHIW).

mother with a university degree (positive) and the mother's number of paid and unpaid hours of work (positive).

Another functioning relating to SIT is attendance to other paid or unpaid activities outside school. Table 10.3 shows a high degree of variation in paid activity attendance across regions.

The probability of attending paid activities (music, painting, sport, languages, computing) not run by the school (Table 10.4) significantly decreases for children in both age groups with regard to their attendance at other unpaid activities not run by the school and, only for 11–13-year-old children, does it significantly increase if the child attends experimental classes and does homework alone. A higher availability of kindergarten is found positively to affect the attendance of paid activities for both age groups. This may be related to the development at an early age of greater experience in doing other activities (such as painting, music, etc.).

We assume that the sum of weekly hours of activity (painting, music, singing, theatre, dance, sport, school magazine, etc.) is a measure of cognitive functioning. On average, taking the whole sample, Italian boys aged 6–13 spend two hours a week in sports and girls one hour (the average number of hours being higher in the Centre and North than in the South of Italy, see Tables 10.5–10.7); girls outweigh boys in the average number of hours spent in music and dance courses.

In order to proxy functionings for LAP, we have used the variables on the frequency with which children play with their parents, meet children of their age, go to the park and their most frequent type of game.[11] We can also observe with whom they play during weekdays and during weekends. Descriptive analysis on this set of variables for children 6–10 years old (Table 10.8) shows variability by gender and location. A low percentage of children play in the park at least once a week; this percentage is higher in the Centre and North than in the South of Italy. More boys than girls play at least sometimes each week with their father in the Centre-North of Italy,

Table 10.4   Probit models on paid activity attendance, by child's age

	Age 6–10	Age 11–13
Boy	−0.110 (−1.00)	0.096 (0.64)
Attend other unpaid activities not run by school	−1.241** (−5.02)	−1.196** (−4.33)
Attends other school activities	0.636** (4.28)	−0.176 (−0.95)
Log kindergarten	0.292** (2.89)	0.325* (2.43)
Number of children in the family	−0.020 (−0.20)	−0.179 (−1.25)
School weekly hours	0.005 (0.45)	−0.006 (−0.39)
More than 59 days absent from school	−0.416 (−1.63)	−0.159 (−0.42)
Private school	−0.199 (−0.83)	0.173 (0.55)
Experimental courses	0.176 (0.75)	0.522* (1.97)
Homework with father	−0.026 (−0.16)	0.233 (1.11)
Homework with mother	0.036 (0.29)	0.270 (1.67)
Homework with sisters/brothers	−0.117 (−0.54)	−0.247 (−0.99)
Homework alone	−0.041 (−0.33)	0.457** (2.70)
Father "white collar" teacher	0.253 (1.53)	0.211 (0.92)
Father manager	0.442 (1.75)	0.225 (0.71)
Father self-employed	0.020 (0.13)	−0.290 (−1.27)
Mother "white collar" – teacher	0.364 (1.76)	0.087 (0.33)
Mother manager	−0.471 (−1.25)	0.769 (1.17)
Mother self-employed	0.371 (1.45)	0.305 (0.92)
Father unemployed	0.012 (0.03)	0.141 (0.31)
Mother unemployed	0.077 (0.16)	0.246 (0.35)
Mother housewife	0.301 (1.05)	−0.022 (−0.06)
Father graduate	0.163 (0.73)	0.437 (1.46)
Father high school	0.109 (0.75)	0.042 (0.20)
Mother graduate	0.047 (0.18)	−0.344 (−1.10)
Mother high school	−0.034 (−0.24)	0.094 (0.49)
Log equivalent family income	0.048 (0.73)	−0.052 (−0.45)
Father paid weekly hours	0.005 (1.15)	0.002 (0.31)
Mother paid weekly hours	−0.003 (−0.43)	−0.005 (−0.66)
Mother unpaid weekly hours	−0.013 (−0.78)	−0.011 (−0.44)
Constant	1.416 (1.26)	3.307 (1.96)
Observations (*n*)	1012	608

Robust z statistics in parentheses; * significant at 5%; ** significant at 1%.
Source: BFSS98 data (merging of two data sets, ISTAT Multipurpose Survey 1998 and Bank of Italy 2000 SHIW).

while more girls than boys play at least sometimes with their father in the South. More boys than girls play at least once a week with their mother in the Centre-North. Children meet other children of the same age more often in the Centre and North of Italy, and this is more often true of boys than girls. The most frequent games for girls in the South of Italy are movement games. Almost 35% of boys and girls play alone on weekdays.

We have defined a new indicator for which values increase with the frequency that children play with either their parents or their peers. A multivariate analysis on this indicator that relates it to family and child

Table 10.5 Average weekly hours in activities: whole sample by age group and gender for Italy as a whole

Age	6–10				11–13			
Hours in	Boys	Girls	Difference	*t*-test	Boys	Girls	GDifference	*t*-test
School magazine	0.02	0.005	0.015	−0.05	0.008	0.007	0.001	−1.18
Other activities	0.07	0.06	0.01	0.95	0.04	0.11	−0.07	0.69
Computing	0.11	0.1	0.01	−0.82	0.09	0.07	0.02	0.22
Languages	0.08	0.11	−0.03	−0.91	0.22	0.07	0.15	−1.91
Gym	2.13	1.3	0.83	−5.7	1.98	1.17	0.81	−3.91
Painting	0.008	0.05	−0.042	−1.49	0.08	0.12	−0.04	0.78
Theatre	0.11	0.03	0.08	−1.38	0.11	0.06	0.05	−0.001
Dancing	0.03	0.25	−0.22	5.26	0.01	0.36	−0.35	3.9
Music	0.15	0.47	−0.32	3.25	0.25	0.3	−0.05	1.68
Singing	0.05	0.05	0	−0.13	0.07	0.12	−0.05	1.68
Observations (*n*)	534	481			301	310		

Source: BFSS98 data (merging of two data sets, ISTAT Multipurpose Survey 1998 and Bank of Italy 2000 SHIW).

Table 10.6 Average weekly hours in activities: whole sample by age group and gender, Centre-North of Italy

Age	6–10				11–13			
Hours in	Boys	Girls	Difference	*t*-test	Boys	Girls	Difference	*t*-test
School magazine	0.02	0.005	0.015	0.86	0	0.01	−0.01	0.94
Other activities	0.005	0.07	−0.065	1.79	0.04	0.17	−0.13	1.13
Computing	0.16	0.08	0.08	−0.92	0.09	0.07	0.02	0.2
Languages	0.08	0.15	−0.07	1.14	0.23	0.09	0.14	−2
Gym	2.6	1.73	0.87	−4.23	2.47	1.68	0.79	−2.96
Painting	0.01	0.06	−0.05	1.08	0.06	0.09	−0.03	0.76
Theatre	0.17	0.04	0.13	−1.38	0.06	0.09	−0.03	1.63
Dancing	0.008	0.25	−0.242	5.02	0.02	0.39	−0.37	2.68
Music	0.13	0.42	−0.29	2.63	0.22	0.29	−0.07	1.03
Singing	0.06	0.08	−0.02	0.64	0.05	0.13	−0.08	1.64
Observations (*n*)	296	258			160	180		

Source: BFSS98 data (merging of two data sets, ISTAT Multipurpose Survey 1998 and Bank of Italy 2000 SHIW).

characteristics for children aged 6–10 (Table 10.9) shows how the frequency of playing with parents or peers is lower, the higher the number of hours at school and the higher the number of days off school. On the other hand, the frequency of play with parents or peers increases with the number of hours spent by mothers in unpaid care and housework activities and with

Table 10.7 Average weekly hours in activities: whole sample by age group and gender, South of Italy

Age	6–10				11–13			
Hours in	Boys	Girls	Difference	*t*-test	Boys	Girls	Difference	*t*-test
School magazine	0.02	0.006	0.014	−0.76	0.02	0	0.02	−1.45
Other activities	0.17	0.05	0.12	−0.78	0.04	0.03	0.01	−0.89
Computing	0.03	0.14	−0.11	−0.01	0.09	0.06	0.03	−0.03
Languages	0.1	0.04	0.06	−2.07	0.21	0.04	0.17	−1.09
Gym	1.39	0.67	0.72	−3.8	1.23	0.48	0.75	−2.94
Painting	0.006	0.02	−0.014	1.22	0.12	0.15	−0.03	0.37
Theatre	0.008	0.02	−0.012	−0.12	0.17	0.03	0.14	−1.19
Dancing	0.07	0.25	−0.18	2.39	0.009	0.31	−0.301	3.02
Music	0.17	0.53	−0.36	1.99	0.29	0.31	−0.02	1.37
Singing	0.03	0.01	0.02	−0.98	0.09	0.11	−0.02	0.68
Observations (*n*)	238	223			141	130		

Source: BFSS98 data (merging of two data sets, ISTAT Multipurpose Survey 1998 and Bank of Italy 2000 SHIW).

Table 10.8 Playing activities by gender and area (%): children aged 6–10

	Italy (whole)		Centre-North		South	
	Girls	Boys	Girls	Boys	Girls	Boys
Park at least once a week	33	31	38	38	29	22
Play with father at least sometimes each week	59	68	54	70	69	65
Play with mother at least sometimes each week	72	74	67	72	84	77
Meet peers at least sometimes each week	66	75	71	79	51	70
Play alone on weekdays	36	34	39	39	32	26
Play alone during holidays	32	26	34	27	32	22
Most frequent game: videos	2	37	27	32	22	42
More frequent Game: building	1	25	13	25	17	26
Parlour games	29	27	37	28	15	19
Role games	4	4	4	5	5	2
Movement games	48	52	61	64	28	38
Drawing	21	12	18	10	28	14
Housework	1	0	1	0	2	0
Toys	6	5	4	5	8	5
Observations (*n*)	376	421	236	272	140	149

Table 10.9 How often does the child play with his/her parents and peers? By ordered probit: variable increases with higher frequency of play

	Frequency of play with parents and peers
	Age 6–10
Boy	−0.103 (−1.08)
Centre-North	0.015 (0.07)
Number of children in family	−0.190* (−2.05)
More than 59 days absent from school	−0.656* (−2.05)
Weekly hours of school	−0.015 (−1.64)
Father "white collar"	−0.097 (−0.68)
Father manager	−0.012 (−0.06)
Father self-employed	−0.004 (−0.03)
Mother "white collar"	0.028 (0.15)
Mother manager	−0.324 (−1.14)
Mother self-employed	0.150 (0.69)
Father unemployed	−0.217 (−0.95)
Mother unemployed	0.183 (0.59)
Mother housewife	−0.132 (−0.60)
Father graduate	0.050 (0.27)
Father high school	0.047 (0.37)
Mother graduate	0.374 (1.84)
Mother high school	0.119 (0.93)
Log equivalent family income	−0.160** (−3.05)
Father paid working hours	−0.001 (−0.41)
Mother paid working hours	0.006 (1.03)
Mother unpaid working hours	0.037* (2.26)
Regional incidence of kindergarten	0.010 (0.07)
Observations (*n*)	938

Robust z statistics in parentheses; * significant at 5%; ** significant at 1%.
Source: our elaboration on BFSS98 data.

her level of education. How often the child plays with their parents or peers is negatively affected by both household equivalent income and the number of children living in it.

10.7. MIMIC model

We have estimated the model described in Section 10.4 using the data set described in Section 10.5.

The indicators for the capability of SIT are the following: attitude toward education (see Table 10.1), a dummy variable equal to 1 if the child has been attending artistic classes (0 otherwise); and a dummy variable equal to 1 if the child has been attending other classes (see Table 10.5), excluding sports classes.

The indicators for LAP are the following: dummy variable equal to 1 if the child has been attending sports classes; and a dummy variable for playing videogames, board games, Lego-type games, movement games or in the playground.

The main regression results are presented in Table 10.10. We report three specifications: specification 1 includes the log of family income but excludes parents' education dummies; specification 2 includes parents' education dummies and excludes income; and specification 3 includes both family income and parents' education dummies. Firstly, we note that the three specifications show similar results, implying that the estimates of the coefficients of the covariates and the factor loading of the latent variable are robust to different specifications. Our preferred specification is the third, because it includes both income and parents' education and it shows that controlling for parents' education, income becomes not significantly different from zero.

Table 10.10 shows regression coefficients for the structural equations of the two capabilities studied. Firstly, we analyse the results for SIT capability. The coefficients show a negative and significant effect for being male and for the number of siblings, whereas there is a positive and significant effect for mother's paid and unpaid hours of work and whether the father is a graduate. In specification 1 the log of family income is significant, but when we include parents' education dummies it loses importance.

As far as the parameters of the covariates on LAP are concerned, we note that being a boy and hours of schooling have a strong positive effect on the capability for leisure and play, while coming from the South and the number of siblings have a negative effect on the same capability. Note that parents' education dummies are not significant in every specification, with the exception of the father's secondary school dummy in the equation for leisure and play.

Table 10.11 presents estimates of the factor loadings for each of the components of the capability for SIT in the measurement equation. It shows that attitudes towards education and performing artistic activities have the highest impact over SIT capability, followed by performing other activities.

Table 10.12 shows the estimates of the factor loadings for the components of the LAP capability. Here, the most important indicators are the dummies for sport and for playing active games, followed by playing videogames.

With regard to the squared multiple correlations for the latent variables, R^2 indicates to what extent the common factors account for the variance of the indicators or how closely the model fits the data (see Table 10.13). Specification 3 has the highest value for R^2; this is not surprising, as it includes more variables than specifications 1 and 2.

The correlation coefficient among the latent variables is positive and significantly different from 0.

Table 10.10 Regression coefficients of the structural equations: γ, γ_2

	Senses, Imagination and Thought (SIT)			Leisure and Play Activities (LAP)		
	Specification 1	Specification 2	Specification 3	Specification 1	Specification 2	Specification 3
Age	−0.006 (0.010)	−0.002 (0.011)	−0.002 (0.011)	−0.007 (0.013)	−0.003 (0.013)	−0.003 (0.013)
Siblings (n)	−0.143** (0.042)	−0.194** (0.044)	−0.185** (0.045)	−0.086* (0.048)	−0.101** (0.051)	−0.096* (0.051)
Boy = 1; 0 otherwise	−0.363** (0.053)	−0.400** (0.055)	−0.394** (0.055)	0.370** (0.060)	0.366** (0.061)	0.372** (0.061)
School hours per week	0.003 (0.004)	0.004 (0.005)	0.004 (0.005)	0.017** (0.006)	0.018** (0.006)	0.017** (0.006)
Father unpaid domestic working hours	−0.018* (0.010)	−0.021* (0.011)	−0.019 (0.011)	−0.007 (0.013)	−0.008 (0.013)	−0.006 (0.013)
Father paid working hours	0.000 (0.002)	0.001 (0.002)	0.001 (0.002)	−0.001 (0.002)	0.000 (0.002)	0.000 (0.002)
Mother unpaid domestic working hours	0.016* (0.009)	0.026** (0.010)	0.024** (0.010)	−0.012 (0.011)	−0.009 (0.012)	−0.011 (0.012)
Mother paid working hours	0.006** (0.003)	0.008** (0.003)	0.007** (0.003)	0.000 (0.003)	0.000 (0.004)	−0.001 (0.004)
Dummy South = 1; 0 otherwise	−0.030 (0.058)	−0.056 (0.061)	−0.046 (0.061)	−0.326** (0.077)	−0.353** (0.077)	−0.338** (0.078)
Log family income	0.054** (0.021)		0.030 (0.022)	0.051* (0.027)		0.027 (0.028)
Dummy father graduate = 1; 0 otherwise		0.178 (0.103)	0.167 (0.102)		0.158 (0.114)	0.148 (0.115)
Dummy mother graduate = 1; 0 otherwise		0.205* (0.107)	0.184 (0.107)		−0.016 (0.128)	−0.029 (0.129)
Dummy secondary school mother		0.066 (0.060)	0.056 (0.060)		0.017 (0.070)	0.013 (0.070)
Dummy secondary school father		0.041 (0.059)	0.032 (0.059)		0.252** (0.071)	0.242** (0.072)
Observations (n)	1504	1504	1504	1504	1504	1504

*Significant at 10% level; **significant at 5% level.

Standard errors in parentheses.

The base category is lower education with respect to degree, Centre-North.

Table 10.11   Estimates of the "loadings" for each of the components of the latent variable "Senses, Imagination and Thought" (SIT) in the measurement equation Λ^{y^I}

	Specification 1	Specification 2	Specification 3
Attitude towards education	1	1	1
Dummy artistic activities = 1; 0 otherwise	1.096 (0.207)**	0.933 (0.183)**	0.952 (0.188)**
Dummy other activities = 1; 0 otherwise	0.693 (0.167)**	0.544 (0.153)**	0.578 (0.156)**

** significant at 5% level, standard errors in parenthesis.

Table 10.12   Estimates of the "loadings" for each of the components of the latent variable "leisure activities and play" (LAP) in the measurement equation $\Lambda^{y^{II}}$

	Specification 1	Specification 2	Specification 3
Dummy sport activities = 1; 0 otherwise	1	1	1
Dummy playing videogames = 1; 0 otherwise	0.351 (0.106)**	0.326 (0.105)**	0.347 (0.106)**
Dummy playing board games = 1; 0 otherwise	0.244 (0.104)**	0.292 (0.100)**	0.276 (0.100)**
Dummy playing Lego-type games = 1; 0 otherwise	0.281 (0.115)**	0.244 (0.109)**	0.240 (0.110)**
Dummy playing active games = 1; 0 otherwise	0.517 (0.113)**	0.504 (0.107)**	0.497 (0.108)**
How often play in playground = 1 if everyday; 6 never	−0.296 (0.085)**	−0.314 (0.081)**	−0.305 (0.081)**

** significant at 5% level, standard errors in parenthesis.

Table 10.13   Latent variables R-squared and correlation coefficients among latent variables

	Specification 1	Specification 2	Specification 3
SIT R-squared	0.252	0.273	0.275
LAP R-squared	0.390	0.404	0.406
Correlation coefficient among latent variables	0.129 (0.026)**	0.141 (0.063)**	0.139 (0.027)**

** Significant at 5% level, standard errors in parenthesis.
SIT: senses, imagination and thought, LAP: leisure activities and play.

10.8. Conclusions

In this chapter we deal with the problem of measuring children's well-being by using the CA with reference to two capabilities: "Senses, Imagination and Thought" (SIT) and "Leisure Activities and Play" (LAP).

We have faced different challenges: firstly, in terms of assembling the type of data necessary to measure these capabilities, and secondly, in terms of the choice of a modelling structure. To tackle the first challenge, we have used a data set (BFSS98) that has been created by matching two different data sets: The Bank of Italy Survey on Income and Wealth (SHIW 2000) and the ISTAT Households, Social Subjects, and Children's conditions (FSS98). With regard to the second issue we have adopted a structural equation modelling (SEM) approach, because capabilities are intrinsically unobserved constructs of which we can only measure some indicators, and SEM allows us to deal with latent variables in a sufficiently flexible way.

Our results are robust to different specifications. A key implication from our results is the strong gender effect in Italy: being a boy implies both a negative effect on the SIT capability and a positive effect on LAP. These two capabilities are also negatively affected by the number of siblings in the household, after having controlled for family income and parents' hours of paid and unpaid work. After controlling for parents' education, family income loses importance in determining children's capabilities.

Acknowledgements

We thank participants at the HDCA Annual Conference in New York (2007), International Association for Research in Income and Wealth Annual IARIW conference (2008) and at the 2007 (Florence) Children's Capabilities Workshop of the HDCA Thematic Group for stimulating comments and discussion. We gratefully acknowledge the highly qualified contribution of Marcello Morciano and Anna Maccagnan in building the matched data sets.

Notes

1. Sen's response in the interview with Saito in March 2001 reported in Saito (2003: 25).
2. Rawls (1980: 546), citation taken from Nussbaum (2003: 53).
3. They used the National Child Development Studies on children born in 1958 controlling for individual, household and neighbourhood variables.
4. Households, Social Subjects and Children's conditions.
5. This age corresponds to children/youth in high school.
6. The above percentage figure exceeds 100% due to the enrolment in schools of foreigners who have not yet been recorded by the Civil Register (Ciccotti et al., 2007: 33).
7. First Report on School Quality by Tuttoscuola (http://www.tuttoscuola.com).
8. "Structural" in this models stands for the assumption that the parameters are not just a descriptive measure of association, but that they reveal an invariant "causal" relation. These techniques do not discover causality in the data. At best they show whether the casual assumptions embedded in a model match a sample of data.

9. This modelling strategy has been extensively used in psychometrics and, more recently, in econometrics (see, for example, Di Tommaso et al., 2007), and is founded upon the specification of a system of equations that establishes the relationship between an unobservable latent variable, a set of observable endogenous indicators and a set of observable exogenous variables (which are believed to be the causes of a specific capability). This approach builds upon the early work of Joreskog and Goldeberger (1975) and Zellner (1970), and has been formalized in the LISREL (Linear Structural Relationships) model of a set of linear structural equations. An excellent review of the literature can be found in Bentler and Weeks (1980), Aigner et al. (1984) and Wansbeek and Meijer (2000).

10. This is the first time these two data sets have been merged. Further details can be found in Addabbo et al. (2007).

11. These variables have been recovered from the matched data set described in Section 10.5.

References

Addabbo, T., Di Tommaso, M.L., Maccagnan, A. and Marciano, M. (2007), "Child Well Being and Family Characteristics. Towards a Measure of Cognitive Capability". Paper presented at the HDCA International Workshop on Children's Capabilities, University of Florence, 18–19 April.

Aigner, D.J., Hsiao, C., Kapteyn, A. and Wansbeek, T. (1984), "Latent Variable Models in Econometrics", in Z. Griliches and M.D. Intriligator (eds), *Handbook in Econometrics*, vol. II, North Holland, Amsterdam, pp. 1323–1393.

Bentler, P.M. and Weeks, D.G. (1980), "Multivariate Analysis with Latent Variables", in P.R. Krishnaiah and L. Kanal (eds), *Handbook of Statistics*, North Holland, Amsterdam, pp. 747–771.

Blau, D.M. (1999), "The Effect of Income on Child Development", *Review of Economics and Statistics*, 81(2): 261–216.

Chevalier, A., Harmon, C., O'Sullivan, V. and Walker, I. (2005) "The Impact of Parental Income and Education on the Schooling of their Children" IZA discussion paper no. 1496, February 2005.

Ciccotti, E. and Sabbadini, M.L. (eds) (2007), "Come cambia la vita dei bambini. Indagine statistica multiscopo sulle famiglie", Quaderni del Centro nazionale di documentazione e analisi per l'infanzia e l'adolescenza, Firenze, Istituto degli Innocenti, n. 42.

Ciccotti, E., Moretti, E. and Ricciotti, R. (eds) (2007), "I numeri italiani. Infanzia e adolescenza in cifre – Edizione 2007", Quaderni del Centro nazionale di documentazione e analisi per l'infanzia e l'adolescenza, Firenze, Istituto degli Innocenti, n. 43.

Clarke-Stewart, A. and Allhusen, V. (2005), *What We Know about Childcare*, Harvard University Press, Cambridge, MA.

Dehejia, R. and Wahba S., (1999), "Causal Effects in Nonexperimental Studies: Reevaluating the Evaluation of Training Programs", *Journal of the American Statistical Association*, December 1999, 94(448): 1053–1062.

Di Tommaso, M.L. (2007), "Measuring the Well-being of Children using a Capability Approach. An Application to Indian Data", *Journal of Socio Economics*, 36: 436–450.

Di Tommaso, M.L., Raiser, M. and Weeks, M. (2007) "Home Grown or Imported? Initial Conditions, External Anchors, and the Determinants of Institutional Reform in the Transition Economies", *Economic Journal*, 117: 858–881.

Duncan, G.J. and Brooks-Gunn, J. (1997) "Income Effects across the Life Span: Integration and Interpretation", in G.J. Duncan and J. Brooks-Gunn (eds), (1997) *Consequences of Growing Up Poor*, Russell Sage Foundation, New York, pp. 596–610.

Elder, G.H., Nguyen, T.V. and Caspi, A. (1985) "Linking Economic Hardship to Children's Lives", *Child Development*, 56(2): 361–375.

Goodman, A. and Sianesi, B. (2005) "Early Education and Children's Outcomes: How Long Do the Impacts Last?", *Fiscal Studies*, 26(4), 513–548.

Heckman, J.J. and Masterov, D.V. (2007), "The Productivity Argument for Investing in Young Children", IZA Discussion Paper no. 2725.

Istituto degli Innocenti (2002), "I servizi educativi per la prima infanzia. Indagine sui nidi d'infanzia e sui servizi educativi 0-3 anni integrativi al nido al 30 settembre 2002", *Quaderni del Centro Nazionale di documentazione e analisi per l'infanzia e l'adolescenza*, IDI, Florence.

Joreskog, K.G. and Goldberger, A.S. (1975), "Estimation of a Model with Multiple Indicators and Multiple Causes of a Single Latent Variable", *Journal of the American Statistical Association*, 70: 631–639.

Krishnakumar, J. (2007), "Going beyond Functionings to Capabilities: An Econometric Model to Explain and Estimate Capabilities", *Journal of Human Development*, 8(1): 39–63.

Krishnakumar, J. and Ballon, P. (2008), "Estimating Basic Capabilities: A Latent Variable Approach Applied to Bolivia", *World Development*, 36, 992–1010.

Kuklys, W. (2005), *Amartya Sen's Capability Approach: Theoretical Insights and Empirical Applications*, Springer, Berlin.

Levy, D. and Duncan, G.J. (2000), "Using Sibling Samples to Assess the Effect of Childhood Family Income on Completed Schooling", *JCPR Working Paper*.

Magnuson, K.A., Ruhm, C.J. and Waldfogel, J. (2004) "Does Prekidergarten Improve School Preparation and Performance?", *NBER Working Paper*, 10452.

Moretti, E. (2004) "Il lavoro minorile in Italia: un approfondimento a partire dall'Indagine ISTAT", in Istituto degli Innocenti (2004) "Bambini e adolescenti che lavorano. Un panorama dall'Italia all'Europa" *Quaderni del Centro Nazionale di documentazione e analisi per l'infanzia e l'adolescenza*, n. 30.

Nussbaum, M.C. (1999), *Sex and Social Justice*, OUP, New York.

Nussbaum, M.C. (2003), "Capabilities as Fundamental Entitlements: Sen and Social Justice", *Feminist Economics*, 9(2–33): 33–59.

Phipps, S. (2002), "The Well-being of Young Canadian Children in International Perspective: A Functionings Approach", *Review of Income and Wealth*, 48(4): 493–513.

Plug, E. and Vijverberg, W. (2003), "Schooling, Family Background, and Adoption: Is It Nature or Is It Nurture?', *Journal of Political Economy*, 111(3): 611–641.

Rawls, J. (1980), "Kantian Constructivism in Moral Theory: The Dewey Lectures", *The Journal of Philosophy*, 7(9): 515–572.

Robeyns, I. (2003), "Sen's Capabilities Approach and Gender Inequalities: Selecting Relevant Capabilities", *Feminist Economics*, 9(2–3): 61–92.

Rosembaum, P.R. and Rubin, D.B. (1983), "The Central Role of the Propensity Score in Observational Studies for Causal Effetcts", *Biometrika*, 70: 41–55.

Rubin, D. (1977), Assignement to a Treatment Group on the Basis of a Covariate, *Journal of Educational Statistics*, 2: 1–26.

Saito, M. (2003), "Amartya Sen's Capability Approach to Education: A Critical Exploration", *Journal of Philosophy of Education*, 37(1): 17–34.

Taylor, B.A., Dearing, E. and McCartney, K. (2004), "Incomes and Outcomes in Early Childhood", *Journal of Human Resources*, 39(4): 980–1007.

UNICEF (2007) *Child Poverty in Perspective: An Overview of Child Well-being in Rich Countries*, Innocenti Report Card 7, Unicef IRC, Florence.

Waldfogel, J. (2002), "Child Care, Women's Employment, and Child Outcomes", *Journal of Population Economics*, 15: 527–548.

Wansbeek, T. and Meijer, E. (2000), *Measurement Error and Latent Variables in Econometrics*, Elsevier Science, North Holland, The Netherlands.

Zellner, A. (1970), "Estimation of Regression Relationships Containing Unobservable Variables", *International Economic Review*, 11: 441–454.

Part III
Policy Implications

11
Rethinking Children's Disabilities through the Capability Lens: A Framework for Analysis and Policy Implications

Jean-Francois Trani, Parul Bakhshi and Mario Biggeri

11.1. Introduction

This chapter has two main aims. The first is to propose a new framework for policy that complements the evolving capabilities approach (CA) developed in Chapter 2. The second is to focus specifically on children with disabilities in developing countries and to revisit current models of disability in this context. The case study of children's well-being in Afghanistan discussed previously in this book is used to illuminate the discussion.

Children and young people with disabilities in developing countries are often very isolated and have little contact with society. A number of children with disabilities are hidden and have no access to education, be it physical access or overcoming social, cultural and religious beliefs and practices. Research shows that children with disabilities are less likely to participate in society and community affairs than their peers (Ehrmann et al., 1995), and children with mental illness and learning difficulties face more participation impediments that those with physical or sensory impairments (Longmuir and Bar-Or, 2000; Law et al., 2004). A large body of literature stresses the importance of social participation by defining it as the interaction between the individual and a disabling or enabling environment. Thus, an increased focus has been put on examining and changing the physical, social, political or institutional environment, in order to enable children with disabilities to participate (Law and Dunn, 1993; Law et al., 1999; Hammal et al., 2004; Welsh et al., 2006; Forsyth et al., 2007; Heah et al., 2007). Development programmes and policies and their underlying frameworks that aim to enhance the participation and empowerment of marginalized groups, including children with disabilities, invariably tend to over-generalize complex issues. There is overarching agreement over what these policy programmes should achieve, but often idealistic goals remain disconnected from the needs of individuals. As a result, vulnerable groups such as children with disabilities become separated from the process and cease to be the central focus. Some studies show that the provision of support at school, for instance, may became a barrier to participation as it reduces the student's opportunities to interact with teachers and peers and can become an obstacle to gaining autonomy (Giangreco et al., 1997; Skar and Tamm, 2001; Pivik et al., 2002; Mihaylov et al., 2004).

In this chapter, we introduce a framework based on the CA developed by Sen (1984, 1999, 2005) and others with the aim of helping policy makers to formulate policies and bridge the gap between research, policy implementation and assessment. This framework focuses on vulnerability from the perspective of increasing inclusion and strengthening empowerment. It reviews the interaction between the individual and social models of disability by giving central focus to human diversity. This framework does not segregate vulnerable groups by providing labels, but takes a more comprehensive view to address vulnerability as a multidimensional dynamic phenomenon with different types of limitations to the "capability" to achieve various "beings and doings", or "functionings" that the vulnerable individual values (Sen, 1992, 1999). In other words, the CA can be a means of overcoming the "dilemma of differences".[1] It focuses on the specificity of an individual situation and needs without attempting to imprison him/her in a binding label. As Sen states, differently (dis)abled people may need different types and different amounts of capability inputs (policies, resources, changes in social norms or infrastructure) to achieve the same levels of well-being (e.g. Sen, 1999; see also Mitra, 2006).

The current impetus of looking at development with a human face invariably means expanding choices and positive freedoms. It is often stated that the CA seems to show limitations when we look at extremely vulnerable groups, such as persons with mental illness and intellectual disability. In this chapter we will argue that this framework remains relevant even for these forms of disability, if we shift the focus from the individual to the household unit and involve direct observers (carers) when considering persons with mental illness and intellectual disability. Theories of justice serve as a basis for policy action in the capability informational space: public policies are therefore responsible for providing the *social and cultural (sense, perceptions, identities, etc. . . .) basis* for capabilities (Nussbaum, 2000: 81). This is especially the case where impairments are preventable, or where disability is socially constructed (Baylies, 2002). Adopting the CA also changes the focus of policy goals and processes, since the effectiveness and relevance of these are gauged in terms of expansion of human capabilities and respecting people's values. The ultimate goal thus shifts dramatically from increasing economic growth to the expanding of human capabilities, from resource-based policies to an in-depth change in the implementation process. Many policy-oriented studies use the CA to extend the informational base, adding and measuring new dimensions of well-being. This is a relevant starting point for the change in policy implementation but, in doing so, they tend to undermine the application of the CA by not using its full potential. Indeed, as emphasized by Sen (1999, 2004, 2005, 2006), there is a need for public scrutiny and reasoning in the application of the CA. We share this approach as we think the process itself is as important as the informational space for policies. Although some of the findings in this chapter may be generalized to a variety of contexts, we apply the framework to the issue of dis/ability among children as an illustration to make the approach operational.

In order to see a meaningful shift in policies, it is crucial to bring changes in the way information is collected as well as in analysing data on disability. For instance, data is sometimes available regarding prevalence rates or the proportion of children with disabilities accessing school, however there is limited data in both developed and developing countries regarding the needs of children with disabilities, which are essential for policy development. There is a need for data that goes beyond mere description and looks at functioning and participation, agency and values (see Chapters 3 and 4). We argue that instruments can measure effective and potential functionings, beings and doings that are valued, barriers to choices as well as available resources. The complementarities between the International Classification of Functioning, Disability and Health (known as ICF; WHO, 2001) that views disability as a combination of individual, institutional and societal factors that define the environment within which a person with impairment evolves on one hand, and the CA on the other, forms a new space within which context specific tools can be designed and inter-country comparisons made possible, provided that cultural specificities are taken into account.

This chapter is divided into five sections. After the present introduction, we review the individual model, the social model and the ICF framework through a CA lens in Section 11.2. In Section 11.3 we present a framework for policies informed by the CA. We subsequently outline the types of data that are needed to overcome existing gaps in broad household surveys of international agencies (such as LSMS, MICS DHS, NLS; see Chapter 3, Section 3.1) or other national household surveys on general living conditions. In Section 11.4, we introduce the example of the National Disability Survey in Afghanistan (NDSA), which attempted to operationalize the CA. In the final Section, 11.5, we discuss the main issues raised and make recommendations for taking the approach forward.

11.2. Rethinking children's disabilities through the CA

It has been acknowledged within the literature and empirical work that the three most relevant models of disability – the individual/medical, the social model and the WHO model ICF – entail diverse and often contrasting policy implications (Terzi, 2004; Trani and Bakhshi, 2008).[2] Indeed, the conceptual framework underlying the identification of disability and its measurement has considerable implications for the estimation of prevalence, analysis and policy making. In this section section we will define the different models and argue that the CA provides a new understanding of disability that reconciles the various views and is more in line with policy-making requirements. The CA is comprehensive, encompasses all dimensions of individual well-being and does not limit its view merely to impairment or to the disabling conditions.

The individual or medical model views disability as divergence from the physical norm. Here disability is understood as being a biological condition intrinsic to the individual, which reduces his/her quality of life and participation in society in comparison to "normal" human functioning (Amundson, 2000; Pfeiffer, 2001). In this model, the measurement of prevalence of disability is based on the evaluation of the number of persons who fall within a series of pre-defined categories of impairments, considered as limitations in health condition across a range of basic functions and body structures. Persons with disability fit neatly into a few categories with clear boundaries (the deaf, the blind, etc.) and are considered as deviant from the norm. From this perspective, prevalence estimates are invariably biased. In fact, censuses or surveys based on self-reporting that use questions that are perceived as stigmatizing lead to under-reporting. Research based on such tools will only focus on the social disadvantages directly linked to the impairment. And policies will only aim to compensate for existing restriction in selected activities instead of reflecting upon the removal of barriers to full participation.

The social model is based on a different paradigm. It does not reject the idea of health limitation, which is the impairment, but considers persons to be "differently abled". This view, which was initially put forward by disability-rights activists, tends to examine the barriers that exist within the social context and prevent a person from achieving the same level of functioning as a non-disabled person. From this perspective it is society that needs to be redesigned in order to take into account disabled persons' needs (Oliver, 1996). The advocates of the social model consider that physical limitations become a disability because society does not accommodate differences in human functioning. Mainstreaming disability concerns is a progressive and sustainable way of redesigning society in order to include people with disabilities. However, the social model has limitations when addressing the issue of prevalence, conducting research and defining policies. Questions based on this model will not be centred solely on impairment, but will include the identification of barriers within the social environment that create the disabling situation. In this regard, policy makers have to address restrictions caused by the environment, and promote participation by ensuring equal rights and opportunities.

In both models, disability is understood as a condition that deviates from a situation considered as being a "normal" state of health. However, a third approach considers that this normal or perfect health situation is an ideal that most people do not experience. In a continuum of health states, each individual presents some deficiency in one or more dimensions of functioning. The ICF model is based on such a view (WHO, 2001). Disability having several dimensions or levels, the ICF is composed of various domains of activities and participation that correspond to the body, the person and the person-in-society. It looks at disability as a combination of different factors that influence the environment within which persons with disability live. In the ICF, the term functioning refers to all the body functions, activities and participation, while disability is similarly an umbrella term for impairments, activity limitations and participation restrictions (WHO, 2001). This system advocates an assessment of two kinds of factors: environmental factors (including the physical environment, the social environment and the impact of attitudes) and personal factors, which correspond to the personality and characteristic attributes of an individual. This view is based on the assumption that functioning is an important outcome, regardless of its determinants. Thus, using the ICF for prevalence measurement in a population-based survey entails a fresh view of the measurement of disability. The ICF consists of a reference scale: its domain codes require the use of qualifiers that identify the presence and record the severity of the functioning problem on a five-point scale (e.g. no impairment, mild, moderate, severe and complete). To take full advantage of this coding, however, requires that a large amount of information be collected: information about activity or participation in sufficient detail to assign ICF domain codes, information about the use of personal assistance and assistive technology, and assessments of five levels of difficulty in both the current environment and within the standardized environment. None of the question sets currently used or recommended by international organizations covers the entire range of information needed to assess all the qualifiers of the ICF. The complexity of disability as a social phenomenon leads to various ways of making the concepts operational and requires a wide range of questions that can be used (Altman, 2001). Research using the ICF identifies a variety of disabling situations combining activity limitations, lack of participation and analysis of causes of exclusion, inequality and poverty (Zaidi and Burchardt, 2005). Comparisons between countries using the ICF are limited by cultural differences and understandings of disability (Miles, 2001; Baylies, 2002; Groce, 2006). This is one of the objectives of the Washington Group on Disability Statistics, which has elaborated a set of questions based on the ICF to be translated in any language and used in any census or national survey to allow for international comparison. However, the ICF does not allow for any analysis of participation and public reasoning, as it is currently used to elaborate a normative instrument to measure disability in any kind of cultural and social context.

The CA offers a general theoretical framework for disability studies that encompasses the social model (Burchardt, 2004; Terzi, 2005; Mitra, 2006; Welch, 2007). It places the definition of disability within the wider spectrum of human development and enhancing freedoms. This view is based on "beings and doings that an individual has reason to value", thus shifting the focus from the specificities of the disabling situation (in the case of ICF on body functions, activities and participation) to establishing equality in terms of possibilities and choices. In this way, this framework is linked to a theory of justice (Sen, 2006, 2009). Amartya Sen's approach provides broader insights into the issues raised by disability, since it proposes to look not at what a person actually does (functionings) but at the range of possibilities (the capabilities set) from which he/she chooses specific functionings (e.g. Sen, 1999). The fact that each individual is asked to assess the level of difficulties faced on each dimension helps assess the situation in a comprehensive and holistic manner. This allows the distinction to be made between capabilities that are intrinsically valuable and others that are also instrumentally relevant. This approach covers the full range of the disability experience, shifting the focus away from limited views in terms of types of impairments only. It focuses on the interplay between individual characteristics and social restrictions and proposes to measure outcomes in terms of expanding people's choices. Limiting the definition to merely a quantitative figure, or to income or institutional access, would entail ignoring the dynamics that exist between the individual and the community (Bakhshi et al., 2006).

To summarise, we argue that there are evident similarities between the various approaches discussed, the emphasis being on the interplay between the individual and the collective. Within the human development perspective, the definition of disability devised, for instance, during NDSA needed to take into account these diverse aspects: the individual's potentialities, the possibilities of "being" what he/she wishes; his/her vulnerabilities, the risk measured as the probability of falling to a lower state of well-being; the opportunities offered by the environment the individual lives in, the agency role of the individual or communities, which looks at the extent to which the person (or the group) considers him/herself as the main actor and decision maker in his/her own life (Bakhshi et al., 2006).

11.3. The capability approach framework for analysis and policy implications

In this section we present a general framework for policy design to expand people's valued capabilities. The capability set is considered within a specific community or social group in other words, we explore the capabilities relevant for a given community or a given social group. Therefore, we argue for the need to define a framework that focuses on the expression of requirements and aspirations of individuals within the group/community. In doing this, as reported by Biggeri and Mehrotra in Chapter 3, we can bypass the debate on whether to endorse a fixed list of capabilities (Nussbaum, 2000 *versus* Sen, 2004; see also Robeyns, 2006; Clark, 2006). We also argue that our approach enriches the framework proposed by Robeyns (2003, 2005). This updated framework has been developed to analyse issues related to children with disabilities, but can be considered as an appropriate tool for policy formulation in a more general context. In Figure 11.1 we present a diagram that illustrates this new framework for policy formulation.

Let us first consider a comprehensive set of valued functionings that form the capability set of a given community. (Figure 11.1, box at far left). These are all potentially valuable functionings that should be guaranteed for all members of the community, and that will be considered for analysis and policies implementation: we will call this the community capability set. The community capability set is composed of individual, collective and social capabilities. Collective capabilities are the capabilities of the group or the community (trade unions, NGOs, community-based organizations, associations, self-help groups, etc.) as they result from collective agency/action of the group.[3] Social capabilities are the supplementary individual capabilities resulting from social interaction between individuals (social agency). The community capability is the aggregation of the various individual capability sets, the collective capability set of the group and the social capability set (Dubois and Trani, 2009).

Two difficulties arise at this point. The first refers to how community capability can emerge from the combination of several individual capabilities – this aggregation problem has not yet been adequately addressed (Anand, 2007; Sandler and Arce, 2007; Dubois and Trani, 2009). A second difficulty is that the community capability set might be neglected by part of the community. In fact, inequalities and exploitation of the most deprived within a given community may go hand in hand with "non-grumbling" endurance and resignation (e.g. Sen, 1984, 1992). For example, a child in bonded labour may value the opportunity to work over other, arguably more ambitious, opportunities such as being able to attend school, due to adaptive preferences. It follows that, in cases where people have adapted, self-assessment may provide an unreliable guide to personal well-being (see also Crocker, 1992; Nussbaum, 2000; Teschl and Comim, 2005; Qizilbash, 2006; Clark, 2009, forthcoming). In order to gauge adequately the community capability set, it may be necessary to consult a representative sample of the population who are able to identify all potential functioning sets, or establish a control group as an impartial point of reference.

This comprehensive community capability set could be used as a road map for identifying areas for public intervention. Nevertheless, in line with Sen, we argue that basic capabilities (and the corresponding human rights)

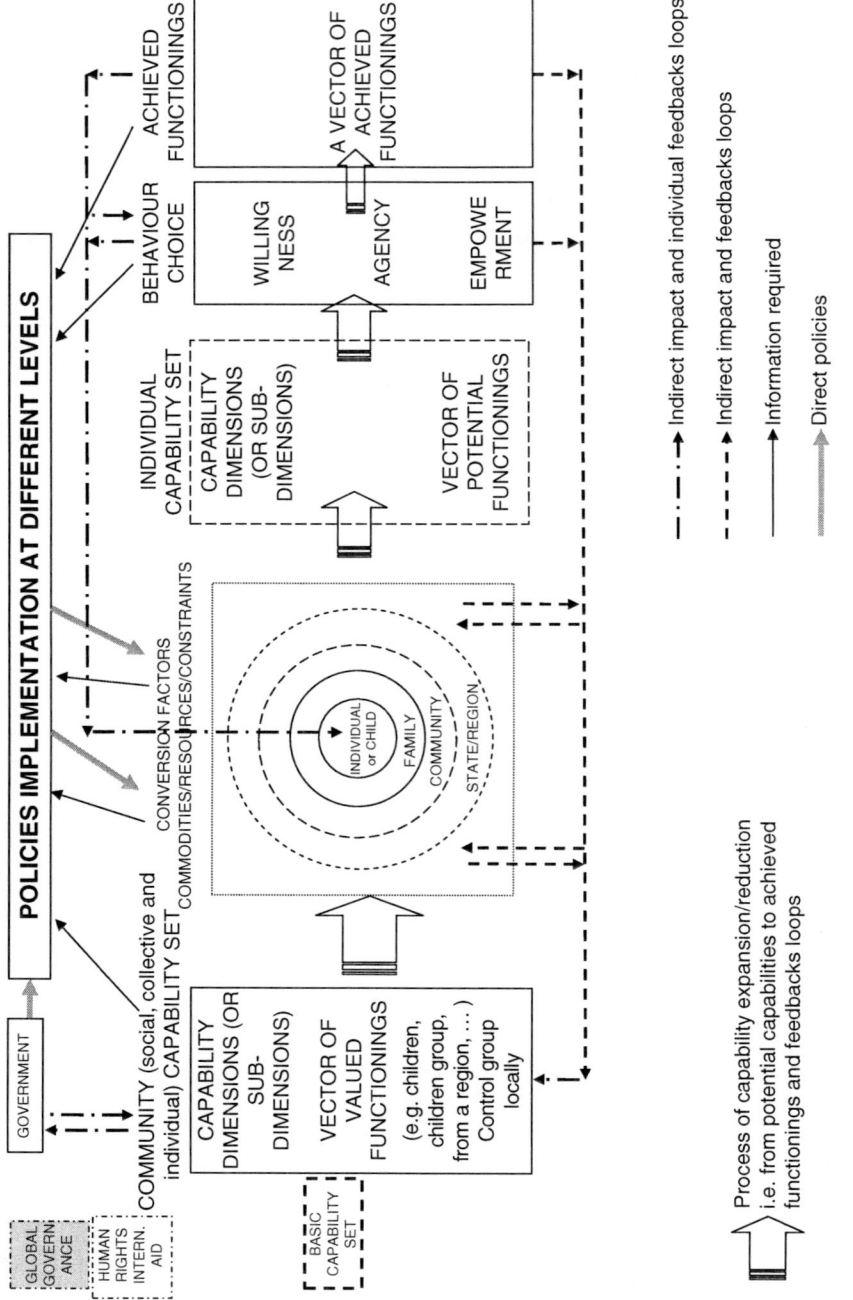

Figure 11.1 The capability framework for policy implications

should be included in the community's potential capability set, as they are minimal requirements for well-being (Sen, 1999, 2005).

On the right-hand side of Figure 11.1 are presented individual children's set of achieved functionings. Following Robeyns (2003), the central part of Figure 11.1 describes the "conversion factors" that govern the person's capability set (i.e. the individual potential functionings and the material or immaterial factors that influence these). The conversion factors exist at four levels: the individual level (age, sex, talent, impairment, etc.); the family level (income, shelter, food ration, support, costs and expenditure); the community level (social capital, traditional norms, solidarity, social participation); and regional or national levels (public goods investment, legal framework, rights and obligations such as tax, military service). Similarly, the conversion factors can be social factors, personal factors or environmental factors. Conversion factors can also be classified in terms of material factors, such as assets, infrastructures, goods and services, and immaterial factors, such as capacities of the individual and social norms, identities and beliefs that can facilitate or impede the benefit of a given capability. Both material and immaterial factors are present at individual, family, community and regional/state levels. All these factors contribute to the determination of individual capability sets.

According to their political and ideological base, conversion factors can constitute resources or constraints. For instance, a national public policy of education is a resource for most children. Similarly, a cooperative organization at the level of the village for agricultural production can be a resource if it serves the interests of the people. A family that provides for their children's well-being or sends them to school (instead of work) is also a precious resource. Family is also important for those seeking support to find work or who need access to food, shelter, cultural or sport activities. For an active individual, in some cultural contexts family can be a constraint when several dependents rely on a single income from one person.

Let us consider a person with disabilities who is a wheelchair user in a major town of a developed country. This person will be able to move around using public transport made available by local, regional or national government. In many cases, this will include access to lifts or ramps to ensure appropriate access to trains, buses and taxis. These products and services may not be strictly necessary for many non-wheelchair users. The adapted pavements in the town, as well as lifts in buses and trains, are regional/state level conversion factors that facilitate the mobility of individuals with disabilities. Disability is an individual conversion factor that makes it harder for a person with the condition to "convert" resources into the capability of being able to move around: even if he/she has the same income as an able-bodied person, he/she will not be able to travel on public transport if there are no lifts to access tube stations, buses or taxis.

In a context such as Afghanistan's rural areas, wheelchairs are rarely available, no public transportation system exists and there are no paved roads: disability and absence of adaptation of the environment make mobility problematic. Community and family support can presumably relieve some of the obstacles as they might try to build a wheelchair using local materials, or try to send someone to the closest major town where wheelchairs might be available. Finally, members of the family can help the person move around on a daily basis. Indeed, family support is a conversion factor that is a major resource in the Afghan context as well as in other societies where family plays a major social role.

In Afghanistan traditional cultural practices are based on the belief that people with disabilities are victims of God's will and black magic (Trani et al., 2009). In both environments, negative perceptions can lead to low self-esteem and isolation. It is therefore difficult for those people with disabilities to "convert" bundles of resources into capabilities or find viable and acceptable coping strategies. As a consequence, policies have to be carefully tailored at the individual level (to reduce the negative impact on valued functionings), the family level (to provide appropriate support to the family) and at the national level (to provide for services – primarily education and healthcare – and to campaign for reducing stigma).

For a given capability set the individual makes choices according to his/her aspirations and agency. These individual choices constitute what Sen (1992) calls the achieved functioning vector. Some of these achieved functionings are instrumental and have an impact on the means to achieve other doings and beings that a given individual or community values. The achieved functionings of various individuals have an influence on the capability set of the community as a whole, as they participate in collective action with potential to influence the well-being of the community; they are the outcome of an ongoing process that either expands or reduces the capability set of the community as defined above. The possibility of expansion (or reduction) depends on the cooperative (or conflicting) relationships between members of the community or in its interaction with other communities. Finally, the understanding of the whole process in any given social, cultural and economic environment calls for the identification of constraints that affect the capability set. If constraints are such that they reduce the capability set, basic capabilities should be protected as a minimum standard of wellbeing. In such a context, principles of good governance and essential rights could constitute guidelines for public action. We argue that policies to expand capabilities can intervene directly in an effort to change the *means* for achieving what people value. The policies that aim to enhance means or instruments are represented in Figure 11.1 by arrows, and have to be designed and implemented at whatever level the problem is encountered – individual, household or community. In the case of mentally disabled children, the family or the caretaker may be central in identifying relevant priorities.

The entire process is dynamic and involves political will at the community level and agency and empowerment at the individual level. The process of capability expansion/reduction proceeds from potential capabilities to individual achieved functioning vectors, as shown by the arrows in Figure 11.1.

Considering the implementation of policy at a national or regional level, we believe that attempts to make the CA operational using the existing information from standard surveys are often not sufficient. Using the CA with traditional survey data can improve information on which policy is conceived, but it does not allow for effective policy planning. In other words, we argue that different types of information are necessary in order to benefit from the full potential of the CA. This implies that data collection has to be based on the CA framework from the outset, and should take into account the values expressed by the people and community alongside information relating to individual agency. Table 11.1 presents a framework for the analysis of different dimensions or capabilities.

Thus, in order to use the CA framework there is a need to collect more data relating to "non-standard" information. This operationalization process indicates that, alongside the assessment of resources, constraints and actual functionings, additional information is required to measure valued capabilities, agency and the choices of individuals and communities. In this respect, Table 11.1 presents a matrix based on the information that has to be collected. As a consequence, survey instruments focusing on capabilities have to be tailored to fit a given social, cultural and economic situation.

11.4. The case of children with disabilities in Afghanistan

In this section we report a simplified version of the framework described in the previous section that draws on a survey in Afghanistan which used the CA to better understand children's disabilities.

The definition devised for the survey was in line with the stated aims, the capabilities framework and other factors within the Afghan context: "Disability is thus the condition that results from the interaction between an individual impairment in functioning and the community and social resources, beliefs and practices that enable or prevent a person from participating in all spheres of social life and taking decisions that are relevant to his/her own future" (Bakhshi et al., 2006: 8).

The survey was designed in 2004, covered all 34 provinces of the country and was conducted in 2005 in an unstable political context and hazardous security conditions. However the need to collect evidence relating to persons with disabilities was essential, according to various stakeholders (including organizations of persons with disabilities, policy makers, international organizations and UN agencies). All stakeholders contributed to

Table 11.1 Re-framing the disability models through the capability approach for policy implementation: the data information matrix

Examples of dimensions/ capabilities and functionings	Capabilities informational space				Individual conversion factors		Household/family level conversion factors		Community level		State/Regional level	
	Achieved functionings	Capabilities relevance for the group (values and priorities)	Agency	Choices	Means (commodities, resources, technology)	Personal impediment	Means (commodities, resources, technology)	Family impediment	Means (commodities, resources, technology)	Community impediment	Means (commodities, resources, technology)	State/Regional impediment
1) Life and physical health	Are you now enjoying ...?/score^	Is ... Important to have for you?/score*	Are you able to change your...?/ score~	Are you willing to have to have ...?/ 0/ 1**	Do you have enough money to buy drugs?/0/1**	0/1**	0/1**	0/1**	0/1**	0/1**	0/1**	0/1**
2) Love and care	score^	score*	score~	0/1**	0/1**	0/1**	0/1**	0/1**	0/1**	0/1**	0/1**	0/1**
3) Mental well-being	score^	score*	score~	0/1**	0/1**	0/1**	0/1**	0/1**	0/1**	0/1**	0/1**	0/1**
4) Bodily integrity and safety	score^	score*	score~	0/1**	0/1**	0/1**	0/1**	0/1**	0/1**	0/1**	0/1**	0/1**
5) Social relations	score^	score*	score~	0/1**	0/1**	0/1**	0/1**	0/1**	0/1**	0/1**	0/1**	0/1**
6) Participation/ information	score^	score*	score~	0/1**	0/1**	0/1**	0/1**	0/1**	0/1**	0/1**	0/1**	0/1**
7) Education	score^	score*	score~	0/1**	0/1**	0/1**	0/1**	0/1**	0/1**	0/1**	0/1**	0/1**
7a Learning to know	score^	score*	score~	0/1**	0/1**	0/1**	0/1**	0/1**	0/1**	0/1**	0/1**	0/1**
7b Learning to be	score^	score*	score~	0/1**	0/1**	0/1**	0/1**	0/1**	0/1**	0/1**	0/1**	0/1**
7c Learning to live together	score^	score*	score~	0/1**	0/1**	0/1**	0/1**	0/1**	0/1**	0/1**	0/1**	0/1**
7d Learning to do	score^	score*	score~	0/1**	0/1**	0/1**	0/1**	0/1**	0/1**	0/1**	0/1**	0/1**

8) Freedom from economic and non-economic exploitation	score^	score*		0/1**	0/1**	0/1**	0/1**	0/1**	0/1**	0/1**
9) Shelter and environment	score^	score*	score~	0/1**	0/1**	0/1**	0/1**	0/1**	0/1**	0/1**
10) Leisure activities	score^	score*	score~	0/1**	0/1**	0/1**	0/1**	0/1**	0/1**	0/1**
11) Respect	score^	score*	score~	0/1**	0/1**	0/1**	0/1**	0/1**	0/1**	0/1**
12) Religion and identity	score^	score*	score~	0/1**	0/1**	0/1**	0/1**	0/1**	0/1**	0/1**
13) Time autonomy and undertake projects	score^	score*	score~	0/1**	0/1**	0/1**	0/1**	0/1**	0/1**	0/1**
14) Mobility	score^	score*	score~	0/1**	0/1**	0/1**	0/1**	0/1**	0/1**	0/1**
Others dimensions	score^	score*	score~	0/1**	0/1**	0/1**	0/1**	0/1**	0/1**	0/1**

Note that for relevant dimensions (e.g. education), it is possible to detail them in sub-dimensions as indicated in grey colour. * Score is given on a scale of measurement of importance of each capability dimension for the respondent. ^ score is given on a scale of measurement of achievement functionings for each capability dimension for the respondent; ~ score is given on a scale of measurement of the level of agency to change the achievement functionings for each capability dimension for the respondent ** 0, 1 variable. Note: "internal" factors, such as personal characteristics (e.g. physical conditions, sex, skills, talents, intelligence, sensitivity, interaction attitude) convert resources (or commodities) into individual functionings. The conversion is also related to "external" factors such as social characteristics (e.g. public policies, institutions, legal rules, traditions, social norms, discriminating practices, gender roles, societal hierarchies, power relations, public goods) and environmental endowments (e.g. infrastructure, country, public infrastructure, climate, pollution).

the design of the study. At the time of our survey, economic and political decisions were made on local and widely varying estimations of disability prevalence (between 3% and 10%). There was no information regarding the numbers, profiles, living conditions and coping strategies of persons with disabilities. Programmes that were run by national and international organizations were often based on intuition and on the capacity to access populations. As a result there was a demand, both on part of the government and disability organizations, for greater knowledge regarding the composition and distribution of these population groups in order to tailor and adapt policies and programmes to the needs of people with disabilities. The study was aimed at providing insights and recommendations for the Government of Afghanistan, even though other NGOs and organizations would benefit from it. From a research perspective the objectives were to (a) measure the prevalence and type of disability; (b) provide insights into the challenges, opportunities and needs of persons with disabilities in Afghanistan pertaining to rehabilitation, education, employment, vocational training, social integration and political participation; (c) identify barriers, difficulties and stigma that persons with disabilities face in everyday life; and (d) provide strategic guidelines to overcome the main challenges and difficulties faced by persons with disabilities. In other words, this survey may be considered a first attempt to operationalize the CA on such a large scale.

The questionnaire was developed in accordance with the framework reported in Table 11.2. Notice that Table 11.2, which is a simplified version of the diagrams in Figure 11.1 and Table 11.1. A large part of the information required by stakeholders was incorporated into the research design and questionnaire. The quality of the information collected partly depends on the validity, reliability and accuracy of the questions asked and the structure of the questionnaire. In line with Afghan cultural norms regarding disability, the questionnaire was composed of a variety of questions that can be used as indicators of the presence of a disabling situation. The questions were arranged in thematic modules and organized in a logical order, ranging from the simplest to the most complex in terms of information required. Sometimes the questions asked were similar to those included in other Afghan questionnaires, to allow comparison over time and/or with different sub-groups of the population.

To build an adequate questionnaire, it is imperative to understand the underlying elements that could provide a framework within which tools should be elaborated and results should be interpreted. Understanding the dynamics that influence the living conditions of persons with disabilities requires an in-depth analysis of the religious, cultural and social aspects, a task that is often complicated by gender, ethnic and economic factors (Groce, 2006).[4]

The first step towards comprehending cultural norms and beliefs is conducting open discussions regarding cultural practices, religious beliefs and

Table 11.2   Pattern for drawing up the questionnaire

Information dimensions	Identifying the resources	Access to these resources	Barriers to these resources	Identifying ways to overcome barriers
Health	Indicator(s): Question(s):	Indicator(s): Question(s):	Indicator(s): Question(s):	Indicator(s): Question(s):
Education	Indicator(s): Question(s):	Indicator(s): Question(s):	Indicator(s): Question(s):	Indicator(s): Question(s):
Employment and income	Indicator(s): Question(s):	Indicator(s): Question(s):	Indicator(s): Question(s):	Indicator(s): Question(s):
Livelihoods	Indicator(s): Question(s):	Indicator(s): Question(s):	Indicator(s): Question(s):	Indicator(s): Question(s):
Social participation	Indicator(s): Question(s):	Indicator(s): Question(s):	Indicator(s): Question(s):	Indicator(s): Question(s):
Love and Care	Indicator(s): Question(s):	Indicator(s): Question(s):	Indicator(s): Question(s):	Indicator(s): Question(s):
Respect	Indicator(s): Question(s):	Indicator(s): Question(s):	Indicator(s): Question(s):	Indicator(s): Question(s):
Awareness	Indicator(s): Question(s):	Indicator(s): Question(s):	Indicator(s): Question(s):	Indicator(s): Question(s):

Source: Our elaboration on Bakhshi et al. (2006).

ways of life using basic qualitative methods such as life stories, focus group discussions, open-ended interviews, word association techniques and case studies. In the Afghanistan survey, this helped us to determine which issues were relevant, acceptable and sensitive regarding disability. We approached groups other than people with disabilities in order to gain a comprehensive view of circumstances of the Afghan population. We tried to decipher the reasons behind stigma and discrimination, to comprehend the plight of women with disabilities and the belief systems and social practices that are prevalent. Three examples below illustrate the reality and complexity of prejudice towards children with disabilities: access to school, love and care and participation in ceremonies reflect the level of acceptation of children with disabilities within the family, the community and society at large. At the same time these examples advocate for a clear space for policy interventions at the community and family levels. Children above the age of 8 were interviewed directly, whereas a caretaker would assist for younger children and children with severe mental illness or intellectual disability.

The new generation of children have more access to school than their parents, but this access is significantly different for persons with disabilities than for the non-disabled (see Table 11.3). The proportion of non-disabled children aged 7 to 14 accessing public school today is almost

Table 11.3 School attendance in Afghanistan

Age group and gender	Non-disabled (%)[**a]	Persons with disabilities (%)[**a]
Age		
7–14	6067 (65.4[**b])	86 (36.1[**b])
15–25	2859 (31.7)	50 (26.8)
26 and above	2360 (25.9[*b])	102 (19.7[*b])
Gender		
Male (7–14)	4067 (68.3[**b])	63 (48.5[**b])
Female (7–14)	2308 (43.2[**b])	14 (15.2[**b])

[a] Chi-squared Pearson for independence; ** significant at $p < 0.01$; * significant at $p < 0.05$.
[b] Test of comparison of proportion between the two groups; ** significant at $p < 0.01$; * significant at $p < 0.05$.
Source: Our elaboration on NDSA (2005).

twice as high (65.4%) as the proportion of children with disabilities (36.1%). Global access to public school is twice as high for non-disabled children than for children with disability below the age of 7, regardless of where they live, their gender or their age group.

Exclusion from education is slightly higher when the child becomes disabled before school age than when disability occurs at an older age. Moreover, the barriers to accessing school are significantly higher for girls with disabilities than for boys with disabilities. In 2005 the gap between people with disabilities (regardless of the age of disability) and the non-disabled (for different age groups) was only highly statistically significant for the generation under 15 years of age. This finding confirms that being disabled before school-starting age is as detrimental to access to school today as it has been over the last 40 years. An explanation of a higher rate of access for children with disabilities before the age of 7 may lie in the considerable enrolment effort made by the Government since 2002. This effort has been seen to mainly benefit non-disabled boys, but there is evidence to show that, to a much lesser extent, girls and children with disabilities have benefited too. However, the effort by policy makers to send children back to school has not been significantly effective for children who became disabled at an early stage, or for girls.

Among children aged 7–14 years, having a disability is the main reason given for receiving no education before seven years of age (53.7%) (see Table 11.4). The absence of an accessible school accounted for 22.4% in this category, whereas for children in the "disabled after age 7 and non-disabled" category this reason was given by 39.1%.

For the current generation, despite increasing numbers of schools and considerable efforts for enrolment, children with disabilities and their families

Table 11.4 Main reasons for not accessing school, by age category and gender

Age group	Main reasons for having received no education	Persons disabled before age 7			Persons disabled after age 7 and non-disabled		
		Male	Female	All	Male	Female	All
7–14	Absence of school	18 (30.6%)	11 (15.3%)	22.4%	56 (47.9%)	64 (34.8%)	39.1%
	Disability	36 (58.1%)	36 (50%)	53.7%	1 (0.9%)	1 (0.5%)	–
	School not for girls	NA	12 (16.7%)	–	NA	75 (41.8%)	–
15–25	Absence of school	3 (8.8%)	6 (25%)	15.5%	48 (40.2%)	105 (44.1%)	42.7%
	Disability	15 (44.1%)	12 (50%)	46.6%	5 (3.9%)	1 (0.5%)	–
	School not for girls	NA	4 (16.7%)	–	NA	66 (33.7%)	–
>26	Absence of school	16 (37.2%)	12 (50%)	41.8%	(197) 45.8%	193 (59.7%)	57.7%
	Disability	19 (44.2%)	2 (8.3%)	31.3%	8 (2.2%)	2 (0.6%)	–
	School not for girls	NA	8 (33.3%)	–	NA	88 (30.3%)	–

NA: not available

Source: Our elaboration on NDSA (2005).

stated their physical or mental condition as the major obstacle to education. Within the 15–25-year age group the absence of school was still the main reason given by those that became disabled after school-starting age and the non-disabled (42.7%). But for persons disabled before age 7, the main reason given for no education was their disability (46.6%). Persons over the age of 25 stated that the main reason for having received no education was the absence of schools in their communities. This was true for persons who became disabled after school-starting age and for the non-disabled (57.7%), as well as for those who were disabled before age 7 (41.8%).

For men and boys who were disabled after age 7 and the non-disabled, absence of a school was the reason most commonly given by all age groups. Other reasons not specified in Table 11.4 were absence of financial means, need for the child to work, bad political situations and the uselessness of school. For boys and men who became disabled before age 7, having a disability was the main reason for having received no education. This was even more evident among boys aged 7 to 14: 58.1% stated disability as the main reason for not receiving any education. For girls and women, there was a third reason for no access to schools: gender discrimination. This reason included the head of the household's belief that either school was not adapted to meet girls' needs or that school was not necessary for girls. Girls themselves indicated that their family considered school unnecessary for girls. For women over 26 years of age, irrespective of their circumstances, the absence of school was the main reason given (59.7%) for no education. For younger girls in this category, this reason seemed less obvious (44.1% for age group 15–25 and 34.8% for age group 7–14). For the youngest group, the fact that school was not necessary for girls was also frequently stated (41.8%) compared with the responses of older women (around 30%). Comparing the above information with the responses concerning girls and women who had become disabled before age 7, the absence of school accounted for 50% of the reason for women over the age of 26, which was close to that of the same generation of women disabled after age 7 or the non-disabled. However, the numbers were substantially less for the 15–25-year-old women (25%) and for the younger groups (15.3%). For the latter, disability was perceived as being a bigger impediment than being a girl, although this was not the case for women over 25 years of age. In general, when there was an absence of any form of school in the area, the other reasons for receiving no education (being disabled or being a girl) became secondary. However, when the structures did exist, the lack of access was attributed to the disability before being ascribed to gender bias.

Considering the instrumental value of education, especially with regard to strengthening the empowerment and agency of children, future adults and workers, our findings call for special attention by policy makers to overcome different impediments to building this capability and expanding opportunities for children. Therefore, efforts to improve access to education will invariably need to take into account the two dimensions mentioned above – lack of infrastructure and the gender issue – simultaneously in order to ensure efficient and sustainable results and to reduce negative social attitudes towards disability. Indeed, social acceptance is paramount in determining the quality of life of persons with disabilities, even more so in societies where family and community are the main support systems. The position and consideration within the family and the community will determine a series of other factors, such as self-esteem, access to education and receiving proper health care in case of need. In Afghanistan, segregation occurs within the private space of the home and women in many Afghan communities interact socially only at rare events such as weddings and funerals (Coleridge, 1998).

Asking about love and care, with two possible answers, was a way to identify the eventuality of rejection of children with disabilities by their family and community. We put forward the hypothesis that children with disabilities may experience lack of love and care or, worse still, ill-treatment and isolation more often than those without disabilities. We did not observe such behaviour based on the responses in Tables 11.5 and 11.6. Even taking account of the possibility that behaviours that might appear "shameful" in the very traditional and religious context of Afghanistan might be under-reported, we found that children with disabilities were well supported, at least within the household. Globally, children with disabilities need more care, including their later years, than do other children. Mothers were the first providers of care, although the person most often mentioned as the second carer was the father. Siblings were also mentioned as the next most likely candidates to care for children with disabilities, although non-disabled children were more likely to mention taking care of themselves. In general, children with disabilities were included and supported by the family.

Children interviewed about the love that they received were asked to provide two answers: they largely mentioned both mothers and fathers. Results are very similar for both disabled and non-disabled children, indicating that stigma does not jeopardize affection within the family circle. No child declared receiving no love from anyone, and furthermore, if we had given a third option, it is likely that siblings and other members of family would have been mentioned as providers of love and affection. Questions about why nobody loved them appeared to be largely irrelevant for children, at least within the family circle.

Communities in Afghanistan are closely knit and the year is punctuated by a number of celebrations. Major ceremonies are those linked to life events, especially marriage, but also funerals and birth ceremonies. People also participate in various religious ceremonies that are major events in the lives of all Afghans, among them Eid, which marks the end of Ramadan and constitutes the most important celebration in the country. It lasts for three days,

Table 11.5   Who takes care of you (your child)?

		First answer		Second answer	
		Non-disabled (%)[**a]	Children with disabilities (%)[**a]	Non-disabled (%)[**a]	Children with disabilities (%)[**a]
Mother	Male	274 (53.1)[*b]	104 (63.8)[*b]	58 (14.6)[*b]	9 (6.5)[*b]
	Female	186 (47.0)[*b]	73 (57.5)[*b]	53 (18.9)	14 (13.2)
Father	Male	58 (11.2)	17 (10.4)	135 (34.0)[*b]	61 (43.9)[*b]
	Female	40 (10.1)	19 (15.0)	97 (34.5)	33 (31.1)
Sister or	Male	28 (5.4)[*b]	17 (10.4)[*b]	57 (14.4)[*b]	31 (22.3) [*b]
brother	Female	23 (5.8)[**b]	18 (14.2)[**b]	38 (13.5)[**b]	29 (27.4)[**b]
Herself/himself/	Male	150 (29.1)[**b]	21 (12.9)[**b]	133 (33.5)[*b]	31 (22.3)[*b]
no one	Female	140 (35.4)[**b]	13 (10.2)[**b]	84 (29.9)[**b]	18 (17.0)[**b]
Other person	Male	6 (1.2)	4 (2.5)	14 (3.5)	7 (5.0)
	Female	7 (1.8)	4 (3.1)	9 (3.2)[**b]	12 (11.3)[**b]

[a] Chi-squared Pearson for independence; ** significant at $p < 0.01$; * significant at $p < 0.05$.
[b] Test of comparison of proportion between the two groups. ** significant at $p < 0.01$; * significant at $p < 0.05$.
Source: Our elaboration on NDSA (2005). Note: children age 5–14 years old were included.

Table 11.6   Who loves you (your child)?

		First answer		Second answer	
		Non-disabled (%)[**a]	Children with disabilities (%)[**a]	Non-disabled (%)[**a]	Children with disabilities (%)[**a]
Mother	Male	431 (83.7)	135 (82.8)	38 (7.7)	13 (8.3)
	Female	320(81.0)	97 (76.4)	31 (8.2)	14 (12.0)
Father	Male	62 (12.0)	20 (12.3)	372 (75.5)	120 (76.4)
	Female	55 (13.9)	22 (17.3)	262 (69.5)	74 (63.2)
Sister or	Male	17 (3.3)	7 (4.3)	57 (11.6)	17 (10.8)
brother	Female	13 (3.3)	2 (1.6)	69 (18.3)	20 (17.1)
No one	Male	0 (0.0)	0 (0.0)	0 (0.0)	0 (0.0)
	Female	1 (0.3)	0 (0.0)	0 (0.0)	0 (0.0)
Other	Male	5 (1.0)	1 (0.6)	26 (5.3)	7 (4.5)
person	Female	6 (1.5)[*b]	6 (4.7)[*b]	15 (4.0)	9 (7.7)

[a] Test Chi 2 of Pearson of independence. ** Significant at $p < 0.01$; * Significant at $p < 0.05$.
[b] Test of comparison of proportion between the two groups. ** Significant at $p < 0.01$; * Significant at $p < 0.05$.
Note: Children age 5–14 years old included.
Source: Our elaboration on NDSA (2005).

starting with the breaking of fast before morning prayer. On this occasion, people who can afford it buy new clothes and families meet for important meals and festivities. The Eid Qurban ceremony takes place in preparation for the pilgrimage to Mecca, and is also an important occasion in the social life of Afghans. People who intend to make the Hajj or pilgrimage, as well as hajjis, who have completed the pilgrimage, sacrifice animals and organize banquets. Such events reinforce the sense of belonging to the community. Therefore, for people who are excluded from these events, this represents segregation from family and community life. The participation of children with disabilities within these various ceremonies can be considered a strong sign of acceptance, as well as respect for their family. This is probably where the perceptions of the causes of disability are important: child victims of accidents such as road or mining accidents are more accepted than those born with disabilities. In the latter case, the stigma attached to the disability is often considered as a curse of God, and therefore affects the social life of the entire family.

As a result, participation in ceremonies is a reflection of social visibility and acceptance. This is true in all ethnic groups. In general, people largely take part in a variety of ceremonies. Yet, a certain proportion of children aged 5 and above with disabilities do not participate – almost 20% of boys and 26.8% of girls (see Table 11.7). These figures are similar in urban and rural areas, indicating that there is no additional exclusion or stigma in villages. Difficulty to reach the venue for children with mobility problems is often a cause of lack of participation. In the case of mental illness and intellectual disability, children and their families are typically not invited. The phenomenon of non-acceptance sometimes leads to a feeling of shame for parents in bringing children and seeing them interacting with others.

In this section, we have tried to illustrate how looking at relevant dimensions of children's capabilities contributes to a better understanding of differences in well-being between disabled and non-disabled children. It is striking that, in the case of Afghanistan, valuable capabilities such as love and care or social participation in collective festivals are quite inclusive of children with disabilities. Whereas access to education, which does not have the same central cultural value within society, but which nonetheless holds crucial instrumental value for the child, has not been generalized for children with disabilities, especially disabled girls.

Table 11.7 Participation in ceremonies for Afghans aged 5–18

	Non-disabled (%)	Persons with disabilities (%)
Participation	914 (95.5)	236 (77.4)
Male	544 (95.9)	143 (80.3)
Female	370 (94.9)	93 (73.2)

Source: Our elaboration on NDSA (2005).

11.5. Conclusions

In this chapter we have argued that the CA can constitute a normative framework to better understand the urgent needs and consequently to formulate policies for differently-abled people, especially children. At the theoretical level, the CA framework helps to overcome some of the limits of existing disability models by shifting the focus from the specificities of the disabling situation, towards establishing equality in terms of possibilities and choices. This in turn helps assess the well-being of the individual in a more comprehensive manner. The framework can also be used as a basis to design tools to identify relevant dimensions of well-being for children, and to look at constraints that limit expansion of their well-being as well as resources available within the community to expand them. Policy makers can thus be better equipped with the knowledge necessary to implement policies to remove existing hurdles.

Considering the implementation of policy at the national or regional level, we further argue that attempts to make the CA operational using existing information from standard surveys are often not sufficient. Using the CA with traditional survey data may help to broaden the informational space for policy – which is considerable – but it is not enough to fully exploit the potential of the CA for policy planning, which requires different types of information such as an in-depth understanding of the value systems expressed by the people of the community as well as information regarding individual agency. The major limitation of this assessment lies in the constraint constituted by the length of interviews: it is always a challenge to ask all the questions needed to cover the various dimensions of capability in a single interview. Research thus faces the task of gauging trade-offs between assembling large data sets and loss of accuracy. The data collected in Afghanistan illustrates the potential of collecting information using a different framework. The three examples on education, love and care, and social participation for children, indicate the type of infrastructural, social and individual impediments to expanding and expressing the capabilities of differently abled people. The future challenges of research are to move forward in the operationalization process by exploring new methodologies for complex data elaboration for more relevant and effective policy planning.

Notes

1. "The dilemma of difference consists in the seemingly unavoidable choice between, on the one hand, identifying children's differences in order to provide for them differentially, with the risk of labelling and dividing, and, on the other hand, accentuating 'sameness' and offering common provision, with the risk of not making available what is relevant to, and needed by, individual children" (Terzi, 2005: 444).

2. For a brief overview of the main models of disability in the context of development, see Harriss-White and Sridhar (2006).
3. On group and collective capabilities, see also Deneulin and Stewart (2002) and Ibrahim (2006).
4. Two of the authors (JFT and PB) spent six months familiarising ourselves with the history of Afghanistan, as well as with cultural and religious aspects of people's lives, in order to understand social rules and to avoid the trap of ethnocentrism. We wanted to comprehend group dynamics and gender relations within the so called "traditional culture" of Afghanistan, where collective identities tend to be more influenced by the way people act and interact.

References

Altman, B.M. (2001), "Definitions of Disability and Their Operationalization, and Measurement in Survey Data: An Update", in B.M. Altman and S.N. Barnatt (eds), *Exploring Theories and Expanding Methodologies: Where We Are and Where We Need to Go*, Elsevier Jai, Oxford, pp. 77–100.

Amundson, R. (2000), "Against Normal Function", *Studies in History and Philosophy of Biological and Biomedical Sciences*, 31(1): 33–53.

Anand, P.B. (2007), "Capability, Sustainability, and Collective Action: An Examination of a River Water Dispute", *Journal of Human Development*, 8(1): 109–132.

Bakhshi, P., Trani, J.-F. and Rolland, C. (2006), *Conducting Surveys on Disability a Comprehensive Toolkit*, Handicap-International, Lyon.

Baylies, C. (2002), "Disability and the Notion of Human Development: Questions of Rights and Capabilities", *Disability and Society*, 17(7): 725–739.

Burchardt, T. (2004), "Capabilities and Disability: The Capabilities Framework and the Social Model of Disability", *Disability and Society*, 19(7): 735–751.

Clark, D.A. (2006), "Capability Approach", in D.A. Clark (ed.), *The Elgar Companion to Development Studies*, Edward Elgar, Cheltenham, pp. 32–45.

Clark, D.A. (2009), "Adaptation, Poverty and Well-Being: Some Issues and Observations with Special Reference to the Capability Approach and Development Studies", *Journal of Human Development and Capabilities*, 10(1): 21–42.

Clark, D.A. (forthcoming), *Adaptation, Poverty and Development*, forthcoming book, typescript.

Coleridge, P. (1998), "Development, Cultural Values, and Disability, The Example of Afghanistan". Paper presented at the Conference Disability Issues: Global Solutions and the Role of Community-Based Rehabilitation' Queen's University, Kingston, Canada, 5–6 March 1998.

Crocker, D. (1992), "Functioning and Capabilities: The Foundations of Sen's and Nussbaum's Development Ethic", *Political Theory*, 20(4): 584–612.

Deneulin, S. and Stewart, F. (2002) "Amartya Sen's Contribution to Development Thinking", *Studies in Comparative International Development*, 37(2): 61–70.

Dubois, J.L. and Trani, J.F. (2009), "Enlarging the Capability Paradigm to Address the Complexity of Disability", *ALTER-European Journal of Disability Research*, 3(3): 2–28.

Ehrmann, L.C., Aeschleman, S.R. and Svanum, S. (1995), "Parental Reports of Community Activity Patterns: A Comparison between Young Children with Disabilities and Their Non-disabled Peers", *Research in Developmental Disabilities*, 16: 331–343.

Forsyth, R., Colver, A., Alvanides, S., Woolley, M. and Lowe, M. (2007), "Participation of Young Severely Disabled Children Is Influenced by Their Intrinsic Impairments and Environment", *Developmental Medicine and Child Neurology*, 49(5): 345–349.

Giangreco, M.F., Edelman, S.W., Luiselli, T.E. and MacFarland, S.Z.C. (1997), "Helping or Hovering? Effects of Instructional Assistant Proximity on Students with Disabilities", *Except Children*, 64(1): 7–18.

Groce, N. (2006), "Cultural Beliefs and Practices", in B.M. Altman and S.N. Barnartt (eds), *International Views on Disability Measures: Moving Toward Comparative Measurement, Research in Social Science and Disability*, Elsevier Jai, Oxford, pp. 41–54.

Hammal, D., Jarvis, S.N. and Colver, A.F. (2004), "Participation of Children with Cerebral Palsy Is Influenced by Where They Live", *Developmental Medicine and Child Neurology*, 46(5): 292–298.

Harriss-White, B. and Sridhar, D. (2006), "Disability and Development", in D.A. Clark (ed.), *The Elgar Companion to Development Studies*, Edward Elgar, Cheltenham, pp. 126–130.

Heah, T., Case, T., McGuire, B. and Law, M. (2007), "Successful Participation: The Lived Experience among Children with Disabilities", *Canadian Journal of Occupational Therapy*, 74(1): 38–47.

Ibrahim, S. (2006), "From Individual to Collective Capabilities: The Capability Approach as a Conceptual Framework for Self-help", *Journal of Human Development and Capabilities*, 7(3): 397–416.

Law, M. and Dunn, W. (1993), "Perspectives on Understanding and Changing the Environments of Children with Disabilities", *Physical and Occupational Therapy in Pediatrics*, 13(3): 1–17.

Law, M., Finkelman, S., Hurley, P., Rosenbaum, P., King, S., King, G. and Hanna, S. (2004), "Participation of Children with Physical Disabilities: Relationships with Diagnosis, Physical Function and Demographic Variables", *Scandinavian Journal of Occupational Therapy*, 11(4): 156–162.

Law, M., Haight, M., Milroy, B., Willms, D., Stewart, D. and Rosenbaum, P. (1999), "Environmental Factors Affecting the Occupations of Children with Physical Disabilities", *Journal of Occupational Science*, 6(3): 102–110.

Longmuir, P.E. and Bar-Or, O. (2000), "Factors Influencing the Physical Activity Levels of Youths with Physical and Sensory Disabilities", *Adapted Physical Activity Quarterly*, 17(1): 40–53.

Mihaylov, S.I., Jarvis, S.N., Colver, A.F. and Bryony, B. (2004), "Identification and Description of Environmental Factors That Influence Participation of Children with Cerebral Palsy", *Developmental Medicine and Child Neurology*, 46(5): 299–304.

Miles, M. (2001), "ICIDH Meets Postmodernism, or 'Incredulity Toward Meta-terminology' ", *Disability World*, 7, (March–April). http://www.disabilityworld.org/03-04_01/resources/icidh.shtml.

Mitra, S. (2006), "The Capability Approach and Disability", *Journal of Disability Policy Studies*, 16(4): 236–247.

Nussbaum, M. (2000), *Women and Human Development: The Capabilities Approach*, CUP, Cambridge.

Oliver M. (1996), *Understanding Disability: From Theory to Practice*, Macmillan, Basingstoke.

Pfeiffer D. (2001), "The Conceptualization of Disability", In B. M. Altman & S. Barnartt (ed.), *Exploring Theories and Expanding Methodologies: Vol. 2. Research in Social Science and Disability*, UK, Elsevier, Oxford, pp. 29–52.

Pivik, J., Mccomas, J. and Lafamme, M. (2002), "Barriers and Facilitators to Inclusive Education", *Except Children*, 69: 97–108.

Qizilbash, M. (2006), "Well-Being, Adaptation and Human Limitations", *Royal Institute of Philosophy Supplements*, 81: 83–110.

Robeyns, I. (2003), *The Capability Approach: An Interdisciplinary Introduction*, University of Amsterdam.

Robeyns, I. (2005), "The Capability Approach: A Theoretical Survey", *Journal of Human Development*, 6(1): 93–114.

Robeyns, I. (2006), "The Capability Approach in Practice", *The Journal of Political Philosophy*, 14(3): 351–376.

Sandler, T. and Arce, D. (2007), "New Face of Public Assistance: Public Goods and Changing Ethics", *Journal of International Development*, 19(4): 527–544.

Sen, A.K. (1984), *Resources, Values and Development*, Basil Blackwell, Oxford.

Sen, A.K. (1992), *Inequality Re-examined*, Clarendon Press, Oxford.

Sen, A.K. (1999), *Development as Freedom*, OUP, Oxford.

Sen, A.K. (2004), "Capabilities, Lists, and Public Reason: Continuing the Conversation", *Feminist Economics*, 10(3): 77–80.

Sen, A.K. (2005), "Human Rights and Capabilities", *Journal of Human Development*, 6(2): 151–166.

Sen, A.K. (2006), "What Do We Want from a Theory of Justice?", *The Journal of Philosophy*, CIII(5): 215–238.

Sen, A.K. (2009), *The Idea of Justice*, Allen Lane, London.

Skar, L. and Tamm, M. (2001), "My Assistant and I: Disabled Children's and Adolescents' Roles and Relationships to Their Assistants", *Disability and Society*, 16(7): 917–931.

Terzi, L. (2004), "The Social Model of Disability: A Philosophical Critique", *Journal of Applied Philosophy*, 21(2): 141–157.

Terzi, L. (2005), "Beyond the Dilemma of Difference: The Capability Approach to Disability and Special Educational Needs", *Journal of Philosophy of Education*, 39(3): 443–459.

Teschl, M. and Comim, F. (2005), "Adaptive Preferences and Capabilities: Some Preliminary Conceptual Explorations", *Review of Social Economy*, 63(2), 229–247.

Trani, J.F. and Bakhshi, P. (2008), "Challenges for Assessing Disability Prevalence: The Case of Afghanistan", *ALTER Revue Européenne de Recherche sur le Handicap*, 2(1): 44–64.

Trani, J.F., Bakhshi, P., Noor, A.A. and Mashkoor, A. (2009) "Lack of a Will or of a Way? Taking A Capability Approach for Analysing Disability Policy Shortcomings and Ensuring Programme Impact in Afghanistan", *European Journal of Development Research*, 21(2): 297–319.

Welch, S.P. (2007), "Applications of a Capability Approach to Disability and the International Classification of Functioning, Disability and Health (ICF)", *Social Work Practice, Journal of Social Work in Disability & Rehabilitation*, 6(1–2): 217–232.

Welsh, B., Jarvis, S., Hammal, D. and Colver, A. (2006), "How Might Districts Identify Local Barriers to Participation for Children with Cerebral Palsy?", *Public Health*, 120(2): 167–175.

World Health Organization (2001), *International Classification of Functioning, Disability and Health*, WHO, Geneva.

Zaidi, A. and Burchardt, T. (2005), "Comparing Incomes when Needs Differ: Equalization for the Extra Costs of Disability in the U.K.", *Review of Income and Wealth*, 51(1): 89–114.

12
Rethinking Access to Education through the Capability Approach: The Case of Street Children

Jérôme Ballet, Augendra Bhukuth and Katia Radja

As emphasized in previous chapters, education is considered by children as one of the most important dimension of their well-being. The intrinsic and instrumental value of education and its role in children's evolving capabilities means it is often at centre of policy approaches for children (for example, as in the Millennium Development Goals). The aim of this chapter is to apply the capability approach (CA) framework in order to assess policies towards education and, in particular, access to education.

In 1990, at the Jontiem Conference in Thailand, international organizations (UNESCO, UNICEF, UNDP and the World Bank), as well as 157 governments, adopted the World Declaration on Education for All, committing them to achieve the *Education for All* objectives by 2000. The target set at this date was not simply a succinct declaration of intent, but implied that these countries were intending to provide universal high-quality education, and were determined to reduce the disparities in access to learning opportunities for groups with particularly low levels of school attendance, such as girls or handicapped people. In 2000 at Dakar, the World Education Forum attended by delegates from 164 countries established a Programme of Action to implement the Jontiem Declaration. The UN summit on *Millennium Development Goals* reinforced the principle of *Education for All* by including it in the targets to be achieved by 2015.[1]

The question of targeting underprivileged populations from the point of view of education has been a topic of discussion (e.g. UNESCO, 2003). The inclusion of certain populations would radically challenge the method proposed to implement this Declaration. This is particularly true for street children.

According to UNICEF (1984), street children constitute a multifaceted phenomenon that can be divided into at least three categories: *children at risk, children on the streets* and *children of the streets*. According to Lalor (1999), the category of children at risk includes the urban poor who form a reservoir of street children. The category of children on the streets is different, and is made up of children who are forced to work on the streets in order to survive. These children generally have a family and return home at night (Le Roux, 1996). The last category is a disparate one, comprising several subcategories of street children: children of the streets, plus abandoned, orphaned and runaway children. Densley and Joss (2000) state that children of the streets regard the street as their home: it is the place where they live, where they work and form bonds with other children of the streets (for a survey on the definition of street children, see, for instance, Le Roux and Smith, 1998).

According to Lalor (1999), these distinctions shed light on the reasons that drive children to migrate onto the streets. Furthermore, Panter-Brick (2003) considers that classifying children is useful as long as the categories are not perceived as discrete and homogeneous. The use of the term "street children" is certainly problematical, but there are few alternatives available – apart from local terms – to refer to this particular group of children (Ennew, 2000; Panter-Brick, 2003).

However, using the general expression "street children" has also tended to blur the distinctions between various different categories of children. From this point of view, the policies for the development of education in the wake of *Education for All* display considerable bias as a result of the assumption that all street children owe their presence on the street to one main cause – poverty. As a result, street children are all assumed to have a problem of access to education, which is conceived as an alternative to both poverty and child labour. The purpose of this chapter is to defend the idea that this all-embracing policy cannot result in the objective of fair educational opportunities for all, because it cannot deal with the complex phenomenon of street children.

In Section 12.1 we will describe the policy initiated in the *Education for All* programme, while in Section 12.2 we will provide a brief discussion of the phenomenon of street children. In Section 12.3 we will look at this phenomenon in the light of the *Education for All* programme as we have described it, and Section 12.4 we will look at what would be involved in taking into account the CA. Then finally, in the Section 12.5, we will try to see how a CA could help in coping with the challenge that street children pose to education and policy design.

12.1. *Education for All* and the poverty hypothesis

The objective of *Education for All* is measured using three main indicators: the gross enrolment rate, the net enrolment rate and the gender gap. The gross enrolment rate measures the proportion of children of school-going age who do actually attend school. The net enrolment rate is a more sophisticated approach to this first measurement, and focuses on the children in the age group corresponding to primary education (6–11 years). These indicators raise many problems, and complementary indicators have therefore been added. We will not dwell here on the difficulties raised by these indicators, or on the complementary measures envisaged; Unterhalter and Brighouse (2007) provide such a discussion. We will concentrate on the hypothesis underlying the political project that has dictated the policies for developing education, and on these policies themselves.

The slow rise in school attendance rates and the fact that adult illiteracy remains high in developing countries reflects the difficulties governments encounter in implementing policy. According to UNESCO, 875 million adults are illiterate and, in a sample of nine countries with the biggest populations (Bangladesh, Brazil, China, Egypt, India, Indonesia, Mexico, Nigeria and Pakistan), 113 million adults are estimated to be illiterate.

These figures clearly demonstrate that there is a gap between the demand and supply of education in most of these countries, despite the efforts that have been undertaken with a view to reducing direct education costs.

One of the reasons advanced is that having parents with inadequate resources encourages children working, which assumes that children are sent to work to increase the family income.[2] There ensues a conflict between paid employment and school attendance. As a result, the fight against poverty is given an important place based on the belief that reducing household budget constraints will automatically boost child school attendance.

From this perspective, the development of access to "education for all" calls for several different measures. First, the availability of education is obviously a central element in children's schooling. In all developing countries, the school attendance rate is higher in urban than in rural areas. This difference may certainly be the outcome of several factors, for instance differences in income level, or even the need for farm labour that urges parents to have their children work instead of sending them to school (Jensen and Nielsen, 1997; Cockburn, 2001). Quite obviously however, the availability of education also plays an indisputable role. As Jensen and Nielsen (1997) note, the low availability of school infrastructures in rural areas, and the long distances that sometimes have to be covered to get to school, constitute a central disincentive to children's school attendance. This first set of factors underlines the importance of the direct and opportunity costs of education. The hypothesis of inadequate resources is increased further as multiple elements are taken into account. In particular, it does not only focus on household income, but also on the budget that governments allocate to the education system.

Restructuring the education system has become a particularly important challenge after a period of damage caused by structural adjustment plans. De-schooling followed policies implemented with a view to reducing public deficits, especially when these policies are translated into a cut in the budget allocated to primary education (Cornia et al., 1987). In some cases, the school system has deteriorated so much that parents have actually had to make contributions to it. For instance, Cornia et al. (1987) note that the deterioration of infrastructures and the absence of money to pay teachers have sometimes led parents to pay the latter in kind (chickens, vegetables, etc.). Canagarajah and Coulombes (1997), in the case of Ghana, point out that, in the absence of salaries, teachers ask pupils to do some work for them in return for education (such as housework, work on land belonging to the teacher, etc.). In many cases these arrangements could not be sustained, which led many parents to take their children out of school. It therefore appears to be important to revive the education system by means of substantial financial support.

Secondly, policies involving financial aid for parents have been developed. These policies seem to make sense insofar as by relieving the poverty of the parents, they could facilitate children's access to education. This policy looks particularly relevant now that it is acknowledged that many children do part-time work while receiving part-time education. In this case, work is often used as a way to finance education (Ersado, 2006). However, this does not seem to be very effective (Psacharopoulos, 1997), as the children's exhaustion generally leads to very poor school results (Mathur, 1996; Akabayashi and Psacharopoulos 1999; Heady, 2003). A policy of aid dependent on children's school attendance is gradually developing, although this policy seems to be having rather limited results. Conditional aid does increase school attendance overall, although it only partially reduces child work. Bourguignon et al. (2003) support this finding on the basis of the Brazilian Bolsa Escola programme. The *Food for Education* programme in Bangladesh has also increased school attendance, but only one third of the increase in school attendance is due to a reduction in child work; the rest of the increase in school attendance has taken place during the children's free time, rather than as a result of reducing their workload (Ravallion and Wodon, 2000). Hazarika and Bedi (2003) come to similar conclusions in the context of rural zones in Pakistan. Boozer and Suri (2001) support these findings in Ghana. An increase of one hour in work time reduces school attendance by 0.38 h. Thus, the question of the number of hours worked by children seems to be crucial. Skoufias and Parker (2001) and Schultz (2004) conclude that the Progresa programme has had significant beneficial effects, both on school attendance and on reducing work, in Mexico. Finally, Guarcello et al. (2005) conclude that there is no significant link between part-time work and lack of education.

Thirdly, adult illiteracy, which is high in most developing countries, is a subject of great concern. Parents' perception of education and school depends on social and cultural attitudes, and in many cases school may be perceived as simply irrelevant (Kabeer, 2003). An education and parent-awareness programme in Calcutta illustrates that the behaviour of parents changes when they become aware of the importance of school education (see CINI-ASHA, 2003). Diallo (2001) highlights the fact that, on the basis of the 1998 national survey in the Ivory Coast, social attitudes play a not inconsiderable role in the decision of whether to send children to work. From this point of view, after controlling for the income variable, the level of education of the parents – and whether they themselves worked during childhood – are important, since they affect their perception of the value of education (see Chapters 2.4, 9 and 15 on the role of parents' capabilities and choice). Emerson and Souza (2003) in the case of Brazil, Wahba (2006) in the case of Egypt, and Dumas and Lambert (2007) in the case of Senegal conclude that social reproduction is significant. A child is more likely to work if his or her parents worked as children. Khanam (2008) also stresses that in rural zones of Bangladesh, educating the parents significantly increases children's access to school. Liebel (2004) also points out that prevailing social attitudes affect the behaviour of the children, who end up thinking that going to work is more important for them than going to school. Madsian (2004) shows in the case of Brazil that such a perception can give rise to aggressive behaviour directed against schools and teachers.

12.2. Understanding the phenomenon of street children

UNICEF (1999) reckon that the ever-increasing number of street children stood at 100–120 million (Pare, 2003, Kerfoot et al., 2007). Their number is obviously very difficult to estimate, for several reasons. On the one hand, it is not easy to assess the phenomenon accurately insofar as street children are mobile and move from one area to another in search of better survival opportunities (Kombarakaran, 2004). On the other hand, very high estimations enable international agencies (mainly UNICEF) to draw the attention of the general public and political decision makers to their work. The calculations provided in support of the phenomenon are symbolic rather than the result of accurate estimations (Ennew, 2000). Finally, the term "street children" is endowed with various meanings. The estimation may therefore differ considerably depending on the meaning adopted.

Using the term "street children" to encompass very different situations has led to considerable confusion. As far as children *on* the streets are concerned, a tendency has emerged to regard "economic poverty" as the main explanatory factor. Such a tendency has developed all the more readily since children *on* the streets do indeed represent the vast majority of street children (Taçon, 1992; Ebigbo, 2003). Some studies on street children conducted in Latin America (Rizzini and Lusk, 1995), as well as in Africa (Aderinto, 2000), suggest that the phenomenon of children *of* the streets is quite marginal, representing only a tenth of the total number of street children. The economic argument concerning children *on* the streets has thus come to be applied to the entire population of street children, and has been taken to be the main explanation of the phenomenon (e.g. Peacock, 1994; Rizzini and Lusk, 1995; Alexandrescu, 1996; Aderinto, 2000; Olley, 2006).

Within the framework of the "poverty" hypothesis, economic poverty contributes to the street child phenomenon in two ways. On the one hand, according to the *luxury axiom* (Basu and Van, 1998), parents send their children to work when their income is not sufficient to provide for their family. Children frequently contribute up to 30% of the family income (ILO, 1996). It should be pointed out that "urban children" quite often work on the streets. On the other hand, many children migrate onto the streets on their own initiative as a result of unsatisfactory living conditions at home. For instance, a study conducted in Nigeria insists on the fact that children deliberately leave their homes to earn a living when their parents are unable to feed them properly (Aderinto, 2000). Hunger then becomes a reason for leaving home. Leaving the household becomes a rational decision that children take to ensure their well-being (Aderinto, 2000). According to Aptekar (1988), in Colombia 48% of street children had left their homes for financial reasons. Many other studies have confirmed the role of economic poverty in the phenomenon of children's migration onto the streets (for instance and among others, Olley (2006) on Nigeria, Alexandrescu (1996) on Rumania, Rizzini and Lusk (1995) on Latin America and Peacock (1994) on Africa).

The massive recourse to the "poverty" hypothesis may thus be explained by the use of a definition of street children that does not make any distinction between *children of the streets* and *children on the streets*.

The role of economic poverty has been discussed on numerous occasions. Blanc (1994) underlines, for example, that if material poverty (defined as income poverty) encourages the phenomenon of street-working children, nevertheless they do not all become street-living children. Aptekar (1988) points out that, in the case of Colombia, even though a not insignificant proportion of children run away from the family home for financial reasons, many others migrate onto the streets on account of domestic violence. In the opinion of Lalor (1999), the main factor that drives children to leave their house is abuse and neglect, following family disintegration, the separation or divorce of their parents, or the death or remarriage of a parent. According to a study conducted in Egypt by UNICEF (1999) in the cities of Cairo and Alexandria, 62% of the children interviewed said they had left their home because of parental neglect, or lack of supervision and affection; 82% of them also said they had deliberately and primarily migrated onto the streets as a result of child abuse, whether by family members or at work. Street children have usually left the parental home to escape from family violence. In such circumstances, helping the parents – when they can be identified – is generally of no use, since their lack of goodwill towards their children is one of the main problems. They can hardly be expected to use the aid supplied appropriately in order to provide their children with education.

Even though the pinpointing of abuse and neglect in families is a significant step forward, it still seems to be inadequate because it focuses entirely on the role of the families in the phenomenon, and overlooks the part played by institutional factors. Education systems are sometimes very violent, and institutional violence, combined with family violence, constitutes a major reason for the existence of street children. For instance in the case of Mauritania, El Michry (2001), Ballet et al. (2004) and Ballet (2006) show that children leave school partly because of violence. This violence arises from educational institutions as often as from parents. Some children run away from that violence, which therefore sustains a breeding ground for street children.

Apart from physical violence, discriminatory practices also make an active contribution to why some children leave school or are excluded. Parents who want to promote the education of their children are often faced by discriminatory practices. For instance, in south-eastern Europe, Roma children are screened out by school entry tests, where they are judged as being mentally retarded and placed in special needs schools or institutions: the so-called "school segregation". The education provided by these schools is generally second rate, so Roma parents usually take their children out of these schools after a few years. This kind of situation is also relevant to understanding many other parts of the world where street children belong to ethnic groups exposed to discrimination.[3] For instance, in the case of Guatemala, Biggeri et al. (2003) highlight the fact that indigenous children are disproportionately represented among children who are absent from both school and work. Their analysis does not offer any explanation for this phenomenon, but it can clearly be related to discriminatory practices in schools (see also previous chapters, especially Chapters 5, 7 and 8).

12.3. Rethinking "Education for All": the capabilities approach

The CA undeniably constitutes an important rethink about development and well-being. However, applying this approach to areas such as health and education is somewhat problematic, although some studies have recently looked into these questions.[4] With regard to education, Sen (e.g. 1992, 1999) underlines the central role that this approach can play in the promotion of capabilities. He argues that education fulfils an instrumental social role through literacy capacities, an instrumental process role through relationships with other people and an empowering and distributive role in increasing the abilities of disadvantaged groups of people. Nussbaum (1997, 2002, 2006) has tackled this aspect of capabilities more thoroughly. In particular, she identifies three capabilities associated with education: critical thinking, the ideal of the world citizen and the development of the narrative imagination.

Other studies have expanded on this line of thinking (e.g. Brighouse, 2000; Saito, 2003; Swift, 2003; Unterhalter and Brighouse, 2003; and a series of contributions edited by Walker and Unterhalter, 2007).

However, Unterhalter (2001) argues that education appears ambiguous in the CA. The CA could be restricted to social opportunities, and in this case the enrolment rate constitutes an appropriate indicator. However, as Unterhalter illustrates well in the case of South Africa, an increase in the enrolment rate of black girls can also be linked to an increase in the risk of being sexually assaulted by their teacher or male students. Limiting the analysis to the enrolment rate, without looking at how the associated risks are regulated, may provide a misleading account of well-being. In this case, the outcome tends to diminish the capabilities of girls rather than boosting them as a result of the harm that can befall them, such as the risk of being contaminated by HIV.

Street children pose a similar problem. Using the enrolment rate is clearly an inadequate measure. More generally, an abusive environment in education is a phenomenon that has a considerable impact on children. Many schools all over the world are oppressive (Lansdown, 2001). From a panel of countries including Sudan, Philippines, the US, Ethiopia and Bangladesh, Boyden et al. (1998) point out that children have reported experience of violence, public humiliation, beating, forcing them to stand in unnatural positions, sexual abuse and even threats of exposure to wild animals. Such experiences have been perpetrated by adults on children with total impunity.

The CA must not, therefore, be restricted to a limited interpretation of social opportunities in the form of the enrolment rate; it must take the whole education system into account. From this point of view, Unterhalter and Brighouse (2007) propose a pertinent scheme that distinguishes between three fields of analysis to be taken into account in the capabilities approach to education: a positional value, an intrinsic value and an instrumental value. The field of the positional value corresponds to the capacity of education to reduce inequalities of class, gender, etc. This involves not what allows children to receive education, but rather how it positions them relative to their competitors. Thus, in the case of access to university, if the number of places is limited, for example to 100, it is better to be classed 99th in a poor system than 101st in a more effective system. The instrumental value corresponds to the capacity of education to facilitate access to social opportunities, such as obtaining employment. Finally, the intrinsic value refers to the benefit that a person can receive from education, independently of his or her instrumental and positional performances. A more highly educated person generally has a more complex mental life, and this enables him or her to discover the pleasure of activities such as reading, music, etc., which leads to greater enthusiasm for activities of this type, which in turn improves his/her agency achievement.

However, whereas the instrumental and positional values of education are compatible with oppressive methods that can, under some circumstances, produce not inconsiderable results, the intrinsic value of education assumes that the method of education must be compatible with the possibility of developing well-being achievement and agency achievement. However, as a study conducted in Bangladesh[5] points out (cited by Lansdown, 2005), the most important quality of teachers reported by children is the absence of violence and physical punishment.

Attempts to determine the intrinsic value of education, without which agency freedom and well-being freedom are fatally reduced, assumes focusing on the methods of education rather than on the level of access to education. From this point of view, the phenomenon of street children is a very significant and extreme example of the lack of serious consideration given to the various types of education.

12.4. Quality of education and intrinsic value

Once they are on the street, children have to work. In this context child work does not constitute an alternative to education, something deliberately decided by parents, but a consequence of certain educational practices. In the case of Mauritania for instance, street children have multiple jobs: they can be fishmongers, delivery boys (or girls), luggage porters, shoe cleaners or cart drivers. When street children are not in a position to earn a decent living by these jobs, they drift into begging or alternative illicit activities that provide them with additional income, such as theft and prostitution. It is relevant to note that street children generally prefer to work, whatever the job, but given the low income that it brings in, illicit activities also appeal to them (Ballet, 2006).

Taking street children into account gives rise to a paradox: the fight against child labour does involve education, but education systems, especially in southern countries, tend to favour the phenomenon of street children who have to work in order to survive. Education as such does not therefore solve the problem. Street children have virtually all attended school at some point. To solve this paradox, it is not enough to develop education quantitatively – it is also necessary to rethink the education system so that it excludes as few children as possible.

The quality of education is also crucial. Brown (2001), in the case of Colombia, and Ersado (2006), in the case of Peru, point out, for instance, that improving the quality of education constitutes an important factor in the duration of children's schooling, especially if school costs increase. The education redeployment policy must therefore involve both qualitative and quantitative aspects. Kabeer et al. (2003) and Bissel (2005) furthermore suggest that some child labour could be eliminated if school quality were to be improved.

Schools are indeed subject to many problems of a dysfunctional nature. Thus, on the basis of studies conducted in six developing countries (Bangladesh, Ecuador, India, Indonesia, Peru and Uganda), Chaudhury et al.

(2006) report a mean teacher absenteeism rate of 19%. They note that this absenteeism is inversely proportional to the *per capita* income in this group of countries, which suggests that teachers are probably absent because they need to combine several sources of income. An absenteeism phenomenon of this type can have the effect of disincentivizing school pupils.

The poor quality of schools is not, however, solely attributable to the absence of the teachers and poor teaching. A pitiful level of school attendance is attributable to inadequate quality in a more general sense. For example if a school does not have lavatories or water, this constitutes an undeniable obstacle to the attendance of girls.

However, even taken in a wider sense, quality as described above remains centred on the positional and instrumental values of education. Any serious attempt to take the intrinsic value of education into account implies defining the quality of education in a way that is not restricted to its material and functional aspects.

As the case of street children clearly demonstrates, it is necessary to raise another problem. The qualitative aspect may not only be tackled in a material fashion, as previous studies have done. It is also and, perhaps above all, necessary to modify teaching methods. As we have said, the phenomenon of street children is partly explained by the violence within school institutions, and this cannot be solved by simply increasing financial means, which may actually constitute a not inconsiderable factor in the occurrence of violent practices (for instance when over-attendance may lead to punitive methods to keep large numbers of schoolchildren under control). Above all, it is necessary to change the cultural attitudes to education, which are sometimes viewed rather like taming. Otherwise, school will come to constitute a breeding ground for the phenomenon of street children, and so will not provide an alternative to child labour since these street children still have to work to survive. Taking the intrinsic value of education seriously into account assumes the development of non-violent and non-excluding models of education.

12.5. Conclusions

To conclude, we would like to point out the main findings of our analysis. A quantitative increase in the access to education cannot constitute a goal in itself, even if it is included as such within the framework of the *Millennium Development Goals*. We prefer to insist on the fact that a serious educational policy must, above all, be a policy of non-violent education. A high rate of access to education may not always reflect this reality.

The presence of street children calls into question the straightforward dichotomy between labour and education on the grounds of the following paradox: education may turn out to be violent. For this reason, the type of education available is an essential factor in the emergence of street children who are forced to work in order to survive. Thus, paradoxically, banking everything on education without thinking this through could have the effect of increasing the number of street children confronted with the need to work to survive. This paradox makes it necessary to rethink education and ensure that it is non-violent. The CA in being a holistic approach to well-being can be used to justify such a point of view. Beyond the instrumental and positional values of education, the intrinsic value matters. Only if this intrinsic value is taken into account seriously will education give the full meaning to the development of the agency freedom of individuals.

Acknowledgements

We would like to express our warmest thanks to Mario Biggeri, Flavio Comin, Benoît Lallau, Nicolas Sirven and Elena Volpi for their helpful and informative criticism on an earlier version of this chapter. We would also like to thank all participants at the "Children capabilities" workshop (held in Florence on 18–19 March 2007) for their reactions and comments.

Notes

1. For an overview of "Education for All" and summary of the Dakar Goals, see Lewin (2006). The Millennium Development Goals and related indicators and targets are summarized in White (2006).
2. There is a lot of evidence in favour of the poverty hypothesis (Basu, 1999; Basu and Tzannatos, 2003; Edmonds, 2005; Edmonds and Pavcnik, 2005; Lachaud, 2008). However, if all poor households are assumed to constitute a uniform category, then the poverty hypothesis seems to be much less robust (Canagarajah and Coulombes, 1997; Jensen and Nielsen, 1997; Ray, 2000; Lieten, 2002).
3. We would like to express our warmest gratitude to Elena Volpi, who pointed out this problem.
4. See, for example, Walker and Unterhalter (2007), Terzi (2008) and Ruger (2010). See also the Human Development and Capability Association's website (www. capabilityapproach.org) for details of other work in these areas.
5. Primary School Performance Monitoring Project, In *Bangladesh: Assessment of the Primary Education Development Programme, Education for Change/Department of Primary and Mass Education*, Dhaka, January 2002.

References

Aderinto, A.A. (2000), "Social Correlates and Coping Measures of Street Children: A Comparative Study of Street and Non-Street Children in South-Western Nigeria", *Child Abuse & Neglect*, 24(9): 1199–1213.

Akabayashi, H. and Psacharopoulos, G. (1999), "The Trade-Off between Child Labour and Human Capital Formation: A Tanzanian Case Study", *The Journal of Development Studies*, 35(5): 120–140.

Alexandrescu, G. (1996), "Programme Note: Street Children in Bucharest", *Childhood, Global Journal of Child Research*, 3(2): 267–270.

Aptekar, L. (1988), "Street Children of Colombia", *Journal of Early Childhood*, 8(3): 225–241.

Aptekar, L. (1994), "Street Children in the Developing World: A Review of their Condition", *Cross-Cultural Research*, 28(3): 195–224.

Ballet, J., Bhukuth, A. and Radja, K. (2004), "Capabilities, Affective Capital and Development: Application to Street Child in Mauritania", 4th Conference on the Capability Approach, *Enhancing Human Security*, 5–7 September 2002, University of Pavia, Italy.

Ballet, J. (2006), "Les enfants des rues: pauvreté monétaire et pauvreté affective", in J. Ballet and B. Hamzetta (eds), *Formes Sociales de Pauvreté en Mauritanie*, L'Harmattan, Paris.

Basu, K. (1999), "Child Labor: Cause, Consequences and Cure, with Remarks on International Labor Standards", *Journal of Economic Literature*, 37(3): 1083–1119.

Basu, K. and Tzannatos, Z. (2003), "The Global Child Problem: What Do We Know and What Can We Do?", *World Bank Economic Review*, 17(2): 147–173.

Basu, K. and Van, P.H. (1998), "The Economics of Child Labour", *American Economic Review*, 88(3): 412–427.

Biggeri, M., Guarcello, L., Lyon, S, and Rosati, F.C. (2003), "The Puzzle of Idle Children: neither in School nor Performing Economic Activity. Evidence from Six Countries", Understanding Children's Work Project, A joint ILO-UNICEF-World Bank research effort, October.

Bissel, S. (2005), "Earning and Learning: Tensions and Compatibility", in B. Weston (ed.), *Child Labor and Human Rights: Making Children Matter*, Lynne Rienner, Boulder, CO and London, pp. 377–399.

Blanc, S.C. (1994), *Urban Children and Distress*, Gordon and Breach Publishers, Luxembourg.

Boyden, J., Ling, B. and Myers, W. (1998), *What Works for Working Children*, UNICEF/Radda Barnen, Stockholm.

Bourguignon, F., Ferreira, F. and Leite, P. (2003), "Conditionnal Cash Transfers, Schooling and Child Labor: Microsimulating Brazil's Bolsa Escola Program", *World Bank Economic Review*, 17(2): 229–254.

Boozer, M. and Suri, T. (2001), "Child Labor and Schooling Decisions in Ghana", Manuscript, Yale University.

Brighouse, H. (2000), *School Choice and Social Justice*, OUP, Oxford.

Brown, D.K. (2001), *Child Labor in Latin America: Policy and Evidence*, Department of Economics, Tufts University, Medford, MA, USA.

Canagarajah, S. and Coulombes, H. (1997), "Child Labour and Schooling in Ghana", Human Development Tech. Report (Africa Region), World Bank, Washington, DC.

Chaudhury, N., Hammer, J., Kremer, M., Miralidharan, K. and Rogers, F.H. (2006), "Missing in Action: Teacher and Health Worker Absence in Developing Countries", *Journal of Economic Perspectives*, 20(1): 91–116.

Cornia, G.A., Jolly, R. and Steward, F. (1987), *Adjustment with Human Face*, Clarendon Press, Oxford.

Cockburn, J. (2001), "The Determinant of Child Labour Supply in Rural Ethiopia", Nuffield College and Centre for the Study of African Economics (CSAE), Oxford University, UK.

CINI-ASHA (2003), "Family Adjustments for Mainstreaming Child Labourers into Formal Schools in Calcutta: The Expérience of CINI-ASHA", in N. Kabeer, G.B. Nambissan and R. Subrahmanian (eds), *Child labour and the Right to Education in South India: Needs versus Rights*, Sage, New Dehli, pp. 335–348.

Densley, K.M. and Joss, D.M. (2000), "Street Children: Causes and Consequences, and Innovative Treatment Approaches", *Work*, 15: 217–225.

Diallo, Y. (2001), "Les déterminants du travail des enfants en Côte d'Ivoire", Document de travail, n. 55, LARE-Efi (GED), Université Montesquieu-Bordeaux IV, http://ged.u-bordeaux4.fr

Dumas, C. and Lambert, S. (2007), "Educational Achievement and Socioeconomic Background: Causality and Mechanisms in Senegal", Working Paper, LEA-INRA.

Ebigbo, P.O. (2003), "Street Children: The Core of Child Abuse and Neglect in Nigeria", *Children, Youth and Environments*, 13(1).

Edmonds, E.V. (2005), "Does Child Labor Decline with Improvements in Economic Status", *Journal of Human Resources*, 40(1): 77–89.

Edmonds, E.V. and Pavcnick, N. (2005), "Child Labor in the Global Economy", *Journal of Economic Perspectives*, 19: 199–220.

Emerson, P.M. and Souza, A.P. (2003), "Is There a Child Labor Trap? Intergenerational Persistence of Child Labor in Brazil", *Economic Development and Cultural Change*, 51(2): 375–398.

El Michry, A.M. (2001), *Enquête sur la Toxicomanie des Enfants et Adolescents à Nouakchott*, mimographe, AEDM, Nouakchott.

Ennew, J. (2000), "Why the Convention Is Not about Street Children", in D. Fotrell (ed.), *Revisiting Children's Rights: 10 years of the UN Convention on the Rights of the Child*, Kluwer Law Int., The Hague/Boston, pp. 169–182.

Ersado, L. (2006), "Child Labor and Schooling Decisions in Urban and Rural Areas: Comparative Evidence from Nepal, Peru, and Zimbabwe", *World Development*, 33(3): 455–480.

Guarcello, L., Rosati, F., Lyon, S. and Valdivia, C. (2005), *Impact of Children's Work on School Attendance and Performance: A Review of School Survey Evidence from Five Countries*, Understanding Children's Work (an inter-agency research co-operative), ILO/UNICEF/World Bank, Florence.

Hazarika, G. and Bedi, A.S. (2003), "Schooling Costs and Child Work in Rural Pakistan", *Journal of Development Studies*, 39(5): 29–64.

Heady, C. (2003), "The Effect of Child Labor and Learning Achievement", *World Development*, 31(2): 385–398.

ILO (1996), *Child Labour Surveys: Results of Methodological Experiments in Four Countries*, ILO, Geneva.

Jensen, P. and Nielsen, H.S. (1997), "Child Labour or School Attendance? Evidence from Zambia", *Journal of Population Economics*, 10: 407–424.

Kabeer, N. (2003), "Deprivation, Discrimination and Delivery: Competing Explanations for Child Labour and Educational Failure in South Asia", in N. Kabeer, G.B. Nambissan, and R. Subrahmanian (eds), *Child labour and the Right to Education in South India: Needs versus Rights*, Sage, New Dehli, pp. 351–393.

Kabeer, N., Nambissan, G.B. and Subrahmanian, R. (eds) (2003), *Child Labour and the Right to Education in South India: Needs versus Rights*, Sage, New Dehli.

Kerfoot, M., Koshyl, V., Roganov, O., Mikhailichenko, K., Gorbova, I., and Pottage, D. (2007), "The Health and Well-Being of Neglected, Abused and Exploited Children: The Kyiv Street Children Project", *Child Abuse & Neglect*, 31: 27–37.

Khanam, R. (2008), "Child Labour and School Attendance: Evidence from Bangladesh", *International Journal of Social Economics*, 35(1/2): 77–98.

Kombarakaran, F.A. (2004), "Street Children in Bombay: Their Stresses and Strategies of Coping", *Children and Youth Services Review*, 26: 853–871.

Lachaud, J.-P. (2008), "Le travail des enfants et le revenu des ménages à Madagascar: Dépendance spatiale et non-linéarité", Document de travail, n. 143, LARE-Efi (GED), Université Montesquieu-Bordeaux IV, http://ged.u-bordeaux4.fr

Lalor, K.J. (1999), "Street Children: A Comparative Perspective", *Child Abuse & Neglect*, 23(8): 759–770.

Lansdown, G. (2001), "Progress in Implementing the Rights in the Convention", in S. Hart et al. (eds), *Children's Rights in Education*, Jessica Kingsley Publishers, London, pp. 37–60.

Lansdown, G. (2005), *The Evolving Capacities of the Child*, Innocenti Insight, UNICEF/Save the Children, Florence.

Lewin, K.M. (2006), "Education for All and the Millennium Development Goals", in D.A. Clark (ed.), *The Elgar Companion to Development Studies*, Edward Elgar, Cheltenham, pp. 145–152.

Le Roux, J. (1996), "Street Children in South Africa: Findings from Interviews on the Background of Street Children in Pretoria, South Africa", *Adolescence*, 31(122): 423–431.

Le Roux, J. and Smith, C.S. (1998) "Causes and Characteristics of the Street Child Phenomenon: A Global Perspective", *Adolescence*, 33(132): 683–688, Winter.

Liebel, M. (2004), *A Will of their Own: Cross-Cultural Perspectives on Working Children*, Zed Books, London and New York.

Lieten, G.K. (2002), "Child Labour and Poverty: The Poverty of Analysis", *The Indian Journal of Labour Economics*, 45(3): 451–464.

Madsian, C. (2004), "Not for Bread Alone: Peanut Vendors in Brazil", in G.K. Lieten (ed.), *Working Children Around the World: Child Rights and Child Reality*, IREWOC and Institute for Human Development, Amsterdam and New Delhi, pp. 128–139.

Mathur, K. (1996), "Les enfants dans l'industrie lapidaire de Jaipur (Rajasthan, Inde)", in B. Schlemmer (ed.), *L'Enfant Exploité: Oppression, Mise au Travail, Prolétarisation*, Karthala Orstom, Paris.

Psacharopoulos, G. (1997), "Child Labor vs Educational Attainment: Some Evidence from Latin America", *Journal of Population Economics*, 10(4): 377–386.

Nussbaum, M.C. (1997), *Cultivating Humanity: A Classical Defence of Reform in Liberal Education*, Harvard University Press, Cambridge, MA.

Nussbaum, M.C. (2002), "Education for Citizenship in an Era of Global Connection", *Studies in Philosophy and Education*, 21(4/5): 289–303.

Nussbaum, M.C. (2006), "Education and Democratic Citizenship: Capabilities and Quality Education", *Journal of Human Development*, 7(3): 385–398.

Olley, B.O. (2006), "Social and Health Behaviors in Youth of the Streets of Ibadan, Nigeria", *Child Abuse & Neglect*, 30(3): 271–282.

Panter-Brick, C. (2003), "Street Children, Human Rights, and Public Health: A Critique and Future Directions", *Children, Youth and Environments*, 13(1): 147–171.

Pare, M. (2003), "Why Have Street Children Disappeared? The Role of International Human Rights Law in Protecting Vulnerable Groups", *International Journal of Children's Rights*, 11(1): 1–32.

Peacock, R. (1994), "Street Children", *Africa Insight*, 24(2): 138–143.

Ravallion, M. and Wodon, Q. (2000), "Does Child Labor Displace Schooling? Evidence on Behavioral Responses to an Enrollment Subsidy", *Economic Journal*, 110(462): 158–176.

Ray, R. (2000), "Child Labor, Child Schooling, and Their Interaction with Adult Labor: Empirical Evidence for Peru and Pakistan", *The World Bank Economic Review*, 14(2): 347–367.

Rizzini, I. and Lusk, M.W. (1995), "Children in the Streets: Latin America's Lost Generation", *Children and Youth Services Review*, 17(3): 391–400.

Ruger, J.P. (2010), *Health and Social Justice*, OUP, Oxford.

Saito, M. (2003), "Amartya Sen's Capability Approach to Education: A Critical Exploration", *Journal of Philosophy of Education*, 37(1): 17–33.

Sen, A.K. (1992), *Inequality Reexamined*, OUP, Oxford.

Sen, A.K. (1999), *Development as Freedom*, OUP, Oxford.

Schultz, P.T. (2004), "School Subsidies for the Poor: Evaluating the Mexican Progresa Poverty Programme", *Journal of Development Economics*, 74(1): 199–250.

Skoufias, E. and Parker, S.W. (2001), "Conditional Cash Transfers and their Impact on Child Work and Schooling: Evidence from the PROGRESA Programme in Mexico", *Economia*, 2(1): 45–96.

Swift, A. (2003), *How Not to Be a Hypocrite: School Choice for the Morally Perplexed*, Routledge, London.

Taçon, P. (1992), *Marco and the Malevolent Monsters*, unpublished paper for presentation to the Organisation of African Unity and its international partners.

Terzi, L. (2008), *Justice and Equality in Education: A Capability Perspective on Disability and Special Education Needs*, Continuum Press, London.

UNICEF (1984), "Latin America Seminar on Community Alternatives for Street Children", Brasilia, Brazil, 12–15 November 1984.

UNICEF (1999), *The State of the World's Children*, New York.

Unterhalter, E. (2001), The capabilities approach and gendered education: An examination of South African complexities. Paper presented at the First Conference on the Capability Approach: *Justice and Poverty, Examining Sen's Capability Approach*, September, St Edmund's College, University of Cambridge, UK.

Unterhalter, E. and Brighouse, H. (2003), "Distribution of What? How Will We Know If We Have Achieved Education for All by 2015?" Paper presented at the Third Conference on the Capability Approach: *From Sustainable Development to Sustainable Freedom*, September, Pavia, Italy.

Unterhalter, E. and Brighouse, H. (2007), "Distribution of What for Social Justice in Education? The Case of Education for All by 2015", M. Walker and E. Unterhalter (eds), *Amartya Sen's Capability Approach and Social Justice in Education*, Palgrave MacMillan, New York, pp. 67–86.

Wahba, J. (2006), "The Influence of Market Wages and Parental History on Child Labour and Schooling in Egypt", *Journal of Population Economics*, 19(4): 823–852.

Walker, M. and Unterhalter, E. (eds) (2007), *Amartya Sen's Capability Approach and Social Justice in Education*, Palgrave Macmillan, Basingstoke.

White, H. (2006), "Millennium Development Goals", in D.A. Clark (ed.), *The Elgar Companion to Development Studies*, Edward Elgar, Cheltenham, pp. 382–389.

13
Re-examining Children's Economic and Non-Economic Activities Using the Capability Approach

Mario Biggeri, Augendra Bhukuth and Jérôme Ballet

13.1. Background

Many case studies in this book deal with the work activities of children (see especially Chapters 5, 7 and 8). This chapter uses the capability approach (CA) to revisit key concepts and highlight the corresponding policy implications.

Children in poor households – particularly in developing countries – typically carry the "burden" of everyday survival from birth. In fact, in many cases a child has almost as much responsibility as an adult for the household's survival, and has to contribute to the family's well-being through income-generating and non-income-generating activities. For many of these children, these activities are often not just a "burden" in themselves, but can result, for instance, in other forms of disadvantage such as being deprived of the opportunity to go to school and learn or to develop other valuable capabilities, thus dramatically undermining their present and future well-being. For other children, however, participating in economic and non-economic activities may lead to new opportunities at the family and community level that improve their present and future well-being. These contrasting situations have given rise to considerable international debate about children's activities, and they lie behind the two main contrasting positions regarding child work. What is in the best interests of the children involved in these activities? What types of work or other activities – and under what conditions – can children develop valuable skills, attitudes and capabilities?

On the one hand, as argued in Chapter 8, there is the abolitionist position, i.e. no child should be allowed to work, because most work is viewed as being detrimental to child development. This position is adopted by most trade unions and by many civil society associations, and is mainly based on the human rights approach and international labour laws.[1] On the other hand is the valorization or regulationist position, i.e. children should be allowed to work under specified conditions if they wish to do so. This approach focuses on improving their working conditions,[2] and is supported by some groups of professionals and activists (see, for example, the Niños y Adolescentes Trabajadores (NATs) movement; Liebel, 2003) and some NGOs (for instance Care&Fair, Step and Kaleen in the carpet industry) that are attempting to improve children's working conditions (Bhukuth et al., 2008). Between these two positions, there is a third more pragmatic approach that is intended to overcome the limitations of both extreme positions. Some international and local NGOs and civil society associations – such as the Global March Against Child Labour and for Education – take this third approach, i.e. campaigning for education and advocating strict rules and their application against the exploitation of child labour, but at the same time accepting light forms of work for children.

We think that this divergence is due, in large part, to differing initial standpoints (see also Myers, 2001). The abolitionist policy arises from a long-term ideal perspective of a world free of child labour in the best interests of the child (Hanson and Vandaele, 2003), whereas the regulationist policy focuses mainly on the present well-being of the children who are working in their communities (Boyden et al., 1998; Myers and Boyden, 1998; Liebel, 2003), and this leads to a sort of trade-off between short-term and long-term policy goals. Another example may help to clarify this trade-off. If you ask a child who belongs to an association of working children (a trade union) if it is right for a child to work, he/she would almost certainly answer "yes". He or she would also demand better conditions in terms of pay, job security, safety at work and some allowances for the particular needs of children, etc. However, if you ask the same child to think about the future, and whether he/she would like his/her son or daughter to work, he/she would reply "no" (for instance, see van den Berge, 2006: 7–8). Similarly, you would get one answer if you were to ask a child about her/his daily needs (i.e. for the next day), but another if you ask about what opportunities a typical child of his/her age should have in their life, i.e. daily needs *versus* equality of opportunities. Although children are ready to work if necessary, they do not view it as a desirable activity for a child (Biggeri et al., 2006).

Although this dichotomy is expounded by advocacy groups, a consensus is gradually emerging that "child work" or "children's work" should be seen as a general term covering the entire spectrum of work and related tasks performed by children, and "child labour" as a subset of children's work that is detrimental to children, and that should be targeted for elimination (ILO, 2002a). Almost everyone in the field agrees that there are certain intolerable forms of child labour that constitute especially serious violations of children's rights, and that must be targeted as a priority for immediate action (Cigno et al., 2003). This implies that there are also some forms of children's employment or work that are not likely to harm their health or development. "Child labour is classified as children's work which is of such a nature or intensity that it is detrimental to their schooling or harmful to their health and development. The concern is with children who are denied their childhood and a future ..." (ILO, 2002b: 3). They work when they are too young, for long hours, and for low wages or even no wage at all, because it is their parents or the subcontractors who are paid. In addition, the working conditions are harmful to their health and to their physical and mental development. They are usually separated from their families, and this debars them from receiving an education. This happens in the case of domestic workers, child bonded labourers and camel jockeys among others. Such child labour can irreversibly damage the child and is in violation of international law, and usually of national legislation (ILO, 2002b: 3).

Everyone recognizes the relevance of distinguishing between child work, which consists of acceptable tasks, and child labour, which should be eliminated, but it is not easy to go beyond this international consensus to reach agreement about where to draw the line. In practice it is difficult to distinguish between different types of child work, and decide when child work/activity is positive or at least acceptable, and when it has to be criticized as having an impact very similar to that of child labour on child well-being. Furthermore, we argue, and this is our main point, that the definitions and categories used in collecting data and in the literature lack any theoretical basis, and therefore lead to problems in terms of consistency. They also have limitations for the analysis of children's work/activity and well-being, especially from a gender perspective. The main problem is that the existing definitions and empirical classifications view the child as passive, and continue to echo adult definitions instead of actively involving children at the heart of analysis.

The aim of this chapter is to re-examine the framework used to investigate the economic and non-economic activities of children using the CA (Sen, 1993, 1995, 1999a), starting from a consideration of children's well-being and social participation. In other words, we are interested in children's activities on the basis of their impact on what children can or cannot "do" and "be" or become. In other words, the focus is on their capabilities and how these "evolve" over time. In particular, we believe that the CA, which is an opportunity-based theory that provides a general normative framework for the evaluation of individual and social well-being, can provide an appropriate theoretical underpinning, and help to reconcile different positions on the subject. These results reviewed in this chapter have several implications for research and policy making.

In Section 13.2, the main classifications of child work are presented and discussed, while in Section 13.3 we use the CA to re-examine children's activities. In Section 13.4, the final section, we present the main results obtained using this approach, and their implications for future research and policies.

13.2. Definitions of child work and the classification of children's activity status: a critique

In the last two decades there has been a considerable increase in research on child work[3] amongst international agencies (e.g. UNICEF, UNESCO, ILO, the World Bank), international NGOs (such as Save the Children) and international research centres (e.g. UNICEF, 2000, 2001; UNESCO, 2001; UN Secretariat 1997).

Almost all analyses of children, and specifically of child work, are based on the UN *Convention on the Rights of the Child* (CRC) (UN CRC, 1989), and on the two ILO conventions on the *Minimum Age* (ILO, 1973: n. 138) and the *Worst Forms of Child Labour* (ILO, 1999: n. 182). Age[4] is the parameter that international instruments generally use to define a child: "A child means every human being below the age of 18 years unless, under the law applicable to the child, majority is attained earlier" (art. 1 of the UN CRC). They accord the rights and protection of a child to people under 18 years of age (UN CRC and ILO, n. 182), and set the minimum age for admission to employment at age 15 (ILO, n. 138, art. 7).[5]

According to ILO (2006), in 2004 the total number of economically active children (between 5 and 17 years of age) worldwide was estimated to be 317.4 million. Around 190.7 million of these children were estimated to be between 5 and 14 years of age; 165.8 million were classified as child workers while 74.4 million were actively engaged in hazardous work.[6]

In accordance with the Minimum Age Convention (ILO, 1973, n. 138, art. 7), most previous studies have defined child work as any form of economic activity performed (whether paid or unpaid) by any person below 15 years of age (and engaged for at least one hour per week). According to the System of National Accounts (SNA, 1993), economic activity is a broad concept that includes most productive activities by children, including unpaid and illegal work, informal sector work and the production of goods for their own use.

> Economic activity covers all market production (paid work) and certain types of non-market production (unpaid work), including production of goods for own use. Therefore, whether paid or unpaid, the activity or occupation could be in the formal or informal sector and in urban or rural areas. However, children engaged in domestic chores within their own households are not considered as economically active. (ILO, 2002a)

In other words, all kinds of work, apart from domestic work in the home, whether it is paid or unpaid, are covered by article 7 of the no. 138 ILO convention.[7] It is also important to note, in view of article 32 (UN CRC), that not all work performed by children is regarded as economic exploitation (Sharon Detrick, 1999: 563). Therefore, the term "child labour" refers only to negative or undesirable forms of work that should be eliminated in accordance with the Minimum Age convention, and especially the Elimination of Worst Forms Convention and article 32 of the UN CRC.

A report from the ILO International Programme on the Elimination of Child Labour (IPEC) classifies four groups of child workers (ILO, 2002a: 29–36) according to their age[8] and the length of time for which they engage in work:

I. Children engaged in an economic activity for at least one hour per week.
II. Children engaged in child labour. This group includes (a) all economically active children from 5 to 11 years of age (at least one hour of economic activity per week); (b) economically active children aged 12 to 14 years, except those doing light work only for less than 14 hours per week; and (c) children aged 15 to 17 years engaged in hazardous work.
III. Children in hazardous work, i.e. work that is likely to harm the health, safety or moral development of a child (including the "unconditionally worst" forms of child labour). In addition to children employed in mining, construction or other hazardous activities, this group includes all children below 18 years of age who work for 43 hours or more per week.[9] They can be considered as a subset of the second category, i.e. children engaged in child labour.
IV. Children engaged in the unconditionally worst forms of child labour, which is a subset of the third category, as defined by ILO Convention No. 182. This includes children in forced or bonded labour, armed conflict, prostitution and pornography, and illicit activities.[10] This last category highlights the fact that age and the time spent doing the work are often not very relevant for estimating child labour when the worst forms of child labour are considered. For instance, if a child is prostituted even for a few hours per week he/she is also classified as being involved in hazardous work.

Although these definitions are important for classifying children's work, it is relevant to note that national statistics, the empirical analyses and the theoretical literature all employ a broader concept of children's work rather than the narrower one of child labour, because of the difficulties in drawing a dividing line between acceptable forms of work, on the one hand, and harmful forms that need to be eliminated, on the other.

Therefore, almost all forms of data collection – empirical analyses, quantitative analyses (mainly econometrics) and theoretical models of child labour-divide the status of children with regard to activity into the following four mutually exclusive categories:

(1) only working, i.e. children who are economically active (for at least one hour per week),[11] and do not attend school;

(2) only studying, i.e. children who go to school but do not work;
(3) working and studying, i.e. children who combine school attendance with work; and
(4) neither working nor studying, or idle (including children doing household chores, apprenticeships, street children).

The definitions of child work, and the division into the four categories described above, can be criticized on at least five grounds.

The first criticism is theoretical. These definitions and classifications are based on a theoretical approach to adults rather than children. More specifically, they do not look at children's well-being in a holistic manner, and the children themselves remain "voiceless".[12] Some categories of activities, despite being detrimental to children, remain "invisible" in the statistics and are ignored by policy makers. These include mostly household chores, and the activities of street children. This theoretical shortcoming and lack of child involvement has led to shortcomings and problems. Here, our main point concerns the conflict between children's household chores and children's well-being and development. This definition, and the consequent division into status categories, does not include household chores in the home according to the SNA.[13] This is despite the fact that the ILO (2002a) acknowledges that "non-economic activities", such as doing household chores, may interfere with a child's school attendance.[14] These activities may conflict, for instance, with formal or informal education just as much as working in the fields or helping in the family business or shop. This means that it is important to recognize that performing domestic chores has a direct bearing on children's capabilities and well-being. It also clearly conflicts with the UN CRC and ILO definitions that recognize children's right to be protected from forms of work that are likely to be hazardous or to interfere with their education, or to be detrimental to the child's health or physical, mental, spiritual, moral or social development.

The second criticism is procedural, since the method applied by definition underestimates the number of children involved in activities that could be detrimental. The paradox is easy to understand by means of an example. Let us consider the case of two 11-year-old male twins, one of whom does more than 30 hours per week of household chores but has no paid activity, and the other of whom does two hours per week of "work" defined by the SNA as falling within the production boundary. The latter is classified as being engaged in economic activity, whereas the former is not, and so is not taken into account in child work statistics.

The third criticism relates to the gender discrimination involved in the definition of child work. For 2000 data, the ILO (2002a: 5) writes "[t]he estimates show that there are no significant gender differences in the global incidence of children at work. In both the 5–9 and 10–14 year age brackets, boys and girls are equally likely to be engaged in economic activity. Only as boys and girls grow older do we observe a widening gap, with more boys working than girls." The 2004 data (ILO, 2006) make it even clearer that for children over 11, boys are more exposed to work than girls. In fact, as we have pointed out, data collected according to these definitions do not include domestic work performed in the home. This implies that children engaged in household chores, often at an intense level, are not taken into account in child work statistics. Therefore, if more boys are economically active than girls, but girls are engaged in household chores to a greater extent, this implies that the ILO statistical estimates are not only misleading but gender biased. By echoing adult definitions, this double burden which reduces female children's capabilities is not taken into consideration. Figure 13.1 provides a graphical representation of the average number of hours spent in child work (i.e. economic activities without making any distinction between work, labour, etc.), and the number of hours spent doing household chores. The children are classified by using the four usual activity status categories, i.e. work only W, work and study WS, study only S and neither working nor studying N; and then the according age group ($1 = 5$–10 and $2 = 11$–17) and gender (male, m and female, f). If the hours spent doing household chores are added to those spent "working", the results are impressive for children in general, and from a gender perspective in particular. In the most extreme example, children's activities can reach 65 hours per week on average in the case of older female children in the "W2f work only" category (50 hours of work plus 15 hours of household chores).[15] For instance, the fact that a child is doing many hours of household chores per day (even if they do not conflict with school hours) reduces his or her educational attainment.[16] Grade repetition, a common phenomenon in developing countries, is closely associated with child work, and with long hours devoted to household chores. These activities often have a negative day-to-day impact on children, leaving them too tired to learn, and reducing their interest in learning. Children who are already contributing economically to their family income may be less interested in academic achievement, resulting in a lack of motivation that affects both their learning and their future prospects. It is important to note that by performing household chores (including other forms of non-market economic activity) children free up other household human resources, mainly involving adults, which can be switched to more productive activities.

The fourth criticism concerns the division of children into four categories, and the ambiguity of the last category that supposedly consists of children who are not at school or work. In fact, this category consists partly of children who, although they are not at school and do not work, are performing high levels of household chores, actively looking for work or who are disabled or severely ill (Biggeri et al., 2003). As a result, interpreting this category is extremely problematic for both theoretical and empirical analysis.

The fifth criticism concerns the reference to the length of work. Children are not always engaged in economic activities all year round. Many of

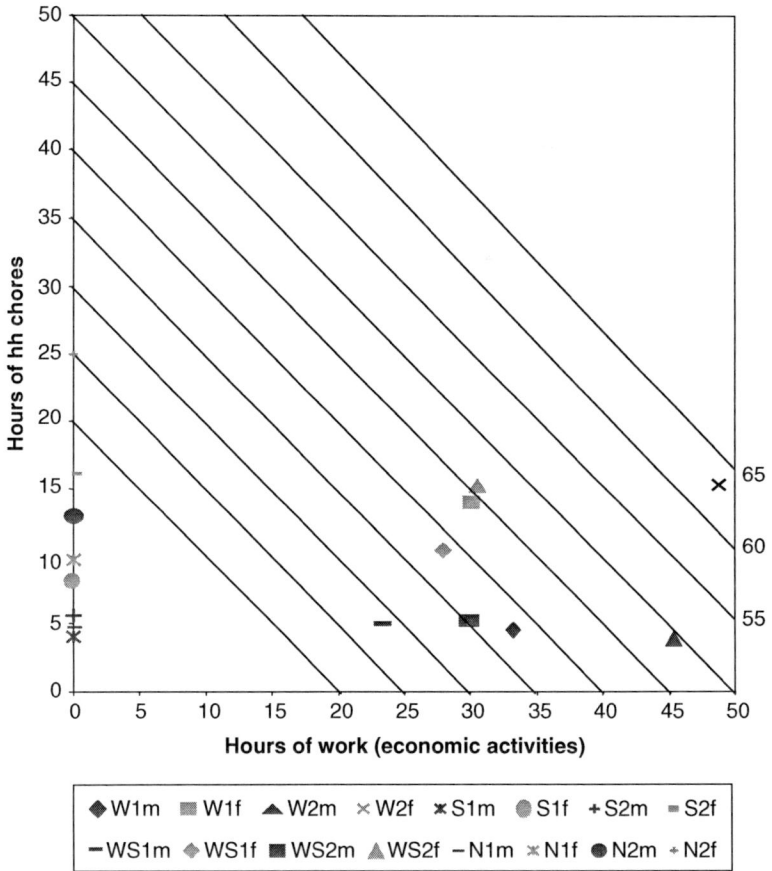

Figure 13.1 Average hours for which children are involved in economic activities (work) and household chores by activity status, age and gender (Guatemala, 2000)
Source: Our elaboration on LSMS Guatemala 2000, Biggeri (2003).

them are employed by their parents for only a small proportion of the year. For instance, in agriculture, child work is very common during the harvest period, but much less common throughout the rest of the year. However, according to the predefined categories, a 14-year-old child engaged in a seasonal activity 15 hours per week is classified as a child labourer, whereas a 14-year-old engaged in activity 10 hours per week all year round is classified as a child worker. According to the definition, the first child is considered to be in a worse situation than the second. However, seasonal activities often coincide with school holiday periods, which means that the impact of this kind of work is not as detrimental for schooling as year-round work.

The main point is that the actual definitions and categories developed for children are derived from statistics originally intended for adults, and have been designed by adults without consulting children or adequately considering how these activities actually affect the lives of the children involved.

13.3. Re-thinking the economic and non-economic activities of children using the capability approach

In applying the CA, we are concerned with what children in developing and developed countries are actually able to "do" and "be" or ultimately become, i.e. with their current and potential capabilities. Therefore, as argued in earlier chapters of this book (especially Chapters 1, 2 and 4), the CA to well-being evaluates policies, and in our case the economic and non-economic activities of children, according to their impact on children's capabilities.

The definitions of the different types of child activities/work, and the categories of children's activity status, can be analysed in terms of constraint on functionings and on capabilities as freedom to achieve in accordance with the child's age and maturity. This implies that there can be types of work/activities that are compatible with child well-being and development. The impact of an activity in terms of a child's capabilities depends on the age of the child, on the type of activity (its harmfulness or exploitativeness, but also on the level of responsibility required, the learning process involved, etc.), on his/her involvement in the activity (i.e. the hours per day or per week worked and how are allocated during the day)[17] and on parents' capabilities and attitudes towards the economic and non-economic activities of their children.

In the case of children, the possibility of converting opportunities or resources into functionings also depends on parents' decisions (and in some cases on those of guardians or teachers), which suggests that the child's conversion factors are subject to further "constraints": on the one hand, children desire to be more autonomous, on the other hand, they require parental care. In a similar vein, children are also subject to an intergenerational transfer of capabilities, and in general to the capabilities of their parents and carers.

The core of our analysis is to understand whether a given child activity is detrimental for child well-being and development, i.e. whether it is damaging or can damage important capabilities, such as education or health, that have intrinsic value and are also instrumental for other functionings. If children are denied the capability or opportunity to achieve a given functioning, this may also constrain other capabilities in a dynamic perspective, which may determine a trade-off in terms of short-term and long-term objectives. Over the course of a life cycle, the relevance of functionings and capabilities, and of the freedom to achieve, can change dramatically, especially in different contexts and in response to key life events. This issue reminds us that in the expansion of each capability or of positive freedom, agency also plays a central role.

As some researchers and practitioners have pointed out, in developing countries work can be an important way to learn a job or form part of the local community (Boyden et al., 1998). Even the ILO accepts that

> Not all work is harmful to children. From a young age, many children help around the home, run errands, or assist their parents in the family farm or business. As they get older they take on light jobs or learn valuable traditional trades. In this way, children acquire the skills and attitudes they will need as future workers and useful members of the community. Light work, carefully monitored, can be an essential part of children's socialization and development process, where they learn to take responsibility, and gain pride in their own accomplishments. Work of this kind is not without risk, but it is not what is generally meant by child labour. (ILO, 2002b: 3)

Although these observations are very important, we should also remember that most of the jobs children do take less than one month to learn (very often two or three days are sufficient). It may take two or three months to learn a more skillful job, but only rarely more than a year to learn difficult jobs (such as carpet weaving, although this rarely takes more than 84 weeks).

On the other hand, the CA leads us to consider exploitative household chores as negative activities, although some types of work/activity and household chores can be done by children if they do not damage key aspects of their well-being. According to children, during Focus Group Discussions (FGDs) (see, for instance, Biggeri et al., 2006),[18] negative activities are exploitative activities that abuse and/or damage any of the following children's capabilities: life and physical health, love and care, mental well-being, bodily integrity and safety, social relations, participation, education, freedom from economic and non-economic exploitation, shelter and environment, leisure activities, respect, religion and identity, time-autonomy and undertaking projects (in terms of interpreting, planning, imagining) and mobility. Furthermore, the children participating to the FGDs decided to define positive activities as those that do not abuse or damage any of these dimensions, and which can facilitate social relations, participation in society, autonomy and respect (including self-respect and self-esteem) and, in the case of older children, fulfil the capability of being able to have paid work (promoting material well-being), which can be a rather important capability in a life characterized by material deprivation.

The CA is much more comprehensive; it takes into account the gender issue, and it is in line with child well-being and development, and with CRC. Obviously such a refinement in multidimensional capability space is complex, and the measurements required for empirical analysis may become complicated.

We explore possible alternative categories of child work for use in the empirical analyses: firstly, we try to think up and use new categories starting from the new definition based on the CA. Secondly, we try to modify the ILO definitions accordingly.

To be acceptable, child work must not interfere negatively with children's capabilities and functionings, which depend on the age and maturity of the child. This implies that the type and the modality of children's economic and non-economic activities should not violate any of the children's relevant capabilities, which means that their functionings and their capabilities must be safeguarded. Childhood life and physical health must be respected, the child must have access to love and care, maintain mental well-being and bodily integrity and safety, and have the ability to form positive social relationships and to participate in community life; the child must also able to access education; be free from economic and non-economic exploitation, and his or her religious beliefs and identity must be respected in the workplace. Children must also work in "a good environment". Finally, the child's work activities must leave enough time for leisure, allow freedom of mobility and sufficient time to undertake projects (daily), including their interpretation and planning, as appropriate to the age and maturity of the child. These categories combine the following: (a) the age of the child and time allocated to the work activity, including the impact on the child's capabilities and actual functionings; with (b) the type of work and its impact on the child's capabilities and functionings. Four categories emerge from this exercise, as shown in Table 13.1.

This means, for example, that a given activity can be acceptable in terms of the type of work involved (e.g. some agricultural activities), but unacceptable in terms of the time devoted to it during the day. In this case it might

Table 13.1　Four categories of children's activities based on the capability approach

		a) Time devoted to the activity according to its impact on the child's capabilities and achieved functionings	
		Acceptable	Unacceptable
b) Type of activity according its impact on the child's capabilities and achieved functionings	Acceptable Unacceptable	Positive Negative	Negative Negative

be considered to have a negative impact, because of its detrimental effect on educational capability. However, if the same work is done during the agricultural season when schools are closed, it may also be acceptable in terms of the time devoted to it, although even seasonal agricultural activity may have some detrimental effects. For example, a child working on a family farm for just few hours per day during the school holiday could end up spreading dangerous pesticides that threaten the capability for good health.

The second option is to modify the ILO definitions. Classifying household chores and other non-economic activities as either child work or child labour calls for compromise,[19] and this substantially reduces the potential of the CA.[20] As a result, the solutions proposed in this exercise are not definitive, but are part of a broader attempt to reach an internationally acceptable consensus on the statistical definition, starting from the ILO definitions of child work and child labour (which includes children involved in hazardous work), and also adding household chores and other non-economic activities that may interfere both with the functionings to be achieved and the capabilities, such as the freedom to achieve.

As our starting point, we take hazardous work, which is defined by the ILO as work that is likely to harm the health, safety or moral development of a child. In addition to children employed in mining, construction or other hazardous activities, this group includes all children below 18 years of age who work for 43 hours or more per week. We can also add children involved in the "unconditional" worst forms of child labour (such as forced or bonded labour, armed conflict, prostitution and pornography, and other illicit activities). These violate most of the capabilities and related functionings that we have already discussed.

In the case of non-hazardous work, the number of the hours worked is also an important question, especially if we are attempting to derive a theoretical definition and delineate classifications from the data to be analysed. According to the literature (Biggeri et al., 2003), a possible threshold might be two or possibly three hours a day of household chores six days a week as a maximum. However, we also have to take into account how much the time allocated to household chores interferes with other achievable and valuable functionings (i.e. capabilities).

Following Biggeri (2003), a child was classified as currently working if he/she:

- worked for someone who is not a member of the household (paid or unpaid); or
- was doing household chores for no more than three hours per day (assuming that the allocation did not interfere with leisure, attending school or the child's health and development); or
- worked for a family farm or business.

Using this new definition, all children can be assigned to five mutually exclusive categories:[21]

I. Work only: children who are economically active (leading to at least some interference with school attendance) or engage in household chores for three or more hours per day.

II. Work and school: children who combine school attendance with work, as defined in (I).

III. School, no work: children who go to school and do not work (they may engage in household chores for less than three hours per day or do work that does not interfere with school attendance).

IV. Light household chores or work: children who do household chores only or do work for less than three hours a day that does not interfere with school attendance.

V. No activities: no work, no school, no household chores.

13.4. Conclusions

The CA is child centred, and so it evaluates children's activities taking into consideration their impact on the well-being of children, and their "well-becoming" in the multidimensional capability space. In particular, any activities that abuse or damage any of the following capabilities are classified as having a "negative" impact: life and physical health, love and care, mental well-being, bodily integrity and safety, social relationships, participation in society, education, freedom from economic and non-economic exploitation, shelter and environment, leisure activities, respect, religion and personal identity, time-autonomy and the ability to undertake projects (in terms of their interpreting and planning) and mobility.

This means that activities, including some work, performed by children or adolescents that do not affect their health or personal development, or interfere with their schooling and other relevant capabilities, may be regarded as positive if they contribute to the children's development and to the welfare of their families.

At first glance this definition may seem more "liberal" in terms of child work and child labour. In reality, by being child centred, this definition is much more comprehensive, and it takes into account the gender issue, as well as being in line with the well-being and development of the children. It also complements the CRC.

Re-examining children's activities within the CA framework leads to conclusions that are relevant in terms of research methods, as well has having policy implications. For instance, in the case of research methods, there is a need to revise the SNA with regard to child activities by including at least household chores within economic activities (despite their being "unpaid"), by either adopting a child-centred approach or taking into account the fact that these free up adult human resources, and so have an economic impact. Moreover, surveys of children's activities need to gather information on functionings and capabilities together with other information (including the number of hours devoted to household chores, the time allocated during the day to different activities, community- and child-centred values, and measuring the constraints on functioning). Finally, the exercise described in this chapter also reminds us of the need to review the various categories and status of children's activities for econometric analysis and theoretical models.

In terms of policy implications, the most relevant result is the one obtained from a gender perspective, since female children are usually involved in household chores to a greater extent. A revision of the statistics will redirect policies towards female children. Furthermore, policies and social arrangements have to be evaluated with regard to the ability to expand children's capabilities and freedom to promote or achieve valuable aspects of being and doing. The consequences are that the activities classified as extremely negative or very negative in Table 13.1 should be banned and prosecuted under law, whereas policies intended to reduce the involvement of children in negative activities may have a trade-off between short-term outcomes (i.e. what helps working children), even though these may at the same time increase children's willingness to take part in these activities (see the discussion of agency as the second best option in van den Berge, 2006), thus running counter to the long-term goal of eliminating negative activities and long-term policies intended to eradicate negative activities for children, but often by means of laws that can lead to an even worse situation for the children and their families (Basu, 1999; Mehrotra and Biggeri, 2002, 2007; van den Berge, 2006; Basu and Lopez-Calva, 2010). We strongly believe that to be really effective these points of view have to reconciled, and thought through and implemented in a "joined-up" manner, i.e. as part of an overall strategy. Only in this way can they can produce key outcomes in the best interests of the children.

Notes

1. This has long been the position of UNICEF.
2. See, for instance, the works of Boyden et al. (1998) and Myers (1999).
3. Articles by the Indian economist Kaushik Basu (1999) and Basu and Van (1998) are relevant here.
4. Age is measured as the number of years completed at the last birthday (ILO, 2003).
5. Members whose economy and educational facilities are insufficiently developed may, after consultation with the organizations of employers and workers concerned, where such exist, initially specify a minimum age of 14 years (ILO n. 138, art.7). Please see Sen 1999b and 2000 on *Decent Work*.
6. Children under five years of age, who are not included in any of these four groups, are generally considered to be too young to work.

7. "Work of a domestic nature (household chores) performed by children in their own households are considered to be non-economic activities and thus outside the "production boundary" as defined by the United Nations System of National Accounts (1993 Rev. 3) for measuring GDP. Our estimates thus do not cover children working in non-economic activities. This is in line with international labour standards that provide for exceptions for household chores in the child's own household. The time children spend on these activities, however, can be substantial. In some cases, school enrolment or attendance is being jeopardized. Unfortunately, data on the extent of non-economic child work are very fragmented and not reliable enough to attempt a global estimation" ILO (2002a: 30). The case is different for the so called "child domestic workers" in other people's households.

8. "Child age groups were broken down in two different ways. For the estimates on economic activity we applied the commonly used age brackets 5–9, 10–14 and 15–17. For the presentation of data on child labour and hazardous child work we cut the first two brackets in a different way, into 5–11 and 12–14" (ILO, 2002a: 29).

9. About 171 million children aged 5–17 were estimated to work in hazardous situations or conditions (ILO, 2002a).

10. There were about 8.4 million children involved in the worst forms of child labour as defined in the ILO Convention (trafficking, forced and bonded labour, armed conflict, prostitution and pornography and illicit activities) ILO (2002a).

11. "In line with the international definition of employment, one hour of work during the reference week is sufficient for classifying a person as at work in economic activity during that week" (ILO, 2002a). In theory, individuals with a structured job, but temporarily absent from work due to illness, vacation or other similar absences are also included in the classification.

12. This voicelessness is due to the legal status of children as minors, excluded from political participation. Furthermore, children working in the informal sector cannot join a union. Almost all trade unions are concerned with adults (mainly men) employed in the formal sector.

13. Work that results in output destined for the market or contributes to national income, i.e. all production actually destined for the market, whether for sale or barter; all goods or services provided free to individual households or collectively to the community by government units or non-profit institutions serving households; all goods produced for own use; own-account production of housing services; and services produced by employing paid domestic staff (UNSD, 2002).

14. From a statistical point of view they are not taken into account because not enough reliable data are available (ILO, 2002a: 30). Furthermore, since questions about domestic chores are not specified in the same way in all questionnaires, and domestic chores are typically not an exhaustive activity category, indicators relating to this type of activity are kept separate from information about child work (Cigno et al., 2002, 2003).

15. Typically girls shoulder a disproportionate burden of the responsibility for housework (Guarcello et al., 2005: 16). See also, for instance, Goldscheider and Waite (1991).

16. See, for instance, Levison and Moe (1998) in the case of Peru.

17. As pointed out elsewhere by Bhukuth (2008), the pleasure of working in non-detrimental activities can rapidly diminish if it is done regularly (for instance, every day).

18. A FGD on children activities was conducted by Biggeri in 2004 at the end of the Global March Against Child Labour and for Education. Eight children from

South Asian countries (Nepal 3, Pakistan 2, India 3) were invited to participate in the FGD (see Biggeri et al., 2006). The group included both boys and girls. All the children (one aged 13 years, one 14, two 15 and four 16) were quite mature, could understand each other and all at least understood a sufficient level of English (five accompanying persons assisted in carrying out the FGD, and were available to help with translation if needed, i.e. they were not participants). These results have been confirmed by another FGD discussion with Children from NATs (Niños y Adolescentes Trabajadores) in Lima in 2009, where the capability of being able to have paid work assumes a positive role if the other capabilities are respected.

19. The real question we raise here is whether household chores should be classified as work or labour. For instance, if the child is deprived of an education, and since cooking food can be harmful (a child could cut or burn him/herself while cooking), then domestic chores must be considered as child labour in terms of their impact on capability.

20. Furthermore, these do not resolve the question of the seasonality of the work; see fifth criticism of the definition.

21. A second possibility for the choice of categories could be as follows:

I. Work only: children who are economically active (and this produces at least some interference with school attendance).

II. Work and school: children who combine school attendance with work, as defined in (I).

III. School, no work: children who go to school but do not work (they may engage in household chores for less than three hours per day, or do work that does not interfere with school attendance).

IV. Household chores only for less than three hours per day that do not interfere with attending school, or with the child's health and development.

V. No activities: no work, no school, and engage in household chores for less than three hours per day or doing work that does not interfere with school attendance.

References

Ballet, J., Bhukuth, A. and Radja, K. (2006), "Travail des enfants, enfants des rues et capabilités: enjeux et questions méthodologiques", *Ethique et Economique*, 4(1): http://Ethique-economique.net

Ballet, J., Bhukuth, A. and Radja, K. (2007), "Fighting Against Child Labour: The Capability Approach Considered", in Rajasekhar (ed.), *Child Labour – Global Perspectives*, Amicus Books-ICFAI University Press, Hyderabad, India, pp. 93–110.

Basu, K. (1999), "Child Labor: Cause, Consequence, and Cure, with Remarks on International Labour Standards", *Journal of Economic Literature*, 37: 1083–1119.

Basu, K. and Lopez-Calva, L. F. (2010), "Functionings and Capabilities", in Kenneth Arrow, Amartya Sen and Kotaro Suzumura (eds.), *Handbook of Social Choice and Welfare*, Vol. 2, Elsevier, Amsterdam.

Basu, K. and Van, P. H. (1998), "The Economics of Child Labour", *American Economic Review*, 88(3): 412–427.

Bhukuth, A. (2008), "Defining Child Labour: A Controversial Debate", *Development in Practice*, 18(3): 385–394.

Bhukuth, A., Ballet, J. and Carimentrand, A. (2008), "Child labour and Responsible Consumers: From Boycotts to Social Labels, illustrated by the Hand-Knotted Carpet Industry", Unpublished paper, University of Versailles St Quentin en Yvelines.

Biggeri, M. (2003) "Children, Child Labour and the Human Capability Approach". Paper presented at the *3rd HDCA Conference*, 7–9 September 2003, Pavia.

Biggeri, M., Guarcello, L., Lyon, S. and Rosati, F.C. (2003), "The Puzzle of 'idle' Children: Neither in School Nor Performing Economic Activity: Evidence from Six Countries", UCW Working Paper, Understanding Children's Work (UCW) Project, ILO/UNICEF/WORLD BANK.

Biggeri, M., Libanora, R., Mariani, S. and Menchini, L. (2006), "Children Conceptualizing Their Capabilities: Results of the Survey During the First Children's World Congress on Child Labour", *Journal of Human Development*, 7(1): 59–83.

Boyden, J., Ling, B. and Myers, W.E. (1998), *What Works for Working Children*, Save the Children Sweden, Rädda Barnen, UNICEF, Stockholm.

Cigno, A., Guarcello, L., Lyon, S., Noguchi, Y. and Rosati, F.C. (2003), "Child Labour Indicators Used by the UCW Project: An Explanatory Note". *UCW WP*, Understanding children's work (UCW) project. http://www.ucw-project.org

Cigno, A., Rosati, F.C. and Tzannatos, Z. (2002), "Child Labour Handbook", SP Discussion Paper, n. 206, The World Bank.

Goldscheider, F.K., and Waite L.J. (1991). *New Families, No Families?*, University of California Press, Berkeley, CA.

Guarcello, L., Lyon, S., Rosati, F.C. and Valdivia, C.A. (2005) "Towards Statistical Standards for Children's Non Economic Work: A Discussion Based on Household Survey Data", UCW Working Paper, Understanding Children's Work (UCW) Project, ILO/UNICEF/WORLD BANK.

Hanson, K. and Vandaele, A. (2003), "Working Children and International Labour Law: A Critical Analysis", *The International Journal of Children's Rights*, 11: 73–146.

ILO (2002a), *Every Child Counts: New Global Estimates on Child Labour*. International Labour Organization, Geneva, 17 July 2002, http://www.ilo.org/public/english/standards/ipec/simpoc/others/globalest.pdf

ILO (2002b), *Combating Child Labour: A Handbook for Labour Inspectors*, International Programme on the Elimination of Child Labour (IPEC), InFocus Programme on Safety and Health at Work and the Environment (SafeWork), International Association of Labour Inspection (IALI), ILO, Geneva.

ILO (2003), *Investing in Every Child: An Economic Study of the Costs and Benefits of Eliminating Child Labour*, Geneva, International Labour Office, http://www.ilo.org/public/english/standards/ipec/ simpoc

ILO (2006), *Global Child Labour Trends: 2000 to 2004*, ILO, Geneva.

Levison, D. and Moe, K. (1998), "Household Work as a Detterrent to Schooling: An Analysis of Adolescent Girls in Peru", *Journal of Developing Area*, 32: 339–356.

Liebel, M. (2003), "Working Children as Social Subjects: the Contribution of working Children's Organisations to Social Transformations", *Childhood*, 10(3): 265–285.

Myers, W.E. (1999), "Considering Child Labour: Changing Terms, Issues and Actors at the International Level", *Childhood*, 6(13): 213–226.

Myers, W.E. (2001), *Appreciating Diverse Approaches to Child Labour*, Department of Human and Community Development, University of California, Davis, CA.

Myers, W.E. and Boyden, J. (1998), *Child Labour: Promoting the Best Interests of Working Children*, Save the Children Alliance, London.

Mehrotra, S. and Biggeri, M. (2002), "The Subterranean Child Labour Force: Subcontracted Home Based Manufacturing in Asia", Innocenti Working Paper, no. 96, UNICEF Innocenti Research Centre, Florence, www.unicef.org/irc

Mehrotra, S. and Biggeri, M. (eds) (2007), *Asian Informal Workers: Global Risks Local Protection*, Routledge, London.

Sen, A.K. (1993), "Capability and Well-being", in M. Nussbaum and A. Sen (eds), *The Quality of Life*, Clarendon Press, Oxford, pp. 30–53.

Sen, A.K. (1995), "Gender Inequality and Theories of Justice", in M. Nussbaum and J. Glover (eds), *Women, Culture and Development: A Study of Human Capabilities*, Clarendon Press, Oxford, pp. 259–273.

Sen, A.K. (1999a), *Development as Freedom*, OUP, Oxford.

Sen, A.K. (1999b), *Address by Mr. Amartya Sen, Nobel Laureate in Economics*, International Labour Conference, 87th Session, 1–17 June.

Sen, A.K. (2000), "Work and Rights", *International Labour Review*. Geneva, ILO, 139(2): 119–129.

Sharon, D. (1999), *A Commentary on the United Nations Convention on the Rights of the Child*, Martinus Nijhoff Publisher, The Hague.

UN (1989), *Convention on the Rights of the Child*, United Nations, New York.

UN Secretariat (1997), "Trial International Classification for International Time Use Activities". Expert Group Meeting on Trial International Classification for Time Use Activities, 13–16 October 1997, New York.

UNESCO (2001), *Education for All and Children Who Are Excluded*, World Education Forum, Dakar, Senegal 26–28 April 2000, Paris, UNESCO.

UNICEF (2000), *Monitoring Progress towards the Goals of the World Summit for Children: End-Decade Multiple Indicator Survey Manual*, United Nations Children's Fund, Division of Evaluation, Policy Planning, New York.

UNICEF (2001), *Progress since the World Summit for Children: A Statistical Review*, United Nations Children's Fund, New York, 17 July 2002, http://www.unicef.org/specialsession/about/sgreport-pdf/sgreport_adapted_stats_eng.pdf

UNSD (2002), *System of National Accounts 1993*. 18 July 2002, United Nations Statistics Division, http://millenniumindicators.un.org/unsd/sna1993/toctop.asp

van den Berge, M.P. (2006), "Working Children: Their Agency and Self-organization", *Éthique et Economique/Ethics and Economics*, 4(1): 1–20.

14
Children's Capabilities: Toward a Framework for Evaluating the Built Environment

JungA Uhm, Ferdinand Lewis and Tridib Banerjee

14.1. Introduction

In this chapter we present a method for evaluating urban planning that considers the impact of environmental and other capabilities on children's well-being. It also focuses on public resources as well as the agency and evolving capabilities of the child. In particular, we are interested in exploring how the production of the built environment – planning and design of the layout, organization and distribution of the physical space – can be better informed by current thinking on the capabilities approach, especially as it pertains to the children and their development.

Historically the production of the built environment has remained in the professional domain of architecture, civil engineering, landscape architecture and real estate development. However, there is very little experience or expertise on how or whether performance of the built environment can be systematically evaluated, especially from the standpoint of consumers or users.

Stimulated by the "healthy cities" initiative around the world, recent interest in the performance of the built environment has increased. Alarmed by the rapid rise in incidence of obesity and diabetes among not only the population generally but also school-age children in particular, non-government organizations (NGOs) like the US-based Robert Wood Johnson Foundation and various government agencies have initiated studies to explore the role of the built environment in promoting or hindering healthy lifestyles.

In this chapter we focus on several assessment or audit tools for measuring the performance of the built environment in promoting healthy lifestyles. These instruments represent a constellation of measures pertaining to various aspects of the built environment that are assumed to influence active living outcomes. In the main these measurement tools reflect conventional wisdom and expert judgements, rather than established theories or empirical evidence. We note here, however, that this is not unusual in the design tradition that goes back to pre-modern times. Historically many normative images of the good city have been advanced (see Lynch, 1984). More recently however, the late Kevin Lynch, a planning professor at MIT, offered a treatise on what he called the "performance criteria" for good city form. Although essentially normative, Lynch's formulations are different from other visionary or aesthetic ideals of a good city, in that they come closest to addressing the more fundamental questions of capability and freedom described by Amartya Sen (1999). Thus we propose to examine these instruments from a capabilities perspective, combining Lynch's requirements for good city form with Sen's formulation of capability as the achievement of substantive "freedoms," and the associated notions of functioning and agency. Our aim is to derive a set of criteria to evaluate the effectiveness of these aforementioned audit tools, especially from the perspective of children's capabilities.

At the end of this chapter we present a framework for assessing the role of the built environment in children's capabilities. We refer to this as a "capability evaluation for the built environment" (or CEBE), noting that none of the existing audit tools have attempted to link the built environment to human functionings. While the main thrust of the chapter is theoretical, it is our hope that the CEBE will be of practical use in undertaking capability evaluations of the built environment's contributions to facilitate children's functionings.

14.2. Capability and good city form

Our work here is part of a theoretical journey that was inspired by Sen's CA, with a further intuition that Sen's ideas might provide a philosophical rationale for Kevin Lynch's arguments about the performance characteristics of good city form. Lynch was aware of the work of Rawls (1974), whom he cites in his work (Lynch, 1984), but it is unlikely that he was aware of the CA or its proximity to his own ideas. Sen's CA was in an incipient stage when Lynch passed away in 1984.[1] It is remarkable, nevertheless, how Lynch's commitment to individual choice and well-being was so similar to that of Sen and Rawls. An apprentice of Frank Lloyd Wright, and trained professionally as a city planner, Lynch never believed in the planner's professional omniscience or the rational determinism of modern planning, or for that matter the authority of planning as a state apparatus (cf. Harvey, 1973; Clark and Dear, 1984). Instead, he believed in individuals' potential for creating and controlling their own environments resulting in a democratic and pluralistic urban form (cf. Sennett, 1971). Sen's CA has inspired many theoretical discussions on topics like "quality of life" or "human development" (e.g. Crocker, 1992; Nussbaum and Sen, 1993; Nussbaum and Glover, 1995; Comim et al., 2008) from many different fields (see also Chapters 1 and 2, this book). However, the philosophical tenets of his basic idea have remained distant from the world of application and practice, especially in the planning and design of the built environment.[2] How to translate the idea of capability into performance criteria for the built environment remains a challenge. While certain contingent concepts have increased the possibilities for the application of the CA, they have yet to resolve difficult notions of freedom, right, functioning and agency that are inextricably linked with Sen's notion of capability. Lynch's work, we believe, brings us closer to a resolution.

14.3. Capability, affordance and behaviour settings

We need not rehash here the extensive literature – indeed an industry – that has been inspired or provoked by Sen's ideas. But we must consider some of the essential features of the CA to build our arguments for this chapter. First, according to Sen, capabilities are defined by substantive freedoms to "choose a life one has reason to value". Furthermore, it is the capabilities or substantive freedoms that should define the relevant "evaluative space" for assessing development or well-being, rather than "utilities" as emphasized by "welfarists" (and "marketists", we might add), or "primary resources" as in the Rawlsian tradition (Sen, 1999: 74). We find this argument appealing because it liberates the well-being argument from the market *versus* planning debate (see Banerjee, 1993; Richardson and Gordon, 1993), between the marketist belief in maximizing collective utilities through the market mechanism, and the public planning imperative of distributive justice in allocation of primary goods. Neither, however, addresses the substantive freedoms to achieve the "functionings" in the sense that Sen (1999) defines:

> The concept of "functionings," which has distinctly Aristotelian roots, reflects the various things a person may value doing or being. The valued functionings may vary from the elementary ones, such as being adequately nourished and being free from avoidable disease, to very complex activities or personal states, such as being able to take part in the life of the community and having self-respect. (p. 75)

Although Sen does not invoke Maslow (1943), it is apparent that valued functionings are likely to range across the Maslovian need hierarchy, as some functionings are contingent on having achieved more basic ones. In any event, Sen proposes that for any given individual the extent of functionings enjoyed and the combinations thereof can be represented by what can be called a "functioning vector". He notes further: "While the combination of a person's functionings reflects her actual *achievements*, the capability set represents the *freedom* to achieve the alternative functioning combinations from which this person can choose" (p. 75).

We may assume that children's functionings would require some form of interaction with the natural and built environment, and the corresponding socio-cultural milieu. In terms of provisioned resources of the built environment, this might include the presence of neighbourhood play spaces, as well as the child's real opportunity to make use of them. These functionings would also require these play spaces to be free of pollutants and other hazards. Furthermore, play spaces can be critical to a child's social network, which in turn encourages the child's engagement with, and understanding of, the environment. Accordingly we draw here from the field of ecological psychology to offer two relevant concepts for considering a child's ability to convert environmental resources to functionings: *affordances*, a notion initially developed by James Gibson (1966) as a cognitive process; and *behaviour settings*, proposed by Roger Barker (1951) as a locus of behaviour, individual or otherwise, but bounded in space and time.

The concept of *affordance* is useful here because it offers a way to consider the human-environment relationship in individual terms. It addresses the relationship between the individual's capabilities and dispositions on the one hand, and the properties of the environment on the other, and the constraints and possibilities afforded by this relationship. A simple example would be the dimension of the risers in a staircase. A 14-inch riser might "afford" climbing by a healthy adult, but may not afford climbing by an elderly person. Affordances in the built environment can also affect children's well-being. For example, a neighbourhood walking path that is free from traffic nonetheless may not afford children's physical activity and play if it is polluted with toxins, or overcrowded, or if it traverses an unsafe social milieu of drug dealing and gang violence.

Behaviour settings describe ecological synomorphy between aggregate or group activities and the environment. Behaviour settings contain affordances to be sure, but the two are different. Affordance describes a constraining or enabling relationship between a characteristic of the individual and a characteristic of the environment, while behaviour settings describe how subsequent and aggregate patterns of activities determine the choices that an individual can make when entering the setting. As Barker pointed out, behaviour settings are characterized by "standing rules of behaviour". For example, a customer entering a café may either sit at a table inside or on the sidewalk, but in either case they will always sit, because that is what people do in cafés. Thus behaviour settings enable us to think of affordances not only in terms of the provision of resources, but also in terms of behavioural outcomes in the aggregate. Thus children who play in streets, thereby risking accidents and social dangers, do so because there is no park in the neighbourhood, but they also do it because the street space provides some affordance and it is where behaviour settings for play customarily occur. It is common to find kids on roller blades playing hockey in neighbourhood streets during summer months when the rinks are closed and the frozen patches of ice are no more. Similarly improvised cricket games with tennis balls are quite common in the neighbourhood streets and alleys of Kolkata, India. Obviously in these instances the street space provides some affordance, albeit with risks of accidents and danger. Another example might be a behaviour setting such as "skateboarding in the parking lot". When the lot is full of cars the affordance of skateboarding is low, but its skateboarding affordance increases after hours when the parking demands on the lot decreases.

The concepts of affordance and behaviour setting also allow us a way to ask important questions about application, for example regarding the responsibility of the state *versus* the private sector in children's capability. We can ask, in the manner of Nussbaum (2000) in regard to Sen's notions of functionings and capabilities: Who is going to provide for the *affordances* and *behaviour settings* – the state, the market, private philanthropy or social capital? These questions remain in the background of our theoretical discussion and pose one of the major policy issues of using the CA in practice. Nonetheless, in the final section of this chapter we will present an application of this theoretical framework to evaluate some of the currently available audit instruments.

14.4. Who provides the means for capability?

Nussbaum (2000) has chosen to circumvent this question, along with those of agency, and property or constitutional rights, in her attempt to develop a prospectus for a CA to gender and development. Sen sees a role for public policy in enhancing these capabilities, however. Indeed, he sees it as a two-way process where capability enhancement – and here we return implicitly to the notion of agency which he discusses, for instance, in the context of women and development – could lead to shaping the direction of public policy in furthering these goals, thus triggering a virtuous circle, so to speak.

How can the built environment enhance capabilities, or in operational terms, increase the possibilities of the number and diversity of valued functioning vectors that depend upon a human–environment relationship? Obviously there is an implicit question of aggregation and priorities in the policy context. Clearly in any given configuration of space or size there can be numerous functioning vectors of use, as in the example of the parking lot above. In other examples the numbers could soon become very large with increasing diversity and size of agglomerations. Is it possible to plan for a utopian balance that maximizes capabilities of every member of the society? And what might be the form of the corresponding built environment?

Of course Sen is aware of these challenges, and he addresses many of these concerns under the rubric of "weights, valuations, and social choice" (Sen, 1999: 76). He admits that the CA allows interpersonal comparison in the evaluative space – and is thus superior to the Rawlsian "primary goods" approach – but Sen also acknowledges the challenge of aggregating "over heterogeneous components". He comments:

> The capability perspective is inescapably pluralist. First, there are differ-ent functionings, some more important than others. Second, there is the issue of what weight to attach to substantive freedom (the capability set) vis-à-vis the actual achievement (the chosen functioning vector). Finally, since it is not claimed that the capability perspective exhausts all relevant concerns for evaluative purposes (we might, for example, attach impor-tance to rules and procedures and not just to freedoms and outcomes), there is the underlying issue of how much weight should be placed on the capabilities, compared with any other relevant considerations. (p. 77)

He argues that its inherent pluralism notwithstanding, this approach is still far superior to the classical utilitarian approach which "values only plea-sure, without taking any direct interest in freedom, rights, creativity or actual living conditions" (p. 77). Sen devotes subsequent discussions on the chal-lenges of priorities and weights, the possibility of partial ordering, and the necessity of social choice in deciding weights pertaining to interpersonal differences in functioning preferences and functioning vectors. There is no need to rehash all those arguments here (see, for instance, Chapters 3–5), but it is important to note that Sen certainly favours a democratic process for assigning priorities and weights, not unlike Rawls' (2001) subsequent formulation of the public conception of justice.

Although Sen has argued earlier that individual capabilities can be enhanced by public policy, his current discussion of the evaluative space of capability is limited to the demand side only. What are the implications of this discussion for the supply side, for the designers, planners and purveyors of the public realm, including market-based responses? We can anticipate Sen's response, i.e. it is the evaluative process that would identify the deficit in capabilities in the form of unmet functionings (see also Chapters 4 and 5). This in turn should provide clues for the kind of improvements that public policy could initiate, thus jump-starting the virtuous circle. There are not many empirical studies that might have indirectly tapped into the func-tioning, freedom and capability nexus (see the HDCA website). The 1976 study of the American quality of life experience (see Campbell et al., 1976) is one such effort that showed deficiency and disparities in the quality of life experiences, and expectations of the American people. Stuart Chapin's (1974) time-budget and activity pattern study devised a quality of life indi-cator from the distribution of one's discretionary and obligatory activities (in other words functioning vectors), and examined the aggregate differences by socio-economic groups and urban settings. Thus for example, controlling for income class, San Francisco residents reported a higher ratio of discretionary *versus* obligatory activities, and a greater variety of discretionary activities (or in other words a larger functioning vectors of value) than say Baltimore residents. In a Los Angeles area study of 22 neighbourhoods in the mid-1970s, Banerjee and Baer (1984) were able to obtain lists of "setting deprivations" and "setting aggravations" (which could be interpreted as obstacles to desired functionings) for different ethnic and income groups. The length of the lists was inversely related to income, as to be expected.

Obviously there are not enough empirical projects that have placed the built environment in the evaluative space of the CA. Our current examination of the existing built environment audit tools is an attempt to address that lacuna. We believe that it is possible to conceptualize "functioning bundles" in addition to "functioning vectors" that include shared or invariant functionings across and within vectors, and among individuals. Sen acknowledges such possibilities. Accordingly, we propose that Kevin Lynch's performance characteristics for good city form can be seen as responding to bundles of universal functionings.

14.5. Children's capabilities along Lynch's criteria

In this section, we examine how the built environment relates to children's functionings. We use Lynch's performance criteria for good city form as a normative framework for the capability evaluation of the built environment. Lynch (1984) offers five basic dimensions as performance characteristics for evaluating the quality of human habitat and their values, which, of course may vary across cultures. Thus any evaluative exercises of the built environment, according to Lynch, should be sensitive to the local context and its inhabitants while serving general dimensions. In this sense, Lynch's criteria can be seen as similar to Nussbaum's (2000) universal list of human capabilities.

14.5.1. Vitality

"An environment is a good habitat if it supports the health and biological well-functioning of the individual and the survival of the species". (Lynch, 1984: 121)

Although children's ill-health can be caused by a complexity of factors, various environmental stressors and hazards are known to present direct and indirect threats to the survival and healthy development of children (see Evans, 2006). When children are in periods of rapid growth and development, their immature body systems tend to bear heavier health burdens that place them at higher risk for long-term harm, far more than for adults (see Bearer, 1995). Accordingly, Lynch tells us that for an environment to be vital, providing opportunities for good health and support for biological well-being, it should be *sustenant, secure, and consonant*. These three operational criteria offer a way to evaluate – in capability terms – what a specific behaviour setting "affords" to promote children's wellbeing in terms of health.

The environmental system should offer the necessities adequate to sustain life. Children living with insufficiently safe water, combined with poor sanitation, for instance, are greatly exposed to diarrhoeal disease and various infections, which further contribute to their malnutrition, making them more susceptible to disease by weakening the immune system (Bartlett, 2005). A high level of environmental stressors such as noise and crowding seems to affect children's cognitive processes (Evans, 2006). To be sustenant, the environment also should be secure from physical harms caused by environmental health hazards, accidents, assaults and the fear of encountering these. Various ambient toxic substances and pollutants are linked to adverse health effects that are particularly severe for children, causing low weight at birth, respiratory illness such as asthma, or decreased lung functions (Bates, 1995). The predominance of automobiles and consequent urban sprawl with growing levels of automobile emissions and traffic-related accidents have led to a variety of health burdens on children, including physical inactivity (Frumkin, 2002). Growing social incivility and unsafe environments seriously limit opportunities for children's outdoor activities and their chances for active use of the body, lacking what Lynch would call a "consonant" human–environment relationship.

14.5.2. Sense

"By the sense of a settlement, I mean the clarity with which it can be perceived and identified, and the ease with which its elements can be linked with other events and places in a coherent mental representation of time and space and that representation can be connected with non-spatial concepts and values". (Lynch, 1984: 131)

Being able to experience the environment and develop attachments to people, animals, things and places are important children's capabilities to which an environment's "sense" can contribute, as Nussbaum (2000) describes. How children perceive, interpret and make use of environmental information to negotiate everyday life will always differ to some degree from child to child. However, Lynch suggests that certain human commonalities create basic constancies in experiencing the same place, and these criteria are useful for describing the environmental experience of particular groups of individual children. According to Lynch (1984), sensible environments are *identifiable, structured, congruent, transparent, legible, unfolding* and *significant*. Each of these characteristics describes what the environment affords the child in terms of Lynch's "coherent mental representations" of the environment.

In Lynch's normative view, the form of a built environment should respond to the human need to identify with places, and further, its structure and organization should support human need for orientation in time and place. For Lynch, and for us, "place" is intrinsic to human existence and imbued with meaning derived from experience, thoughts, memories, emotions and social relationships (Tuan, 1977). A *sense* of place arises when individuals attach meaning to a place, reflected in a sense of "belonging" or identification of the self with it (Relph, 1976). Thus place identity becomes interwoven with a child's sense of self, and an interactive relationship grows between functionings of children and environmental resources (Proshansky and Fabian, 1987; Altman and Low, 1992). Children tend to identify place with potential activities or its use for them (Aitken and Ginsburg, 1998). They explore and manipulate environments by trying out ideas on it, and in the process, acquire environmental knowledge and skills. Such engagements help them develop personal attitudes toward the world, and a fundamental self-awareness. Clearly these require a "congruence" in the child–environment relationship. Moreover, the "structure" and other features of the environment should afford "transparency" and "legibility" that evoke what Lynch (1960) famously called "imageability". A child's image of the environment helps him/her to orient in time and space, and to organize his/her activities and knowledge of the environment in memory. We note that Lynch was not arguing that environments should be designed in a way that imposes meanings, but rather that the individual's sense of an environment should have an "open-endedness" that allows meaning to "unfold" as it is experienced, and without overloading our sensory system (p. 139).

14.5.3. Fit

"The fit of a settlement refers to how well its spatial and temporal pattern matches the customary behaviour of its inhabitants. It is the match between action and form in its behaviour settings and behaviour circuits". (Lynch, 1984: 151)

Environmental fit is closely related to the aforementioned notions of *affordances* and the "synomorphic" nature of *behaviour settings* – which, we argue, can be seen as linking functionings with the form of the environment.

Lynch's normative arguments considered both constraints and opportunities particular to an individual in the setting (i.e. affordances) and overall and salient characteristics of behaviour in its setting (i.e. behaviour settings),[3] suggesting that the fit of the environment should be *stable, manipulatable* and *resilient*. The stability of the environment reduces uncertainty and conflict through the match between built form and our behavioural expectations. It is important, Lynch argues, to understand what is expected of the environment in which children grow up, and it is essential that designers and planners consider the perspectives of the child. Various studies continue to support this position, trying to uncover children's environmental needs and preferences (see e.g. van Vliet, 1981; Lieberg, 1997; Talen and Coffindaffer, 1999). Most notably, Lynch's UNESCO-sponsored "Growing Up in Cities" (1977) study documented and analysed children's needs and perspectives on their immediate relationship to the environment. Twenty-five years later the study was revived by Louise Chawla and others (2002), with added emphasis on participatory research. These two studies have collectively revealed a set of environmental values shared by children across different parts of the world. In addition to articulating their needs, children described environments responsive to their functionings, such as those offering diverse activities, social interactions and safe and free movement.[4] Studies by Robin Moore (1986) and Chawla and Heft (2002) have shown that the two most frequently identified characteristics that children value in their everyday environments correspond to Lynch's performance dimensions of "accessibility" and "diversity" (see also Chawla, 2002).

Lynch argues that the environment should also be "manipulable", or adaptable to the changing needs of its residents, and also be resilient to future changes. However, many pre-programmed settings designed for children tend to be rigid, affording no room for the creativity that children require, leaving such settings unused and deserted (see Gold, 1972). Studies show that children value what Lynch calls "manipulable" environments, in which they can assert control (Lynch and Lukashok, 1996). By affording creative activities and explorations, the environment plays an educative role that stimulates children's environmental learning (Carr and Lynch, 1968; Southworth and Southworth, 1974).

14.5.4. Access

"Access is one fundamental advantage of an urban settlement... it is a matter of potential reach, and the obstacle to it may be physical, financial, social, or psychological". (Lynch, 1984: 203)

The environment enhances children's capabilities by affording access to social activities, material resources, places and information. Increasing their choices is more significant than simply maximizing accessibility. Lynch suggests that the environment should offer its users access to *diverse* opportunities in an *equitable* manner and that accessibility should be *locally manageable*. Children's access to healthy learning and developmental opportunities is closely linked to their freedom of independent mobility (among other freedoms). Being able to move around freely promotes children's functioning opportunities such as acquiring environmental knowledge, engaging with other children and adults and developing self-esteem and control (van Vliet, 1981; Prezza et al., 2001; Rissotto and Tonucci, 2002). Inasmuch as they encourage children's active use of the body, mind and senses (in Lynch's terms), children's independent mobility is also an essential condition for improving their health and well-being and thus obtaining a "just" environment for children (O'brien et al., 2000: 258).

In recent years, an alarming rise in childhood obesity and associated health risks has generated increasing interest in creating environments that promote physical activity. In particular, the idea of employing environmental design to encourage children's walking to school has gained widespread support. Yet, we argue that while studies examining children's travel to school grow in number, the children remain invisible as a subject in these studies, as they mostly focus on environmental conditions believed to encourage parents to let their kids walk to school (see e.g. McMillan, 2003; Braza, Shoemaker, and Seeley, 2004; Kerr et al., 2006). Thus interventions in the built environment to increase physical activity invariably focus on *qualities of objects of the built environment*, such as crosswalk striping and shade trees, for instance, rather than on opportunities for desired functionings that are afforded in the child's relationship to his or her environment. This is the built environment equivalent of providing a Rawlsian equality of general use resources, which, as Sen argued, cannot in themselves describe how they are able to be converted by individuals into well-being. While we recognize that almost any programme to increase children's physical activity probably makes the situation no worse, we will go further to assert that our profession's ongoing misapprehension of the affordance relationship between children, their environments and capabilities amounts to a kind of institutionalized neglect.

14.5.5. Control

> ... "a good settlement is one in which place control is certain, responsible, and congruent, both to its users (present, potential, and future) and also to structure of the problems of the place". (Lynch, 1984: 220)

Lynch argues that control of the environment in the hands of its immediate users is the key to achieving "fit". Hence, for children, being able to express their needs and concerns about their everyday environment and to participate in shaping the decisions that affect their environment are important capabilities. Children's participation may not only foster their competence by exercising control over place, but also improve their environmental knowledge and consequent responsibilities (Chawla and Heft, 2002: 202). However, necessary consensus to promote children's participation is not yet present. Questions about the appropriateness of involving children in the decision-making process and the capacity of children in exercising such responsibilities largely suggest participation as the domain of adults' activities (Matthews et al., 1999). Also, the variable needs of children, which fluctuate between being dependent and in need of having care and being autonomous and entitled to their own opinion, present a potential tension between protection and participation (Bartlett et al., 1999; Jans, 2004). In Western developed societies children's role is limited and remains at the level of "manipulation", "decoration" or "tokenism", which is non-participation according to Hart's (1992) "ladder of participation" model (adopted from Arnstein, 1969). As heightened parental anxiety today puts children under constant adult surveillance, particularly in the developed world, adult perspectives on the protection and control of children continue to dominate the development of children's environments. Consequently, children are constrained by limited mobility and forced into increasingly fragmented adult-determined "token spaces", where the environment is little more than a physical expression of what Sen refers to as "unfreedoms" (Matthews, 1992; see also Chapters 2, 3, 5 and 6 in this book).

By participatory capabilities of children we mean the competence and freedom they might have to pursue the functionings they value or desire. In other words, it relates to broader notions of agency as discussed in Chapter 2. Of course, due weight must be given to the age and maturity of the child in shaping participatory experiences, but neither must the child's abilities be eclipsed by adult needs in this regard. For planning and urban policy to consider the child and their spaces, it will be necessary to accept that children have agency, and are fully capable users of the environment, although the meanings of agency and capability are different – and we argue, necessarily so – from those of adults. In the most practical terms, this re-conception of children's agency and capability is of fundamental importance in determining the ways in which children might participate in the planning and design process (see Simpson, 1997; Jans, 2004), toward creating "child friendly cities" (c.f. UNICEF, 2004).

Based on the literature we have reviewed in this chapter, Table 14.1 below presents children's built environment capabilities, employing Lynch's performance criteria as a frame of reference in evaluating children's environment in the capability space. This organization of children's capabilities is modelled on Nussbaum's list of human functionings (Nussbaum, 2000). Nussbaum's list relies upon a universal list of capabilities that rises above the challenges of aggregation, valuations, weights and, ultimately, social choice, which requires more investigation than we can take up here. Here we use Nussbaum's list of capabilities in a way that explicitly includes the role of the environment, thus creating a set of categories that describe the interface between Lynch and Sen.

14.6. Capability-based evaluation: a synthesis

In this section we present our synthesis of Sen's CA and Lynch's criteria for "good city form" in a comprehensive framework that includes a

Table 14.1 Lynch's performance dimensions and children's built environment capabilities

Lynch's dimensions	Built environment features	Nussbaum's central human capabilities	Existing discourses on children's environment	Children's capabilities
Vitality	Sustenant Secure Consonant	Life Bodily health Bodily integrity	Creating healthy cities Promoting sustainable development Improving the level of physical activities	Being able to be born healthy and to maintain health Able to lead a normal length of life
			Ensuring the safety of child pedestrians from traffic and crime	Being secure against bodily accidents and assaults
Sense	Identifiable Structured Congruent Transparent Legible Unfolding Significant	Senses, Imagination, and Thought Emotions	Understanding children's experience of place Promoting children's environmental knowledge and competence	Able to make sense of place in relation to self Able to experience sensory environment Able to imagine and develop meaning
Fit	Stable Manipulable Resilient	Play	Creating a child-friendly environment Ensuring children's opportunities to play Creating an effective learning environment	Able to cognitively and physically engage with environment Able to manipulate environment Able to predict events in settings, and relate to them
Control	Certain Congruent Responsible Intermittently loose	Control over one's environment	Recognizing children's agency Recognizing children's role in planning and designing their environment	Being able to participate in environmental decision making Able to take responsibility for one's environment

				Able to perceive and understand environmental operations and controls
Access	Diverse Equitable Locally manageable	Bodily integrity Affiliation	Creating a safe, walkable neighbourhood	Able to engage in social, physical, sensory and cognitive activities
			Encouraging children's participation in social activities	Being able to move freely from place to place
			Allowing access to green spaces	

mapping of four Active Living Audit tools chosen for illustrative purposes (see Table 14.2). We will call this framework a form-based CA. As noted previously, these audit tools were developed by scholars to evaluate the role of the built environment in promoting physical activity and active living. Here we examine the extent to which aspects of these audit tools may satisfy the form-based CA to evaluate the built environment. In developing this framework we use Lynch's performance characteristics of good city form to organize the basic children's capabilities, which are derived from Nussbaum's original list of universal categories she developed in addressing gender and development (Nussbaum, 2000; Uhm and Banerjee, 2006). These capabilities are presented in the top two rows of the table, labelled as "capabilities". The following four rows, labelled "Built Environment Audit Tools", represent the four Active Living Audit tools[5] and the extent to which aspects of these tools correspond to the children's capabilities, as categorized under Lynch's performance dimensions. The final row at the bottom represents our contribution toward a capability-based audit system for children and the built environment.

The objective of the chapter is to suggest how to assess the built environment's contribution to improving children's capability. Our method employs the conceptual model of children's capabilities, as described above, for comparison with resource-based measures from four audits, each of which gathers the sorts of data commonly used by planning scholars and professionals in evaluating the built environment's contribution to health. Each audit was initially studied as a separate subject, and then analysed for its commonalities to the others regarding underlying egalitarian assumptions about what ought to be distributed equally by the built environment. The analysis represented in Table 14.1 further delineated our focus on children, and with that we compared measures called for by each element of each

Table 14.2 Capability and built environment audits according to Lynch's performance characteristics of good city form

		Vitality	Sense	Fit	Control	Access
Capabilities	**Nussbaum's Universal Capabilities**	Life; bodily health; Bodily integrity	Senses; imagination; thought and emotion	Play	Control over one's environment	Bodily integrity; affiliation; other species
	Children's Capabilities	Being able to be born healthy and to maintain health; able to lead a life of normal length; being secure against bodily accidents and assaults	Able to make sense of place in relation to self; able to experience sensory environment; able to imagine and develop meaning	Able to cognitively and physically engage with environment; able to manipulate environment; able to predict events in settings and relate to them	Being able to participate in environmental decision making; able to take responsibility for one's environment; able to perceive and understand environmental operation and control	Being able to engage in social, physical, sensory and cognitive activities; being able to move freely from place to place
Built Environment Audits – Tools – methods and data collected	**St. Louise Audit (2004)** (phone survey of inhabitants)	• age • general health • walking frequency • walking distance • perception of change in amount of exercise over time	• access to information about facilities Perception of: • facilities on exercise habits • places for walking • accessibility and maintenance of facilities	• presence of destinations and facilities (i.e, schools, day care, playground, and sports field) Perception of: • pedestrian environment	• visibility of environmental information and physical/social order.	• local social commitments • role of social commitments on exercise habits • reasons for non-use of facilities Perception of: • social capital in local community • social dimensions of exercise • unsupervised dogs

Irvine – Minnesota Audit (2006) (specialist observation/ inventory)	• amount and locations of crosswalks • elements of crosswalks • speed limits and traffic slowing measures • outdoor lighting • number and location of front porches • places and amount of shade	• public art • billboards location • monuments, markers and banners • buildings heights • amount and location of abandoned buildings, lots, and barred windows • undifferentiated spaces and building types • graffiti, litter, visible dumpsters, overhead wiring • "adult uses"	• presence and attractiveness of public spaces • undesirable land uses • barriers to pedestrians • sidewalk amenities • steepness of street • safety and convenience of street crossing	• presence of traffic and pedestrian control system • ways to overcome barriers to pedestrians	• crossings • features of crossings • level of pedestrianization • mixed uses • exercise facilities • stationary socializing places • barriers to continuous movement • continuity and maintenance of sidewalks • permanent street closings • pedestrian access points
Neighborhood Walkability Survey (2003) (inhabitants survey)	Perception of: • walking difficulty • barriers to continuous movement	Perception of: • proximity to various destinations • attractiveness of residential homes	Perception of: • walking destinations (i.e., schools, park, rec. center, and gym)	Satisfaction with: • accessibility to and presence of services, businesses, and transits	Perception of: • walking difficulty • transit access • access to local services and shopping

Table 14.2 (Continued)

		Vitality	Sense	Fit	Control	Access
		• presence of excessive auto exhaust pollution, location and amount of shade	• local street systems and traffic environment supportive of walking • social disorders that discourage walking	• quality of local schools and businesses • pedestrian and social activities	• barriers to continuous movement • sidewalk continuity and maintenance location and amounts of trees • continuity of streets	• crossing needs • bike lanes • location, height, and number of trees • perceptions of threat from crime
	Survey of the Physical Environment (2002) (specialist observation/ inventory)	• parking restriction • traffic slowing devices • number of driveway crossovers • outdoor lighting • "eyes on the Street"	• views • maintenance of residential yards • litter • maintenance of public landscape	• presence, type and condition of paths for walking and cycling	Perception of: • attractiveness and easiness for walking and cycling	
Capabilities Audit- methods and additional data	CEBE (Children's travel journals, children's cognitive mapping/photo	Parent description of child: • physical abilities of child regarding stamina, weight, etc.	Child's perceptions: • child's sense of orientation in place and time	Child's use and perceptions: • child's experience of environment	Child's needs and concerns: • child's sense of empowerment and self-esteem	Child's perception of: • causes of changes to setting • historical significance of place

data participatory field observation, parent descriptions of child and specialist observation of environment)

- child's physical disabilities (if any)

Specialist observations/ inventory of:

- design codes, standards, ordinance
- air pollutant levels

- child's congnitive identification with environment
- child's perceptions of special and beautiful places
- child's perceptions of threatening places

Specialist observations/ inventory of:

- views significant to children
- child's perceptions of role of facilities in exercise habits

- child's perception of and preference for outdoor play environment

Specialist observations/ inventory of:

- child's behaviors in outdoor settings

- child's sense of social inclusiveness
- child's perception of an ideal environment

Specialist observations/ inventory of:

- child's special places (i.e., forts, tree houses, etc.)
- child's role in local environmental decision making

- pedestrian safety
- attractiveness of views
- location and amount of greenery
- waste and leftover spaces
- engagement of children's curiosity with features of setting

Specialist observations/ inventory of:

- incongruities of use, worn paths, improvised uses, etc.
- local ordinances regarding speed limits, leash laws, pedestrian safety, etc.
- children's uses of crosswalks, sidewalks, median, etc.
- socialization in transit
- "waste spaces"

audit, and then compared these to the measures required by our capability model.

Our longer-term aim is to develop a framework for evaluating capabilities in the relationship between the built environment and human beings, or what we refer to as "capability evaluation for the built environment" (or CEBE). The CEBE will build on current evaluation instruments, by expanding their descriptions of how the built environment relates to human functionings. The aim of this section is to articulate the types of information that would be needed to undertake a CEBE.

We do not evaluate the environment itself here, but rather attempt to demonstrate the types of data necessary to conduct such an assessment.

14.7. Analysis

We first categorized each of the four Active Living Audits according to their major and minor concerns, and identified a set of measures that all four have in common. We achieved this by describing the specific measures suggested by each of the four audits according to what it *observes* ("landscaping", or "bike lanes", or "sidewalk continuity", etc.) and the *mode* of observation. Methodologically, the four audits used either (a) a survey instrument, either in person or over the telephone; or (b) field observations made by specialists trained for the audit. The four audits consider children as a user group, but only through the perspective of the adult respondents and their responses. We were to discover that the surveys focused on human perceptions about environmental features, by and large, without being physically present in the actual environment (i.e. interviews were not conducted in the field) and the specialist field observers focused on the built environment exclusive of its human inhabitants, as though the specialist were the only person in the neighbourhood. Furthermore, none of these methods require interviews with children or observations of their functionings, although certain measures involving walking to school and such activities are by implication *about* children and their functionings.

We identified 12 categories of measures common to all four audits, obtained from a collective total of 157 different measures. The following are the 12 common measures:

(1) educational facilities and land use;
(2) commercial facilities and land use;
(3) transportation facilities and land use;
(4) presence of cul-de-sacs and permanent street closings;
(5) number of street trees;
(6) condition or maintenance of sidewalks;
(7) presence and/or use of alternative paths;
(8) presence of sidewalks and types of barriers to route choices;

(9) presence/use of bike lanes;
(10) parking facilities: number, visibility, prominence;
(11) proportion of windows at street level; and
(12) presence of visual hazards.

With this initial set of 12 categories it quickly became clear from a capability perspective that all of these measures interact or are interconnected, so that for example the presence of bike lanes (#9) could delimit route choices (#8), thus supporting Sen's observation that "the lack of one functioning affects another" (Sen, 1999: 4, 40, 43, 195, 284). However, these linkages would not be useful to urban planners and designers without further reclassification of the 157 measures according to their roles in influencing children's functionings.

Reclassification of the audits' measures within our children's capabilities model produced a more fine-grained analysis of these measures (i.e. their strengths as well as the lacunae that children's capabilities measures could address) by considering them according to Sen's three indicators of well-being: (1) Millsian utilities; (2) Rawlsian primary goods or general resources; and (3) capabilities. Utilitarian measures, for example, gather information on the effect on inhabitants, from "consumption" of some feature of the environment, and are identified by their *observations of the preference fulfillment or satisfactions accompanying consumption of some feature of the environment* ("Are the buildings attractive or not?", etc.).

Another criterion for identifying utility data was that *they call for an averaging of the preferences and behaviours,* either by inhabitants or specialist observers, and do not consider unique dispositions (i.e. functioning desires) of inhabitants. This approach is quite common in planning and urban design research. The utility *versus* resources distinction appeared more subtly, but perhaps even more profoundly, in the method by which data are intended to be gathered by the four audits. Thus, while an inventory of neighbourhood lawn maintenance may seem a clear matter of resource distribution, if the data are gathered from the perceptions of inhabitants rather than from specialist observations we can assume that the inhabitant is averaging his or her preferences. Similarly, if the specialist observer is asked to average the preferences of inhabitants for hilly *versus* flat terrain, we can assume that he or she is averaging preference and therefore methodologically dealing in utilities.

Resource measures focus on features of the environment as consumable commodities. *A criterion for identifying resource-based measures was the presence or absence of resources* to the exclusion of individual *dispositions* that might make the resource more or less fungible ("number of trees per block", "amount of shade", etc.). It must be kept in mind that the same criterion applies whether the measure treats a resource simply as an object ("presence of sidewalks") or it includes the *quality of the resource* ("condition of side-walks"). This requirement is necessary because the CEBE approach considers resources only in terms of their actual or potential relationship to individual dispositions, and in that relationship neither the resource nor the quality of that resource can describe its fungibility.

Once the utility and resource measures were differentiated and re-categorized in the capability framework, we began the process of teasing out capability measures. Each resource measure was considered in an affordance "template", that is, a conversion relationship between a child and the features of the resource that make it convertible. We classified these affordance relationships between a child and an environment, according to Lynch's performance dimensions of good city form (five major categories, 19 minor), as shown in Table 14.2; the capability measures are shown in the bottom row. These, we believe, offer a cogent set of criteria for evaluating children's built environment capabilities.

By way of examples of the sorts of children's dispositions that can be useful in a CEBE audit of the built environment, consider children's spatial curiosity at certain developmental stages (Hart, 1979);[6] children's poor health habits as shaped by poor access to health care (Borders et al., 2003; Bauman et al., 2006); gender disparities related to childhood obesity (Borders et al., 2006); "setting aggravations" such as pollutants or traffic hazards constricting the child's ability to convert resources to well-being (Banerjee and Baer, 1984); or the highly valued "favourite places" of late adolescents – the location of which are often kept from parents – used by the children as "emotional regulators" (Korpela et al., 2002). The point is that in order to include capability data, an audit must not stop at a description of a "resource environment" (Sloane et al., 2006), but must be evaluated in relation to the individual whose dispositions make the resources more or less convertible to well-being.[7]

Again, our purpose in articulating capability data types was not to make built environment audits necessarily more comprehensive (although it could conceivably have that effect), but specifically to evaluate whether a location – a neighbourhood, let's say – serves to maximize a child's real opportunities to pursue functionings of his or her choice.

14.8. Summary and conclusions

Our principal aims in this chapter were to link Amartya Sen's CA to Kevin Lynch's theory of good city form, to suggest Lynchean criteria evaluating the capability of urban children and to examine how or whether current studies of the person–environment relationship aim to achieve this, or fail to do so. We have focused on children, and on how to identify the relevant capabilities that should define the evaluative space of the built environment.

We have taken guidance from Lynch to define these relevant capabilities in terms of performance characteristics of built form, and have used this essential framework to evaluate some of the currently available Active Living audit tools. We offer this research as background for future work, both scholarly and in the field, investigating the relationship between the city and children's well-being.

Notes

1. Nowhere in his notes, writings and teachings can we find any mention of Sen's work.
2. Even though the construction of the Human Development Index (HDI), was inspired by his work, Sen (1993, 2006), however, argues that the HDI is only a partial use of the CA that conceals many aspects of human development.
3. See Chawla and Heft (2002). And, indeed, Lynch was strongly influenced by the environmental ecology research going on in his lifetime, and depends heavily upon some of its techniques in his field research methods.
4. See the concluding chapter in Chawla et al. (2002) for further details.
5. Each of the four audits were sponsored by the Robert Wood Johnson Foundation's well-known "Active Living" initiative (Active Living Research, 2006).
6. "Children seem to find as much enjoyment in getting to places as they do in being there. In fact, there often is no "there"; they are just exploring" (Hart, 1979: 40).
7. Other example of children's dispositions that could be usefully employed in a capability audit of an environment might be the child's willingness to walk to school or use of park facilities in the light of parents' perception of social threats (Prezza et al., 2005); gender disparities in parents' willingness to let children explore the neighbourhood (McMillan et al., 2006); the sense of ownership and identity that children project onto particular elements of neighbourhoods (Min and Lee, 2006); or how children's bias towards places differ from their parents' (Gearin and Kahle, 2006).

References

Active Living Research (2006), Retrieved 29 January 2007 (http://www.activelivingresearch.org/).
Aitken, S.C. and Ginsburg, S.P. (1998), "Children's Characterization of Place", *Association of Pacific Coast Geographers Yearbook*, 50: 69–86.
Altman, I. and Low, S.M. (1992), *Place Attachment*, Plenum Press, New York.
Arnstein, S. (1969), "The Ladder of Citizen Participation", *Journal of the American Institute of Planners*, 35: 216–224.
Banerjee, T. (1993), "Market Planning, Market Planners, and Planner Market", *Journal of the American Planning Association*, 59(3): 347–352.
Banerjee, T. and Baer, W. (1984), *Beyond the Neighbourhood Unit: Residential Environments and Public Policy*, Plenum Press, New York and London.
Barker, R. (1951), *One Boy's Day: A Specimen Record of Behaviour*, Harper, New York.
Bartlett, S. (2005), Water, Sanitation and Urban Children: The Need to Go Beyond "Improved" Provision [electronic Version], *Children, Youth and Environments*, 15: 115–137. Retrieved 15 February 2007 (http://www.colorado.edu/journals/cye).

Bartlett, S., Hart, R., Satterthwaite, D., de la Barra, X. and Missair, A. (1999), *Cities for Children: Children's Rights, Poverty and Urban Management*, Earthscan, London.

Bates, D.V. (1995), "The Effects of Air Pollution on Children", *Environmental Health Perspectives*, 103(Suppl. 6), 49–53.

Bauman, L.J., Silver, E.J. and Stein, R.E.K. (2006), "Cumulative Social Disadvantage and Child Health", *Pediatrics*, 117: 1321–1328.

Bearer, C.F. (1995), "How Are Children Different from Adults?", *Environmental Health Perspectives*, 103(Suppl. 6): 7–12.

Borders, T.F., Brannon-Goedeke, A., Arif A. and Xu, K.T. (2003), "Parents' Reports of Children's Medical Care Access: Are there Mexican-American Versus Non-Hispanic White Disparities?", *Medical Care*, 42: 884–892.

Borders, T.F., Rohrer, J.E. and Cardelli, K.M. (2006), "Gender-Specific Disparities in Obesity", *Journal of Community Health*, 31(1): 57–68.

Braza, M., Shoemaker, W. and Seeley, A. (2004), "Neighbourhood Design and Rates of Walking and Biking to Elementary School in 34 California Communities", *American Journal of Health Promotion*, 19(12): 128–136.

Campbell, A., Converse, P. and Rogers, W. (1976), *The Quality of American Life: Perceptions, Evaluations, and Satisfactions*, Russell Sage Foundation, New York.

Carr, S. and Lynch, K. (1968), "Where Learning Happens", *Daedalus*, 97(4): 1277–1291.

Chapin, S. (1974), *Human Activity Patterns in the City: Things People Do in Time and Space*, Wiley, New York.

Chawla, L. (ed.) (2002), *Growing Up in an Urbanising World*, Earthscan, London.

Chawla, L. and Heft, H. (2002), "Children's Competence and the Ecology of Communities: A Functional Approach to the Evaluation of Participation", *Journal of Environmental Psychology*, 22: 201–216.

Clark, G. and Dear, M. (1984), *State Apparatus: Structure and Language of Legitimacy*, Allen & Unwin, Boston.

Comim, F., Qizilbash, M. and Alkire, S. (eds) (2008), *The Capability Approach: Concepts, Measures and Applications*, Cambridge University Press, Cambridge.

Crocker, D.A. (1992), "Functioning and Capability: The Foundation of Sen's and Nussbaum's Development Ethic", *Political Theory*, 20(4): 584–612.

Evans, G.W. (2006), "Child Development and the Physical Environment", *Annual Review of Psychology*, 67: 423–451.

Frumkin, H. (2002), "Urban Sprawl and Public Health", *Public Health Report*, 17: 201–217.

Gearin E. and Kahle, C. (2006), "Teen and Adult Perceptions of Urban Green Space in Los Angeles", *Children, Youth and Environments*, 16(1): 25–48.

Gibson, J.J. (1966), *The Senses Considered as Perceptual Systems* (pp. xiv, 335), Houghton Mifflin, Boston.

Gold, J. (1972), "Non-use of Neighbourhood Parks" , *Journal of the American Institute of Planners*, 38: 369–378.

Hart, R. (1992), *Children's Participation: From Tokenism to Citizenship*, UNICEF, Florence.

Hart, R. (ed.) (1979), *Children's Experience of Place*, Knopf, New York.

Harvey, D. (1973), *Social Justice and the City*, Johns Hopkins University Press, Baltimore.

Jans, M. (2004), "Children as Citizens: Towards a Contemporary Notion of Child Participation", *Childhood*, 11(1): 27–44.

Kerr, J., Rosenberg, D., Sallis, J.F., Saelens, B.E., Frank, L.D. and Conway, T.L. (2006), "Active Commuting to School: Associations with Environment and Parental Concerns", *Medicine & Science in Sports & Exercise*, 38(4): 787–794.

Korpela, K., Kytta, M. and Hartig, T. (2002), "Restorative Experience, Self-Regulation, and Children's Place Preferences", *Journal of Environmental Psychology*, 22: 387–398.

Lieberg, M. (1997), "Youth in their Local Environment", in R. Camstra (ed.), *Growing Up in A Changing Urban Landscape*, Van Gorcum, Assen, pp. 90–108.

Lynch, K. (1960), *The Image of the City*, MIT Press, Cambridge, MA.

Lynch, K. (1984), *Good City Form* [11th paperback edn], MIT Press, Cambridge, Mass.

Lynch, K. (ed.) (1977), *Growing Up in Cities: Studies of the Spatial Environment of Adolescence in Cracow, Melbourne, Mexico City, Salta, Toulca, and Warszawa*, MIT Press, Cambridge.

Lynch, K. and Lukashok, A.K. (1996), "Some Childhood Memories of the City", in T. Banerjee and M. Southworth (eds), *City Sense and City Design: Writings and Projects of Kevin Lynch*, MIT Press, Cambridge, London, pp. 154–173.

Maslow, A.H. (1943), "A Theory of Human Motivation", *Psychological Review*, 50: 370–396.

Matthews, H. (1992), *Making Sense of Place; Children's Understanding of Large- Scale Environments*, Harvester Wheatsheaf, Hemel Hempstead.

Matthews, H., Limb, M. and Taylor, M. (1999), "Young People's Participation and Representation in Society", *Geoforum*, 30: 135–144.

McMillan, T., Day, K., Boarnet, M., Alfonzo, M. and Anderson, C. (2006), "Johnny Walks to School – Does Jane? Sex Difference in Children's Active Travel to School" [electronic version], *Children, Youth and Environments*, 16: 75–89 (retrieved 19 January 2007 from http//:www.colorado.edu/journals/cye/).

McMillan, T. (2003), *Walking and Urban Form: Modeling and Testing Parental Decision about Children's Travel*, Unpublished PhD dissertation, University of California, Irvine.

Min, B. and Lee, J. (2006), "Children's Neighbourhood Place As a Psychological and Behavioural Domain", *Journal of Environmental Psychology*, 26: 51–71.

Moore, R.C. (1986), *Childhood's Domain: Play and Place in Child Development*, Croom Helm, London and Dover, NH.

Nussbaum, M.C. (2000), *Women and Human Development: The Capabilities Approach*, CUP, Cambridge and New York.

Nussbaum, M.C. and Glover, J. (eds) (1995), *Women, Culture and Development*, Clarendon Press, Oxford.

Nussbaum, M.C. and Sen, A.K. (eds) (1993), *The Quality of Life*, Clarendon Press, Oxford.

O'Brien, M., Jones, D., Sloan, D. and Rustin, M. (2000), "Children's Independent Spatial Mobility in the Urban Public Realm", *Childhood*, 7(3): 257–277.

Prezza, M., Alparone, F.R., Cristallo, C. and Luigi, S. (2005), "Parental Perception of Social Risk and of Positive Potentiality of Outdoor Autonomy for Children: The Development of Two Instruments", *Journal of Environmental Psychology*, 25: 437–453.

Prezza, M., Pilloni, S., Morabito, C., Sersante, C., Romana, F., Maria, A. et al. (2001), "The Influence of Psychosocial and Environmental Factors on Children's Independent Mobility and Relationship to Peer Frequentation", *Journal of Community & Applied Social Psychology*, 11(6): 435–450.

Proshansky, H.M. and Fabian, A.K. (1987), "The Development of Place Identity in Child", in C.S. Weinstein and T.G. David (eds), *Spaces for Children: The Built Environment and Child Development*, Plenum Press, New York and London, pp. 21–40.

Rawls, J. (1974), *A Theory of Justice*, Harvard University Press, Cambridge, MA.

Rawls, J. (2001), *Justice as Fairness: A Restatement*, E. Kelly (ed.), Harvard University Press, Cambridge, MA.

Relph, E. (1976), *Place and Placelessness*, Pion, London.

Richardson, H. and Gordon, P. (1993), "Market Planning: Oxymoron or Common Sense?", *Journal of the American Planning Association*, 59(3): 347–352.

Rissotto, A. and Tonucci, F. (2002), "Freedom of Movement and Environmental Knowledge in Elementary School Children", *Journal of Environmental Psychology*, 22(1): 65–77.

Sen, A.K. (1993), "Capability and Well-being", in M.C. Nussbaum and A.K. Sen (eds), *The Quality of Life*, Clarendon Press, Oxford, pp. 30–53.

Sen, A.K. (1999), *Development as Freedom*, Knopf, New York.

Sen, A.K. (2006), "Human Development Index", in D.A. Clark (ed.), *The Elgar Companion to Development Studies*, Edward Elgar, Cheltenham, pp. 256–260.

Sennett, R. (1971), *Use of Disorder: Personal Identity and City Life*, Vintage Books, New York.

Simpson, B. (1997), "Towards the Participation of Children and Young People in Urban Planning and Design", *Urban Studies*, 34(5–6): 907–925.

Sloane, D., Nascimento, L., Flynn, G., Lewis, L., Guinyard, J.J., Galloway-Gilliam, L. et al. (2006), "Assessing Resource Environments to Target Prevention Interventions in Community Chronic Disease Control", *Journal of Health Care for the Poor and Underserved*, 17(2): 146–158.

Southworth, M. and Southworth, S. (1974), "The Educative City", in G. Coates (ed.), *Alternative Learning Environments*, Dowden, Hutchinson & Ross, Inc., Stroudsberg, pp. 274–281

Talen, E. and Coffindaffer, M. (1999), "The Utopianism of Children: An Empirical Study of Children's Neighbourhood Design Preference", *Journal of Planning Education and Research*, 18: 321–331.

Tuan, Y.-f. (1977), *Space and Place: The Perspective of Experience*, University of Minnesota Press, Minneapolis.

Uhm, A.J. and Banerjee, T. (2006), *Conceptualizing the Child Friendly Neighbourhood: A Question of Form, Family, and Functioning*, Paper presented at the 1st International Symposium on Environment, Behaviour, and Society, Sydney, Australia.

UNICEF (2004), *Building Child Friendly Cities: A Framework for Action*, UNICEF Innocenti Research Center, Florence.

Van Vliet, W. (1981), "Neighbourhood Evaluations by City and Suburban Children", *Journal of the American Planning Association*, 47(4): 458–466.

Part IV
Conclusions

15
Developing Children's Capabilities: The Role of Emotions and Parenting Style

Flavio Comim

15.1. Introduction

The general argument that pervades this book is that using the CA to address children's issues can provide a fruitful path to evaluate and promote their development. Different chapters delve into distinct methodologies and perspectives, illustrating the diversity of solutions that can be found by applying the CA to children's development. In particular, several chapters in this book support a view of children not as passive beneficiaries of adults' concerns but as agents, with dreams and choices of their own.

The CA provides a humanistic way of thinking about public policies that entails government's actions and the participation of the general public. In addition, it brings into perspective the cognitive role of emotions and a view of human values that are essential for the design of new human development policies. The main objective of this penultimate chapter is to consider some of the results presented in earlier chapters and to explore how these results can be used to shape policy and practice. Before advancing some concrete solutions, it is useful to review some of the analyses presented in the book and focus on some core issues that may provide a good illustration of incorporating key conclusions into practice.

15.2. Towards a child-centred capability approach

When narrowly interpreted, the CA is mostly seen as a new informational space for normative evaluations of well-being or states of affairs. This narrow interpretation is, however, important for focusing our attention on the choice of new domains and variables in understanding children's development and limitations. Instead of representing people merely as a locus of utilities, resources or subjective viewpoints, the CA proposes to see them according to what they are able to be and to do, with their respective liberties that are considered important to them.[1] Children are, by definition, beings in movement, and a contextualization of their well-being in terms of beings and doings follows to a certain extent a close correspondence with the nature of being a child – animated beings in development rather than simply a locus of utilities or resources. By doing so, it brings to human development a perspective centred on the promotion of agency and autonomy as part of human flourishing (see Chapter 2).

On the other hand, when broadly interpreted, the CA represents a revival of concerns about human dignity and social justice in shaping development policies, providing not merely a new informational space for understanding and evaluating human well-being as a set of freedoms but, most importantly, a new perspective for thinking about life purposes, human values, public reasoning and social organization. Whereas much has already been said about the issue of children's choices,[2] the emphasis here is about how children's autonomy is shaped with human values that foster identities and attitudes as future citizens.

When human life is understood as a succession of temporal stages, childhood becomes the pillar towards the construction of a decent society. Participatory processes have become the main engine of human development but, quite often, children are denied involvement, when a critical examination of oneself and the others' points of view (the basis of an examined participation) is an ability that should be part of the early development of children as soon as they are able to speak. Methodologies for capturing children's voices have been presented in this book (Chapters 4–6), offering a wide range of alternatives for identifying normative dimensions for assessing children's capabilities, with focus on issues of agency, autonomy, love and care.

The benefits of a child-centred approach to human development are multiple. Firstly, it brings conceptual attention to the role of capability dynamics (i.e. evolving capabilities, see especially Chapter 2) and to processes of capability building. Secondly, it deepens our understanding of a different range of social injustices that seem much more subtle but are in fact very damaging, as they often occur over the whole of a human life. Thirdly, it throws new light on the role of families in human development. Fourthly, it stimulates integrated analysis, considering how multiple stakeholders, such as families, schools or government can affect children's well-being. Fifthly, it highlights the importance of studying the links between well-being and time allocation. Whereas many poor children are forced to grow up quickly to face the world, many others are accorded considerable protection for many years. For children, time is the essence of the matter of being a child. Children need time with their parents, time for playing, time for being creative and happy during which they are protected from the world. Finally, a child-centred approach emphasizes the development of emotions as part of growing up and structuring capabilities. Children need to be prepared for moral interaction. They need a grasp of simple facts to notice the feelings of living creatures. As they grow older, their moral abilities need to become more complex to differentiate a wide range of situations, attributing emotions to others.

The implications of a child-centred approach to the development of child-friendly policies are striking. When children's agency is recognized, as capable human beings, they can be seen as part of the solution and not merely as part of the problem. Moreover, policies can overcome a short-term rescue strategy moving towards the provision of freedoms, allowing a long-term approach to children's development of capabilities. The chapters addressing street children issues in this book illuminate the contexts in which supporting children's agency provides innovative solutions to their development.

The temporal perspective added by a child-centred CA invites us to consider the processes under which everyday relationships are built and how they impact on children. Understanding the temporal and spatial dimensions of capabilities can throw new light on the approach, bringing elements of subjectivity that are necessary for delving into people's views of their own problems.

Many education systems are still constituted by a utilitarian view of the world, centred on the notion of human capital and transmission of transferable skills. A child-centred CA can examine the utilitarian foundations of educational systems, focusing on the importance of tackling learning life skills that should teach children to be more autonomous, to cooperate, to live in society with the aim of fostering children to flourish as human beings, learning how to dream and to have aspirations about a better world.

In what has been said, two elements are crucial during childhood: namely, the role of emotions and the importance of families and caregivers (including teachers and tutors) in promoting children's well-being and evolving capabilities. In what follows, we briefly examine these elements to consider how practices and policies can be improved.

15.3. The role of emotions during childhood

If emotions are central to the building of children's ethical reasoning, as often argued by Martha Nussbaum (1995, 1997, 2006), practices and policies need to be changed to investigate their links with emotions. Most importantly, new practices and policies can be seen differently under this new light. For instance, a father singing nursery songs to his baby daughter can be seen as part of the building of her moral life and, as such, can be understood as an important practice that should be respected and supported by policy makers.

Emotions get a bad press from utilitarians. They are normally considered unsuitable for deliberation from a rationalistic point of view. But, as Nussbaum has convincingly argued in her books on this issue, emotions have a cognitive role that is fundamental for our deliberative beliefs. Emotions enable people to perceive features in a situation that are worthy of value. Only solipsistic individuals would live in a world without emotions. The human sense of value is built upon interactions for which emotional cognition plays an important role. Without emotions our actions would be different. As put by Nussbaum (1995: 74):

> Appropriate emotions are useful in showing us what we might do and also morally valuable in their own right, as recognitions of the character of the situation before us. Furthermore, they motivate appropriate action. Of course, not always emotions are good guides for action, for instance, when they are not based on a true view of the facts. But this caveat would also be applicable for other sorts of beliefs based on facts or conjectures.

Understanding the role of emotions in shaping human values and rationality allows us to see children's responses to oppression and abandonment, quite often qualified merely as childhood misbehaviours, in a new light. Children's moral development needs to be nourished and strategies and policies for that have to be part of new ways of promoting children's capabilities. Children's misbehaviours should be seen as part of their upbringing, and causes that relate to their families, nurseries, schools and neighbourhoods need to be investigated. Blaming the victims might be the easiest but it is rarely the best option.

Thinking about emotions brings into analysis a wide range of policies for children's development that can be classified into the following categories:

I Micro: they are bottom-up, shaped by people in their daily actions and ordinary affairs rather than by guidelines established by far-away bureaucracies.

II Practical: they are seen as defined by practical and concrete instances rather than based on abstract ideas. Being grounded on daily affairs means that they are manifested in concrete actions rather than on large policy-making strategies.

III Integrated: they are seen as part of relationships among children, families, schools and other agents. As a result, policies should be viewed in terms of their synergies, complementarities and trade-offs. Sectorial policies do not seem more effective than integrated policies.

IV Diverse: policies motivated by recognition of the role of emotions in shaping children's moral reasoning can be diverse because people live a variety of situations that shape their emotions.

As illustrations we could mention policies informed by the acknowledgement of the cognitive role of emotions for children[3]:

- singing a nursery song to children;
- reading books that develop their literary imagination[4];
- carrying out a genuine dialogue with children;
- choosing a "provocative and perceptive" teacher for stimulating children's minds; and
- choosing stories to read to children that foster human identity.

Thinking about the formation of children's values in relation to their emotions can illuminate how different functionings and capabilities are ranked by children. Values are formed very early in life and are part of individuals' motivations. Values can fulfil several roles. They are important for defining people's views, opinions and criteria for social engagement. They are the basis for individual and organizational behavioural choice.[5] Their psychological nature helps people to rationalize their experiences, assisting them in keeping their self-esteem. Different values are part of integrated systems that evolve as people get older.[6] As children become teenagers they are exposed to different situations and experiences.

In particular, it is interesting to note that values are mostly formed by concrete life experiences. On the one hand, values may influence behaviours by shaping attitudes and cultures. On the other hand, concrete behaviour can influence values. This acknowledgement is relevant for considering how different policies can be constituted by practices rather than by abstract guidelines.

15.4. Parenting style

Families are very important to the promotion of children's capabilities. This is not merely a theoretical observation but a practical consideration, because it is to a large extent through families that policies benefiting children are implemented. Families are networks of love and care that follow different arrangements.[7] It is within families that children can be subjected to moral and physical abuses and have their development compromised or challenged (as resilience can have a role). Therefore, thinking about families is a first step towards considering how children's autonomy can be shaped and how individuals can be brought up as moral agents.

Individuals' emotions are influenced by their families' practices. Families' influence is characterized according to the level of interaction between parents and children. Early socialization that families provide to their children influences future development, such as self-regulation of their emotions, critical thinking and behaviour. It is also relevant in shaping how children internalize values introduced by their parents' behaviour. It is within early socialization that children internalize their values and how they should behave and relate towards others. It is from this initial set of values that children redefine their perception of reality and future behaviour. Emotions are shaped during this period and children start organizing in their minds the importance of (a) moral rules; (b) his or her actions; and (c) impacts on others (see Hoffmann, 1994).

Focusing on emotions, families and values to address children's issues invites us to consider the role of parenting style in developing children's capabilities. The impacts of parental practices and styles on children can be wide open, influencing children's academic performance and their sense of independence, cooperation and social empathy.

Negative parental practices can include negligence, physical and psychological abuse, inconsistent discipline and punishment, overbearing monitoring and negative communication. Many of these practices are not fully understood or rationalized by parents who do not realize their importance to the development of their children. For instance, negligence, the parental attitude characterized by omission, lack of attention, lack of concern, absence and lack of affection towards their children, is often rarely seen as a form of violence (see Darling and Steinberg, 1993). Similarly, negative communication, based on threats, shouting, swearing, insults and ironies can be transformed into the routine form of communication between parents and children, promoting aggressive behaviour in the family.

Parental practices are consolidated into parenting styles that register certain behavioural patterns among parents. The most influential styles are as follows:

- Authoritative: parental control with understanding, open communication, respect, emotional support. Parents offer clear guidelines and love.
- Authoritarian: rigorous assessment of children's behaviour, with rigid norms, strict punishment and little sympathy for children's difficulties. Parents do not offer emotional support.
- Permissive: parents condone all actions and behaviour carried out by children. They offer love and sympathy but no control and concern with limits. Sometimes parents who feel absentees try to compensate for their absence by being permissive.
- Negligence: lack of interest and involvement. Parents spend little time with their families, with low levels of support and control.

The message behind this classification is straightforward: daily actions might be invisible to people who are responsible for children's development, but when understood as part of a style they can reveal that children might be subjected to all forms of socialization patterns that can, to a large extent, explain constraints and shortcomings in promoting children's capabilities.

The parenting style most conducive to human development is the authoritative, showing how children need not only love, help, support and dialogue, but also supervision, rules and clear guidelines about what can and what can't be done in order to promote their autonomy and well-being (see Shaffer, 1989). This result is very important for informing children-friendly policies that depend on parents for their implementation.

15.5. Children-centred public policies

Focusing on childhood development can help us reconsider which policies are appropriate for promoting children's capabilities and which stakeholders should be involved. Public policies usually tend to be seen from within a utilitarian tradition, according to which governments are the only moral agents for allocation of responsibilities.[8] Part of the argument used to transfer responsibilities to governments can be fairly attributed to the fact that governments have the instruments for changing social realities, whereas quite often individuals have only very limited means at their disposal. However, it is precisely when individuals feel their lack of control over social reality that governments are less accountable and less likely to perform the much-needed actions to change this reality. Collective action then becomes impossible. Individuals end up not seeing the relevance of their participation and blaming governments for failures that are often socially built.

Within the Basic Needs perspective, different normative criteria are specified for rethinking a list of reasoned human needs[9] within local cultures, claiming that universal needs can be translated into different local satisfier characteristics. However, in its latest format of "basic needs", this approach called for a universal normative mode that very much reduced the importance of people's self-expression, leading to a view of public policy centred on the provision of public goods, such as health and education. Within this framework, individuals also seem to struggle to find a place to be recognized as moral agents in which responsibility and values can be made meaningful.[10]

The CA represents a positive turn towards new forms of reasoned participation and internal scrutiny of development. In its applied format, namely, the Human Development perspective, it gave life to a wide variety of analyses addressing a rich range of topics, from gender inequality to governance or from poverty to climate change. The search for criteria of social justice as a means for qualifying development combines an emphasis on individuals' autonomy with arguments for democracy and public reasoning in shaping public policies. Within a children-centred public policy focused on the promotion of their capabilities, this perspective is redirected towards considerations that see individuals in their full trajectories as human beings. By doing so, inter-temporal elements are naturally included and more importance is given to earlier policies towards the promotion of children's capabilities. The relevance of age is normally underestimated in the patterning of individuals' life courses.

Childhood is a phenomenon that should not be taken for granted by human development. Children are not simply "becomings", they are also "beings" with values, personalities, imagination, feelings and dreams. And need to be respected as such by having their views considered as standards for assessing and monitoring their development. When children are considered reliable informants they become relevant for development analysis. In this book several chapters explore methodologies that tackle children as having much to offer to research. As a result, different techniques offer perspectives for understanding and intervening with real-life policies that invite citizens and children themselves to overcome the stigma of being part of the problem in an effort to become part of the solution.[11]

Children-centred public policies do not need to be restricted to government policies. They should involve families, schools and children themselves. Governments are important for macro policies, but to a large extent much of what happens to children can be improved by micro policies, namely, by changing parental and school practices, by allowing children opportunities for self-improvement, by focusing on early stages of children's lives and what happens next, by understanding how daily-life attitudes can have large impacts in the future. Children are co-constructors of society and need to be respected as such, as we will see in this book's "final remarks".

Notes

1. This is also the case independently from the CA, having been interpreted as a contrasting or complementary perspective towards others. For this discussion between different interpretations of the approach, see Sen (1992).
2. See, for instance, Nussbaum (2006) for further discussions.
3. These recommendations appear in several books written by Nussbaum that are cited in this chapter. They are re-contextualized as part of policy-making strategies.
4. Nussbaum (1997: 92, 106) argues that "Literary understanding ... promotes habits of mind that lead toward social equality in that they contribute to the dismantling of the stereotypes that support group hatred" and "If literature is a representation of human possibilities, the works of literature we choose will inevitably respond to and further develop our sense of who we are and might be."
5. See, for instance, Kluckhohn (1951).
6. See Schwartz (1994).
7. This broad definition allows consideration of homosexual parental arrangements or single parental arrangements. On the other hand, it reminds us that we can be part of a traditional parental arrangement but not be part of a family if the functions of care and love are not exercised.
8. The argument can be seen from the perspective of governments in which individuals would find "all sorts of excuses" for allocating their responsibilities to governments. For an interesting discussion about the state as a moral agent see Robert Goodin, (1995, Chapter 2).

9. See, for instance, Doyal and Gough (1991).
10. See the excellent discussion by Gasper (2004) for further analysis on the basic needs approach.
11. See the excellent collection of papers in the book edited by Greene and Hogan (2005).

References

Darling, N. and Steinberg, L. (1993), "Parenting Style as Context: An Integrative Model", *Psychological Bulletin*, 113: 487–496.

Doyal, L. and Gough, I. (1991), *A Theory of Need*, Macmillan, London.

Gasper, D. (2004), *The Ethics of Development*, Edinburgh University Press, Edinburgh.

Goodin, R. (1995), *Utilitarianism as a Public Philosophy*, CUP, Cambridge.

Greene, S. and Hogan, D. (2005), *Researching Children's Experience: Approaches and Methods*, Sage, London.

Hoffmann, M.L. (1994), "Discipline and Internalisation", *Developmental Psychology*, 30: 26–28.

Kluckhohn, C.K. (1951), "Values and Value Orientation in the Theory of Action", in T. Parsons and E. Shilds (eds), *Toward a General Theory of Action*, Harvard University Press, Cambridge, MA, pp. 388–433.

Nussbaum, M. (1995), "Aristotle, Nature and Ethics", in J.H.J. Altham and R. Harrison (eds), *World, Mind and Ethics*, Cambridge University Press, Cambridge, pp. 86–131.

Nussbaum, M. (1997), *Cultivating Humanity: A Classical Defense of Reform in Liberal Education*, Harvard University Press, Cambridge, MA.

Nussbaum, M. (2006), *Frontiers of Justice: Disability, Nationality, Species Membership*, The Belknap Press of Harvard University, Cambridge, MA.

Schwartz, S. (1994), "Are There Universal Aspects in the Structure and Contents of Human Values?", *Journal of Social Issues*, 50: 19–45.

Sen, A.K. (1992), *Inequality Re-examined*, OUP, Oxford.

Shaffer, D. (1989), *Development Psychology: Childhood and Adolescence*, Brooks, Cole Publishing Company, Pacific Grove, CA.

16
Final Remarks and Conclusions: The Promotion of Children's Active Participation

Mario Biggeri, Flavio Comim and Jérôme Ballet

This book tries to show that a new conceptual framework and shift in policy design is required to help promote children's well-being and enhance their "evolving capabilities". The arguments in this book have been developed and refined following workshops, seminars and conferences held over a number of years and are likely to be the subject of future debate. The chapters in this book represent a wide range of perspectives and have been written by people from various countries with different disciplinary backgrounds, methodologies and life experiences. However, all are committed to working towards a more just world in which children can be respected as active agents in their own right. For this reason we would like to end this book with some thoughts that put our commitment to changing the world through a "child-centred CA" into perspective. We also reflect on the goals that need to be achieved to make this a reality.

The CA is a way to think about our lives in our societies and how we can engage as human beings in a struggle for justice and dignity for all. As we look at the world with critical minds it is impossible to hide from the many injustices and forms of exploitation that befall children. Children are amongst the most vulnerable and unprotected members of society, often subject to hunger, physical and moral abuses or are denied the most basic rights to a life with dignity.

Thinking about "beings" and "doings" is not just a strategy for broadening the information base beyond utility or resources, but a way of engaging with individuals in order to reflect upon the things that are relevant to their daily lives and close to their hearts and minds. The use of the CA for addressing children's issues acknowledges several arguments for seeing children's priorities and potentialities as part of the solution for a more just world.

If development relies on people's freedom to make decisions and advance key objectives in order to be agents of change, children will need the freedom to be educated, to be loved and cared for, to speak in public without shame, to be respected and to have freedom of expression and association (amongst many other capabilities).[1] However it is also by being agents that people (including children) can build the environment in which they can be educated, loved and cared for and speak freely, and so on. In this sense, it is important to point out also that policy instruments are not necessarily a panacea. They need to be tailored and complemented with other instruments to reach the goal of capability expansion. As a matter of fact, as argued by Amartya Sen, "What opportunities children have today and will have tomorrow, in line with what they can be reasonably expected to want, is a matter of public policy and social programmes, involving a great many agencies" (Sen, 2007: p. 10). In this perspective, the responsibility of policy makers is to create an environment – by including children themselves in the process – which facilitates the ability of children to pursue worthwhile and flourishing lives. It is important, however, to strike a balance between the expansion of intrinsic and instrumental capabilities on the one hand, and short-term *versus* long-term objectives that may conflict and yield trade-offs, on the other. The capacity to balance and complement short-term and long-term perspectives is a reality that needs to be addressed by different disciplines.

Most of the chapters, from different fields and perspectives, recognize that children are beings endowed with different degrees of autonomy that should be respected in formulating policies that are targeted at them. Such policies should encourage proactive behaviour of children in decision-making processes. Indeed, fostering their participation is a key part in the process of evolving capabilities in order to take into account their priorities, their values and aspirations. For instance, education in a Human Development and Capability perspective should not be reduced to learning mathematics or developing literature skills, but should also incorporate life-learning skills; it should teach children to be more autonomous and to cooperate and to interact with others and with the "world". Moreover, in the task of educating their children, parents and tutors could be more autonomy supportive (e.g. giving an internal frame of reference, providing a meaningful rationale, allowing choices, encouraging self-perspective and critical thinking).

As far as the question of autonomy is concerned, the process by which choices are made is even more important than choices themselves. In other words, it is relevant to internalize freedom of choice through the choice process, and not through choices themselves. It follows that it is necessary to provide children with learning, as well as a voice in the learning process, in terms of choice-guiding rules. These must be the subject of an argued discussion with children, who will thus come to participate in the elaboration of decision rules concerning them. While the capacity to aspire relates to the aspiration as such, the capability to aspire is connected with freedom to aspire, which entails examining the process behind aspirations.[2] Therefore, it is not just a question of opening up multiple opportunities, even if this can be the starting point in case of deprivations, but seeing to it that, amongst a set of limited and achievable choices, children may develop a capability to aspire through their involvement in the decision making process.

We have seen that applying the CA to children encourages a rethinking of the CA itself through a new perspective that calls for a far more dynamic approach. It opens new perspectives on the role of interaction among different capabilities for the same individual; it also raises the possibility of children as capable agents (at different levels of maturity) and highlights the need to take into account the interrelation of capabilities among adults and children and between children.

These arguments, as emphasized in the Chapter 15 have strong policy implications and unlock new frontiers for research regarding agency and empowerment, participation and methods to participate regarding the relationships of the child with his/her parents and family, friends, school teachers, caregivers, community and society. In particular, looking at children's issues generates several key insights about the use of the approach and our own actions:

- analyses of different conceptions of well-being and well-becoming, and how these evolve along with one's age and life experiences;
- research on synergies between different capabilities, especially those with high instrumental significance, should be promoted;
- policy-making decisions cannot be understood outside the context of people's values;
- concerns about the freedom and the process aspect of capabilities should receive increasing attention and should address the links between individuals and the societies in which they live; and
- concepts such as action/interaction, autonomy/heteronomy, restriction/tutorial and products/processes, that are highlighted when discussing children's issues, should be part of general concerns about the application of the CA.

Overall, the book is a tentative to committing to a single strategy for making the CA operational. Instead, the focus is on processes and adapting qualitative and/or quantitative methods or exploring new methodologies for complex data elaboration for more relevant and effective policy planning.

When examining the capability deprivation of children, we do not appear to live in "a world fit for children" – to paraphrase the UN (2002) – in which many children are able to flourish or even achieve a minimally decent form of life. But this is no reason to treat children as incapable or passive sufferers without recognizing that they might part of the solution for achieving a better life with dignity. For this reason, children should be seen, so we argue, as part of the process, i.e. as agents and social actors. In this respect we build upon the observations made by Sen and Landsdown regarding the development of people and children: "The people have to be seen ... as being actively involved – given the opportunity – in shaping their own destiny, and not just as passive recipients of the fruits of cunning development programs" (Sen, 1999: 53). Moreover, "There is no lower age limit imposed on the exercise of the right to participate. It extends therefore to any child who has a view on a matter of concern to them" (Lansdown, 2001: 2). Indeed, as stressed by Lansdown, there are many issues that even very small children are capable of understanding and to which they can contribute thoughtful opinions.

This is why, in this book, we have tried to be concrete and positive, raising policies and conclusions that can inspire new approaches for improving the lives of millions of children all over the world. We have delved into the role of civil society and international organizations in paving the way for children to flourish and expand their capabilities in a good and sustainable environment.[3] For the sake of this we have to promote values and good societies able to listen to children as full citizens and thus to actively engage with them to explore solutions for a better future. Children's social participation needs to be visible in public contexts – a clear manifestation of their citizenship and inclusion in a society that includes a full range of rights and opportunities. These considerations push us in the direction of the self-determination human rights approach (Freeman, 1998).

If, as Sen argues, democracy means to participate in a public deliberation (Sen, 2006; Crocker, 2007), society should aim to form capable agents.[4] Therefore, the process to acquire communicative competences (Habermas, 1981), including dialogical attitudes and argumentative practice, become central. Indeed, the development of a democratic society implies the promotion of critical, creative and care thinking in its citizens so to enhance their autonomy and at the same time open their minds to confrontation with different perspectives and points of view (Santi, 2007). Promoting children's active participation means also socializing children towards an "understanding of their own competencies", i.e. to a sense of responsibility and skills in planning, designing, monitoring and managing social contexts (Matthews, 2003) and thus participating in changing factors affecting children's evolving capabilities (Prout, 2005).

Thinking in terms of beings and doings invites us to consider not only what governments should do to promote children's freedoms, but what each of us can do in our daily lives to respect children and promote fair conditions that help them live with dignity. Policies for children's equal opportunities can be part of governments' strategies and of our daily practices (including professional competences, adequate structures), as teachers, parents, academics, doctors and so on.[5]

Whether a child can effectively participate in society and evolve capabilities over time depends on several conditions, including access to information, necessary training, openness of parents and other adults to dialogue and learning from other children, and having access to safe spaces in the family, community and society that fosters appropriate dialogue. It also depends on the given socio-cultural, economic and political context. Most of all, authentic and meaningful participation requires a radical shift in adult thinking and behaviour – from an exclusionary to an inclusionary approach to children and their capabilities – from a world defined solely by adults to one in which children contribute to building the kind of world they want to live in (UNICEF, 2002: 5; see also the new report UNICEF, 2011).

Children's collective actions and identity[6] constitute the start of this new process of emancipation (which also includes responsibilities). Participation and peaceful struggle for recognition are preconditions for empowerment and for realizing and claiming new rights. Over the last century, women and people with disabilities have launched important and reasonably successful political movements that have reformed many societies.[7] The hope is that children's movements with the support of adults and involvement of government will be able to promote further reform, especially in terms of creating new instruments for participation and deliberation – at least at the local level – that incorporate social monitoring, appropriate forms of communication and alliances with NGOs and civil society.

Notes

1. As stated in the first Human Development Report (UNDP, 1990: 11), "the most basic capabilities for human development are to lead long and healthy lives, to be knowledgeable, to have access to the resources needed for a decent standard of living and to be able to participate in the life of the community. Without these, many choices are simply not available, and many opportunities in life remain inaccessible." According to Sen and Dreze, participation has also an intrinsic value for the quality of life. Indeed being able to do something not only for oneself but also for other members of the society is one of the elementary freedoms which people have reason to value. The popular appeal of many social movements in India confirms that this basic capability is highly valued even among people who lead very deprived lives in material terms (Sen and Dreze, 2002: 359).
2. Moreover the capability to aspire assumes an important role in children's well-being and well-becoming (Hart, 2010).
3. Children may flourish regardless of adverse circumstances thanks to their resilience (a very important strategy to handle the lack of resources, barriers, ability and care). This, however, cannot be an excuse to not listen to children voices and/or to change those adverse circumstances. The word is from latin *resalio* and has been introduced in sociology by Emmy Werner. The theory of resilience and risk tries to explain why some children respond better than others to stress and adversity throughout internal protective factors (self-esteem and internal locus of control) and external factors (such as social supports from family and community, such as positive role models or health services) (Luthar and Zigler, 1991).
4. Around the world there are some significant and reasonably successful examples of Municipal Councils of Children (an instrument adopted by local administration to

promote children's participation). See also the EU Charter of Fundamental Rights (proclamation at Parliament in Strasbourg, 12 December 2007).
5. The *Ombudsman's* action (i.e. free spokesperson for children) should help to move these objectives forward.
6. Chapters 7, 8 and 13 suggest that the role of NATs and GMACLE is already very important.
7. These movements have typically embraced equality of opportunity as the final objective independently from biological data. It is our hope that the defining political movement of the twenty-first century and next major campaign for change will focus on equality of opportunity for children, as argued by Don Milani (Scuola di Barbiana, 1967). For many countries much progress remains to be made, while for many others attention to the safeguards is needed: recent crises demonstrate that any social achievement is not for ever.

References

Crocker, D.A. (2007), "Deliberative Participation in Local Development", *Journal of Human. Development*, 8(3): 431–455.

Freeman, M. (1998), "The Sociology of Childhood and Children's Rights", *International Journal of Children's Rights*, 6(4): 433–444.

Habermas, J. (1981), *The Theory of Communicative Action, Vol. 1: Reason and the Rationalization of Society*, Beacon Press, Boston.

Hart, C. S. (2010), *Aspirations Re-Examined: A Capability Approach to Widening Participation in Higher Education*, Doctoral Thesis, University of Cambridge, Cambridge.

Lansdown, G. (2001), "Promoting Children's Participation in Democratic Decision-Making", *Innocenti Insight*, UNICEF Innocenti Research Centre, Florence.

Luthar, S. and Zigler, E. (1991), "Vulnerability and Competence: A Review of Research on Resilience in Childhood", *American Journal of Orthopsychiatry*, 61(1):6–22.

Matthews, H. (2003), "Children and Regeneration: Setting and Agenda for Community Participation and Integration", *Children & Society*, 17: 264–276.

Prout, A. (2005), *The Future of Childhood*, Routledge, London.

Santi, M. (2007), "Democracy and Inquiry. The Internalization of Collaborative Rules in a Community of Philosophical Discourse", in D. Camhy (ed.), *Philosophical Foundations of Innovative Learning*, Academia Verlag, Saint Augustin, FL.

Scuola di Barbiana (1967), *Lettera a Una Professoressa*, Firenze, Libreria Editrice Fiorentina.

Sen, A. K. (1999), *Development as Freedom*, OUP, Oxford.

Sen, A. K. (2006), "What Do We Want from a Theory of Justice?", *The Journal of Philosophy*, CIII(5): 215–238.

Sen, A. K. (2007), "Children and Human Rights", *Indian Journal of Human Development*, 1(2): 1–11.

Sen, A. K. and Dreze, J. (2002), *India: Development and Participation*, Oxford University Press, New Delhi.

UN (2002), *A World Fit for Children*. A/S-27/19/Rev.1. 12 July 2002, United Nations Children's Fund, http://www.unicef.org/specialsession/documentation/documents/A-S27-19-Rev1E-annex.pdf.

UNICEF (2002), *State of the World Children 2003*, UNICEF, New York.

UNICEF (2011), *State of the World Children 2011*, UNICEF, New York.

UNDP (1990), *Human Development Report*, OUP, New York.

Author Index

Subject Index